The Copywrights

The Copywrights

INTELLECTUAL PROPERTY AND
THE LITERARY IMAGINATION

Paul K. Saint-Amour

Cornell University Press

Ithaca and London

Copyright © 2003 by Cornell University

All rights reserved. Except for quotations in a review, and similar instances of fair use, this book, or parts thereof, must not be reproduced in any form without permission in writing from the publisher. For information, address Cornell University Press, Sage House, 512 East State Street, Ithaca, New York 14850.

First published 2003 by Cornell University Press
First printing, Cornell Paperbacks, 2010
Printed in the United States of America

Library of Congress Cataloging-in-Publication Data
Saint-Amour, Paul K.
  The Copywrights : Intellectual property and the literary imagination / Paul K. Saint-Amour.
    p. cm.
  Includes bibliographical references and index.
    ISBN 0-8014-4077-7 (cloth : alk. paper)
    1. English literature—History and criticism. 2. Law and literature—History—19th century. 3. Law and literature—History—20th century. 4. Wilde, Oscar, 1854–1900—Authorship. 5. Joyce, James, 1882–1941—Authorship. 6. Copyright—Great Britain. I. Title.
  PR468.L38 S25 2003
  820.9'355—dc21   2002014617

Cornell University Press strives to use environmentally responsible suppliers and materials to the fullest extent possible in the publishing of its books. Such materials include vegetable-based, low-VOC inks and acid-free papers that are recycled, totally chlorine-free, or partly composed of nonwood fibers. For further information, visit our website at www.cornellpress.cornell.edu.

Cloth printing   10 9 8 7 6 5 4 3 2 1

*For Alison,
my bright particular star*

Contents

Preface	ix
Introduction: Intellectual Property and Critique	1
1. Neoclassicisms: The Tectonics of Literary Value	23
2. Committing Copyright: The Royal Copyright Commission of 1876–78	53
3. Oscar Wilde: Literary Property, Orality, and Crimes of Writing	90
4. The Reign of the Dead: Hauntologies of Postmortem Copyright	121
5. James Joyce, Copywright: Modernist Literary Property Metadiscourse	159
Conclusion: Copyright, Trauma, and the Work of Mourning	199
Appendix: A Collection of Nineteenth-Century Centos	221
Notes	235
Index	269

Preface

This book's curious title-word, *copywrights,* is an example of what Lewis Carroll's Humpty Dumpty called a "portmanteau" word—one into which multiple meanings have been "packed up." One might imagine the project of this book as a gradual unpacking of its title-word, along with the legal, economic, and cultural formations to which it refers. Although the word *copywrights* principally suggests *copyright,* the latter, more conventional term fails to do justice to the law's vast range of extralegal functions and implications. I mean the deformation of *copyright* in my title to suggest how the integrity of the law is warped or even burst by the multiple discourses that intersect in it but cannot be contained by it. *Copywrights,* then, is meant to be a sort of impossible object, a finite sign for the nearly infinite array of categories, agendas, and phenomena that collide in the space of copyright. Unpacking the interior of such an object presents certain challenges to anyone who would also map its emboxed and paradoxical space. Though all the interlocking chambers in a portmanteau exist simultaneously, the nature of their adjacency can only be perceived across the time of their opening. As a result, we will have to visit various categories and questions attaching to copyright more than once in order to trace their relation to one another. In addition, copyright's morphology has continued to change over time, and in a relation of tangled and agonized reciprocity with the discourses that comprise it. We will have to attend to copyright's historical contingencies and trajectories even as we attempt to track its structural involutions, its double lust for quarantine and collapse. By the end, I hope, a space that is bigger on the inside than on the outside will have slowly turned itself inside-out. Which is nothing more than what every book does in the course of being read.

But let me at least roughly unpack my title-word here. Already out of the unlatched trunk is *copyright,* a word that describes both a right and the body of law that confers that right. Because of the many homonyms and homophones of the word *right, copyright* is already a much punned-upon term and therefore gratifyingly susceptible to the portmanteau form; one is tempted to say that the semantic openness of the word *copyright* vexes two

Preface

key assumptions of the law the word denotes—namely, that linguistic expression can be owned, and that its circulation can be controlled. For many, the word *copyright* resonates with the normative functions and transgressions of the law, as in the titles of Siva Vaidhyanathan's book *Copyrights and Copywrongs* (2001) and Richard M. Stallman's 1993 *Wired* article, "Copywrong." Stallman has also mapped a political axis onto copyright in his coinage, *Copyleft,* an open source, free software licensing practice that opposes the conservatism its title implicitly finds in the law. My title-word takes as its stem the word *wright,* descended from the Old English *wryhta,* a worker or maker, as in *wheelwright* or *playwright;* and *wright* is itself a homophone for what wordwrights do: write. The word *copywrights,* in its own semantic openness, should suggest not only the many varieties of maker and worker involved in producing informational copies but also the makers of copyright—the legislators and judges and publishers and authors and constituencies who have shaped the law since its inception nearly three centuries ago. Finally, though it leaves no typographical trace in my title, I hope the reader will also hear the word *rites* attached to the notion of copying and begin to consider the ritual functions attaching to literature, to the copying of literature, and to copyright law itself.

The portmanteau I have taken for my title is the more fitting given my contention that copyright is a formation whose inside is both more extensive and more complex than its exterior suggests or even permits—that copyright is, in other words, a kind of conceptual portmanteau. Though the law purports to govern a narrow range of human transactions, this book shows that, to the contrary, copyright has attained a stunningly broad bandwidth of influence, shaping not just our experiences as producers and consumers of information but also our aesthetic and normative categories, our psychological and affective lives. The ensuing pages will pay special attention to these extralegal functions of the law: to its preference for certain models of authorship and invention over others; to its tendency to stigmatize and, in some cases, stimulate modes of creation that fall outside these preferences; to its growing presence in the Western literary imaginary and its capacity to underwrite literary forms and narrative itineraries; to the role of postmortem copyright in safeguarding a deceased person's creative corpus and thereby facilitating the work of mourning; and to the danger that long postmortem copyright terms can pose to free speech, freedom of expression, fresh creation, and the griefwork of those who are not the legatees of dead creators. In the terms unpacked from our portmanteau, I will consider how the rights explicitly conferred by the law alternately shelter and maim the rites in which the law more covertly participates. I will retrace the steps by which the makers and shapers of copyright came to value and reward the creative modes of certain kinds of wright above others, as well as the steps taken by those written out of legitimacy to write back to the law, whether by quietly mapping its biases and expropriations or by directly and publicly antagonizing it. And I will consider, as much as possible, the normative question of where the present law does right by those it protects—creative individuals, creative collectivities, the public sphere, and the public domain—and where it wrongly infringes the very rights it was initially designed to uphold.

Despite its clearly polemical aspects, this is before anything else a work of literary criticism and literary and legal history; while it advocates a "thinner," or less extensive, copyright regime than the present one, it does so without proposing specific legal reforms. Readers interested in considering the pragmatics of particular copyright reforms might consult those proposed in chapter 13 of James Boyle's *Shamans, Software, and Spleens: Law and the Construction of the Information Society* (1996); I briefly address Boyle's proposals at the end of my second chapter. I would also direct the reader to the work of Lawrence Lessig, the law professor and public domain activist who has led two attempts to overturn the 1998 Sonny Bono Copyright Term Extension Act on constitutional grounds. Chapter 14 of Lessig's recent book, *The Future of Ideas: The Fate of the Commons in a Connected World* (2001), contains proposals for scaling back the present copyright and patent regimes in order to restore the law's capacity to foster innovation. And I would bring the reader's attention to three cyberlaw organizations—the Electronic Frontier Federation (EFF), the Digital Future Coalition (DFC), and the Berkman Center for Internet and Society at Harvard Law School—that defend civil liberties, initiate court cases, and coordinate public campaigns in the space limned by digital media, intellectual property law, the public domain, and matters of privacy and free speech. Although the specific advocacy of these individuals and organizations has crucially informed the present book, I am most immediately concerned with making the general case, amid a climate hospitable to extensive or "thick" copyright protection, for the urgent necessity of "thinning" copyright. Only after the prevailing disposition toward copyright has shifted in this direction will legislation that thins the current copyright laws have any hope of passing.

I am fortunate in having undertaken this project with the encouragement of several remarkable teachers and scholars. They deserve much credit for the strength of what follows but should not be held accountable for its shortcomings. Robert Polhemus was a wise and supportive counselor throughout, a wellspring of friendship and adviserly concern. For the habitability and sanity of my time at Stanford, and for its happy fruition, I owe him a world of thanks. Michael Tratner exercised tremendous influence over this project, particularly during initial phases when it was more concerned with the intersections of financial and intertextual models of debtorship; though the book's emphasis on debtorship has since diminished, I am happy to say that my debts to Michael have not. George Dekker shared his inimitable skills as both close reader and broad conceptual critic, always challenging me to higher standards of care and rigor. And Hilary Schor has been a terrific friend, mentor, and advocate; her interest in my work and her enthusiasm

Preface

for the profession we share have sustained me throughout the years I have worked on this book.

Some of the people who have influenced this project most are those who have challenged me through their writing and through the example of their public advocacy. I have been inspired by a wide variety of work being done on the cultural ramifications of intellectual property law by literary and legal scholars, lawyers, and free speech and public domain advocates and activists such as John Perry Barlow, James Boyle, Rosemary Coombe, Esther Dyson, Wendy Gordon, Peter Jaszi, Dennis Karjala, Susan Kornfield, Lawrence Lessig, Jessica Litman, Charles Nesson, Timothy Phillips, Margaret Radin, Mark Rose, Marc Rotenberg, Pamela Samuelson, Vandana Shiva, Robert Spoo, Richard Stallman, Susan Stewart, Siva Vaidhyanathan, Martha Woodmansee, and Jonathan Zittrain. I hope this book will contribute to the conversations about culture and intellectual property that many of these individuals have helped to initiate and focus.

In its early stages, this project benefited from the critical input of some very talented graduate student peers at Stanford University. The members of the Hippogryph Dissertation Reading Group—Caroline Bicks, Edmund Campos, Barbara Fuchs, Sujata Iyengar, and Richard Menke—buoyed me up with friendly encouragement even as they pointed out lapses in my prose and reasoning. I passed many fruitful, caffeine-laden hours conversing with Brendon Reay about intertextuality, ideology, and 1980s action films. My department-mate Caroline Bicks was an intellectual and emotional mainstay during both the serene and the turbulent seasons of our graduate years. Her friendship and Brendon's were among the chief blessings of those seasons. Participants in several incarnations of the Victorian Studies Reading Group—Helen Blythe, Kenneth Brewer, Jason Camlot, Jeff Erickson, Lisa Jenkins, Stephanie Kuduk, Diana Maltz, Tim Wandling, Kate Washington—lavished time and critical attention on several chapters, and all of us were the better for the tutelage and example of Regenia Gagnier.

I am grateful, too, to colleagues and friends who commented on part or all of the manuscript at subsequent stages in its revision: Michael Blackie, Marlene Briggs, Joe Bristow, Erin Carlston, Catherine Fisk, Matthew Harray, Ned Schantz, Mary Beth Tegan. And I owe particular thanks to Simon Stern, who shared his compendious knowledge of intellectual property law and criticism with me, teaching me more over email and one memorable afternoon's coffee than a whole raft of books could have done; I learned of Viereck's *The House of the Vampire* through him.

A Stanford Humanities Center fellowship, generously endowed by Theodore and Frances Geballe, enabled me to finish the dissertation out of which this book grew. The 1996–97 fellows were an extraordinary group, as much for their warmth as for their critical acumen, and the climate they created nurtured this project as much as did their questions and suggestions. The staff then at the Center—Susan Dunn, Susan Sebbard, Susan Dambrau, and

Preface

Gwen Lorraine—fostered this informal and collegial atmosphere, as did the Center's director, Keith Baker; they all have my thanks. I completed major revisions to this book during a fellowship year at the Society for the Humanities at Cornell University. I am grateful to Mary Ahl, Linda Allen, and Lisa Patti for helping to make that a smooth and productive time.

I want especially to thank my colleagues in the Pomona College English Department—Martha Andresen, Daniel Birkholz, Toni Clark, Edward Copeland, Kathleen Fitzpatrick, Rena Fraden, Paul Mann, Cristanne Miller, Arden Reed, Valorie Thomas, and Steve Young—for their personal and intellectual fellowship and for granting me an extra semester's leave, over and above a sabbatical year, during which time I was able to put the finishing touches on this book. All of us are indebted to Barbara Clonts, whose great care makes our work possible, and whose warmth makes it a greater pleasure. And I am deeply grateful to my colleagues Jay Atlas, Susana Chavez-Silverman, Ron Cluett, Kevin Platt, Marc Redfield, and Gary Wilder for their exemplary senses of humor and fortitude, their encouragement, their intelligence, and their friendship.

I benefited enormously from the comments of Robert Spoo and Mark Osteen, who read the manuscript for Cornell University Press. Both were as rigorous and as knowledgeable as they were generous in their response to my work. I am grateful to Bernhard Kendler for his interest in and support of this book. And I would like to thank Teresa Jesionowski and Kristin Herbert for their assistance in editing the manuscript and Jane Marsh Dieckmann for her work in preparing the index.

Finally—and fundamentally—I wish to express my love and gratitude to my mother, Constance Saint-Amour; my sister, Renée Saint-Amour; my daughters, Claire and Julia; and my wife, Alison Buttenheim. They have reminded me unfalteringly of the best reasons, both within and without the profession, for carrying on.

Chapter 3 of this book first appeared in a slightly shorter form as an article, "Oscar Wilde: Orality, Literary Property, and Literary Crime," in *Nineteenth-Century Literature* 55 (June 2000).

PAUL K. SAINT-AMOUR

Claremont, California

The sentimentalist is he who would enjoy reality without incurring the immense debtorship for a thing done.
  — GEORGE MEREDITH, *The Ordeal of Richard Feverel* (1859)

For a sentimentalist is simply one who desires to have the luxury of an emotion without paying for it.
  — OSCAR WILDE, *Epistola: In Carcere et Vinculis* (1897)

The sentimentalist is he who would enjoy without incurring the immense debtorship for a thing done.
  — JAMES JOYCE, *Ulysses* (1922)

The Copywrights

Introduction: Intellectual Property and Critique

How does newness enter the world?
Once new expressions, ideas, and inventions appear, how are they best bestowed upon the public? With what rewards and protections should their creators be induced to share their creations? What varieties of creator and creation should warrant these rewards and protections? Which aspects of a new work should be protected, to what degree, and for how long? And how should these inducements for creative individuals be balanced with concerns such as free speech and expression, intellectual freedom, and future innovation?

These are the crucial questions to which intellectual property law addresses itself. Its statutes and case law together tell a story about the function, nature, origins, itinerary, and destination of innovation. Given the highly technical ways in which it gets encoded and debated, that story is, at its heart, almost improbably colorful. In the midst of all the privatizing energies of capitalism, it posits the existence of a "public domain," a common lode of ideas and expressions that can be mined freely by all, and which intellectual property law exists to enrich. The law undertakes this enrichment of the public domain, fascinatingly, by charting a detour through private property: in order to provide creators with an incentive to create and to share their creations with society, it assigns them a temporary monopoly, akin to a property right, in particular uses of the creation—its reproduction, distribution, adaptation, and, in some cases, its public performance and display. This monopoly privilege, or intellectual property right, is alienable in the sense that its original holder may sell it, mortgage it, bequeath it, or divide it equitably in divorce; it circulates, then, like most tangible property, rather than being an inalienable right. Unlike tangible property, however, it is not perpetual but strictly temporary, expiring at the end of a set term as if it were an organic form reaching the end of its life span.[1] Patents, which protect inventions, expire after the relatively short term of 20 years in most countries.

[1]

Copyrights, which protect most other forms of intellectual property, last much longer—currently, in most developed nations, for the length of the author's life plus 70 years, or 95 years from publication in the case of anonymous works, pseudonymous works, and works made for hire.

When the copyright in a work expires, the work joins the public domain. More precisely, the end of copyright releases the *protected* aspects of the work into the public domain, as some unprotected, communal property aspects have resided there since its publication. Though patents protect ideas, copyright law applies only to original expression—*not* to ideas, procedures, processes, systems, methods of operation, concepts, principles, facts, discoveries, or preexistent expression incorporated in the new work. So what actually happens when a copyrighted work lapses into the public domain is the reunion of its temporarily privatized elements with the elements that have been public property all along. In addition, "fair use" or "fair dealing" provisions in many countries make even copyrighted expression reproducible for purposes such as commentary, criticism, teaching, research, scholarship, reporting, and parody. These exemptions, along with the partial and temporary nature of copyright protection, demonstrate copyright's ultimate subordination of private property to both the public domain and the public discourse it exists to fecundate, and on whose behalf it creates the incentive of monopoly privilege.

One could hardly daydream a stranger and more imaginative narrative than the one traced by intellectual property law, replete as it is with postmortem estates, hybrid and organic property forms, cultural recycling, loopholes, first sunderings, and final reunions. Nor, in many ways, could one hope for a more elegant and seemingly just balance between personal incentive and public weal, individual and collective legacy, privacy and publication. So long as it remains undisclosed, the fruit of the creative act—the text or image or composition or contraption—possesses the status of a secret: confected in private, it remains the absolute and exclusive property of its creator. Yet the society at large cannot benefit from the work of creative people unless that work is published. In the long-term interests of the public, copyrights and patents create a temporary bubble of exclusivity around published artifacts and public inventions: the physical text or object can be bought, owned, borrowed, lent, sold, or destroyed, but never copied, at least not beyond the allowances of fair use, without the creator's permission. This monopoly privilege should not be so extensive that it chills public discourse through the privatization of ideas. Nor should it be perpetual, lest it prevent future creators from building on past creations and thereby injure the public good. But it cannot be so perfunctory or so brief that creators are better off guarding their innovations in secret or ceasing to innovate altogether. Embodying these delicate balances, intellectual property is a frail gondola that ferries innovation from the private to the public sphere, from the genius to the commons. Yet for all that this narrative seems to posit individual genius as the mystified source of innovation, it also recognizes and defends the collective as both the destination *and* source of creation. Patent and copyright regimes demand that new works exhibit a certain degree of "originality" in order to qualify for the monopoly privilege. But by creating a terminal property form, they also acknowledge that prior inventions and expressions are at least part of the raw material for future innovation, that creation ex nihilo, if it exists at all, is always compounded with reuse and recombination. Intellectual property law recognizes, in other words, that creation is social rather than solipsistic.

Since its inception in the early eighteenth century, monopoly copyright has been a crucial element in the legal and economic infrastructures that undergird cultural production. By creating a temporary monopoly in the reproduction of new work within its jurisdiction, copyright established spatial and temporal horizons within which new works could be published without the threat of competing editions. This guarantee protected publishers' investments in new works and gave them legal recourse against pirated editions, at least within the boundaries of national and colonial copyright regimes and international accords. By granting creators limited property rights in their creations, copyright also helped emancipate writers from their dependence on aristocratic patrons, eventually giving them financial leverage in their relationships with publishers; in this respect, copyright was indispensable to the development of the "author" as a propertied, professional, and financially self-sufficient figure. But copyright has done more than simply stabilize a legal and commercial environment hospitable to the modern author. By establishing the criteria that make a work eligible for protection, along with the nature and duration of the protection, copyright has shaped not only the field on which the figure of the author moves but the identity of that figure as well. Authors, according to the law, win the laurel of intellectual property through the creation of *original expression*. Though it may seem counterintuitive, this consecration of originality actually reflects copyright's recognition of the social nature of creation: the law makes original expression the sole category of intellectual property protection because, in order to maintain a rich public domain, it refuses to grant property rights in ideas, or in expressions whose copyright has already lapsed. In the eyes of the law, then, an author is a person who wins an intangible, temporary, and predominantly alienable property through a highly specific kind of creation, one that society deems sufficiently valuable to warrant the incentive and reward of exclusive rights.[2]

Copyright law, as I have described it here, seems nothing but admirable. It helps sustain creative professions by giving creative laborers a property right in what they produce; it balances that right against the needs of both the public and future innovation by making it temporary; it creates a private property in the replication and dissemination of expression but not ideas, and thus stops short of chilling public discourse; it provides fair use easements in intellectual property rights for a range of purposes; and it rewards creative individuals without, apparently, overtaxing the collective. However, as this book will demonstrate, the above description of copyright is a highly idealized one, positing an ideally stable set of balances among the law's interested parties and principles. In reality, copyright's constitutive balances are highly precarious and extremely susceptible to change through legislative reform, judicial practice, and rightsholder lobbying. Having imagined copyright in an ideal state, one must ask what changes would result in cultural production, public discourse, free speech, and the public domain if the law were to achieve different equilibria. What would happen, say, if the monopoly privileges the law awards were to become considerably less temporary through repeated term extensions? What if the conceptual space of "expression" were to expand its boundaries, encroaching on the space of "idea"? What if creators could only obtain intellectual property rights in a new work once it had been approved by a regime of state censorship? Or if fair use provisions for critical, pedagogical, scholarly, reportorial, or parodic deployments of copyrighted work were to wither and thus license a private censorship by rightsholders? What would happen if the public domain were no longer the authorizing power that copyright served? What if the public domain were instead subordinated to the perceived sovereignty of private intellectual property and its overconsecrated sponsor, original genius? Or what if the law's historical orientation toward the creative individual were to result in a blindness toward the collective sources of even "original" expression, or in a failure to recognize noncorporate communities—communities that gradually, collectively, and publicly create a text, artifact, or practice—as legitimate authors and proprietors?

For many scholars and critics of intellectual property law, the foregoing questions are not hypothetical but rhetorical, describing conditions that have intensified during the last 150 years and, in most cases, persist today. During that period, perhaps the most striking trend across a number of national and international copyright regimes has been "copyright creep," a tendency toward frequent and increasingly substantial term extensions. In the U.S., the last 40 years have seen a massive transition away from domestic industrial manufacturing and toward intellectual-property-reliant sectors such as pharmaceuticals, biotechnology, computer platforms and software, and the culture industry. As a key guarantor of the nation's postindustrial, informational economy, copyright has flourished in tandem with it: during the same 40 years, the U.S. copyright term has been extended 11 times.[3] Most recently, the 1998 Sonny Bono Copyright Term Extension Act lengthened the U.S. copyright term from 50 to 70 years after an individual author's death, or from 75 to 95 years from publication for "work-for-hire," thus guaranteeing that virtually nothing will enter the public domain for the next 20 years.[4] The results of this "maximalist" tendency in U.S. intellectual property legislation are complex. As copyright protection expands in both extent and duration, the public domain of materials freely available to artists, teachers, scholars, and the general public diminishes. Longer copyright terms do, of course, benefit individual innovators and their heirs; but creative individuals also suffer from the impoverishment of the public domain, from which the raw materials of future innovation have been withheld in favor of longer terms. Meanwhile, the hyperextension of intellectual property rights carried out in the name of individual authors and artists works less equivocally to secure lucrative corporate holdings. As a result of the Bono Act, for instance, the Disney character Mickey Mouse, who first appeared in the 1928 film *Steamboat Willie*, will enter the public domain in 2024 instead of 2004. The example may appear frivolous, but if we consider the character's global recognition and appeal and the vast financial resources an organization like the Walt Disney Company can devote to legislative lobbying, the Bono Act can be seen for what it is: less an incentive to creative individuals, or even a consolation to their heirs, than a corporate special interest giveaway. Disney would no doubt respond that it deserves to reap continued rewards for the continuing risks it takes in marketing Mickey and its other intellectual properties. But such an argument reduces the production of meaning in mass culture to a unidirectional, monologic process that begins and ends with the Walt Disney Company. If instead we understand the meaning of Mickey and other mass-cultural characters as a dialogic, reciprocal, even agonistic effect—as the sum total of fantasies and transactions by consumers, producers, parodists, collectors, detractors, scholars, appropriationists—then the superprivatization of such collaboratively produced figures begins to seem bizarrely inappropriate.

It is also lamentably so, in that trademarks and copyrighted characters like Mickey Mouse (and Joe Camel, and the Marlboro Man) are increasingly seen by courts as legally immune to parody, despite a recent Supreme Court case affirming that parody may qualify for fair use exemptions as a variety of "comment or criticism," so long as the parody criticizes the same work it mimics.[5] Such immunity impoverishes not only the public domain but the syntactical range of criticism-through-reproduction; in effect, free speech and the possibilities of critical retort are infringed on so that intellectual property will not be. As a result, a legal canon initially conceived as a wary concession by the public domain to individual creators "for the advancement of learning" has been inverted into a grudging concession by corporate owners to a shrinking public domain.[6] Rosemary Coombe has made such an argument at greater length:

> For subjects in contemporary consumer societies . . . political action must involve a critical engagement with commodified cultural forms. In the current climate, intellectual property laws often operate to stifle dialogic practice in the public sphere, preventing us from using the most powerful, prevalent, and accessible cultural forms to express alternative visions of social worlds. . . . If, as

human selves, in human communities, we are constituted by and constitute ourselves with shared cultural vehicles (as many of us are weary of having to assert), then it is important that legal theorists consider the nature of the cultural forms that "we" "share" in consumer societies, and the recognition that the law affords them.[7]

As a growing number of scholars have argued, a law grounded in the figure of the individual genius-creator is ill equipped to recognize a dynamic and intersubjective model of meaning or value, much less a notion of the subject as constituted by and with other subjects in relation to "shared cultural vehicles." Yet if copyright law seems inflexibly wed to an eighteenth-century metaphysics of authorship, it has remained flexible enough in adapting that metaphysics to serve special interests, advancing corporate holdings and private censorship beneath the standard of individual genius.

The phenomenon of "copyright creep," however much one might regret its reapportioning of public and private domains, appears to have resulted from the influence of the private sector on the legislative climate, rather than from some privatizing drive inherent in copyright's metaphysics. If anything, the rash of term extensions in the twentieth century indicates a legislative drift away from stipulations in the law's inaugural statutes that copyright create a property strictly limited in its duration. But in large part, these term extensions have been rationalized by invoking the figure of the individual creator, whose original creations can only be induced, it is argued, through stronger, more extensive intellectual property rights that will persist long enough to benefit many generations of heirs. Insofar as copyright's initial statutes are premised on an individual model of creation, on the criterion of originality, and on the assumption that innovation depends on the private incentives of property and profit, the recent maximalism might be seen as latent in copyright's genome from the start, awaiting a complex of environmental conditions to activate its expression. I suggested above that the limitation of copyright to "original expression" actually indicates the law's commitment to a social model of innovation. But although it may have been established as a category of circumscription, original expression was consecrated by the Romantic cult of the individual genius, and that legacy of Romanticism, at least, has proven both durable and adaptable. So much so that a scholarly critique of the concept of original genius as a historically contingent ideological formation faces a peculiar problem of reflexivity: the originality cult thrives in the very institutional contexts where such scholarship is produced and evaluated. As a result, academics whose work interrogates hegemonic models of authorship tend nevertheless to deploy that same dominant rhetoric of original genius within the competitive circuits of the profession, particularly in hard-sell hyperbolic genres such as the letter of recommendation and the jacket-copy blurb.

The relationship between copyright law and the Romantic figure of the original genius, however, is not a simple or straightforward one. Martha Woodmansee has shown that copyright and the Romantic model of genius were interdependent formations during the late eighteenth century; yet copyright law has never limited its protection to works of the radical, visionary originality celebrated by the likes of Edward Young and William Wordsworth. The "original expression" a work must exhibit in order to win copyright is not a transcendent iconoclasm or singularity but something more modest: the absence of verbatim copying and the demonstrable presence of a modicum of creativity. That copyright law does not reward labor *tout court* is obvious in the kind of textual production it prohibits—namely, infringement—which may involve work, but clearly not the right kind of work. Along less transgressive lines, the U.S. Supreme Court decided in 1991 that alphabetical listings (e.g., in telephone books) are not copyright because the work of compiling and alphabetizing names, numbers, and addresses is not an "original" or "creative" enough transformation of public domain information.[8] Still, the threshold of innovation is set well below Wordsworthian notions of originality: the changes made to an existing text in new "derivative" works (translations, dramatizations, editorial revisions, abridgments, condensations, and annotations) are eligible for their own copyright status as "original works of authorship." Copyright does not even stipulate that "original" works be different from preexisting ones, only that they be the products of creative exertion rather than outright copying. Judge Learned Hand imagined an extreme case of "independent creation" to illustrate copyright's emphasis on the work of original expression rather than on radical originality:

> Borrowed the work must indeed not be, for a plagiarist is not himself *pro tanto* an "author"; but if by some magic a man who had never known it were to compose anew Keats's "Ode on a Grecian Urn," he would be an "author," and, if he copyrighted it, others may not copy that poem, though they might of course copy Keats's.[9]

If the hypothetical is a little hard to accept, it owes partly to the burden of proof Learned Hand's imaginary poet would have in demonstrating his or her lack of familiarity with Keats's ode, particularly now that charges of "subconscious infringement" have been successfully prosecuted in copyright suits.[10] But we balk at the idea of an identical yet noninfringing ode for another reason as well: Western culture still largely imagines authorship, particularly of "imaginative" works such as poems, novels, and musical compositions, to be a unique expression of a unique self. If we laugh at Learned Hand's imaginary scenario, we do so both to affirm our belief that such a thing could never actually happen and to ward off its insinuation that the self and its expressions might not be unique. Though the scenario asserts copyright's indifference to the uniqueness of persons or their works, intellectual property law is frequently employed to assert just the opposite: that the self and its expressions are singular, inimitable, authentic, and utterly original; that each of us is a Keats. And when the relatively thin requirements of originality native to copyright are hitched to the Romantic notion of radical originality, copyright no longer functions simply to reward modest creative labor; instead, it has been enlisted in the protection and consecration of a model of the self as original genius.

Still, what could possibly be so objectionable about a legal, aesthetic, or even academic regime that celebrates original genius? Nothing at all, one might respond, so long as that celebration does not take place at the expense of other sources, sites, and models of creation. Historically, though, the concept of original genius has been impatient of valorization *among,* and has insisted rather on valorization *over.* In his Preface to the second edition of *Lyrical Ballads,* Wordsworth defined the poet as "a man ... endowed with more lively sensibility, more enthusiasm and tenderness, who has a greater knowledge of human nature, and a more comprehensive soul, than are supposed to be common among mankind."[11] Though the description only admits of a difference of degree between the genius and the average person, the refrain of "more" and "greater" sings cumulatively of a difference in kind. That fundamental difference, in academic as well as legal and aesthetic discourse, has more often been invoked to justify an exemption from, or even a dominion over, the common and the commons than to bind genius to their defense; the rights and entitlements of genius tend to claim an inverse, rather than a proportional, relation to those of the masses, the public domain, and the public sphere. This narrative of election and exemption repeats itself, furthermore, at the level of designation: the claim that a work is "original" bestows on it a magical, mystified aura that acquits the claimant of any further burden of proof. Such a claim implies an epistemological depth by appeal to a mythological surface. To be designated radically original, a work must break detectably with its antecedents, and in order to make such a claim, the claimant purports to know not just the *best* that has been known and thought but *all* that has been known and thought. Thus, while the laurel of originality is supposedly reserved for "incomparable" works, it can only credibly be awarded after the most thoroughgoing global comparison—a comparison no claimant is in much of a position to undertake. In more general terms, originality is a property licensed by its vaunted self-sufficiency and heterodoxy but only really attainable by the most external, contingent, and generally orthodox means possible. Once it is denominated original, however, the work puts on the near-invulnerable glamour of the self-generating, self-legislating Romantic artifact. Dissevered not only from the more collective sources and modes of its own production but from the hypothetical nature of its originality, it attains the theological rank of a "classic," a "masterpiece," a work of "genius." What ought to have been a rhizomatic process of evaluation has become an indwelling, monolithic *value.*

The self-replicating power of the concepts of originality and original genius has given them the status of fact in Western culture. This seeming facticity of the concepts is the veil behind which they hide their own factitiousness—their status as artifact, artifice, ideological formation. In this sense, the concept of radical originality duplicates the same commodity form it helps underwrite, sustaining the illusion of its autochthony and autonomy by concealing the social and economic conditions of its production and proliferation. This concealment, moreover, can work effectively to naturalize dominant powers and power structures so that they may both legitimate and replicate themselves. Where art forks into "highbrow" and "lowbrow," elite and proletarian, originality acts as a kind of gatekeeper to the high road, remaining *the* indispensable criterion for the formation of high aesthetic canons and the ruling-class ideologies they tend to ratify. But to link originality with hegemony in such a way must be the starting point, not the ending point, of any study like the present one. That germinal connection opens out into a bouquet of difficulties: how does one confront literature's implicit beautiful lies—and culture's perhaps more explicit ones—about the spontaneous self-generation of "original" art without falling back on some notion of a privileged origin? Can source-hunting, for instance, or unmasking "sole authorship" as collaboration do more than bolster those lies by exfoliating "false" claims of originality back to "true" claims? Does a deprivileging of origins thwart the indispensable projects of validating labor and detecting historical causalities? How does one account for the appearance of new ideas and expressions in the world, if not through genius and originality? And more strategically, does even a partial assault on the notion of original genius deprive the Left of a potent, imaginative means to solidarity-building, as Richard Rorty has argued?[12] Can individual agency and moral autonomy survive a critique of original genius, or does such a critique fatally impoverish its own lexicon for galvanizing transformative energies?

I will not attempt to answer these questions here, as it is the work of the following chapters to address them in a more site-specific manner. In response to the foregoing skepticisms about the ideological constitution and deployment of originality as a sign, however, one might always object that originality nonetheless "happens." We are schooled, at least, to experience the originality of important works as an enduring strangeness, a calcified power to shock—like the signature of a sudden climatological change encoded in a fossil record or embedded in sediment. Even if we reject the notion that originality can be discerned in an individual work or person, a ghostly version of the idea survives in many historical methods. Cultural critics continue to record the ventilation of the familiar by the unfamiliar through the transom of newness—new events and inventions, epistemic shifts and seachanges in ideas, attitudes, styles, movements, modes of production and consumption, lifeworlds, dominant paradigms, regimes of knowledge. This book itself supposes that we can distinguish the stirrings, if not the precise geneses, of emerging intellectual currents such as Romanticism, marginalist economics, and intellectual property maximalism and metadiscourse from the chop and swell of contemporary circumstances and ideas. Imprecision does not obviate newness: that we can seldom pinpoint the moment when the mast first breaks the horizon is no argument against the arrival of the ship. I would respond: just so. Creation, invention, originality do happen, and a good thing too. But the sources and channels of those originary "happenings" are more radically unknowable than we like to admit. By the time we experience an idea or expression *as* original—really, in order for us to experience it that way—it has passed through the sieves and screens of institution and ideology: critical, educational, legal, economic, and political structures of selection and valorization. I am not suggesting that originality is some noumenon that exists beyond the reach of human apperception, but that it is only ever meaningfully a dialogical cultural phenomenon—a complexly intersubjective, intertextual product of social processes of consensus, contestation, distortion, and occlusion. The gesture by which this social process misrecognizes itself as noumenal or theological is the ideological gesture par excellence, and thus the central domain of critique. To return to the nautical figure, the gaze of culture is not restricted to first sightings of newness; it also chooses which vessels to track. Those it rejects, it forgets; those it selects, it exaggerates, whether by consecration or execration, and makes dreadnoughts of them. The originality effect, a hypermnesia that fetishizes an elite pantheon of "originals," can only occur alongside an amnesia about the precursors and contemporaries of those same originals: the great individuals loom largely because others are blotted out, forgotten. Yes, originality happens *as an effect,* but, viewed up close, it dissolves into its constituent pixels; like the televisual image, it is a composite to which we habitually impute a naive and spontaneous holism. This study examines the historical uses of that holism, its strategies of self-constitution and consecration, its durable allure, its embarrassing internal discontinuities, and its proliferating metadiscourses and counterdiscourses. It attempts to provide a sense of why the idea of "original genius" and the legal, economic, and cultural structures that sustain it and depend on it have been at once the pride and scandal of modernity.

Although copyright has long been understood as an important force in the modern literary marketplace, its cultural role in shaping models of authorship, literary value, and literary crime has emerged much more recently. One early attempt to relate literary property law and the cultural construction of authorship was Benjamin Kaplan's *An Unhurried View of Copyright* (1967), which adduced an intimate symbiosis between copyright and the Romantic "cult of originality." Kaplan went on to predict, or hope for, a waning of that cult along with its legal symbiont, copyright maximalism. Noting the rise of collaborative authorship, aleatory musical composition, computer-generation, and global communications networks, he observed that "not only is the relationship between author and audience radically changed but the author's pretensions to individual ownership and achievement are at a discount: his dependence on the past is better appreciated; he is seen somewhat as a tradition-bearing 'singer of tales,' as a kind of teacher peculiarly indebted to his teachers before him." Such a discounting of the originality cult, Kaplan concluded, would probably "abate feelings of proprietorship and modify conceptions of copyright, especially those bearing on plagiarism"—a possibility he welcomed, given his stated "low-protectionist bias."[13] Even more inaugural for later scholars of copyright and its cultural correlates was another late-sixties text, Michel Foucault's "Qu'est-ce qu'un auteur?" (1969), which calls in its famous opening *praeteritio* for a "sociohistorical analysis of the author's persona":

> Certainly it would be worth examining how the author became individualized in a culture like ours, what status he has been given, at what moment studies of authenticity and attribution began, in what kind of system of valorization the author was involved, at what point we began to recount the lives of authors rather than of heroes, and how this fundamental category of "the-man-and-his-work criticism" began.[14]

However brief, Foucault's suggestion has enjoyed a long critical afterlife, prompting work on the history of the writerly profession, literary property law, the publishing industry, and mythologies of authorship.[15] Building on both Foucault's and Kaplan's work, Martha Woodmansee's "The Genius and the Copyright: Economic and Legal Conditions of the Emergence of the 'Author'" (1984) demonstrated the interpenetration of eighteenth-century copyright law and nascent Romantic notions of original genius as well as the dependence of both on the changing economics of the book trade.[16] Mark Rose's *Authors and Owners: The Invention of Copyright* (1993) took a sustained look at decisive eighteenth-century British copyright cases to illustrate the socioeconomic contingencies of the law's founding decisions and to argue that copyright is, finally, "an archaic and cumbersome system of cultural regulation" and "an institution built on intellectual quicksand: the essentially religious concept of originality, the notion that certain extraordinary beings called authors conjure works out of thin air."[17] By demonstrating how copyright law and literary culture interdependently construct the author as original genius and as possessive individual, these studies have, in turn, helped draw attention within legal scholarship to the biases the Romantic author-figure builds into intellectual property law. In recent work, Peter Jaszi, James Boyle, Rosemary Coombe, and other legal scholars have criticized the law's infrastructural inability, given its reliance on individualist models of authorship, to comprehend and reward collaborative invention and creation.[18]

The Copywrights

Although they are both literary critics, Woodmansee and Rose foregrounded legal over literary discourse, in their above-mentioned work, in order to see how the laws pertaining to the literary marketplace underwrote aesthetic categories and criteria conventionally held to be disjunct from the market. The result has been a growing body of literary historical scholarship that attends to the conceptual bases and gradual elaboration of copyright—its landmark cases, domestic reforms, international accords, economic rationales, and legal metaphysics—as they affected not only the economics but the evaluative paradigms of the literary marketplace. In attending to copyright as an infrastructural force in cultural production, however, such work tends to treat literary texts as largely incidental to copyright—as passive counters circulating on a field constituted and delimited by intellectual property law and other market forces. This is not to say that the roles literary figures played in promoting copyright have been neglected. The activities of Wordsworth, Thomas Carlyle, Robert Southey, Thomas Arnold, Thomas Noon Talfourd, and others in supporting the Copyright Act of 1842, for instance, are well known. So is the fact that Charles Dickens, on a tour of the U.S. that same year, publicly denounced the widespread American piracy of works by foreign authors and pleaded for the U.S. to participate in international copyright accords.[19] But the literary texts that get discussed in relation to copyright tend to be confined to overtly polemical or occasional texts—Wordsworth's pro-copyright-extension sonnets, "A Plea for Authors, May 1838" and "A Poet to His Grandchild," say, or Mark Twain's unpublished dialogue "The Great Republic's Peanut Stand"—that directly address literary property debates.[20] The present study argues that copyright's presence *within* literary texts is far more pervasive than has previously been recognized. As the property form most "proper" to literary texts, copyright has incontestably shaped the commercial and evaluative circulation of literature. But it has done more: as its spatial, temporal, and economic domains have expanded, copyright's presence in the late-modern literary imaginary has also intensified. Yet this is not to suggest that the previously secure and autonomous space of the literary has been passively "invaded" by copyright. The literary texts I discuss in this book are not occupied by copyright so much as preoccupied with it: rather than accepting the fiction that copyright law is utterly external to literariness and literary culture, they recognize copyright as mutually constitutive with the literary, as forming one horizon, at least, of literary possibility. They recognize, too, that copyright law need not be accorded a naturalized, nonnegotiable facticity over and against literary contingency, but that it is a crucial subject of literary meditation and, if need be, contestation. Neither recognition is quiescent; these are textual spaces where lettered discourse wrestles, or is made to wrestle, with its vexed status as property.

The focal literary texts of the ensuing chapters may seem a motley assemblage, consisting of several anonymous patchwork poems, or "centos," written between 1850 and 1900; a series of Victorian essays defending plagiarism; lecture notes, a tale, and a letter by Oscar Wilde; George Sylvester Viereck's 1907 thriller *The House of the Vampire;* and James Joyce's *Ulysses* (1922). Most of them deliberate in some way on the question of value in relation to originality. But what really unites these texts is more specific: they are intimately conversant with their own embattled status as literary property. One critical truism has it that modernist literary texts, in particular, tend to turn away from the sociopolitical world and toward the aesthetic realm of style, form, allusion, and so on in a gesture of tightening self-contemplation—that they are Hubbles trained on their own literary navels. Without either accepting or disputing this narrative, the present book makes the more sharply focused claim that since copyright law's inception, a growing number and range of texts (both "literary" and "nonliterary") register a self-awareness about their status as literary property. I would hardly insist that this self-awareness is historically coextensive with *modernism,* though one of this book's focal texts—Joyce's *Ulysses*—sits at the core of the current modernist canon, and partly, I will argue, as a result of its proprietary self-consciousness. But to the extent that intellectual property law and the economic and cultural views that legitimate it are central formations of modernity, I suggest that this copyright metadiscourse—a discourse whose subject is its own literary property status—is one feature of the *modern* text, and one that remains undertheorized. Unlike more ingrown kinds of formal self-consciousness or metafiction, it is directed both inward, at the text's patterns and principles of construction, and outward, at the legal, economic, and ideological operations that protect and commodify the text. In that sense, we might think of copyright metadiscourse as a literary energy whose vector is always socioeconomic.

The notion that an imaginative work might be internally engaged with its legal status as property, and therefore with its economic status as commodity, is hardly daring in the present era of appropriationist artists such as Hans Haacke, Kathy Acker, Raymond Federman, Dan O'Neill, Bonnie Vierthaler, Sherrie Levine, Jeff Koons, Negativland, ®™ark, Plunderphonics, Illegal Art, the Kopyright Liberation Front, The Evolution Control Committee—individuals and groups whose work parades and often theorizes its redeployments of source material as well as its legal and economic status, joking at the expense of intellectual property orthodoxy and Romantic models of authorship, and in some cases deliberately courting infringement suits. But in looking at Anglo-American letters in the late nineteenth and early twentieth centuries, we are looking, arguably, at the halcyon days of the autonomous aesthetic, a period during which the legal and economic institutions circumscribing art tended to be viewed as incidental, rather than instrumental, to the production of aesthetic value. To find intellectual property law firmly ensconced in the period's literary imaginary, whether in overt or covert deployments, is to trace a fissure in the apparently flawless surface of the self-governing, self-delighting aesthetic, a place where the aesthetic demonstrably fails to be at one with itself by admitting its contingency on the property and commodity status of the literary artifact. This phenomenon helps explain why I have chosen to focus this study on the second half of the nineteenth century and the first few decades of the twentieth. Scholarly investigations of intellectual property have tended, understandably, to dwell on two periods: the eighteenth century, which was the birth-century of modern copyright law and the Romantic concept of original genius to which it remains closely knit; and the late twentieth century, when "information" grew more dematerialized, monopolized, anonymous, accelerated, and increasingly central to first-world economies, thereby precipitating a variety of crises in concepts of originality and authenticity and in their legal safeguards. (These ongoing crises, one could add, partly constitute the condition of postmodernity.) By comparison, critical studies of copyright in the nineteenth and early twentieth centuries are scarce.[21] But if the eighteenth century witnessed the birth of copyright in Britain, the nineteenth saw its adolescence, replete with growth spurts and growing pains in the form of term extensions and prolonged debates about the desirability of monopoly copyright versus a royalty system. By the early years of the twentieth century, both domestic and international copyright regimes had been standardized, centralized, and bureaucratized in Britain and the U.S.: the state-granted temporary monopoly had survived generations of skepticism and dissent and would go on, later in the century, to achieve global hegemony through the Berne Convention, the World Intellectual Property Organization, GATT, and the World Trade Organization's Agreement on Trade-Related Aspects of Intellectual Property Rights, Including Trade in Counterfeit Goods (TRIPS). The consolidation, consecration, and extension of intellectual property regimes in late modernity are legible, I will argue, in a number of the contemporary works of imaginative literature those regimes protected.

The project's primary texts share a second feature: they all participate, though ambivalently in some cases, in a critique of copyright. Some engage in a simultaneous critique of the Romantic figure of original genius that sponsors intellectual property law. One, G. S. Viereck's *The House of the Vampire*, rejects the notion that unpublished works belong absolutely to their creators, but does this explicitly in the service of the Romantic genius: the "overmen," for Viereck, must be free to appropriate the innovations of lesser people if the race is to thrive. It is tempting to join all these texts in a single tradition of dissent against private intellectual property, but for a number of reasons I have resisted doing so. For one thing, the intertextual connections would not sustain it: though both Viereck and James Joyce overtly donned the Wildean mantle, the other direct links that would suggest something deliberate enough to be deemed a "tradition" are not to be found. For another, the political affinities of the people in question ranged from socialism to free trade liberalism to fascism and are simply too divergent to cluster believably under the rubric of a single tradition or countertradition. During the nineteenth century, monopoly-copyright law and its model of individual creation transcended the status of an argument and became consecrated and codified as a dominant discourse—that is, as an argument that needed to be made less and less because it had attained the apparent status of self-evident truth, had fossilized into an indispensable precondition of life as we know it. Richard Terdiman offers this concise description of the dominant or hegemonic discourse:

> The inherent tendency of a dominant discourse is to "go without saying." The dominant is the discourse whose presence is defined by *the social impossibility of its absence*. Because of that implicit potential toward automatism, the dominant is the discourse which, being everywhere, comes from nowhere: to it is granted the structural privilege of appearing to be unaware of the very question of its own legitimacy. Bourdieu calls this self-assured divorce from consciousness of its own contingency "genesis amnesia." And it is one of the conditions of possibility of that assumption of (false) totalization by which the dominant tends to efface anything which does not fall within its own orbit or appear consonant with its own interests.[22]

If hegemonic discourse naturalizes its dominance by forgetting its origins and refusing to recognize even the possibility of dissent, a counterdiscourse works to revive supposedly settled arguments, to remember the forgotten origins of the dominant on its behalf, and to assail its self-evidence by suggesting what contingencies, contradictions, and occultations are involved in "going without saying." Given that hegemonic signs and practices function as shibboleths—passwords that construct membership in a social formation—a counterdiscourse might be imagined as a complex of signs and practices that construct exclusion or dissent from that membership, even a refusal of it. This book's primary texts, we could say, participate in a counterdiscourse to the hegemony of private literary property discourse, united only in what they variously refuse or contest. However, opposition entails its own kinds of contingencies; Terdiman reminds us that, "like all subversive thought, the counterdiscourse is intensely—if surreptitiously—parasitic upon its antagonist."[23] We will want to be attentive, then, not only to the different modes of refusal, contestation, and exclusion exhibited by these texts, but also to their dependence on the dominant, and to the reciprocal dependence of the orthodox on the heterodox. And we will want to ask whether the counterdiscourse—always by definition a minority discourse, we should remember—wants nothing more than to become a new hegemony, and wonder what the perils of such an ambition might be.

The chapters that follow are, in essence, case studies in literary property metadiscourse and counterdiscourse. The first, "Neoclassicisms: The Tectonics of Literary Value," builds on Howard Caygill's and John Guillory's contention that the discourses of aesthetics and political economy were "separated at birth" and continued to exhibit certain rhetorical and logical congruences during the nineteenth century despite having parted disciplinary ways in the late eighteenth. "Neoclassicisms" makes the case that the mid-Victorian rise of a copyright counterdiscourse in imaginative literature should be understood dialectically with the period's economic value theory. Around 1870, the so-called neoclassical revolution in economics shifted theoretical emphasis from the scene of production to the scene of consumption, from abundance to scarcity, from labor to desire. Its proponents said that the value of a commodity inheres not in the quantity or even quality of labor that creates it but in the amount and nature of consumer desire for that commodity. Precisely this argument structures the defense-of-plagiarism essay that flourished between 1840 and 1900: its writers justified plagiarism on the grounds that literary value arises not in the scene of writing so much as the scene of reading, and that any mode of literary production is legitimate so long as the text edifies an audience that demands it. Though in its extreme form this argument underwrote a lamentable kind of consumer sovereignty, it also prompted crucial meditations about the collective nature of cultural production. The writers of both plagiarism defenses and poetic centos insisted that literary value arises not only from individual genius but also from the collective sources and destinations of literary creation—from the precursor texts that writers reproduce and modify, from a rich public domain that makes such texts available, and from the readerly communities that interpret and evaluate new works. Chapter 2, "Committing Copyright," traces the rhetoric of both marginal economics and free trade doctrine through the 1876–78 Royal Commission on Copyright, the last concerted attempt from within the British government to abolish monopoly copyright, and the public debates it sparked. In the subsequent rewriting of the Commission's highly conflicted report as consensual and incontrovertible, I read the production of an ideological closure about monopoly copyright at the turn of the century, a closure that later critics of monopoly-copyright maximalism have had hard work to contest.

In the work of Oscar Wilde, the nineteenth-century counterdiscourse to private literary property found its most spectacular expressions. My chapter on Wilde treats his celebration and commission of plagiarism in light of both his professed socialism and his disposition toward talk over writing, while also understanding Wilde's resuscitated "orality," at least in part, as a strategic hallucination by lettered culture of a pure and wholly alien origin. I demonstrate that Wilde's 1886 lecture on Chatterton, which he heavily plagiarized from two biographies of the poet, thematizes its own transgressive mode of composition in its discussion of the poet, writing itself into a glorified and implicitly collective Romantic genealogy. The chapter then turns to Wilde's "The Portrait of Mr. W. H." (1889), a tale about a literary theory that only one person can believe at a time. I read the tale as a critical parable about literary property, one that deplores copyright's transformation of expression into an alienable property form that circulates like a material object, from one sole owner to the next. Both "Mr. W. H." and the Chatterton lecture, I suggest, reject private literary property in favor of the public property of discourse in oral cultures and in the public domain obliquely canonized by Wilde's 1897 prison letter and intellectual testament, *De Profundis*.

Although my discussions of Wilde, the centonists, the plagiarism apologists, and the anti-copyright Commissioners reanimate a minority discourse opposed to the culture of monopoly copyright, I elsewhere address less straightforwardly antagonistic relations between copyright and the cultural imaginary. In "The Reign of the Dead," I argue that limited postmortem copyright can participate in the cultural work of mourning, establishing a fixed period of time during which an author's estate remains in a commemorative stasis, watched over by the legatees whom it benefits. The overextension of copyright terms, however, unduly prolongs this mourning period, granting the estates and intentions of long-deceased authors a legal afterlife at the expense of what Thomas Jefferson called "the usufruct of the living."[24] Developing this connection between copyright and undeath, the chapter takes as its primary text Viereck's *The House of the Vampire*, which appeared just as European copyright regimes were adopting postmortem terms. The vampire of the title drains his victims of ideas rather than blood, stealing their unwritten plays and poems from their minds while they sleep and publishing them under his own name. By likening plagiarism to vampirism, ideas to blood, the novel echoes Wilde's "The Portrait of Mr. W. H." in lamenting the reification and commodification of expression under intellectual property law. It also engages in certain of what Derrida has called "hauntological" operations, using the spectrality and liminality of its central figure to question and contaminate the ontological distinctions—idea versus expression, writer versus reader, origination versus appropriation—that copyright takes to be fundamentally stable.

Chapter 5, "James Joyce, Copywright: Modernist Literary Property Metadiscourse," focuses on *Ulysses,* a cardinal text of interwar modernism and a key work of metafiction, or fiction that dwells on its own fictiveness. My discussion of *Ulysses* projects its metafictive geometries into the dimension of literary property, arguing that the novel thinks exhaustively about its identity as property and commodity as well as about its replications and breaches of literary formal convention. This analysis takes its cue in part from the complex publishing history of Joyce's novel: *Ulysses* was effectively denied U.S. copyright status from 1921 to 1934 on the grounds of its putative obscenity, and the text itself is rife with oblique references to its conflicted designations as both obscenity and literary property. The novel's "Oxen of the Sun" episode, in particular, reproduces several of copyright's central narratives and categories, but with critical and parodic differences. In my discussion of "Oxen," I show how the terminal narratives of gestation, parturition, and literary tradition that structure the episode are paired with the equally terminal narrative of copyright, observing that "Oxen" concludes with a celebratory portrait of public domain discourse after performing an encyclopedic range of fair use borrowings from its many source texts. The episode, I maintain, is concerned to parody not only its literary sources but copyright law itself, while simultaneously performing appropriative parody as a potent form of critical discourse and thus as an arguably fair use of sources. The chapter ends with a thought experiment that imagines how *Ulysses* might have been different had it been published under a millennial copyright regime rather than under 1922 conditions, suggesting how the state censorship still in place in the interwar period has given way to a less visible, but no less repressive, private censorship. In the book's conclusion, I consider two more recent texts—Spider Robinson's "Melancholy Elephants" (1982) and Alice Randall's *The Wind Done Gone* (2001)—that illustrate the high stakes of private censorship licensed by stronger and stronger copyright regimes. Both Robinson's story and the legal action surrounding Randall's novel illustrate, in quite distinct ways, copyright's role in facilitating or obstructing the personal and communal working-through of historical trauma. More obliquely, they suggest that maximalist copyright regimes might not only obstruct or facilitate the working-through of extant trauma, but also precipitate new traumas by making catastrophic incursions on the public domain, the public sphere, and the therapeutic and political potential of transformative redeployments that rely on the openness of those spaces.

To the extent this book formulates a critique of dominant intellectual property regimes, their consecration of original genius and possessive individualism, and their threat to public discourse and the public domain, it may appear to nominate the majority of its primary texts as its own precursors, assembling a loose genealogy of circumspection and dissent in order to install itself at the contemporary end. I want to acknowledge that so hermetic and teleological an approach would be an intellectually dangerous one and to insist that it is not my intention simply to present a self-aggrandizing prehistory of my own critique. My aim in undertaking this project has been to illustrate an ongoing recognition, since the messy inception of copyright, that the ascendant concepts and conventions of literary property are neither inevitable nor unassailable but, rather, that they result from isolated material conditions, historically contingent mythologies of authorship, and tendentious economic and political motives on the parts of legislators and lobbyists. An important corollary must follow such a statement: any genealogy of dissent is itself site-specific, contingent, tendentious. I will end this introduction, then, by attempting to situate this book within several contexts—critical, disciplinary, historical—while acknowledging my own necessarily partial view of its influences and presuppositions.

Because the critique I am undertaking strives to locate intellectual property law at the crossroads of jurisprudence, economics, aesthetics, and politics, the work with which it is in dialogue also tends to be interdisciplinary. Where both Woodmansee and Rose (and others, including Margareta de Grazia, N. N. Feltes, and Chris Vanden Bossche) have routed literary scholarship through legal and economic inquiries, a number of legal scholars of copyright have adopted cultural studies approaches in pointing up the occlusions and blindnesses of the law.[25] James Boyle is similarly interested in forms of innovations the law fails to recognize, but he approaches the problem specifically from the vantage of a Critical Legal Studies (CLS) critique of liberal categories of self and property and the intractable dualisms on which these categories are founded.[26] Rosemary Coombe, in her powerful study *The Cultural Life of Intellectual Properties: Authorship, Appropriation, and the Law* (1998), calls for a new interdisciplinary approach she calls a "Critical Cultural Legal Studies": a synthesis that brings the socially, politically, and ethically contextualizing energies of cultural studies to bear on legal discourse, while at the same time insisting on both the inescapably political and contingent nature of the law (à la CLS) and legal theory's responsibility to the actual social relations and lifeworlds of those whom the law governs. In framing a Critical Cultural Legal Studies, Coombe warns of the immanent Romanticism of a certain vocabulary of power and the difficulties of finding an adequate lexicon of transgression when intellectual property is involved:

> Practices of authorial power and appropriation, authorized meanings and alternative renderings, owners' interest and others' needs cannot be addressed simply in terms of dichotomies like domination and resistance, however. Romantic celebrations of insurrectionary alterity, long popular in cultural studies, cannot capture the dangerous nuances of cultural appropriation in circumstances where the very resources with which people express difference are the properties of others. Acts of trangression, though multiply motivated, are also shaped by the juridical fields of power in which they intervene.[27]

Outside extremely narrow parameters, intellectual property law has a low tolerance for practices that criticize or parody its basic tenets—practices it recodes, belittles, and criminalizes as piracy and infringement. (Plagiarism, as we will see, is an ethical rather than a legal transgression, not being necessarily a violation of copyright; however, because plagiarism and infringement overlap in cases where the plagiarist copies and disseminates copyrighted material, the two are often conflated.) In a sense, this is just a fancy way of saying that you can seldom criticize the law by breaking it and yet expect the law to forgive your infraction as criticism. Law is not an argument so much as an instrument of self-enforcement; thus, even breaking the law confirms the logic and categories of the law, which work to criminalize any transgressive act of dissent. In the case of property law, this circularity tightens further: criticizing standards of ownership can lapse into a near-absurdity when some of the most effective critical pathways—counterappropriation or parody, for example—are by definition *already owned* by someone else. My sympathies with CLS become apparent here: if we see law as the unassailable embodiment of self-evident truths, rather than as an ideologically fraught, idiosyncratic, and highly contingent apparatus, then intellectual property law—all law, in fact—is invulnerable to critique, susceptible only to confirmation, consecration, and occasional reverent modification.

At its most basic level, the law of copyrights, patents, and trademarks creates economic incentives, which have been criticized exclusive even of their ethical, political, and cultural effects. In the nineteenth century, the most vocal economic criticisms of British intellectual property law came from the radical free trade quarter and reached a crescendo during the 1876–78 Royal Commission on Copyright, which I discuss in chapter 2. Though unsuccessful at the time, arguments launched against monopoly copyright during that Commission have remained influential during the twentieth century. In 1934, economist Arnold Plant cited Commissioner Louis Mallet's objection that, whereas tangible property "exists in order to provide against the evils of natural scarcity," copyright artificially "creates scarcity in order to create property."[28] Plant went on to propose a version of Mallet's alternative to extensive monopoly copyright: a five-year period of exclusive protection followed by a compulsory license or royalty system. He even speculated that the Anglo-American patent system might be partly responsible for the Great Depression during which he wrote.[29] Stephen Breyer's 1970 article, "The Uneasy Case for Copyright," stopped short of recommending the abolition of copyright but did find that "none of the noneconomic goals served by copyright law [e.g., the author's moral rights, Lockean natural rights in property] seems an adequate justification for a copyright system." Written during Congressional debates that resulted in the extension of copyright from a 56-year maximum (28-year term plus 28-year renewal) to the length of the author's life plus 50 years, the article deployed a social cost-benefit analysis of copyright's effect on the publishing industry and concluded that even the 56-year period was too long, that educational fair use provisions should be broadened, and that software should not be patentable.[30] (Since 1970, U.S. law has gone counter to all three suggestions; Breyer, meanwhile, became the 108th Justice of the Supreme Court.) More recent economic critiques of copyright range from radical free market or "anarcho-capitalist" approaches to Marxist historical materialism.[31] However, rather than deploying strictly economic or econometric methods, I have investigated the political economic assumptions immanent within copyright law and its aesthetic correlates, particularly in my discussion of nineteenth-century economics and literary value. In doing so, I partly take my cue from work by cultural critics (Regenia Gagnier, Mark Osteen, Marc Shell, Martha Woodmansee, and others) working under the rubric of "the New Economic Criticism."[32] I join these writers in viewing aesthetics and economics as dialectically susceptible to one another's suppositions and terminologies, and the conventional firewall be-

Intellectual Property and Critique

tween the two discourses as a deterrent mythology. This view entails not only attending to material conditions and economic worldviews as hypostases of aesthetics but, perhaps less obviously, thinking about how realms of feeling, bias, projection, and imagination can inflect economic thought for good and ill.

Feminist legal scholar Drucilla Cornell has made a similar point about the interdependence of ethics and aesthetics, arguing that "The moment of [ethical] commitment is aesthetic in its orientation. It demands not only the capacity for judgment but also the ability to dream of what-is-not-yet. The ethical cannot be reduced to an aesthetic, but neither can it do without the aesthetic."[33] The ability to dream of what-is-not-yet is never more crucial than during periods of catastrophic change, particularly when the law has yet to digest that change. Imaginative acts of prediction, projection, extrapolation, admonition should inform any ethically motivated assault on present orthodoxies. In the final pages of his critical short history of copyright law, Benjamin Kaplan presciently imagined coming technological changes that would alter conceptions and conventions of authorship and intellectual ownership. The technological and social context of much recent copyright critique, including my own study, is contained in his forecast:

> You must imagine, at the eventual heart of things to come, linked or integrated systems or networks of computers capable of storing faithful simulacra of the entire treasure of the accumulated knowledge and artistic production of past ages, and of taking into the store new intelligence of all sorts as produced. The systems will have a prodigious capacity for manipulating the store in useful ways, for selecting portions of it upon call and transmitting them to any distance, where they will be converted as desired forms directly or indirectly cognizable, whether as printed pages, phonorecords, tapes, transient displays of sights or sounds, or hieroglyphs for further machine uses. Lasers, microwave channels, satellites improving on Comsat's Early Bird, and, no doubt, many devices now unnamable, will operate as ganglions to extend the reach of the systems to the ultimate users as well as to provide a copious array of additional services.
>
> Conceived as conduits or highways for the transmission of signals, the systems will have intense responsibilities of a "public utility" type enforced by law—if indeed the systems (or some of them) will not come under direct government ownership and control. . . . Meanwhile we have to observe that the electronic systems need not, and probably will not, remain national; they will be linked, possibly with the aid of automatic translation, in world-wide networks.[34]

Kaplan's prophecy, with its attendant warnings about the ethical dangers of copyright maximalism, appeared in 1967. In 1969—also the year of Foucault's "Qu'est-ce qu'un auteur?"—the ARPANET military communications network would come online, developing over successive decades into the present Internet. The "communications age" Kaplan saw himself inhabiting would become the vaunted "information age" during which my own book, like many of its immediate antecedents, was written. Unlike many contemporary intellectual property critics, however, I am wary of accepting the so-called digital revolution as the end toward which history tends, or as in itself sufficiently "revolutionary." Raw technology, however sophisticated and accessible, is not identical with emancipation; it provides nothing more than an imaginative prompt, and perhaps one tool among many, for the societies that use it to emancipate themselves by more thoughtful and systematic means. The Internet is not an argument, and to mistake it for an ethical or political articulation is to accept the widespread fetishization of "information" as a magical, sourceless, costless panacea. (Though appealing at a visceral level, *Wired*-generation slogans like "Information wants to be free" simply beg the question of who is misattributing his or her own desires to the fetish-category of "information.") Rather than become infatuated with what is, I want to recur to Cornell's idea of dreaming through aesthetic projection toward ethical commitment. Those dreams of what-is-not-yet will include both utopian ideals and cautionary dystopias—places we do and do not wish to inhabit—along with a sense of how we might arrive there by holding or altering our present course. Investigating the aesthetic musings, forecasts, and protests of the past is one way of quickening our own meditations about what-is-not-yet; this book hopes to aid that quickening.

[1]

Neoclassicisms: The Tectonics of Literary Value

> Whether a diamond was found accidentally or was obtained from a diamond pit with the employment of a thousand days of labor is completely irrelevant for its value. In general, no one in practical life asks for the history of the origin of a good in estimating its value, but considers solely the services that the good will render him and which he would have to forgo if he did not have it at his command.
> — CARL MENGER, *Principles of Economics* (1871)

> Uncut diamonds, artistically speaking, may be legitimately taken away from their idiot-possessor, provided the thief will well and truly cut them, thus giving them a new brilliance. This is not a theft, properly speaking: rather it is a duty. It is good that diamonds should be stolen, be they yours, ours, or another's, provided only—this is essential—that the new possessor exhibits them to better advantage. They may already have been pebbles in some barbarous toilet; it is the artist's business to steal them thence, and make of them a *parure* for a queen.
> — E. F. BENSON, "Plagiarism" (1899)

Diamonds are a value theorist's best friend. Fruitlessly beautiful, they provide an extreme case among commodities whose value is out of all proportion to their usefulness. In his *Wealth of Nations* (1776), the classical political economist Adam Smith famously used the diamond to illustrate just this point: "Nothing is more useful than water: but it will purchase scarce any thing; scarce any thing can be had in exchange for it. A diamond, on the contrary, has scarce any value in use; but a very great quantity of other goods may frequently be had in exchange for it."[1] While the invention of the diamond-tipped drill and the diamond anvil cell may have blunted Smith's point slightly, the value of the diamond still resides far more in exchange than in use. But locating the diamond's value in exchange raises a further question: what is the source and measure of exchange value? Are diamonds valuable in exchange because they are costly to mine, cut, set, and market? Because they are scarce? Because they have come to signal the purchaser's disposable income and thus, according to a familiarly circular logic, must remain expensive to perpetuate that symbolic function? However they account for its particular exchange value, economists invoke the diamond not as an exception to general patterns of valuation but as an extreme case that illuminates the general one. Thinking through examples like diamonds and water, value theorists like Smith have attempted to fathom the fundamental principles— the origin and nature of value itself—that undergird phenomena like price, exchange, demand, and distribution. Robert Heilbroner sums it up attractively: value is the "deep structure" that imparts "orderly configurations to the empirical world, akin to the arcs created in iron filings under the influence of a magnet."[2]

Though Adam Smith eventually argued for a cost-of-production theory, he was at heart a proponent of the labor theory of value, which identified labor as "alone the ultimate and real standard by which the value of all commodities can at all times and places be estimated and compared. It is their real price; money is their nominal price only."[3] Thus the value of diamonds inhered in the laborious process of wresting them from the earth and fluctuated according to the fertility or barrenness of the mines. The classical political economists writing after Smith tried to account for additional factors like scarcity, demand, and abstinence, revising the labor theory of value without rejecting it. But by the 1870s, Carl Menger, William Stanley Jevons, and other economists of the emerging "neoclassical" or "marginalist" school had completely discarded the labor theory of value in favor of a subjectivist, utility-based calculus that located value in consumer pleasure. The diamond, they said, named its price in proportion neither to its usefulness nor to the amount of labor spent finding, mining, or refining it, but according to the pleasure ("utility") it gave its purchaser. Consumers were, they argued, oblivious to an object's origin and conditions of production; as Menger put it, they considered solely the services and pleasures that the good would render them and that they would forgo if they did not have it at their disposal. This extreme late-Victorian shift in value theory—away from labor and the scene of production, toward desire and the scene of consumption—responded to equally dramatic changes in industrial European economies. No longer living amid the late mercantilism and early industrialism that informed Smith's *Wealth of Nations,* the neoclassical economists observed both staple and luxury goods being produced with growing quality and efficiency and a burgeoning advertising culture stimulating consumer demand for these abundant goods. Although its object of scrutiny was supposedly "deep structural," value theory had shown itself spectacularly responsive to the changing conditions of the marketplace; new patterns of iron filings had seemed, at least, to necessitate a new magnet.

Political economy is not the only discourse to assume that an arc of iron filings implies the presence of a magnet. Western aesthetics, too, has meditated on the organizing principles that bestow value and patterns of valuation on art objects, aesthetic experiences and conventions, art institutions, and artists themselves. Radiating outward from this central preoccupation with value, aesthetics and economics share a number of contiguities. Both discourses address labor and desire in their attempts to define and assess value. Both respond to conditions of paucity and plenitude in the markets that circumscribe them. And both must choose whether or not to emphasize the social and material relations that underlie the various productions, exchanges, and consumptions they survey. Just as the political economists did with the commodity, modern writers on aesthetics have inquired into the source of the art object's value. How much of it comes from the raw materials of art, how much from the artist's labor (or from the artist's genius, if genius is taken to be distinct from labor), and how much from consumer demand? Are there different kinds of artistic labor, producing different kinds or amounts of artistic value? Can we distinguish between use value and exchange value in art as we do in commerce?

This chapter begins by investigating the twin discourses of economic and aesthetic value—their proximate origins, homologies, divergences, and reunions—with a specific emphasis on problems of and at the origin, reading the cardinal literary value of originality in the light of extraliterary debates on the origin of value in both the artwork and the commodity. Because economics and aesthetics borrow terminology from one another, their metaphors often appear to mix: artists incur debts of language, while economists descant on the harmony and genius fostered by the distribution of labor. Brushing aside these crossings as "merely" figural neglects the fact that metaphor is always an economic function in at least one sense: as Kurt Heinzelman points out in *The Economics of the Imagination,* the etymology of "metaphor"—to transfer or bear across—signals its identity as a form of exchange.[4] This is not, however, to make metaphor the tenant farmer of economics; exchange may be central to economics, but it is hardly endemic to it. Nor does metaphor operate exclusively within the bounds of imaginative literature. As writers in the Critical Economics movement have lately reminded their fellow economists, the dismal science relies crucially (and often all too unselfconsciously) on putatively "aesthetic" modes and rhetorical devices—trope, narrative, allegory, exemplum—that not only ornament but help constitute economic discursive practices.[5] My aim in what follows is to treat neither economics nor aesthetics as ontologically prior to the other, but to address their conceptual and rhetorical interpenetrations in order to illustrate how changing ideas of value have been applied not only to material commodities such as diamonds and iron and water but also to "intangible" ones such as imaginative literature.

Just such an interpenetration or crossing is legible in this chapter's second epigraph, an excerpt from the novelist E. F. Benson's article "Plagiarism," which appeared in *The Nineteenth Century* in 1899. Likening rough-hewn literary ideas to uncut diamonds, Benson claims that such raw gems "may be legitimately taken away from their idiot-possessor" so long as better writers rework them to advantage. Theft becomes a "duty" provided that the thieves add value to the art object, exhibiting it to better advantage and thus making it more pleasurable to consume.[6] The passage enacts what it urges by stealing the example of the diamond from its better-known setting in political-economic value theory and exhibiting it anew in a defense of plagiarism. But even more strikingly, Benson's rant resonates with the core argument of neoclassical economics, removing value from the scene of production and relocating it in the scene of exhibition, appreciation, and consumption. The diamond's itinerary—from the "barbarous toilet" of its "idiot-possessor" to "a *parure* [ornamental headdress] for a queen" by way of licensed, even duty-bound, appropriation—resonates, too, with the more sinister late-nineteenth-century uses of neoclassical economics to rationalize aristocratic privilege and sanction imperial seizure. As the marginalist economist Francis Edgeworth wrote in 1881, the means of pleasure tend to (and, by implication, should) go to those with the greatest and most highly evolved capacity for enjoyment: "In the general advance, the most advanced should advance most . . . the happiness of some of the lower classes may be sacrificed to that of the higher classes."[7] In the decades before and after the so-called neoclassical revolution of the 1870s, Benson and dozens of other writers were introducing homologous paradigms into literary discourse through their explicitly consumerist defenses of plagiarism.

This chapter understands two kinds of late-nineteenth-century neoclassicism—quantitative, consumerist economics and appropriative, consumerist literary aesthetics—as coeval phenomena. After discussing the mingled origins of aesthetics and economics in Britain in eighteenth-century moral philosophy, I trace productivist theories of value—theories that root value in the scene of an object's production—through political economy, aesthetics, and early copyright debates and the rise of consumerist value theory concurrently in economics and literary aesthetics. The economic critique of productivism launched by the likes of Menger and Jevons finds its aesthetic correlate in two increasingly popular antiproductivist literary forms: the aforementioned defense of plagiarism and a radically intertextual poetic form called the "cento," both of which endorsed a recombinant rather than a radically originary view of literary creation. The growing counterdiscourse to both originality and literary property law embodied in these two forms is catalyzed by the demise of the labor theory of value, and in turn catalyzes more extravagant appropriations and recombinations in work by Wilde and, after him, a number of prominent modernist writers. Theirs was not the neoclassicism of Horace or Pope, which cherished formal imitation and generic convention, but a latter-day neoclassicism that celebrated profligate literary borrowing. The chapter concludes with a consideration of the ethical benefits and damages bound up in a consumerist critique of originality and literary property law.

Theories of Value

Despite the frequent blurring of artwork and commodity in both art markets and numerous postmodern installations, Western culture has consecrated certain distinctions between art and the market: art supposedly occupies an "outside" to the economic realm, a space that fosters beauty, generosity, and spontaneity against the tabulations and drab parsimonies of the market. Adopting this view, the literary anthropologist Lewis Hyde ascribes art's social value to its independence from the marketplace. Though he admits that works of art can behave like commodities, he finds that the essence of art is the gift, a principle of free circulation rather than private accumulation: "a work of art can survive without the market, but where there is no gift there is no art."[8] But where Hyde rather dubiously maintains that art can do without the market, Howard Caygill and John Guillory have recently pointed out that the eighteenth-century market could *not* do without art in imagining itself—that aesthetics and political economy were in effect "separated at birth," insofar as early political economists used aesthetic criteria such as beauty and harmony both to judge social organizations and to explain people's willingness to forgo such considerations as simple utility or immediate gratification.[9] Following Caygill's lead, Guillory locates the shared genesis of modern aesthetics and economics in the moral philosophy of Adam Smith, whose *Theory of Moral Sentiments* (1759) made the aesthetic disposition (a "love of system" and "regard to the beauty of order, of art and contrivance") nothing less than "the secret motive of the most serious and important pursuits of both private and public life."[10] Hume, in his *Treatise of Human Nature,* had observed that an object pleases its owner by suggesting "the pleasure or conveniency which it is fitted to promote." But Smith noted that we often value the object's fitness for its end—its beauty—more than the end itself. This tendency to value means over ends, beauty over utility, leads us to desire more means (beautiful objects) than we have ends (needs met by usefulness), and in turn begets jealousy, ambition, commerce, industry, technology, progress, society itself. In making this argument, Smith was careful, too, to lodge a claim of originality, saying that the means-over-ends phenomenon "has not, so far as I know, been yet taken notice of by any body."[11]

The Copywrights

But while Smith's "original" revision of Hume offered an explanation for *why* people value objects, it did not provide a *measure* of value, either economic or aesthetic. Though he had touched on the subject in earlier works, Smith did not quantify value until his *Wealth of Nations* articulated the labor theory of value in 1776. The theory—not "original" this time, since he inherited it from William Petty, John Locke, Richard Cantillon, and more remotely from Aristotle's *Politics*—made labor the sole measure of value, as it was ultimately the source of everything that possessed value.

> Labour was the first price, the original purchase-money that was paid for all things. It was not by gold or by silver, but by labour, that all the wealth of the world was originally purchased; and its value, to those who possess it, and who want to exchange it for some new productions, is precisely equal to the quantity of labour which it can enable them to purchase or command.... Labour, therefore, it appears evidently, is the only universal, as well as the only accurate measure of value, or the only standard by which we can compare the values of different commodities at all times and at all places.[12]

The *Theory of Moral Sentiments,* for all its emphasis on beauty, had rooted value in utility: more than anything, it said, we value beauty, which is a fetishization of a thing's usefulness or fitness for a purpose. By grounding value in the quantum of labor required to produce a commodity, *Wealth of Nations* left the vague domain of use value in favor of a precise theory of exchange value, bracketing the question of aesthetics altogether. After this abandonment of beauty, Guillory writes, the labor theory of value "can never find its way back to, or include within its formula for price, the 'beauty' of the commodity" described by the *Theory*.[13] Though Smith let the earlier book's meditation on utility and beauty stand in new editions as late as 1790, the aesthetic disposition never reappeared in his political-economic work after *Wealth of Nations*. Offered in the *Theory of Moral Sentiments* as exemplary of all commodities, the work of art had become an exceptional case and was almost entirely set aside by later political economists. The long dissociation of commodity and artwork, political economy and aesthetics, had begun.

If pre-Smithian political economists regarded all labor as artful, their contemporaries in legal circles were arguing about whether art was laborious, and specifically about what kinds of art were sufficiently laborious to merit protection by nascent intellectual property laws. Even before Smith fully endorsed the labor theory of value, a version of the theory was being adduced in support of the developing copyright canon. Though the statute that codified British copyright law in 1710 was entitled "An Act for the Encouragement of Learning," the law was more often defended and interpreted as an incentive to intellectual *labor.* As Smith himself wrote in his *Lectures on Jurisprudence* (1762–63), copyright provided "an encouragement to the labours of learned men"; though he regarded it, as he did all monopolies, with suspicion, Smith conceded that the law was "perhaps as well adapted to the real value of the work as any other."[14] Though Smith never tied copyright explicitly to a labor theory of value, other writers of the period—both judges and journalists—did make such a connection in debates over the nature and extent of copyright. Like Smith's labor theory of value, these arguments drew heavily on Locke's famous defense of private property in *Two Treatises of Government* (1690):

> Though the Earth, and all the inferior Creatures be common to all Men, yet every Man has a *Property* in his own *Person*. This no Body has any Right to but himself. The *Labour* of his Body, and the *Work* of his Hands, we may say, are properly his. Whatsoever then he removes out of the State that Nature hath provided, and left it in, he hath mixed his *Labour* with, and joyned to it something that is his own, and thereby makes it his *Property*. . . . 'tis *Labour* indeed that *puts the difference of value* on every thing; and let any one consider, what the difference is between an Acre of Land planted with Tobacco, or Sugar, sown with Wheat or Barley; and an Acre of the same Land lying in common, without any Husbandry upon it, and he will find, that the improvement of *labour makes* the far greater part of *the value*.[15]

Whereas political economists like Cantillon and Smith used Locke's rationale of private property to advance the labor theory of value, copyright theorists deployed it in defense of private literary property. In two key eighteenth-century copyright cases, *Tonson v. Collins* (1761) and *Millar v. Taylor* (1769), advocates of perpetual copyright invoked Locke's theory in claiming that legitimate appropriations from the commons by intellectual labor should result in an intangible property no less private, and no less permanent, than tangible property.[16] Again echoing Locke, William Enfield wrote in his *Observations on Literary Property* (1774), "Labour gives a man a natural right of property in that which he produces: literary compositions are the effect of labour; authors have therefore a natural right of property in their works."[17] By articulating and protecting that "natural right of property," copyright would simply ensure the value of what authors had wrought by their labor.

Earlier copyright cases, too, had borne the mark of this literary labor theory of value. In 1720, defendants in the infringement case *Burnet v. Tonson* argued that translations were new works and thus free from copyrights protecting works in their original languages. Though Lord Chancellor Macclesfield ruled for the plaintiff in order to prevent the text in question (Burnet's infamous *Archaeologia Philosophia*) from appearing in English, his decision conceded that "a translation might not be the same with the reprinting of the original, on account that the translator has bestowed his care and pains upon it."[18] The care and pains of "original labor"—that is, intellectual labor beyond the simple reprinting of a pirated edition—soon became the criterion separating "new works" from infringements of old ones. In later debates, copyright would be enlisted by Wordsworth and others to protect a much more extreme and mystified originality; but during the eighteenth century, landmark copyright cases relied on a much more modest definition of originality to decide which kinds of literary labor garnered the "natural right of property." The decision for *Gyles v. Wilcox* (1740) established abridgements as new works on the grounds that they required a skilled labor of the abridger, whose "invention, learning, and judgment" earned him the title of "author."[19] And in 1785, Lord Mansfield made a similar ruling regarding maps in *Sayre v. Moore,* granting maps "new work" status even if they were mostly collations of previous maps. His introductory words to *Sayre* explicitly tied copyright to the work of authorship; copyright, said Mansfield, ensured "that men of ability, who have employed their time for the service of the community, may not be deprived of their just merits, and the reward for their ingenuity and labour."[20]

But while some debaters and legislators were advancing an aesthetic labor theory of value that dovetailed with the logic of the copyright debates, others of the new professional class created by copyright—the authors themselves—were developing a competing theory of value. Though they put the same premium on originality that copyright theorists did, these proto-Romantics celebrated the inspired, spontaneous creations of original genius rather than the hard-won products of original labor. Their emerging doctrine found an early exponent in the poet Edward Young, whose *Conjectures on Original Composition* (1759) appeared the same year as Smith's *Theory of Moral Sentiments.*[21] In his tract, Young paid lip service to labor-based theories of literary value, likening genius to a "master-workman" and averring that "moderns, by the longevity of their labors, might one day become ancients themselves." In his youth, Young had avowed himself a neoclassicist and had labored to become imitable (or "ancient") by imitating prior poets. In most of his *Conjectures,* though, he allied labor with the classicism he now denounced, maligning the study of classical texts as imitative, toilsome, and invention-killing. Worthy literature, he insisted, could not be manufactured from raw materials taken from the ancients through study and imitation but must spring into bloom ex nihilo and sui generis:

> An original may be said to be of a vegetable nature: it rises spontaneously from the vital root of genius; it grows, it is not made; imitations are often a sort of manufacture wrought up by those mechanics, art and labor, out of pre-existent materials not their own. . . . Nor is it strange; for what, for the most part, mean we by genius but the power of accomplishing great things without the means generally reputed necessary to that end? A genius differs from a good understanding, as a magician from a good architect; that raises his structure by means invisible, this by the skillful use of common tools. Hence genius has ever been supposed to partake of something of the Divine.[22]

Neoclassicisms

While Adam Smith was equating beauty with "the order, the regular and harmonious movement of the system, the machine or economy by means of which [satisfaction] is produced," Young gave beauty's origins as anti-industrial, antimechanical, antisystemic—as organic, vegetable, magical, divine.[23] Rather than dwelling on means to the exclusion of ends, the creator in Young's vision leapt to glorious ends through insufficient means, much as Young's idol, Shakespeare, had miraculously written his plays with little Latin and less Greek. Imitation, translation, and writing by ancient rules were impoverished, belated activities best left to workman-like classicists of Pope's ilk; genius had "untrodden ground" to break, yet it would blaze its trails by inspiration, the divine effortlessness.[24]

Having rejected literary classicism, classical economics, and the labor theory of value both discourses shared, Young and like-minded writers founded a Romantic countertradition to all three, one that emphasized not only inspiration over labor but individual heterodoxy over convention, continuity, and social relations. In other words, the Romantic conception of authorship revolted against the very market conditions—mechanical reproduction, textual commodification, logics of equivalency, labor-based copyright laws—that had made authorship professionally viable in the first place. In this sense, the nascent Romantic strain of British aesthetics had begun to reject political economy before political economy could reject it. That strain, incubated by Young and others, would prove contagious. Though the reasons for it are unclear, *Conjectures* did not make immediate waves in England. But Young's text had appeared in two German translations by 1761 and, as Martha Woodmansee has shown, helped spark the *Genieperiode* of German Romanticism by influencing the likes of Herder, Goethe, Fichte.[25] Kant's *Critique of Judgment* (1790) echoed Young in its contention that beautiful art was only possible through genius, "a *talent* for producing that for which no definite rule can be given; it is not a mere aptitude for what can be learned by a rule. Hence *originality* must be its first property. . . . Everyone is agreed that genius is entirely opposed to the *spirit of imitation*."[26] Elaborating on the distinction between imitative and original art, Kant suggested that the two differed not only in degree but in kind or "spirit": the labor of original creation was a different order of labor from that of imitation, producing a kind of value beyond imitation's reach. Twenty-five years after this "Critique of the Aesthetical Judgment," Wordsworth in turn echoed Kant (probably through Coleridge) by prefacing the first collected edition of his *Poems* with a paean to genius, originality, and aesthetic value:

> [E]very author, as far as he is great and at the same time *original*, has had the task of *creating* the taste by which he will be enjoyed . . . . Of genius the only proof is, the act of doing well what is worthy to be done, and what was never done before: Of genius, in the fine arts, the only infallible sign is the widening of the sphere of human sensibility, for the delight, honour, and benefit of hu-

man nature. Genius is the introduction of a new element into the intellectual universe: or, if that be not allowed, it is the application of powers to objects on which they had not before been exercised, or the employment of them in such a manner as to produce effects hitherto unknown.[27]

For both Kant and Wordsworth, geniuses were the rule-breakers who fashioned new rules—were so original that they had to invent their public's capacity to enjoy their work. Genius, then, was earliness personified: not only did geniuses do things before anyone else, they antedated even their own comprehensibility and consumability. Genius was more than a property of originals; it was the mystified origin itself—of ideas, taste, rules, value, the future—and of intellectual property.

In the mid-nineteenth century, the Romantics, whose precursors had departed from the labor-based logic of copyright during the previous century, returned to that territory to secure their literary winnings. In 1814, the copyright term had been extended from its original term (14 years, plus an additional 14 if the author were still alive) to a firm 28 years from publication, or the duration of the author's lifetime, whichever was longer. Sponsored by the Whig M.P. Thomas Noon Talfourd, an 1837 Copyright Bill sought to extend copyright again, this time to the term of the author's life plus 60 years. After being struck down repeatedly, the bill finally passed in revised form in 1842, granting authors a copyright of either 42 years from publication or life plus 7 years, whichever was longer. Chris Vanden Bossche's analysis of the 1837–1842 debates suggests they were, at heart, a standoff between productivist and consumerist theories of literary value. The proponents of the bill were primarily publishers and authors, including such prominent names as Wordsworth, Carlyle, Southey, Dickens, Robert Browning, and Thomas Arnold; as famous "producers" of literature, they emphasized the productivist Romantic values of original genius, authenticity, organicism, and durability. Consumer desires should not influence the copyright term, they argued, because the average reader chose works that satisfied only "an accidental passing taste or want." But since original, enduring literature would not appeal to readers in search of immediate gratification, it needed time for its value to be recognized. Such a time lapse would require longer copyright terms to encourage authors who, in Talfourd's words, "create the taste which should appreciate and reward them" (the echo of Wordsworth seems calculated; Talfourd, himself a literary man, proved a powerful and allusive rhetorician).[28] But while the Talfourd Bill's proponents fought for copyright extension from a productivist standpoint, they sustained Young's rewriting of production as creation, continuing to invoke an imaginative labor that was neither manual nor mechanical. An extended copyright term, they argued, would turn literary property into a hereditary estate, making it the exceptional laurel won by the exceptional labor of original literary creation.

The bill's opponents, by contrast, were less interested in fostering a scarce canon of immortal texts than in disseminating knowledge to a working-class readership. Borrowing much of their rhetoric from the radical Society for the Diffusion of Useful Knowledge, they grounded literary value not in an author's original genius but in the text's consumer utility—its availability, cheapness, and capacity to give instruction, comfort, and happiness to its readers. Monopoly copyright, they insisted, diminished consumer utility by impairing the free market dynamics that kept prices low. In the words of Thomas Babington Macaulay, who opposed Talfourd, copyright was "a tax on readers for the purpose of giving a bounty to writers," and ought therefore to be pruned rather than unbound.[29] According to Macaulay's fellow critics, copyright also set authors above other literary workers (editors, bookbinders, printers, illustrators) by granting them literary property rights instead of wages.[30] So long as it garnered different rewards, authorial labor would be held to differ in kind from manual labor; inflated with this false difference, the lone figure of the author-proprietor would always blot out the collaborative scenes of literary production. Though the consumer "utility" advocated by the Talfourd Bill's opponents was not yet the hedonic calculus later postulated by the maginalist economists and the plagiarism apologists, it anticipated those neoclassicisms in an important way. By looking to the conditions of consumption—cheapness, availability, convenience, usefulness—as the primary source of literary value, the anti-Talfourdians helped shift the proving ground of value in general from production to consumption. Of course, their attack on the disproportionate rewards won by literary labor doubled as a defense of manual labor, whose importance and dignity they saw belittled by authorial property incentives. But rather than assail copyright's Romantic constructions of authorship from the diminished promontory of the labor theory of value, they dug into the newer turf of consumer utility. As a result, they contributed to a series of demand-side critiques of private intellectual property that unwittingly helped pave the way for the consumer hedonics of neoclassical economics.[31]

Though labor-based theories of value had begun eroding in mid-eighteenth-century aesthetics thanks to proto-Romantics like Young, they remained integral to political-economic debates for another hundred years. Smith's most prominent disciple, David Ricardo, kept labor at the center of his own meditations on value. By finessing Smith's theory, Ricardo was able to describe the "equipment" owned by the capitalist—the valuable "means of production"—as a repository of past labor, arguing that a commodity's value was the sum of the present and stored-up labor used to make it. Yet even in Ricardo's work, the labor theory was on the defensive, often against art in particular. In order to preserve a general labor theory of value, Ricardo quarantined it from exceptional cases such as unique artworks and other scarce or unreproducible objects:

> There are some commodities, the value of which is determined by their scarcity alone. No labour can increase the quantity of such goods, and therefore their value cannot be lowered by an increased supply. Some rare statues and pictures, scarce books and coins, wines of a peculiar quality, which can be made only from grapes grown on particular soil, of which there is a very limited quantity, are of this description. Their value is wholly independent of the quantity of labour originally necessary to produce them, and varies with the varying wealth and inclinations of those who are desirous to possess them.[32]

By dividing rarities from commodities that were limitlessly reproducible by labor, Ricardo made a point not only about quantities of labor but about the nature of labor involved in producing unique artworks. Because the scarcity of such works gave them a value unrelated to the amount of labor exerted by the artist, that artistic labor became different in *kind*—became, in a way that would have gratified Young and Talfourd, the mystified labor of creation rather than the rationalized and quantifiable labor of production.[33] But although Ricardo's exemption of unique artworks from a baser commodity status appeared to ratify the Romantic doctrine of inspiration-over-labor, it also rejected the artist-centered aspect of that doctrine: art, Ricardo said, was not valuable because an original genius created it but because of the conditions of scarcity that circumscribed it. Thus the source of the artwork's value shifted—as it had threatened to do in the Talfourd Bill debates—from the divinely gifted Romantic author to the art consumers, whose "varying wealth and inclinations" gave art a value disconnected from the artist's labor. In attempting to rescue the labor theory of value, Ricardo was completing the schism between political economy and aesthetics begun by Smith.

The labor theory of value started to lose favor among political economists during the first half of the nineteenth century, when writers like Samuel Bailey and J. R. McCulloch attacked Ricardo's work, and Nassau William Senior revised it past recognition. The "neoclassical" or "marginalist" school that arose out of these critiques and revisions began its full-scale makeover of political economy during the 1870s, with the work of William Stanley Jevons in England, Carl Menger in Austria, and Léon Walras in France. Though differing in some specifics, the work of these writers helped precipitate a fundamental shift in economic notions of both value and social relations. This shift began with a focus on the scene of individual consumption rather than on the social scene of production. Using the mathematical approaches that became their hallmark, the marginalists posited a "law of diminishing marginal utility" that traced the consumer's falling desire for increasing numbers of a particular commodity. In their focus on the scene of consumption, they regarded the commodity not as a repository of labor but as "any object, substance, action, or service which can afford pleasure or ward off pain." The value of a commodity, consequently, was a function not

Neoclassicisms

of the labor required to produce it but of its "utility"—its power to please or palliate; as Jevons wrote, "[labour's] *value must be determined by the value of the produce, not the value of the produce by that of the labour.*"[34] According to the marginalist view, individuals sought to maximize their utility, or pleasure, by fulfilling first their basic needs and desires and then their more esoteric, idiosyncratic ones. Because utility, then, was ultimately a subjective matter, no standard of "intersubjectivity" was deemed possible or even desirable. The best economics could do was to extrapolate roughly from individual utility to aggregate valuations, declining any more specific provisions for the collective good. Embracing a quantitative science of individual consumer choices and desires, the marginalists forbore to make social or ethical judgments; at Jevons's behest, they retired the "political" side of political economy in both name and practice.

Yet if the marginalist revolution of the 1870s divorced economics from ethics, it also renewed the long-dormant tie between economics and aesthetics by grounding value in individual sensations (the Greek *aisthesis*, whence *aesthetics*) and by generalizing the artwork's condition of scarcity for all commodities. Where political economists such as Ricardo had increasingly exiled scarce or unreproducible objects from their labor-based theories of value, the marginalists readmitted such objects to the center of their calculus: the value of *all* objects, they said, was determined not by the quantum of labor required to produce them, but by what Ricardo had sidelined as the "inclination of those who are desirous to possess them"—the idiosyncratic desires of consumers. Because consumers' desires for a particular commodity varied according to its availability, value was a function primarily of scarcity. And since consumers' desires, once sated, were always succeeded by new, unsatisfied ones—the supply of new desires being the only inexhaustible supply—insatiable consumers were held to exist in a permanent field of scarcity, their limitless desires contending with a limited supply of desirable commodities. The marginalists shook the commodity loose from its scene of production by locating its value in its powers of pleasure-giving. Like the work of art, the commodity acquired a glamour of autonomy—what Marx called "commodity fetishism"—insofar as its power to afford pleasure or ward off pain flowed from a forgotten, occulted, or mystified origin. As I argue in the following section, this new affinity, or even identity, in conceptions of commodity and artwork can also be discerned in a series of nineteenth-century meditations on the nature of literary originality and literary value. Some of the texts belonging to this minority counterdiscourse deployed the pleasure-centered, consumerist logic of marginalism to decriminalize and ultimately valorize plagiarism as well as other, less taboo forms of literary appropriation. Others contributed to a critique of the law and ideology of private literary property underwritten by classical economics during the eighteenth century. Both of these gestures—the hedonic assault on plagiarism's moral stigma and the critique of private literary property law—eventually converged in certain fin-de-siècle literatures and helped underwrite later acts of recirculation, appropriation, and critique.

Literary Hedonics

Jevons's preface to the second edition (1879) of *The Theory of Political Economy* provides a microcosmic example of the shift his economic work helped license in the realm of aesthetics—the shift from a Romantic emphasis on originality to a demand-side emphasis on readerly consumer satisfaction. Whereas the preface to the 1871 edition had announced the heterodoxy of Jevons's theory, "sketched out, almost irrespective of previous opinions," the second preface is deflated, almost apologetic: "the question is not so much whether the theory given in this volume is true, but whether there is really any novelty in it." The answer—an implicit *no*—is followed by a roster of precursors. Disappointed to learn that "Gossen has completely anticipated me as regards the general principles and method of the theory of Economics," Jevons must find solace in having promulgated ideas he didn't pioneer but that might have remained obscure without him.

> I have carefully pointed out, both in the first edition and in this, certain passages of Bentham, Senior, Jennings, and other authors, from which my system was, more or less consciously, developed. I cannot claim to be totally indifferent to the rights of priority; and from the year 1862, when my theory was first published in outline, I have often pleased myself with the thought that it was at once a novel and an important theory. From what I have now stated in this preface it is evident that novelty can no longer be attributed to the leading features of the theory. Much is clearly due to Dupuit, and of the rest a great share must be assigned to Gossen. Regret may easily be swallowed up in satisfaction if I succeed eventually in making that understood and valued which has been so sadly neglected.

Echoing the very arguments advanced by his book, Jevons shifts the value of his work from the Romantic-productivist claim of "priority" to the consumerist claim of utility—the work's capacity to bring the value of "satisfaction" both to its author and to its readers. Rather than denigrate his own contribution as belated or borrowed, Jevons attempted to draw strength from his precursors. From the second edition onward, he appended a list of "Mathematico-Economic Writings" by like-minded economists, as if to legitimate his own approach by creating a tradition for himself to inherit—as he called it, a "filiation of ideas."[35] The "rights of priority" became a matter of indifference compared with the validating power of an intellectual genealogy. In Jevons's own preface, neoclassical economics had sponsored literary neoclassicism.

While the forerunners of Jevonsian economics were writing around mid-century, a previously unseen kind of article had begun to appear in British and American literary journals: the defense of plagiarism. These articles used a language and logic strikingly similar to those of the nascent neoclassical economics to transfer literary value from priority to utility—in this case, a *readerly* hedonics—claiming that the origins of ideas and expressions mattered less than their capacity to satisfy and edify the reader. Like the marginalists' writings, they discarded the labor theory of value in favor of idiosyncratic consumer desire, putting a new emphasis on taste and choice. They also posited a reading public with an insatiable appetite for novelty, at the same time broadening the category of novelty to include any forgotten ideas and expressions restored to readers through rediscovery, renovation, or plagiarism. The writers of these articles—some of them prominent figures such as the novelist E. F. Benson and the folklorist Andrew Lang—attempted to destigmatize plagiarism on the grounds that new ideas and expressions were increasingly scarce in their belated epoch and that even the great minds of earlier periods had alluded, imitated, and stolen. As F. J. Hudleston wrote for *Tinsleys' Magazine* in 1889, "[literary appropriation] is perfectly justifiable, for if there was nothing new under the sun in the time of Solomon, the same may very well hold good in the present day."[36] The broad project of the defenses of plagiarism was to overhaul the Romantic mythology of original genius, remaking genius as a function of assimilation and recombination rather than a fountainhead of fresh invention.[37] One of these writers, W. H. Davenport Adams, summed up the transformation in a phrase that would have seemed both perverse and paradoxical to Edward Young and Romantics of his stripe: "a good imitation is the most perfect originality."[38]

The arguments advanced by these plagiarism apologists locate even late-twentieth-century critiques of originality squarely within a nineteenth-century "filiation of ideas." One apologist, A. Mitchell, wrote that "What is often termed originality, is more a manufactured article than a natural product.... An original thinker may be considered as one who has grown mentally fat upon the food great minds in all ages of the world have afforded him."[39] Mitchell's stance, at least, may seem poststructuralist, but the sentences appeared in *The Knickerbocker* in 1854, the year Gossen published the *Entwicklung der Gesetze des menschlichen Verkehrs* that so dismayingly anticipated Jevons's work. According to Mitchell, literary originality was not some organic embodiment of pure innovation but a commodity—a "manufactured article"—proceeding from an unspecified source and destined for consumption. To that end, the primary work of writers, as the neoclassical economists were to say of all individuals, was no longer production but consumption—in this case, growing "mentally fat" on tradition. The obsessive peristaltic language in this and other plagiarism defenses registers the emerging idea that literary production was simply a function of literary consumption. Poor readers were necessarily poor thinkers and writers, since "The mind grows by what it feeds upon, and no man can be an original thinker without a good deal of knowledge.... knowledge is of little value unless it is well digested.... Minds, like stomachs, have little relish for food they cannot digest."[40] In 1888, Fred Ford attributed critics' persistent charges of plagiarism to "literary indigestion,"[41] and in 1899, E. F. Benson's extended meditation on writing as eating appeared in *The Nineteenth Century:*

> Indigestion is the mother of remorse; shellfish bring near to us the sense of sin.... the same phenomenon is incontrovertibly shown in the case of literary and artistic digestion, and the sense of sin consequent thereon. There exist in this world great masses of admirable literary food, the inherited treasury of the race. On these we feed ... and without them we starve. But it is necessary that we should assimilate what we take, the food must be digested. That done, it becomes a part of us, it enters into our muscles, our bones, our brains, it has caused and is causing to make us grow in our own small manner, and the words we use, and the things we write, and the songs we sing, are the inevitable outcome of the nourishment we have received.... if we [digest tradition], we shall get, by assimilation of our food, not a plagiarised imitation of our original, but a manner which, but for it, could never have been ours.... No amount of dissimulation will conceal from ourselves the fact that we have stolen unintelligently, that we have not digested properly.[42]

Contra Edward Young, writers were told not to avoid the debased and "borrowed knowledge" of others' works, but to feast well on tradition and digest it properly—to bite off all that Young would eschew. Though literary super-consumption was endorsed as the shortest route to originality—a "manner" that was finally "our own"—consumption, not creation, occupied the discursive foreground. At the hands of Mitchell, Ford, Benson, and other apologists of plagiarism, readers and writers received a message that defied Young's proto-Romanticism: at the eatery of literature, you are what you read. According to their evolving consumerist aesthetic, invention had become a by-product of feasting on the public domain—on those "great masses of admirable literary food" that constituted "the inherited treasury of the race."

By imagining writing as a pleasurable deglutition, the Victorian plagiarism apologists effectively remade production in the image of consumption, conferring the sumptuary pleasures of reading on the act of writing. In fact, pleasure itself—Jevonsian "utility"—became the key term in the new aesthetic calculus, replacing original genius as the source and standard of literary value. Because plagiarized ideas and expressions lost none of their power to please readers in the moment of their consumption, the more extreme of the apologists regarded plagiarism as no less valuable than original literature. As a result, they decriminalized plagiarism in their writings, retooling it as a kind of benefaction that required its own variety of genius. The most aggressive and protracted of these rewritings is the long entry under "plagiarism" in William S. Walsh's *Handy-Book of Literary Curiosities* (1892):

Is plagiarism a crime? For ourselves we confess that we hold it only a venial offense—unless, of course, it is found out. If a man thrills us with the joy and gladness of a great thought, what matter where he got it? We might have passed our lives in ignorance thereof. The discoverer is as great a benefactor as the originator. And then, to be Irish, the originator may not have originated it. . . . But now mark what far-reaching benefits accrued from Disraeli's plagiarism. In the first place, he gave a great deal of pleasure to his hearers which he could not have given otherwise. The review article was better than anything he could have offered himself, otherwise he would not have filched it. Now, the pleasure was an actual pleasure; when the moment had fled, it could not be retracted or embittered by any subsequent development. Then he gave his critics the pleasure of detecting him—a great delight accorded to a worthy and deserving and very hard-worked class. The whole of England was aroused, amused, and interested. In fact, Disraeli proved himself an all-round benefactor.[43]

The episode Walsh cheekily describes had occurred in 1852 when Benjamin Disraeli, then Chancellor of the Exchequer, was found to have cribbed his funeral oration over Wellington from Thiers's 1829 encomium for Marshal Gouvion de Saint-Cyr. Disraeli's plagiarism, which became a staple in the apologists' articles, had raised a predictable howl from the anti-Disraeli *Globe*: "We have seen him snatch a wreath of faded French artificial flowers for the pall of Wellington, with an audacity of larceny unsurpassed in Grub Street."[44] Walsh's defense of the plagiarism, even forty years after the fact, went against the prevailing public view of plagiarism as a "larceny." But most interesting is Walsh's enumeration of the various "pleasures" the incident had afforded the British public. Far from being less valuable than Thiers's original composition, Disraeli's plagiarism had not only pleased its hearers but added the pleasures of detection and public spectacle to the mix. As a result of his larcenous benefaction, the British public was that much more "aroused, amused, and interested" than Thiers's initial readers.

This hedonic line of argument neither began nor ended with Walsh's *Handy-Book*. In 1874, an anonymous writer for *The Leisure Hour* defended *Ossian*, MacPherson's forged and partly plagiarized Scots epic, for the unabated pleasure it continued to give him: "I now, although convinced of the imposture, find pleasure in reading MacPherson."[45] In the U.S., Ralph Waldo Emerson anticipated Walsh in 1876, writing that "If an author give us just distinctions, inspiring lessons, or imaginative poetry, it is not so important to us whose they are. If we are fired and guided by these, we know him as a benefactor, and shall return to him as long as he serves us well."[46] Cut adrift from the substrate of its source, the text became a pleasure-parcel; the author, in Emerson's formulation, was more a private postman than an originator, earning customers' loyalty through years of reliable service. In 1887 Andrew Lang argued that even the most hackneyed plot devices could still, in the right hands, become "a novel that would soothe pain and charm exile"—that is, a perfect example of the Jevonsian commodity, "any object, substance, action, or service which can afford pleasure or ward off pain."[47] And in a 1904 article pointedly entitled "The Art of Plagiarism," Edward Wright made the following claims: "the men who first conceive an idea, a situation, a melody, a colour scheme, an effect in sculpture, are insignificant. The men who best conceive these things are great. . . . A poet is not essentially an inventor. . . . He is a singer. So long as he sings with sincerity and clearness, with charm or grandeur, it matters nothing to his fame where he finds the subject-matter of his song."[48] Literary labor theories of value, which evaluated the conditions of literary production and esteemed the labor of original composition most highly, had been challenged by a readerly hedonics that countenanced plagiarism for the sake of pleasure.

Having identified both reading and writing as explicitly pleasurable acts of individual consumption, the apologists now schooled readers in how to enjoy the consumerist talents of authors, talents legible in such textual qualities as deftness of selection, rightness of taste, elegance of integration. As W. H. Adams wrote in an 1892 number of *The Gentleman's Magazine*, "The scholar will hardly impute [extensive literary borrowing] as a reproach; he feels a rare and genuine pleasure in following the poet in his researches in many fields; in observing with what care he selects the finest growths—in admiring the taste and elegance with which he weaves them in his own garlands."[49] Where the Edward Young strain of Romanticism had celebrated the poet's ex nihilo "invention," the apologists restored the original meaning of *invenire*: to come upon. No longer poets in the literal sense of "makers," writers were just more "tasteful" shoppers and arrangers than their readers were—or, to return to the peristaltic metaphor, better digesters and incorporators of literary nourishment. What they bestowed on their readerly fellow consumers was the "rare and genuine pleasure" of a mimetic consumption, an act of reading whose primary aim was to appreciate the writer's anterior acts of reading and recombination. Writing was a record of reading, and the new literary product nothing more than an agglomeration of prior consumptions.

This emerging view of authorship as a primarily consumptive act belonged, as I have indicated, to a minority discourse during the nineteenth century, a century during which the Romantic figure of the author as original genius continued to dominate both aesthetics and literary property law. Nonetheless, the counterdiscourse I have described was both more vital and more varied than is generally recognized, manifesting itself not only in legislative movements and defenses of plagiarism but in the flux of popular literary form as well. The counterdiscourse to Romantic authorship can be discerned, for example, in the growing popularity of the "cento" or "mosaic" or "patchwork" form of poetry over the course of the nineteenth century. Charles Bombaugh's *Gleanings from the Harvest-fields of Literature, Science and Art* (1860) defines the cento as "a work wholly composed of verses, or passages promiscuously taken from other authors and disposed in a new form or order, so as to compose a new work and a new meaning."⁵⁰ Its rigid rules of composition, set down in the fourth century C.E. by the Roman poet Ausonius, gave the cento classical constraints: its constituent parts could be taken from one author or many; single lines or even full couplets could be mined from a particular source, but consecutive couplets must come from different source texts.⁵¹ In a sense, the cento represents the ultimate neoclassical form: it not only pushes imitation to the point of verbatim (if piecemeal) copying, it also reinforces traditional poetic forms by quarrying its component lines from metrically identical source poems.⁵² The famous centos Bombaugh cites were largely religious—classical recuperations, such as lives of Christ assembled from lines of Homer and Virgil, or devotional verse cobbled together from disparate lines of scripture. The classical tradition had thrived during the eighteenth century and continued in the early nineteenth, with examples like the 1806 *Brontes: A Cento, to the Memory of the Late Viscount Nelson, Duke of Bronté*, which remobilized some 300 lines of extant Latin verse to recount Nelson's naval victories, death, and funeral. But in addition to such offerings, Bombaugh's *Gleanings* contains a cento with more recent source texts, one that displays its compiler's encounters with contemporary rather than classical poetry:

MOSAIC POETRY

I only knew she came and went	*Lowell.*
Like troutlets in a pool;	*Hood.*
She was a phantom of delight,	*Wordsworth.*
And I was like a fool.	*Eastman.*
"One kiss, dear maid," I said and sighed,	*Coleridge.*
"Out of those lips unshorn."	*Longfellow.*
She shook her ringlets round her head,	*Stoddard.*
And laughed in merry scorn.	*Tennyson.*
Ring out, wild bells, to the wild sky	*Tennyson.*
You hear them, oh my heart?	*Alice Carey.*
'Tis twelve at night by the castle clock,	*Coleridge.*
Beloved, we must part!	*Alice Carey.*
"Come back! come back!" she cried in grief,	*Campbell.*
"My eyes are dim with tears—	*Bayard Taylor.*
How shall I live through all the days,	*Mrs. Osgood.*
All through a hundred years?"	*T. S. Perry.*
'Twas in the prime of summer time,	*Hood.*
She blessed me with her hand;	*Hoyt.*
We strayed together, deeply blest,	*Mrs. Edwards.*
Into the Dreaming Land.	*Cornwall.*
The laughing bridal roses blow,	*Patmore.*
To dress her dark brown hair;	*Bayard Taylor.*

The Copywrights

> No maiden may with her compare,   *Brailsford.*
> Most beautiful, most rare!   *Read.*
>
> I clasped it on her sweet cold hand,   *Browning.*
> The precious golden link;   *Smith.*
> I calmed her fears, and she was calm,   *Coleridge.*
> "Drink, pretty creature, drink!"   *Wordsworth.*
>
> And so I won my Genevieve,   *Coleridge.*
> And walked in Paradise;   *Hervey.*
> The fairest thing that ever grew   *Wordsworth.*
> Atween me and the skies.   *Osgood.*[53]

This cento's amiable puzzle-effects—its bizarre marriage of lines by unkindred poets, its thematic wink at the nuptial nature of its form, its lapses into incoherence or bathos ("I only knew she came and went / Like troutlets in a pool")—belie its complex construction of authorship. Unsigned and generically titled, the poem declines a discreet identity of its own, suggesting instead that the literary object is the sum of its maker's readerly acts of consumption, just as the maker's identity is at once constituted and eclipsed by those acts of reading. Those readings are memorialized by the column of source authors provided by the cento's anonymous writer (or rather, redactor), a column that acts as both a parody of the parallel columns used in plagiarism allegations and a rather miscellaneous poetic mini-canon. But while the list of authors glorifies them as near-scriptural sources, it also deconsecrates the canonized writers by demonstrating that even "immortal" poetic lines depend partly on context for their effects and can be altered beyond recognition when grafted onto less exalted lines. Even more heretically, the source column insinuates that poetic titans like Wordsworth and Coleridge might themselves be nothing more than gifted centonists—an allegation partly true, at least, in the case of Coleridge, whose extensive plagiarisms had been publicly exposed during the 1830s. If the cento paid a lavish tribute to its sources, it also levied a tax on their claims of originality.

By naming its multiple "authors," the cento printed in *Gleanings* also identified the kind of pleasure its readers were meant to enjoy—what W. H. Adams would call the "rare and genuine pleasure in following the poet in his researches in many fields"—the pleasure of a recursive or mimetic consumption. By supplying a partial answer key to the *poème à clef*, the redactor challenged the reader to retrace his or her steps through the garden of poetic history, admiring the "taste and elegance" with which the found blossoms had been woven into new garlands. Insofar as it records its maker's gleanings from the harvest fields of literature, the cento also reproduces Bombaugh's book in miniature: *Gleanings* (subtitled *A Melange of Excerpta*) is nothing if not a monument to its "collator's" literary super-consumption, his ability to digest and redact language into categories as diverse as "Para-

Neoclassicisms

nomasia," "Churchyard Verse," "Moslem Wisdom," and "Nothing New Under the Sun." In fact, the epigraphs of *Gleanings* make the whole book out to be a kind of cento—"A fountain set round with a rim of old, mossy stones, and paved in its bed with a sort of mosaic-work of variously colored pebbles (HOUSE OF SEVEN GABLES)." And like the cento it includes, Bombaugh's collection specifies not only its source authors but the kind of pleasure it intends for its readers. Another epigraph portrays the book as an inexhaustible smorgasbord to suit literary consumers' idiosyncratic desires: "It is a regular omnibus: there is something in it to everybody's taste. Those who like fat can have it; so can they who like lean; as well as those who prefer sugar, and those who choose pepper (MYSTERIES OF PARIS)."[54]

Over the course of the century, both the cento and the prefabricated scrapbook or "digest" continued to proliferate in Britain and the U.S. As the amount and variety of printed matter increased to the point of perceived excess, a demand arose for collections of literary gems rescued from the oblivion of superfluity by keen-eyed collators and gathered under headings like "The Witchery of Wit," "The Bright Side," "Youth and Age," "Pastimes of the Pen." As a result, archives of Victorian publications teem with "gleanings" from various fields: *Pisgah Sights & Gospel Gleanings; Churchyard Gleanings; Gleanings on Gardens; Science Gleanings in Many Fields; Geology Gleanings; Gleanings for Leisure Hours: A Set of Conversational Cards in Prose & Verse; Gleanings from the Poets, for Cottage Homes*. Predictably, the activities of collation and creation mingled in both the digest's principles of construction and its internal meditations about the nature of authorship. Frederick Saunders, who compiled a best-selling literary miscellany called *Salad for the Solitary: by an Epicure* (1853; rpt. 1872, 1886), named a second after the cento form, his *Mosaics* (1859). The book's opening chapter, "Author-Craft," is typical of mid- and late-century popular literary digests in the way it embraces seemingly incompatible views of authorship:

> An author is a kind of anomaly in the human family—living apart from his race, and inhabiting an ideal world with feelings and impulses peculiarly his own. With the commonplace things of every day life he has generally but little sympathy—anti-social, isolate, and indulging in ascetic exclusiveness that at once induces our mingled pity and admiration.... Whatever their social peculiarities or defects, yet, if authors are, in a certain sense, the inspired among men, ought we not to reverence and love them? ... Genius is a ray from heaven; its very name indicates its connection with all that is *genial* upon earth, and its celestial mission is to foster and perpetuate a love of the beautiful and to multiply the gentle amenities of life.
>
> Authors, again, have been styled lamps, exhausting themselves to give light to others: to bees, industriously collecting honey from the flowers, which they treasure up in the hive of books to sweeten and solace life. Author-craft is an imitative as well as a creative art; an original thinker is one who portrays the

works of the great Author of the universe—the compiler, one who ingeniously adapts or rearranges the thoughts and illustrations of others; both in their degree may be said to exhibit creative power.⁵⁵

The first passage is standard Romantic author worship and might have been excerpted from Edward Young's *Conjectures* in its construction of the author as an exceptional, visionary genius. The second, while it retains the category of original creation, makes it an effect of collection, imitation, compilation, adaptation, rearrangement—the activities, say, of a Frederick Saunders. Ultimately the second model, in its inclusiveness and radical heterogeneity, overwhelms the first by absorbing it: Young's organic, autochthonous model of genius can make no allowances for craft, influence, learning, or gathering, whereas Saunders's description of the author as honeybee can still accommodate original creation as one among many modes of authorial production. Despite their genuflections to original genius through homage and quotation, *Mosaics* and its genre-mates sought to reconfigure authorship in the image not of the writers they quoted but of their compilers: the author as miscellanist, the author as miscellany.

1890 saw an expanded edition of Bombaugh's *Gleanings*, whose introduction quantitatively boasted that "while [the volume] has been nearly doubled in size, it has been more than doubled in literary value," and served up a whole banquet of self-descriptors: "miscellanea," "collectanea," "scripscrapologia," "olla podrida," "hotch-potch," "omnium-gatherum."⁵⁶ True to its ostentatious plenitude, the 1890 edition doubles its offerings of centos, among them "Life," whose first line is, a little wickedly, taken from Edward Young:

LIFE

1.—Why all this toil for triumphs of an hour?
2.—Life's a short summer, man a flower.
3.—By turns we catch the vital breath and die—
4.—The cradle and the tomb, alas! so nigh.
5.—To be is better far than not to be,
6.—Though all man's life may seem a tragedy.
7.—But light cares speak when mighty griefs are dumb;
8.—The bottom is but shallow whence they come.
9.—Your fate is but the common fate of all,
10.—Unmingled joys, here, to no man befall.
11.—Nature to each allots his proper sphere,
12.—Fortune makes folly her peculiar care.
13.—Custom does not often reason overrule
14.—And throw a cruel sunshine on a fool.
15.—Live well, how long or short permit, to heaven;
16.—They who forgive most, shall be most forgiven.
17.—Sin may be clasped so close we cannot see its face—

18.—Vile intercourse where virtue has not place.
19.—Then keep each passion down, however dear,
20.—Thou pendulum, betwixt a smile and tear;
21.—Her sensual snares let faithless pleasure lay,
22.—With craft and skill, to ruin and betray.
23.—Soar not too high to fall, but stop to rise;
24.—We masters grow of all that we despise.
25.—Oh then renounce that impious self-esteem;
26.—Riches have wings and grandeur is a dream.
27.—Think not ambition wise, because 'tis brave,
28.—The paths of glory lead but to the grave.
29.—What is ambition? 'Tis a glorious cheat,
30.—Only destructive to the brave and great.
31.—What's all the gaudy glitter of a crown?
32.—The way to bliss lies not on beds of down.
33.—How long we live, not years but actions tell;
34.—That man lives twice who lives the first life well.
35.—Make then, while yet ye may, your God your friend,
36.—Whom Christians worship, yet not comprehend.
37.—The trust that's given guard, and to yourself be just;
38.—For, live we how we can, yet die we must.

---

1. Young. 2. Dr. Johnson. 3. Pope. 4. Prior. 5. Sewell. 6. Spenser. 7. Daniel. 8. Sir Walter Raleigh. 9. Longfellow. 10. Southwell. 11. Congreve. 12. Churchill. 13. Rochester. 14. Armstrong. 15. Milton. 16. Bailey. 17. Trench. 18. Somerville. 19. Thomson. 20. Byron. 21. Smollett. 22. Crabbe. 23. Massinger. 24. Cowley. 25. Beattie. 26. Cowper. 27. Sir Walter Davenant. 28. Gray. 29. Willis. 30. Addison. 31. Dryden. 32. Francis Quarles. 33. Watkins. 34. Herrick. 35. William Mason. 36. Hill. 37. Dana. 38. Shakespeare.

Still another volume of miscellanea, William T. Dobson's *Literary Frivolities, Fancies, Follies, and Frolics* (1880), includes "Life" in its extensive collection of "Centones or Mosaics." Unlike Bombaugh's *Gleanings*, however, Dobson's book provides details of the cento's provenance: "'Life' is said to have occupied a year's laborious search among the voluminous writings of thirty-eight leading poets of the past and present times. The compilation first appeared in the *San Francisco Times* and was the work of Mrs. H. A. Deming." Though Dobson's note foregrounds the laboriousness of the poem's birth, it is the labor of "searching" and "compiling" rather than "writing" or "composing"—the labor of the reader or scholar rather than that of the original genius. (In similar terms, he both belittles and lauds another cento that appeared in the *People's Friend* of May 1871 as "laborious trifling ... evincing great patience and research.")[57] Dobson's remarks make the finished 38-line cento seem lavishly, even laughably out of proportion to the year-long labor of its compilation, and insinuate that cento-making is necessarily an activity for the leisured classes. In its nineteenth-century resurgence, the cento enabled the members of this prime readerly demographic to write back through the activity of reading, to produce a literature of extravagant consumption.[58] The resulting poems rewrite consumption as authorship without erasing or subordinating the fact of consumption; as such, they are portraits of a model of identity just emerging in the late nineteenth century, one for which the act of production is secondary to that of consumption, the act of writing a function of reading. The centonist's mode of authorial attribution diverges, too, from productivist Romantic orthodoxy: though some centos are attached to the proper names of their supposed collators (Mrs. H. A. Deming, Sir Fretful Plagiary), that attribution is a "soft" attribution, seldom verifiable, often overwhelmed by the identities of the source authors and immune to the temptations of the "man-and-his-work-criticism" decried by Foucault.

Although Victorian centos share certain consumerist affinities with the defenses of plagiarism, they commit neither the moral transgression of plagiarism nor the legal one of copyright infringement. Those centos that do not identify their source authors in attribution columns tend to alert readers to their recombinative nature through their titles ("Cento from Pope"), or through the inclusions of giveaway lines such as "His was a grief too deep for tears" and "The proper study of mankind is man" (see examples in appendix). By exonerating itself of plagiarism, the cento seems to open itself to the charge of infringement—that is, of having reprinted the protected expression of another author without consulting or remunerating that author. Obviously, the cento's reuse of a single line from a source poem is unlikely to cannibalize the market for authorized editions of that poem, the primary violation against which copyright protects a work. But in the more severe copyright climate of our own day, we are used to acknowledgments pages bearing copyright permissions to quote equally brief excerpts from protected works. The absence of such permissions in nineteenth-century centos testifies not to their legal transgressiveness, but to the fact that they were written under a more open copyright regime than the present one. In quoting from both protected and public domains, these centos exemplify the kind of technically "fresh" creation from prior works that is possible under a thinner copyright regime than our own, and perhaps constitute a sort of embodied plea, in the wake of the 1842 Copyright Act, that literary property laws not thicken further.[59] Finally, by demonstrating the uses of recirculated expression, Victorian centos anticipated the doctrine of "fair dealing" or "fair use"—the exemption of certain kinds of textual reproduction from infringement—which had yet to be formalized in Anglo-American copyright law. But in a sense, they already went beyond the eventual provisions of that doctrine. Where fair use now permits the quotation of protected works for such purposes as teaching, scholarship, criticism, and parody, the cento's quotations do not fall clearly under any of these rubrics; nor do they constitute the sort of "political" speech that might mitigate intellectual property rights. Rather, the cento asserts the intrinsic value of textual *appropriation*—in the nonstigmatized sense of "making something one's own"—as a mode of fresh creation, legitimating the very sort of noncritical, nonparodic appropriation that would be prohibited by millennial copyright regimes.

The centonists, the gleaners and collators, and the plagiarism apologists hinted that all texts were to some extent centos of prior texts and all writers conduits for anterior ideas and expression. Emerson wrote that "there is no pure originality. All minds quote," adding that "We expect a great man to be a good reader; or in proportion to the spontaneous power should be the assimilating power."[60] Accordingly, many late-nineteenth-century critics began to focus less on writers' powers of generation and more on their powers of consumption, redaction, and recontextualization. To demonstrate his own "assimilating power," Lang confessed to plagiarizing a passage from Zulu and suggested that the word *plagiarist* could be defined as "any successful author."[61] In 1888, the American Fred Ford concurred, writing that "Our plagiarisms cease only with life," while Oscar Wilde announced, around the same time, that plagiarism was "the privilege of the appreciative man"—a privilege he claimed in his works.[62] Remarkably, the neoclassical disposition of the Victorian apologists and centonists did not perish with their generation but persisted in a number of Anglo-American modernist writers. In works by Joyce, Eliot, Pound, Moore, and others, certain traits of an obscure Victorian counterdiscourse—the apologists' and centonists' bent toward imitation, quotation, appropriation, and recombination—found more celebrated expressions. The critic Edmund Wilson recognized the link between modernism (which he called Symbolism) and cento-making in *Axel's Castle* (1931): "in reading Eliot and Pound, we are sometimes visited by uneasy recollections of Ausonius, in the fourth century, composing Greek-and-Latin macaronics and piecing together poetic mosaics out of verses from Virgil."[63] As we will see in chapter 5, Joyce's *Ulysses* is, if not strictly a cento, radically intertextual, and its infrastructural deployment of the *Odyssey* is a broadly neoclassical gesture. And as innumerable poststructuralist writings and postmodern works attest, the notion that there is no radical originality—that all minds always quote—retains its currency for a wide range of critics, theorists, and artists. Paradoxically, the apologists' marginal and counterdiscursive demotion of originality helped lay the conceptual groundwork for several generations-worth of more highly visible critical and creative innovation.

Literary Property

So far I have been discussing the neoclassicisms of the marginalist economists, the Victorian centonists, and the plagiarism apologists as crucial counterdiscourses to the increasingly hegemonic status of intellectual property law during the nineteenth century. But what of the ethical costs of a sumptuary aesthetic that, say, condones plagiarism in the name of pleasure and individual choice, or one that subordinates the scene of production to the scene of consumption? Recently, several critics and intellectual historians have excoriated Jevonsian marginalism for washing its hands of ethics, adding that this same gesture of "normative evisceration" was duplicated in contemporary writings on aesthetics.[64] Whereas political economists from Smith to J. S. Mill had appraised and theorized both the quantitative laws and the social relations involved in labor, capital, rents, and exchange, Jevons and other neoclassical economists focused on the scene of individual consumer desire, extrapolating from it to a mathematics of aggregate demand. This shift toward "mathematico-economics" entailed a shift away from ethics and social relations, now set aside as belonging to a separate intellectual sphere. Jevons was careful to circumscribe his interests, showing how a "calculus of utility" led people to supply their basic wants with the least amount of labor possible and to devote their excess energy to the accumulation of wealth. Although he conceded that "A higher calculus of moral right and wrong would be needed to show how [the laborer] may best employ that wealth for the good of others as well as himself," he made no attempt to develop this higher calculus. For Jevons, ethics was what occupied the contemplative few while the rest of humanity (economists included) were busy producing and consuming according to their internal calculus of utility: "we may certainly say, with Francis Bacon, 'while philosophers are disputing whether virtue or pleasure be the proper aim of life, do you provide yourself with the instruments of either.'"[65] Regenia Gagnier has argued that neoclassical economists and Paterian aesthetics "converge in their promotion of subjectivism, individualism, passive consumption, and ultimately formalism."[66] Instead of scrutinizing the art object's conditions of production as John Ruskin, William Morris, and others had done, Walter Pater turned his attention to the nuances of art consumption—the fleeting sensations and ruminations of the private reader, viewer, and listener. According to this reading, Pater was the Jevons of aesthetics, forsaking the social for the solipsistic, the ethical for the pleasurable.

The nineteenth-century writers who exonerated plagiarists on the basis of a pleasure-calculus are certainly vulnerable to such a critique. By evaluating literature on purely consumerist grounds, they appeared to shelve any concern for how literary works were produced and by whom. As long as the text delivered its cargo of readerly pleasure, the conditions of the writer's or printer's or binder's or papermaker's lives, whether posh or impoverished, remained behind the veil of a seemingly autonomous product. The apologists also chose to ignore plagiarism's real financial effects in a market society—its capacity to infringe not just on copyrights but on writers' livelihoods by sapping the market for their work, although this effect resulted more often from large-scale piracy than from plagiarism. At a broader level, plagiarists failed or refused to honor other writers' labor through conventional channels of acknowledgment and financial reward. Profiting in revenue and reputation from purloined literary work, the plagiarist alienated fellow writers from the fruits of their own labor. And as we have seen in the example of E. F. Benson's diamond metaphor, the apologists sometimes followed the marginalist economists in perpetuating an imperialist rhetoric that justified expropriation by an often racist hierarchy of pleasure capacities.

Yet at the same time that they participated in a certain "normative evisceration" of literary value, the plagiarism apologists were building a critique of their own, one that embraced ethical considerations as much as their plagiarism endorsements often shunted them aside. In defending or redefining plagiarism, the apologists concurrently attacked the conventions and metaphysics of private literary property law during a period when that law was becoming more extensive, more widely accepted, and more thoroughly integrated into the commercial and ideological matrices of industrial capitalism and British colonialism. The logic of this assault may be difficult to follow, given the distinction between plagiarism and copyright infringement: whereas the infringer transgresses copyright law by making unauthorized copies of a protected work, the plagiarist is guilty of misattribution regardless of whether the copied work is under copyright or in the public domain. Infringers break the law, whereas plagiarists commit moral transgressions even in cases where their copying is, strictly speaking, permitted by the law. But though the term *plagiarus* had denoted literary theft (literally, "kidnapping") since Martial used it in the first century C.E., the powerful moral stigma that had attached to plagiarism by the nineteenth century depended on a relatively recent idea: that writers could own, profit by, and control the disposal of their language as if it were real property. Although copyright law did not forbid plagiarism per se, the rise of copyright was a central prop to the economic and cultural developments that had turned plagiarism into a cardinal literary sin. To destigmatize plagiarism, as the apologists attempted to do, was implicitly to criticize the regime of intellectual property laws that had fixed and darkened the stigma of plagiarism by making originality the cardinal virtue of letters. Defending plagiarism could signify in broader, more overtly political ways as well: by the late nineteenth century, monopoly copyright had become such an important buttress to the social hierarchies cherished by industrial capitalism that to attack the law, even obliquely, was to invite charges that one was "communistical"—that one stood in a dissenting relation to the possessive individualism of the age.

As critics of private literary ownership, the plagiarism apologists had a common cause with the opponents of the Talfourd Copyright Bill. But the two critiques did not run entirely in tandem. The anti-Talfourdians had attacked copyright primarily from a consumerist angle, arguing that authorial monopolies in texts robbed readers of cheap, edifying books. The apologists, however, were themselves professional writers and apt to fold literary production into their critique. Though they used a consumerist logic to condone plagiarism, their most outlandish gesture was to collapse the distinction between literary consumption and production. Writing, they implied, was a belated form of reading; individuals were not divisible into readers and writers, consumers and producers, but instead were nodes in an unceasing circulation of ideas and language. Since originality was an effect, not a fact, of such circulation (a "manufactured article" rather than a "natural product"), the traditional conception of literary property was indefensible. Here is the anonymous *Leisure Hour* writer—the one who exonerated Macpherson's *Ossian* for its pleasure-giving power—delivering a prescient attack on private literary ownership by describing a kind of intellectual fluid dynamics:

> In the republic of letters may not a good thing once uttered be considered the property of all? At the feast of reason and the flow of soul, who is to be blamed for helping himself first? . . . [Coleridge] helped himself to the thoughts of others without scruple, but he also gave away, it must be added, in the same open-handed, generous way. He was, it must be admitted, a plagiarist, but he could plead the excuse of the Yankee who was charged with walking off with another man's umbrella—that he bought a new one once a year, put it into circulation, and then considered himself free of the umbrella-stands of his friends for the rest of the twelvemonth.[67]

Imagining a "republic of letters" (against copyright's petty principalities, perhaps), the writer constructs a communal system of literary property based on circulation rather than accumulation. Participants in such a system would be, like the essayist, anonymous points of reciprocity and "flow" rather than titled proprietors of private literary hoards. Published in 1874, the article looks forward to late-century critiques like Wilde's, which defy the logic of private literary accumulation not only by guiltless appropriation but by donation: depositing an idea or expression (troped here by an umbrella) in the communal account licenses one to make eventual withdrawals without penalty. The common-fund model of intellectual property recurs in several essays by other plagiarism apologists—Ford's "That 'Bugbear,' Plagiarism" (1888) and Adams's "Imitators and Plagiarists" (1892):

> If in perusing the work of others we find an idea which is agreeable to us, then that idea immediately becomes our property; not merely by the right of eminent domain, but by the same right that was exercised by the person from whose work we took the idea—that of helping ourselves out of the common store of knowledge—the accumulation of the ages—which is our birthright.[68]

> All those great men whom we see at various epochs dominating over their age are bound to their generation and to the preceding generations, not by threads invisible, but by powerful ties which become perceptible as soon as we care to look for them. A great idea is of slow growth, nor does it attain to its full de-

velopment until it has passed through many minds. Then, at last, it finds the necessary expression, and is made over to the ages as the general possession of mankind.[69]

This notion of a continuum of shared exchange—a writerly joint checking account or gift economy or public domain—becomes a point of resemblance among otherwise divergent modernists. Such accounting recognizes only one form of criminal expropriation: that of seizing an idea or expression out of the public domain and calling it one's own. This private seizure of avowedly communal property may just be the modernist gesture par excellence. Still, however bizarrely they were replicated, marginal countergestures like the ones we have been tracing went on to influence more prominent literary movements and forms. With Wilde, and later Pound, Eliot, Joyce, and other appropriative modernists, literary antiproperty began to take root in new elite literatures—and, arguably, to accrue a cultural capital of its own.

In seeking to recover several late-Victorian counterdiscourses to private literary property law, this chapter left the legislative terrain of copyright with the passage of the 1842 Copyright Act. In later chapters on Wilde, Viereck, and Joyce, I will consider in greater depth the literary critique of copyright and the increasing familiarity of literary works with their intellectual property status. First, however, we need to return to copyright law itself in order to learn what debates were going on in legislative circles, as well as in the public sphere, about intellectual property during the second half of the nineteenth century. For although most accounts of modern British copyright law pass quickly over the period between the 1842 and 1911 Acts as one of unruffled consolidation and unchallenged hegemony, this is manifestly not the case. Though copyright did achieve a form of ideological closure during the late nineteenth century, it did so despite, rather than in the absence of, organized resistance. Remarkably, this resistance did not come principally from the far Left, from a subcultural fringe, or from a consortium of academics, librarians, and free speech advocates, as would be the case today. Instead, it came from a bloc of powerful free trade radicals affiliated with the Board of Trade—men who were knights, factory owners, and administrators of empire, and whose antimonopoly doctrine was diametrically opposed to intellectual property laws that created even temporary monopolies in the reproduction and dissemination of expression. The flat royalty system with which these men proposed to replace monopoly copyright seems, in retrospect, cumbersome and potentially inequitable. Far more interesting is the simple fact that intellectual property law was assaulted by members of the same well-educated governing and industrial classes whom it is generally thought to have benefited most. That such a politically and commercially powerful group could be so trenchantly opposed to a property form already

The Copywrights

over 150 years old illustrates the extent to which postmortem monopoly copyright was still an open question even among the ruling elite, and attests to the degree of ideological closure copyright has achieved *since* it was attacked by the free trade radicals. Their efforts to contest and overturn monopoly copyright coalesced around the 1876–78 Royal Commission on Copyright, to which we now turn.

[2]

Committing Copyright: The Royal Copyright Commission of 1876–78

> I am quite sure that the selfish principle, or I will say the self-regardful principle, is enshrined and glorified by means of copyright, in a way which is most dangerous; and I should be most thankful if we could get quit of it, or get it curtailed by means of the royalty system.
> — R. A. MACFIE, TESTIMONY TO THE COMMISSION

> I take it that the proposal really amounts to this . . . that people with smaller amounts of money shall have no disadvantages from their smaller amounts of money. It is communistic practically: it is simply equalising the advantages of wealth and poverty.
> — HERBERT SPENCER, TESTIMONY TO THE COMMISSION

Matthew Arnold, poet of ignorant armies, called it "a great battle."[1] On the face of things, though, the Royal Copyright Commission hearings of 1876–78 were a civil-enough business: only the murmur of learned men in well-appointed chambers, the scratching of a secretary's stylus. Certainly the witness roll could boast some titanic figures: a quorum of major names in British and American publishing appeared (John Blackwood, John Boosey, R. W. Routledge, John Murray, William Longman, G. H. Putnam, Alexander Macmillan), as did several prominent men of letters (Herbert Spencer, T. H. Huxley, John Tyndall, and Arnold himself). The composer Arthur Sullivan made a statement; a minister from the French Embassy testified once, and the Permanent Secretary of the Board of Trade appeared eight times. But there is little in the main text of the Commission's Report to suggest a titanic clash of opinions. Finally submitted on May 24, 1878, the Report stated

[53]

flatly that "copyright should continue to be treated by law as a proprietary right, and that it is not expedient to substitute for this a right to a royalty, or any other of a similar kind."[2] It then went on to recommend an extension of copyright to the length of the author's life plus 30 years. Throughout, the report has a decisive, vatic ring—fitting, given the mandarin cast of its signatories: J. A. Froude, Anthony Trollope, and James Fitzjames Stephen sat among Baronets, Earls, and Knights in the Commissioners' benches. Yet outside the rhetoric of unanimity, contention teemed: of the fifteen Commissioners, ten attached dissenting statements to the main text. Although some of these appended remarks took issue with minor points of the Report, a handful registered serious reservations, and one—Sir Louis Mallet's eleven-page critique of the ethics, economics, and metaphysics of copyright law—all but repudiated the Report's central conclusions. With its dissenting appendices, then, the Report of the Commissioners documents a profound disagreement among some of the major figures of its time on the subject of intellectual property law. J. A. Froude, one of the few nondissenting signatories, observed correctly that "the real question at issue was whether copyright itself was to be maintained or abandoned."[3] But the debate, deliberation, and discord harbored by the Commission strayed far beyond the strict ambit of copyright. During two years of intermittent hearings, the Commission played host to basic ideological battles over the *doxa* of free trade, the purpose and extent of property rights, the nature of the public-private dichotomy, the circuits of British national and imperial identity, the social value of literature, and the definition of value itself.

Any one of these mêlées makes the 1876–78 Copyright Commission a fascinating object of study.[4] But the Commission was not simply an occasion for the staging and restaging of familiar ideological skirmishes. It also quickly congealed into an ideological formation of its own: the Report of the Commissioners was used by later disputants as a kind of Q.E.D. for the wisdom of monopoly copyright and the folly of its assailants. In 1891 a more moderate reformer could cite the signally discordant 1878 report as a "practically unanimous" ratification of copyright. By 1899 the historian Augustine Birrell would dismiss the royalty system proposed by the antimonopoly Commissioners as a "preposterous scheme, which reeks of our adorable 'Civil Service,'" a scheme "based on the supposed misery of our poor population, sorely standing in need of the literature of the hour. It was knocked on the head by Mr. Herbert Spencer, and other eminent men who gave evidence before the Copyright Commission."[5] For Birrell as for later historians of copyright, the 1878 Report demonstrated conclusively that the dominant conception of copyright was as inevitable as it was just, and that any attempt to curtail or abolish it was little more than a perverse, "communistic" fantasy. Most recently, Brad Sherman and Lionel Bently, in their admirable project of "de-naturalizing" intellectual property law by contesting its claims to closure and inevitability, pass over the dissenting reports entirely. Instead, they contend that "by the 1850s there was a widespread consensus both as to the form that copyright law should take and agreement that the grant of property rights in things such as artistic and literary works was a worthwhile and valuable exercise."[6]

But none of these later oversights or misreadings changes the fact that the 1876–78 Royal Copyright Commission comprised—and was largely intended to comprise—a serious attempt *from within the government* to abolish copyright law or at the very least to rethink its immanent ideology and economics from the standpoint of free trade, and, at least putatively, in the name of the public interest. As it turns out, it may have been the last such attempt: the subsequent history of copyright reform in Britain, as in the United States, has consisted mostly of extensions in the length and breadth of protection. I want to suggest that these extensions have built on the *perceived* finality and unanimity of the 1878 Report, reading it as irrefutable testimony that monopoly copyright embodies the best compromise between individual creative incentives and the public interest. Copyright as we know it, I will argue, habitually rewrites the differences that compose its own history into a self-serving affidavit, conveniently forgetting or misrepresenting once vital alternatives and counterarguments. To some extent, this revisionary gesture of self-legitimation is endemic to all canons, legal and otherwise: in any "progressive," teleological model of history, once-viable alternatives are first stigmatized as dead ends or nearly avoided perils and subsequently buried by the dominant discourse. But in the case of copyright, I would hazard, this retrospective bias is unusually strong—the more so as our present information society relies increasingly on intellectual property laws to secure revenue generated by copyrighted material. Restoring the 1878 Report, then, to its political and socioeconomic contexts—and to its genesis in two years of ideologically divisive hearings—might stir a hundred-year-old counterdiscourse out of hibernation and thus help build a contemporary case for radical copyright reform. Before turning to the Commission and its legacy, however, we need to trace its conceptual roots back some thirty years, to the first Victorian quarrel over the ethics and economics of copyright.

Monopoly, Monopsony, and Free Trade

Though the Royal Copyright Commission was initiated in 1875 and convened the following year, its central preoccupations and arguments dated back, in key ways, to 1842. That year saw the inception of Britain's first postmortem copyright term with the passage of the Talfourd Bill. Since 1814, copyright had lasted 28 years or until the author's death; with the 1842 Act, the term was extended to 42 years or the duration of the author's life plus 7 years, whichever was longer. For the first time, a piece of literary property could explicitly outlive its progenitor, and the literary estate effectively came into being. Talfourd's chief opponents in the debates—a group he disdainfully called the "Doctrinaire party"—were radicals, liberals, and reformist Whigs united under the banner of free trade. They argued that copyright law, like all monopolies, protected artificially high prices, thus robbing book purchasers of the benefits of unfettered competition. This "Doctrinaire party" made no concerted attempt to abolish copyright altogether; after all, even Adam Smith, the father of laissez-faire political economics, had deemed copyright "a proper and adequate reward of merit" (though at a time when protection lasted only a maximum of 28 years from publication).[7] But the free traders would no more brook an extension of the copyright term than they would countenance high tariffs on imported corn. Their resistance to copyright extension collapsed, however, when the 1841 election that ousted Talfourd also brought a Tory majority to the House of Lords. Trimmed from the proposed life-plus-60-year term by Macaulay, the bill passed easily. Its basic provisions would survive even the assault of the radical Commissioners in 1876–78, remaining intact until a further term extension in 1911.

The free trade radicals may have lost the battle over copyright, but they had more dramatic victories ahead. As Chris Vanden Bossche has observed, the Talfourd Bill debates of 1837–42 occurred simultaneously with the anti-Corn-Law agitation that thrust free trade advocates Richard Cobden, John Bright, and C. P. Villiers into the national consciousness. Both debates shared the rhetoric of free trade versus monopoly and in some cases were even argued analogically.[8] (The mixed lexicon of "food material" and "food intellectual" would remain in play throughout the 1876–78 Commission hearings.) Formed in 1838, the Anti-Corn-Law League had achieved partial tariff reform in 1842 and, in the wake of the English rains and Irish Famine of 1845, won the full repeal of the Corn Laws in 1846. In essence, the League held that the Corn Laws—high tariffs on imported corn—had failed as domestic agricultural protections, surviving as a malicious bread tax that favored the landed population at the expense of the working poor.[9] Only the repeal of the domestic corn monopoly, they argued, would free working-class consumers from spending the bulk of their income on food. The structure of that argument was replicated in a subsequent free trade initiative that more closely resembled the copyright issue: the movement to abolish the taxes on paper, newspapers, and newspaper advertising. As Mallet and company were later to say of copyright and the book trade, the threefold "Taxes on Knowledge" made daily newspapers unaffordable for the working class and much of the middle class, who either had to hire out papers or read them in public houses. Cobden knew that the radical case for universal male suffrage was fettered without an educated working-class electorate. He wrote to Bright in 1853 that "The stamp [tax on newspapers] lies at the bottom of the great mound of ignorance and helplessness which bars the path of political and social progress in this country."[10] With Cobden and Bright on its committee, The Association for Promoting the Repeal of the Taxes on Knowledge eventually succeeded in wearing down all three excise duties by 1861. By then, the once heretical doctrine of free trade had become orthodoxy; even Disraeli, a vocal critic of free trade, acknowledged that, as of the elections of 1852, "the principle of unrestricted competition was entirely and finally adopted as the principle of our commercial code."[11]

The future copyright abolitionists of 1878—Mallet, Farrer, and Macfie—were rooted in the common turf of Cobdenite radicalism. In 1862, a few years before his death, Cobden had written of British patent law, "I have a growing doubt of the value and justice of the system, whether as regards the interests of the public or the inventors."[12] His doubts were shared by Robert Andrew Macfie, a Scottish sugar refiner and unswerving Cobdenite. Having retired from the sugar industry in 1863, Macfie sat as M.P. for Leith Burghs from 1868 to 1874, during which time he led a nearly successful campaign to abolish patent law. As Fritz Machlup and Edith Penrose have shown, this movement on behalf of "free trade in inventions" was not a British eccentricity but a trend that swept through Europe between 1850 and 1875. Such a movement is hard to imagine today, when intellectual property laws have a kind of monolithic facticity. But during those years, Chancellor Bismarck denounced the principle of patent law, and Prussia and Switzerland repeatedly refused to adopt patent regimes; in 1869, Holland, known as the capital of the free trade movement, went so far as to repeal its patent law.[13]

Of course, the antipatent view was not universally held, even by radical free traders. In the 1862 edition of his *Principles of Political Economy,* John Stuart Mill had famously dismissed the patent abolition movement as a travesty of free trade advocacy:

> It would be a gross immorality in the law to set everybody free to use a person's work without his consent, and without giving him an equivalent. I have seen with real alarm several recent attempts, in quarters carrying some authority, to impugn the principle of patents altogether; attempts which, if practically successful, would enthrone free stealing under the prostituted name of free trade, and make the men of brains, still more than at present, the needy retainers and dependents of the men of money-bags.[14]

Speaking before Parliament in May 1868, Macfie made a line-by-line rebuttal to Mill's endorsement of patent law (though himself an M.P. for Westminster at the time, Mill was absent from the session). Macfie expressed doubt as to whether the current system really gave inventors an "equivalent" for their works in any meaningful sense. To begin with, patent law recognized the first patentee as sole inventor: latecomers to the registration office went home empty-handed, even if they had labored longer, harder, and earlier than the patent holder, and the resulting disputes over priority often led to expensive litigation that sapped all parties of resources. Second, inventors who could not afford to register or litigate their patents became beholden to wealthy capitalist financiers, frequently losing their patents outright in the process; hence, inventors were already the "dependents of the men of money-bags." Third, the sole proprietor "invents often along with others, and always in consequence of knowledge which he derives from the common store"; the monopoly of patents, in Macfie's view, not only rewarded individuals for appropriations from others and from the public domain but obstructed subsequent inventors by limiting their access to new methods and technologies. Finally, where Mill had lamented the "prostituted name of free trade," Macfie retorted that the monopoly powers vested in patent holders "raise prices," "hurt trade," and cause "general inconvenience"—the very evils that Mill's own free trade advocacy professed to combat.[15]

As would be the case in the Copyright Commission hearings, the central question was not *whether* to accept free trade principles, but rather *whose* definition of free trade was the most persuasive and beneficial. For a season, at least, Macfie's seemed to dominate: in 1869, the *Economist* reported that "It is probable enough that the Patent-Laws will be abolished ere long," and the *Times* that "the day is at hand when this branch of our legislation will be wiped out of the statute-book."[16] Backed by inventors, political economists, noblemen, and several influential newspapers, Macfie seemed likely to prevail. But by 1874, the patent abolitionists could only get a compromise bill, halving patent terms from 14 to 7 years and adding a few new restrictions, through the House of Lords. The same bill was withdrawn in the Commons.[17] A recrudescence of militarism and nationalism in Europe—the Franco-German War, the Crimean War, the War of Italian Independence—along with the severe depression that hit England in 1873, had soured the heyday of free trade with a resurgence of protectionism, one easy way to recoup wartime expenses.[18] As tariffs went back up throughout Europe, so did patents, and though patent reform bills were subsequently introduced, the movement for abolition never recovered its former strength.[19]

Throughout the patent controversy, Macfie had distinguished repeatedly (if a little naively) between patents and copyrights: "There can be no rival claimant to the authorship of any particular book; many persons may honestly and indisputably claim originality in an invention." One could favor copyright and impugn patents, he maintained, without inconsistency.[20] But he had already set his sights on patent law's sister canon: the *Abolition of Patents* collection of 1869 also begins to build the case against monopolistic copyrights in a forty-page appendix. When the patent abolition movement failed in 1874, Macfie was free to develop the alternative to copyright at which he had hinted five years before. Once again, he carried the benison of the now dead Cobden. As he told the Copyright Commission, "It is possible that one might convince one's self by argument, that on the whole the interests of the public would be promoted by abolishing copyright; that, I believe, was Mr. Cobden's opinion; he told me he was against copyright." But this time his approach differed importantly from Cobden's: if he could abolish the monopoly principle of copyright, he would replace it with a system of royalties.[21]

Macfie was not the first to propose the replacement of monopoly copyright with royalties. In 1837, Thomas Watts, then Keeper of Printed Books at the British Museum, had suggested a similar royalty scheme of "compulsory license" as an alternative to the first Talfourd Bill.[22] Even Mill had mentioned royalties in his *Principles of Political Economy*, if only to reject them as ultimately inferior to the patent model.[23] In the appendix to *Abolition of Patents*, Macfie proposed to grant the author an exclusive right to print for only one year, long enough to recoup the costs of production from first-edition receipts. Thereafter, anyone could reprint the work by paying the author a 5 percent royalty on the retail price, provided the text was not altered. The royalty would be guaranteed by a government stamp, without which it would be a penal offense to sell the book. Macfie saw manifold advantages to the royalty system. The U.S. and Canada, he claimed, were more likely to accept such a model than the existing monopoly form; an international copyright agreement with the rest of the Anglophone world, long desired by British writers and publishers, might finally be possible. There would be benefits, too, for the domestic reading public: instead of withholding cheap editions until sales of expensive ones had fallen off, first publishers would take advantage of their one-year monopoly by issuing both the expensive "*de luxe*" and the more affordable "people's" editions simultaneously. For the first time, the working population would have unobstructed access to the literature du jour:

> Whereas now under monopoly a new book of intrinsic value is seldom or almost never possessed by, or even seen in the houses of, the labouring population, there would under royalties be a tendency to cheapness which might be confidently relied on as the means of bringing such works within reach of the masses—not when they are stale, but when they are fresh . . . this is no more than the practical recognition of a taste universal among men and women, whether it concerns food material or food intellectual. Let us work it for the good of our race.[24]

Strangely, "race" for Macfie was no more specific a category than "subjects of the British Empire": contrasting the "Chinese system of open literature" to the British form of monopoly copyright, he insisted that an empire-wide royalty system would benefit all the ethnicities and classes within its purview.[25] (As I will show later, a wider circulation of books also meant a greater ease of disseminating the identities, loyalties, and ideologies encoded in those books.) In a presciently neoclassical gesture, Macfie imagined a society of consuming individuals united by their "taste universal" for freshness and novelty—an appetite whose universality could engulf even the particularities of the category "race."

The Copywrights

The peculiar state of the British publishing industry—in which the "fresh" versus "stale" dichotomy had become infrastructural—deserves a brief digression that, once again, takes us back to 1842. The passage of the Talfourd Bill was not the only major event of that year in the British publishing world; it also saw the humble beginnings, on Bloomsbury's Upper King Street, of what quickly became a juggernaut in the world of Victorian letters: Mudie's Circulating Library. There, for a guinea a year (21 shillings), Londoners could purchase unlimited borrowing privileges—as long as they borrowed only one volume at a time. Within a few years, Mudie's had grown to such dominance that it circulated not only books, but (as George Moore famously complained) morals: if the library's censors deemed a book unsuitable for young female readers, Mudie's would refuse to stock it.[26] The library had risen to this paternalist stature by cunningly institutionalizing a particular literary form—the three-volume (or "triple-decker") novel, made popular by Walter Scott. The triple-decker suited Mudie's not only because it could cover thrice the readerly ground of a single-volume issue but because its high retail price forced most readers to borrow rather than buy. At 31 shillings 6 pence (31*s.* 6*d.*) the triple-decker was prohibitively dear for all but the super-wealthy; most middle-class and working-class readers had no choice but to borrow—provided they could afford the guinea-a-year borrower's fee.[27] Having established an oligopoly on lending, Mudie's and its few competitors also built a consumer monopoly—that is, a *monopsony*—on first-run publications, often buying out entire first-edition printings of promising titles. The monopsony, in turn, gave the libraries leverage to demand special privileges of publishers, including 50 percent discounts on new titles and promises not to publish cheap editions (at 6*s.*, 3*s.* 6*d.*, or even 2*d.*) until borrower demand for the first edition had been tapped out. When Charles Edward Mudie turned his circulating library into a limited liability company in 1864, some of these same publishers became its principal shareholders: the close embrace of monopoly and monopsony tightened, further squeezing the consumers caught in between.

Recalling the recent abolition of the Taxes on Knowledge, Macfie wrote that "We should legislate so as to accomplish, in regard to books, at least such an expansion as has been attained in regard to newspapers." That latter expansion had legalized the penny press, and the number of working-class newspaper readers was increasing daily as a result. Dropping the monopoly form of copyright, Macfie imagined, would break the circulating libraries' profitable, regressive stranglehold on the publishing industry by ending the sole reign of the triple-decker first edition. Authors would still be guaranteed a fair percentage for their labors, and first publishers would have economic incentives to make cheap first editions available to the laboring classes without the alienating delays built into the current system. In the preamble to his royalty scheme, Macfie warned fellow radical reformers that the socially uplifting aims of their books would come to little without a publishing industry in harmony with those aims:

> I appeal with equal directness to philanthropists, especially all those who have the power of representing to their fellows what a folly and mistake it is to write books with a view to the moral, social, and religious welfare of men, and yet to rest satisfied with a system of law and trade that find [*sic*] the recompenses of authorship and of publishing ventures in a limited sale of dear books instead of an extensive sale of cheap ones—of a few good books at a large profit instead of many good books at a small![28]

The debate over "a few books at a large profit" versus "many good books at a small" became central in the 1876–78 Commission hearings. Macfie would find allies in Commissioners like H. D. Wolff, who told John Blackwood that "the present system by which books are published at a high price, and by which different profits are made before they get to the public, is an artificial system which is prejudicial to the public" (*Min.* 299). But he would also meet strong opposition in Commissioners and witnesses who saw the multitiered publishing process as the only way to winnow the "good" books—those with the "intrinsic value" Macfie himself sought—from the ephemera. More to the point, many of these opponents regarded copyright law not as an artificial monopoly but as the just articulation of an absolute, natural right of authors in their creations. Literary property, they held, was neither a convention nor a bundle of rights that could be adjusted to balance the interests of author, publisher, and consumer; it was the incontestable entitlement of authorship.

This debate constituted the "great battle" Matthew Arnold discerned in the 1876–78 Copyright Commission—an essentially domestic battle over the nature and extent of literary property law. The Commission itself, however, was precipitated by developments in the realm of colonial and international copyright. In 1875, a Canadian Copyright Act empowered Canadian publishers to reprint British books by paying the copyright holders a fixed royalty. The printers were also required to obtain permission from the copyright holder before printing and were forbidden from exporting the (cheap) Canadian reprint to Britain.[29] The Act prompted the formation of the Commission by way of two discrete reactions. Edward Jenkins, a Liberal M.P., saw the Act as a dangerous flaw in the surface of imperial unity. A staunch imperialist despite his Canadian birth, Jenkins worried that the absence of an empire-wide copyright regime would license more menacing autonomies in Britain's colonies and dominions. Along with fellow members of the Association for the Protection of the Rights of Authors (Thomas Hardy, Mary Elizabeth Braddon, Ellen Price Wood, Charles Reade, and Charles Dickens the younger), he lobbied Disraeli to appoint a royal commission or a parliamentary committee of inquiry on copyright.[30] The Association asked that the government not only consider the question of international and intercolonial copyright but also update and clarify aspects of the domestic law, such as protection for journalism and dramatization of novels. (Interestingly, no one made any mention of extending the *term* of copyright.) Disraeli listened indulgently to a long-winded speech of Reade's, flattered the company by shaking a few hands, and promised to give the matter his "most entire attention" in the fullness of time, adding that "I should think there must be a mass of information in the possession of the Government" before new legislation would be drawn up.[31] That "mass of information"—the Royal Copyright Commission minutes—would arrive three years later, in a Blue Book eight hundred pages long.

At the same time, T. H. Farrer, a dogmatic Cobdenite and Secretary of the Board of Trade, saw in the Canadian Act an opportunity to strike a blow for free trade. Why, he asked, should British readers continue to pay several times what colonial readers did for the same books? And if Canada could replace a monopoly regime with a system of royalties, why not Britain—particularly in the interest of imperial uniformity desired by the likes of Jenkins?[32] The Board of Trade, too, clamored for a Commission, which was appointed in March 1876. As Froude would later put it, "English authors and the publishers of their writings have been indicted before a Royal Commission.... The chief prosecutor is no less a person than the Secretary of the Board of Trade, the department of Government which is specially charged with the administration of copyright."[33] Froude's rhetorical gesture—rewriting parliamentary hearings as a criminal trial—registers the high political and emotional stakes of the Commission. Its report on the nature and future of literary property—and hence on the definitions of literary crime—would be awaited like a verdict.

The Commission

The Royal Commission on Copyright first convened on May 8, 1876, in chambers at 13 Delahay Street, Westminster. At the witness stand stood Charles Trevelyan, a zealous Whig reformer and laissez-faire advocate who had made the rounds of the Indian Civil Service, served as Assistant Secretary to the Treasury under Gladstone, and wound up as governor-president of Madras.[34] He had also been drawn as "Sir Gregory Hardlines" in Commissioner Trollope's *The Three Clerks* (1857). Trevelyan delivered the Board of Trade's opening salvo against monopoly copyright, touching on all the cardinal points of the free trade argument that Macfie, Farrer, and other witnesses would reprise in the coming months. Declaring literature to be "more important in influencing the character of the nation, and of the individuals of whom it is composed, than anything else," he went on to deplore the reign of the "monster joint-stock circulating library," along with the staggered, stratified system of publication it had institutionalized, as the single greatest impediment to national improvement (*Min.* 263–64). An affordable mass literature, he argued, was urgently needed to fulfill the legacy of the 1867 Reform Bill and the 1870 Educational Act:

> We have established suffrage on the household basis, and it is of quite as much importance, perhaps of more importance, that the body of the people should receive sound instruction on political and economic subjects, and be able to appreciate our general literature, as that it should be appreciated by the upper classes. We have also provided a very expensive system of national education, and yet the necessary supplement of a cheap popular literature is entirely wanting. No doubt the people get it at last, but they get it after great delay, they get it after the first interest has evaporated . . . . I believe that the illiterate, semi-stolid character of our agricultural labourers, and of the lower class of our work-people in towns, is in a considerable degree owing to the dearness and inaccessibility of books. (*Min.* 260, 266)

For Trevelyan, as for Macfie, the monopoly of the circulating libraries was founded on the monopoly form of copyright. "All this would be remedied," he told Commissioner H. D. Wolff, "if free trade were established by remunerating authors in proportion to the sale of their books, instead of by a monopoly" (*Min.* 264). The royalty system he endorsed would centralize authorial remuneration, separating it from the local scene of publishing: the government would secure authors their 10 percent or 12.5 percent retail royalty from publishers, who would be free to reprint and compete in the literary marketplace with whatever editions they could sell. Such a system, in Trevelyan's view, would "reconcile [authors'] just reward with the interests of the public, that is to say, with the diffusion of literature . . . authors would, in a manner, be in partnership with the public for the sale of their works, instead of holding a monopoly against them" (*Min.* 260–61).

But although he made clear that monopoly copyright in Britain was a "monstrous evil," Trevelyan took care to propose the royalty system only for the colonies, knowing the resistance it would meet at home (*Min.* 260). This feint to the colonial was partly a thin-end-of-the-wedge strategy, and when pressed he admitted to hoping the royalty scheme would be "thus gradually brought about in England likewise" (*Min.* 261). More immediately, Trevelyan thought a royalty system the best way to ensure the circulation of cheap colonial reprints. As a veteran of the Indian Civil Service, he was especially attuned to techniques of imperial administration and thus to the role played by literature in the growth, naturalization, and upkeep of empire.[35] In fact, what Trevelyan's testimony makes clearest is how intimately the question of copyright—even domestic copyright—was linked to the circuits of imperial governance. Of course, this link between copyright and empire

The Copywrights

had been part of the copyright discussion, though in a different form, since the debates of 1837–42. Writing in support of the Talfourd Bill, the associationist Archibald Alison had insisted that

> It is not sufficient for England to refer to the works of Milton, Shakespeare, Johnson, or Scott; she must prolong the race of these great men, or her intellectual career will speedily come to a close. Short and fleeting indeed is the period of transcendent greatness allotted to any nation in any branch of thought. The moment it stops, it begins to recede; and to every empire which has made intellectual triumphs, is prescribed the same law which was felt by Napoleon in Europe and the British in India, that conquest is essential to existence.

Only "by giving something like perpetuity to the rights of authorship," Alison maintained, could "the talent of the empire" reclaim that "masculine independence of thought" central to intellectual, and thus territorial, conquest.[36] The distance between Alison's rhetoric and Trevelyan's is the distance between forms of domination—between raw territorial conquest and education as a stronger, subtler bulwark of imperial occupation. For Alison, Milton and Shakespeare inspired the conquerors; for Trevelyan, they quelled the conquered by subjecting them to the conqueror's canon:

> Since the year 1835, when through Macaulay's help, and Lord William Bentinck's statesmanlike courage, the resolution was come to to make English literature and science the basis of Indian education, English education has been spreading in India in a wonderful manner, and at this moment it is no exaggeration to say that English is the language of education for the upper and middle classes in India . . . and it is rapidly spreading among high and low; English is also the principal language of official proceedings; and it is the language of business to a very great extent; and our English classical writers, not merely those whose copyrights have expired, but living writers, or those recently dead, are read in India to a greater extent than they are in England. . . . the entire staple of Indian high education is our English classical authors—Johnson, Addison, Macaulay, Milton, Shakspeare, and so forth—so that it is of the most essential importance that our English classics should be provided in a cheap form for the use of the people of India. (*Min.* 3)[37]

Of course, Trevelyan nowhere identifies education with social control, but the right to rule is so basic to the discussion as to require no articulation; the room, remember, was full of former colonial secretaries and other imperial administrators. That assumed right is legible, too, in the tautological formulations of Trevelyan's argument: since we conquerors decided to use our literature to educate Indians, that literature has indeed educated Indians. Because English classics are a staple in Indian education, English classics must be available as a staple to Indians. In both cases, the familiarly silent term is "the better to rule." If a cheap press at home could speed the production of British "national character," a cheap press in the colonies would speed the reproduction of that national character among colonized populations through British modes of education and through the intellectual and moral rigor they were thought to instill. Copyright reform would help make colonial subjects a more British—and thus a more governable—people.

Once the royalty system had taken root in the colonies and dominions, Trevelyan implied, it would be both difficult and unfair to keep it out of Britain. Domestic readers would not submit indefinitely to the circulating library oligopoly and the inflated book prices it supported, especially when cheap first editions were available everywhere else in the British empire. But Trevelyan's critique of the current copyright regime did not stop at the particulars of colonial education and domestic publishing; it also targeted the reigning notion that copyright conferred an absolute (if temporally limited) property right upon its holder. In the centerpiece of his testimony, he described literary property as radically contingent—in its present form, the result merely of a historical "vogue" for monopoly—and thus potentially renegotiable:

> Copyright is a modern development of the principle of property, which happened first to be applied, in this case, by granting a monopoly. It was the fashion of the day. Monopolies were then in vogue. . . . All property whatever, even the most solid of all, namely landed property, is the creature of the law, and is modified by considerations of public expediency. Copyright is the last born of property, and is subject in a special manner to limitations having reference to the public interest. In the year 1842 the conditions under which copyrights were held were entirely changed, and they are liable to be changed again in accordance with the interests, not only of the authors, but of the public. (*Min.* 262, 265)

The depiction of property as a "creature of law" was not in itself new; among political economists, Mill had most recently argued that "Even what a person has produced by his individual toil, unaided by any one, he cannot keep, unless by the permission of society."[38] By limiting the term of literary proprietorship, copyright acts of the past had granted societal permission but curtailed the duration of authorial "keeping" in the public interest. What Trevelyan called into question, though, was not the length, but the *nature* of that keeping. Whereas other forms of property ownership amounted to a monopoly of an object's use and disposal, he saw full monopoly in literary property—that "last born" kind of property he dubbed "subject in special manner to limitations"—as incompatible with the public interest. Later in the hearings, T. H. Huxley would make the more orthodox claim that property rights, once granted, were absolute: "a man shall make any contract which he pleases with regard to the disposal of his property" (*Min.* 562). Trevelyan's testimony flew in the face of that plenary model of ownership. Even once society had granted it, the "right to keep" literary property was not an absolute right but a bundle of rights; Trevelyan wanted to remove the monopoly strand from that bundle.[39]

The Copywrights

Unluckily for those who wished to abolish monopoly copyright, the most articulate pro-royalty witness—Trevelyan—spoke at the very outset of the Commission's hearings, never to reappear. Macfie's testimony began well enough, with the witness presenting copies of his 1869 royalty proposal to the Commissioners, but quickly devolved into a scattered monologue. Having paused to reacquaint himself with his own proposal, Macfie meandered off on long tangents about the need for a parcel post, the importance of precut edges in books, and the economy of paper covers and narrower margins. He confused things further by altering his original provision of a year's protection for a book's first edition. Instead, he proposed, authors should go to a government official with a sum representing their desired remuneration plus the cost of producing the first edition. If the official approved the sum, the first edition would be protected from competitors until that sum was realized, so long as the cover price of the book was judged moderate and affordable. After the author had made the target sum, the book would be opened to all publishers on a 5 percent royalty to the author, for the current term of copyright. The impulse behind Macfie's amendment seems fair-minded enough: monopoly would last just long enough for the author and first publisher to recover their sunk costs plus a modest profit, and authorship would become more like the professions that paid on an hourly basis, rather than a form of speculation that could leave writers either affluent or destitute. Nonetheless, the complication of a new government office to negotiate prices and profits for every new book seemed more like interventionist price-fixing than free trade. As Froude later asked, "What would Mr. Macfie say if it were proposed to appoint a public officer to look into the business of his merchants, his own among them, to overhaul his prices, to examine his profits, to test his income against some arbitrary measurement of his time and labour and cut it down till it is fairly proportioned to the estimated value of Mr. Macfie's services to the State?"[40] Rather than press Macfie on the free trade issue in the hearings, however, the Commissioners let him exhaust himself with rattling off cost-of-printing figures. He ended his testimony with a plea for mandatory alphabetical indexes.

Froude's question, though it was not framed until the Commission had adjourned, struck at a central dissonance in Macfie's pro-royalty case without absolutely discrediting that case. The dissonance lay in an entrepreneur's use (Macfie was a sugar refiner) of an entrepreneurial doctrine (free trade had been foremost a manufacturer's creed) to strip the authorial profession of its entrepreneurial qualities. By marshaling authorship toward a wage-oriented, professional model rather than a venture-based, speculative one, Macfie's royalty scheme would deny authors the very liberties and opportunities that free trade was designed to promote and protect—the opportunity to reap profits disproportionate to one's labor and the liberty to keep or dispose of those profits as one wished. Such contradictions commonly arose when the categories of physical property (labor, rent, estate, usufruct) were imposed on the realm of intellectual property: as difficult as it might be to ascertain, say, the value of labor or the limits of ownership in the physical world, those difficulties ballooned in the more abstract case of intellectual property. The legal and procedural containers of such abstract property were bound, in themselves, to try the temper of free trade. But even more centrally, the apparent contradictions of Macfie's scheme mark the limits of the laissez-faire doctrine in promoting anything more than the most perfunctory collectivism. Froude was right: Macfie's royalty scheme may have been many things, but it was not free trade in any common form. The free trader in Macfie had come to grief against a still more radical propensity: in order really to defend the public weal against commercial monopolies, Macfie had resorted to corrective forms of intervention that looked remarkably like state socialism.

Froude recognized this slippage in his retrospective essay on the Commission, asking "Has the Board of Trade been converted to Socialism?"[41] So did the social theorist and naturalist Herbert Spencer, who rejected the royalty system as a needless concession to poorer readers with an inflated sense of entitlement. Such a system, in his view, would erode the constitutive differences of the moneyed and less-moneyed classes and thus the very basis of a naturally stratified society. "I take it that the proposal really amounts to this," he said:

> that whereas, at present, the poorer class of readers are inconvenienced by having to wait for a cheap edition a certain number of years, they shall, by this arrangement, be advantaged by having a cheap edition forthwith; which is to say that people with smaller amounts of money shall have no disadvantages from their smaller amounts of money. It is communistic practically: it is simply equalising the advantages of wealth and poverty. (*Min.* 284)

Spencer, the self-styled "social evolutionist" who had coined the phrase "survival of the fittest," regarded money as a reliable index of social worth and work and its unequal distribution as the appropriate outcome of a Darwinist society. So long as that society's markets remained unfettered by state intervention, the fittest contestants—ideas, books, people, classes—would eventually rise to the top. Royalty copyright, he argued, would skew that natural verdict by narrowing the range of an author's potential profits and enforcing artificial cheapness in books—all in order to give unearned advantages to the poor. Using Macfie's own laissez-faire doctrine against him, Spencer objected that the proposed system was "distinctly opposed to the principles of free trade" in its attempt to "secure cheap books by legislative arrangements" (*Min.* 540).

Among other things, Spencer's testimony illustrates the vast heterogeneity of views assembled under the rubric of free trade. For Macfie and Trevelyan, free trade's chief allure lay in delivering the lowest price to the consumer through competition. Since small margins were only profitable in great volumes, free trade also promoted widespread distribution and could therefore power the education and betterment of the underclasses. To Spencer, however, laissez-faire appealed as the socioeconomic twin of biological Darwinism. Protectionism should be as scarce in trade as in the state of nature, and the superior should be as free to dominate. Rather than close the gap between rich and poor, Spencer's free trade naturalized it as an expression of humanity's built-in mechanisms of differentiation and advancement. At its extremes, such a view enshrined the very social hierarchies that Darwinism could also be used to relativize; at its mildest, it unburdened literature of accountability to the public at large. Spencer found allies among the other advocates of the "divine rights of authordom." John Tyndall told the Commission, "I think it perfectly fair for an author, if he thinks fit, to write a work that appeals to the wealthier classes of humanity" (*Min.* 573). And though Huxley would later denounce Spencer's social Darwinism as unempirical, he defended books for consolidating, rather than dissolving, intellectual and socioeconomic elites. When asked whether he would not prefer a wider readership for his own books, he replied, "I do not care much about it; if I have half a dozen careful readers I would rather have them than all the rest of the world put together." Like Spencer, he felt the public had as little right to demand the "cheapest possible rate" in books as in "beef, mutton, or potatoes" (*Min.* 565). His own *Man's Place in Nature,* like a rare caviar or cut of loin, would likely be wasted on the masses.

If Macfie's royalty scheme claimed a "free trade" affiliation, the pro-copyright party would counter it with a "freer-trade-than-thine" strategy. Having stigmatized the royalty system as price-fixing, Huxley and Spencer attempted to lift the stigma of monopoly from the current copyright system. Far from being a mere "favour which the State confers upon the author," Huxley argued, copyright protected authors' "absolute right" in their works. Having thus rejected the "bundle" theory of rights, he added that "the application of the word 'monopoly' to persons who possess rights under the copyright law is an entire mistake; it is merely a contrivance arising out of the peculiar nature of book property, to put that property upon the same footing as other kinds of property" (*Min.* 562). Spencer's argument proved more sophisticated and was immediately adopted by the pro-copyright Commissioners.[42] He began by conceding that all property rights were a form of monopoly, but protested that copyright was no more so than the others. Authors claimed no monopoly in a subject, only "that part of the value of the article which has been given to it by his shaping process, which is what any artisan does" (*Min.* 540). In a letter to Commissioner Froude, he defined monopoly as "an arrangement under which a person . . . is given by law the exclusive use of certain natural products, or agencies, or facilities, which, in the absence of such law, would be open to all." A free trader would look not to become dependent upon the monopolist but only to obtain equal access to those products, agencies, and facilities. Spencer then ingeniously applied his definitions to the book trade:

Does the so-called monopolist (the author) forbid the so-called free-trader (the reprinter) to use any of those appliances or processes, intellectual or mechanical, by which books are produced? No. These remain open to all. Does the so-called free-trader wish simply to use these open facilities independently, just as he might do if the so-called monopolist and his works were absent? No. He wishes to be dependent; he wishes to get advantages which he could not have were the so-called monopolist and his works absent. Instead of complaining, as the true free-trader does, that the monopolist is an obstacle put in his way, this pseudo free-trader complains that he may not utilise certain aids which have arisen from the labour of the man whom he calls a monopolist.[43]

In one inspired gesture, Spencer dissociated copyright from monopoly and the pro-royalty party from "true" free trade. The first point was particularly bold, given that Adam Smith, Macaulay, and Mill had conceived of copyright as a monopoly, however tolerable. But the second point provided the strategic *coup de grace* the pro-copyrightists needed. No longer the righteous radicals, Macfie and his fellow "pseudo free-traders" were recast by Spencer as shoddy apostates of the right religion, misappropriating the rhetoric of "true" free trade to promote a parasitic regime of reprints. Spencer's argument registered his indifference to the "public weal" championed by Macfie and Trevelyan: his rejoinder betrayed no interest in breaking the library oligopoly, in making books affordable to the masses, in educating the new working-class electorate. But he had succeeded in shifting the ground of the debate to the more passional domain of orthodoxy—the seemingly imperiled orthodoxy of free trade.

Since the pro-copyright surge happened late in the Commission hearings, it fell to the pro-royalty party's last witness—T. H. Farrer of the Board of Trade—to control the damages. Having observed a number of prior testimonies, he began by summarizing the existent law and recapping issues raised by earlier witnesses. Though he avoided the topic of royalties early in his testimony, his attitude toward copyright absolutists was clear enough: "This right or property is a creature of the statute law, and the statute law which makes it, can modify it" (*Min.* 405). He went on to argue that copyright had always been constructed on the "bundle" model of rights. Whereas real property was perpetual and indivisible (here he contradicted Trevelyan), literary property consisted only in a temporary right to prevent the multiplication of copies. When Farrer finally broached the royalty question, he used Trevelyan's tactic of admitting them through the back door of colonial and international copyright. Neither the U.S. nor Canada nor the colonies, he said, were likely to accept the British monopoly copyright system, devoted as they were to cheap literature; but they would very likely take up an international system of royalties. Domestic royalties, he admitted, were impractical for the present, because they would require a complicated array of governmental machinery. But even that difficulty was not "insuperable." If the royalty system had been taken up earlier in the country's history, he conjectured, it might already "have given to the author a larger market, and to the public cheaper literature" (*Min.* 468).

Farrer's subsequent appearances gave both the pro- and antimonopoly Commissioners a last public opportunity to demonstrate and consolidate their views. Louis Mallet's long interrogation of Farrer was more duet than deposition, with each man giving the other openings to state his more extreme positions. In his questions, Mallet made clear his own opposition to a monopoly that favored publishers, his preference for royalties, even his willingness to consider abolishing copyright altogether; in his responses, Farrer insisted that copyright reform need not benefit the public at the expense of authors, though he observed that the best books were seldom written out of monetary motives. But if Mallet's sympathies were passionately aired, the antipathies of Commissioners James Fitzjames Stephen, J. A. Froude, and William Smith were even more so. Stephen in particular accused Farrer of considering the public good at the expense of the author's and simple cheapness at the expense of literary worth and gravity:

> *Sir J. Stephen*—Do you think it a matter of great congratulation and high importance that 370,000 copies of a particular novel should be sold at an extremely small price throughout America?
>
> *Mr. Farrer*—It would depend on what the novel was; some novels are the best of books.
>
> *Sir J. Stephen*—Do you think for instance . . . that the public is seriously injured and a great loss inflicted upon it because it has to pay 2*s.* 8*d.* for the "Sketches by Boz" and "Pickwick" instead of 1*s.* 3*d.*?
>
> *Mr. Farrer*—Yes, I certainly do. I think that both "Sketches by Boz" and "Pickwick" are excellent books in their way, and I should be very glad to see them in every cottage in the country, which they are more likely to be if they are sold at 1*s.* 3*d.* than if they are sold at 2*s.* 8*d.*
>
> *Sir J. Stephen*—You consider that to cheapen all books indiscriminately as much as you possibly can is in itself a highly desirable object?
>
> *Mr. Farrer*—Yes, I do; because on the whole we must trust to the public demand purifying itself; and reading almost any book is a better thing than most of the pleasures of our lower orders. (*Min.* 520–21)

As the exchange suggests, the battle over copyright also harbored a debate over the social and literary value of the novel versus more "improving" sorts of literature—the histories of Froude, say, or the natural histories of Spencer. As the largest single genre at Mudie's, and the likeliest to be taken up by working-class readers, the novel stood to widen its circulation more than other forms if monopoly copyright and the circulating library oligopoly were abolished; consequently, the pro-royalty faction championed prose fiction as a potentially didactic, morally improving literature for the masses.[44] Stephen and several other defenders of the extant law, however, insisted on the frivolity of fiction as against the gravity of less popular forms (religion, science, history, biography, philosophy, political economy). Writers in these more serious and valorous categories, they argued, could not expect the widespread sales enjoyed by novels, and therefore needed a long-term monopoly copyright to remunerate them over time.

Despite his lengthy and increasingly ardent testimony, Farrer helped seal the doom of the royalty system. He had read the depositions of Spencer and Huxley and claimed that Spencer's facts were "consistent with that principle of a royalty which I have not myself suggested, but which is the special subject of Mr. Spencer's attack" (*Min.* 580). But he neglected to show how Spencer's evidence supported royalties, a scheme which at any rate he suddenly seemed to disown.[45] Even earlier in his testimony, his espousal of domestic royalties had remained provisional, tempered by the qualifier "impracticable" and by his willingness to tinker with the existing monopoly form. When pressed about how a royalty system might be implemented, he demurred: "I am not come prepared with any scheme in detail for collecting royalties. I have not thought it out; and it could scarcely be thought out without the assistance given by the criticism of the trade on an actual Bill" (*Min.* 530). Farrer's Board of Trade, though in an ideal position to draft such a bill, never did so. With such a tepid key witness, the pro-royalty party had hardly needed its many assailants.

Farrer's last testimonial appearance on May 8, 1877, marked the end of the Commission's hearings. No records were kept of the ensuing deliberations, but a handful of newspaper notices tracked the Commissioners' progress. The *Times* of July 13 reported that the Commission was not likely to make its report until the following year. "Meanwhile the Commissioners are endeavouring to find a basis for their Report by formulating a series of resolutions. These resolutions, we are informed, are now about 70 in number. It is probable that they will reach 100."[46] By November each Commissioner had a draft Report in hand, but the final meeting was delayed until May 11, 1878; the complete Report, with its 294 resolutions and its raft of dissenting attachments, reached the Home Secretary of the Board of Trade two weeks later.[47]

In its pages, the Commissioners advised Her Majesty to retain the monopoly form of copyright and to extend its term in Britain and the royal dominions to author's life plus 30 years, the current length of German copyright, or to an international standard if one were ever established. A fixed postmortem term, they argued, would be easier to enforce because the date of an author's death was easier to verify than the date of a particular work's first publication. Such an amendment would also prevent the republication of the earlier, flawed editions that came out of copyright before later, corrected ones. The wholesale expiration of an author's copyrights, too, would enable publishers to release "complete works" editions all at once, rather than piecemeal. In addition, abridgments, dramatizations, lectures, adaptations, translations, and musical compositions should fall under the 30-year postmortem term, and newspaper copyright should be standardized. Further recommendations were made about copyrights in paintings, sculpture, photography, and architecture and about the registration and deposit of copies. As for imperial protection, the Report suggested giving empire-wide copyright to books published anywhere within the royal dominion—it being "highly desirable that the literature of this country should be placed within easy reach of the colonies"—but advised that cheap colonial reprints should not be imported to Britain without the author's permission (*Rep.* 192). Finally, the Commissioners urged Parliament to pursue an international copyright accord with the reluctant U.S., adding that, in the meantime, U.S. writers should continue to enjoy copyright in Britain as a show of British good faith and principles.

The Report's page-long dismissal of the domestic royalty scheme gave suitably little hint of the "great battle" that had occurred over the nature and future of copyright. It was, rather, a recommendatory document—one that existed to illuminate a single path of legislative action by shutting off those byways it deemed irrelevant. After briefly rehearsing the arguments for and against the adoption of royalties, the Commissioners wrote that "we think it unnecessary to discuss the subject in greater detail, or to point out the practical difficulties which the introduction of such a scheme would necessarily involve, or how those difficulties might possibly be more or less obviated, because we are unable, after carefully considering the subject, to recommend for adoption this change in the existing law" (*Rep.* 171). The Commission had spent long hours listening to an array of royalty advocates—Trevelyan, Macfie, Farrer, the publisher and bookseller Thomas Bosworth—as well as to their energetic opponents and must have further debated the scheme in its post-hearing deliberations.[48] But with the vote against royalties finally cast, the majority of Commissioners set out not only to reject the scheme for the present but to annul it fully. Thus, the Report devoted just enough space to the royalty debate to appear thorough, but not enough to leave Macfie's scheme standing as a viable proposal worthy of further investigation.

By December 1878, Commissioners Jenkins and Herschell had turned the Report's recommendations into a "Bill to *codify* and amend the law of copyright," and by July of the following year, the "Manners Bill" had been read in Parliament.[49] But the bill stalled when Parliament dissolved in 1880, and for a time the domestic issue was overshadowed by developments in the international copyright sphere—the Berne Convention of 1886, the Canadian Act of 1889, and the 1891 Chace Act in the U.S. Still, despite the long delay in domestic reform, the basic resolutions of the 1876–78 Commission continued to guide the debates in various Select Committees on copyright all the way through the Copyright Act of 1911, which gave authors a protection term of life plus 50 years, in accordance with the amended Berne Convention.[50] Though the 1911 Act did not pass unopposed, the debates leading up to its passage bore little trace of the fundamental critique advanced in the

1870s by Macfie, Trevelyan, Farrer, Bosworth, Mallet, and other copyright dissenters.

Dissenting Reports

The vaunted "unanimity" of the 1878 Copyright Commission Report breaks down in its own appendixes, in the Separate Reports attached by ten of the Commissioners. Half of these lodge localized, if important, complaints. James Stephen opposed copyright in pictures and statues, as well as tighter restrictions on abridgment and dramatization; Trollope and Daldy objected that authors should be able to repress piracies even if they had failed to register a text with the British Museum. The more fundamental objections were raised by those sympathetic to Macfie's free trade assault on monopoly copyright. Charles Young, John Rose, and Edward Jenkins sided with Louis Mallet in preferring a copyright term of 50 years after registration to the 30-year postmortem term recommended by the main Report. Mallet and his supporters noted that the proposed term gave authors' earliest (and often weakest) productions a longer protection than their later, more accomplished works, while also irrelevantly rewarding writers' personal longevity in the coin of copyright. A term measured from registration would not only compel authors to register their works, but would also provide for anonymous or collaborative works better than a copyright keyed to a single author's life span. Mallet, again, led several dissenters (Young, Rose, and H. D. Wolff) against the resolution prohibiting the British import of cheap colonial reprints. The main Report held that authors would only give permission for colonial reprints if they knew those cheaper editions would not return to Britain and compete with the more expensive domestic editions. Such a prohibition made colonial publishers' profits dependent on high prices at home: in effect, domestic readers were being taxed to keep colonial subjects supplied with cheap books. As Mallet wrote in his Separate Report, the prohibition "renders exile a condition of easy access by Englishmen to the contemporary literature of their own language, and causes England to be the only country in which English books are scarce and dear" (*Rep.* 218). Empire-wide competition among editions, Rose added, would remove "obstacles to the enlarged dissemination, as well as to the permanent acquisition, of literary works, by the masses, on terms within the reach of their means" (*Rep.* 208).

H. D. Wolff's Separate Report lobbed a last protest at Mudie's, whose continuing stranglehold on British letters had hardly been mentioned, much less endangered, by the main Report. Though the *DNB* claims that Wolff "only dissent[ed] on some points of detail" from the Commission's Report, he in fact denounced all its resolutions on colonial and international copyright. Restricting the importation of colonial reprints, he wrote, sustained "a system which has and can have no analogy in any other trade—*viz.*, that of circulating libraries"—which artificially kept book prices well above the cost of production. Like Macfie, Trevelyan, and Mallet, he argued that the widespread sale of a cheap first edition would benefit the author, "while reader and student might, by the purchase of new books, pursue their studies under far more favourable conditions than are compatible with the hurried and superficial perusal of works hired, for a few days, volume by volume, from a subscription library" (*Rep.* 209). By his scathing indictment of Mudie's and others, Wolff registered his disappointment that despite its hundreds of hours in session, the Commission had failed to abolish the last de facto Tax on Knowledge: the circulating library oligopoly.

But the most substantive statement of dissent was penned by the economist and statesman Louis Mallet, who refused outright to sign the Report of the Commissioners. Affiliated with the Board of Trade from a young age, Mallet had become a protégé of Cobden's and on the master's death had taken up the mantle of arch-free-trader within the government. (He would later assist John Morley in writing the first biography of Cobden.) During the Copyright Commission's hearings, he had played sheepdog to the frequently wayward pro-royalty witnesses, remaining a staunch critic of monopoly copyright even when Farrer was faltering. He had shown symptoms of his skepticisms in his questions: Did monopoly copyright benefit the consumer as much as the producer? How could the royalty system be made more feasible? If the territory of copyright were extended by international agreements, why not shrink the length of the term proportionally? Using these questions as a frame, he would reject the Commission's chief recommendations on domestic, colonial, and international copyright.[51] But before the main Report had even reached the Board of Trade's Home Secretary, the *Times* had gotten wind of a more fundamental defection: "Sir L. Mallet, we learn, almost calls in question the principle of a copyright law."[52]

As an economist of Jevonsian stripe, Mallet had subjected monopoly copyright to neoclassical analysis and found it untenable. In his view, "the claim of an author to [an absolute] right of property in his published work rests upon a radical economic fallacy, *viz.*, a misconception of the nature of the law of value" (*Rep.* 210).[53] According to classical economics, value was instilled in an object through labor, which in turn claimed property rights (or an equivalent) as its reward. But for Mallet, as for Jevons, this labor theory could not explain the dependence of exchange value on consumer demand. In a section of his dissenting Report that reads more like a manifesto for neoclassical economics than a critique of copyright, he attempted to rewrite not only value but property itself as a function of scarcity. He began with the marginalist claim that "it is only from a limitation of supply that there can be any value in exchange." When supplies were naturally scarce, property rights (a form of monopoly) were necessary for the public good: without property, "the progressive increase of an unlimited demand operating on a limited supply would lead to the dissolution of society." By contrast,

> In that which is absolutely unlimited, in the air, in sunlight, in the forces of nature, such as heat, electricity, magnetism, &c., there is no natural exchangeable value, and therefore no property; in that which, although not absolutely unlimited in itself, nevertheless exceeds all probable or possible demands in exchange, there can be little or no value, and little or no property, e.g., in the sea, in the water of large or unfrequented streams, in the game of a wild country, or in the fish of the sea. *It is in fact scarcity which creates value, and renders property necessary. Property exists in order to provide against the evils of natural scarcity. A limitation of supply by artificial causes, creates scarcity in order to create property.* To limit that which is in its nature unlimited, and thereby to confer an exchangeable value on that which, without such interference, would be the gratuitous possession of mankind, is to create an artificial monopoly which has no warrant in the nature of things, which serves to produce scarcity where there ought to be abundance, and to confine the few gifts which were intended for all. (*Rep.* 210; emphasis added)

Mallet's key distinction is between natural and artificial scarcity. In cases of natural scarcity, property is a desirable alternative to bloody warfare over the limited resource. Property rights, then, are defensible as a means to the end of the public good. But when property becomes an end in itself, Mallet implies, it supplants and often imperils the public good. Manufacturing scarcity (through a monopoly, say) out of a nondepletable resource might create property, but for property's sake, not the public's. Raising private property to the status of an end in itself cordons off even the few communal plenitudes—the natural "gifts" among which Mallet set ideas and their expression.

Having rejected the absolute-property-rights rationale for copyright, Mallet considered that the temporary monopoly currently in effect might be necessary to induce writers to write, and thus prevent either "a diminished supply or a deterioration in quality" of books. But the sole justification for such an incentive rationale, he argued, was "to ensure for a community the best possible literature at the cheapest possible price." In his view, as in Wolff's and Macfie's, British copyright law had failed disgracefully to achieve that aim; thanks to the current law, "It may indeed be said without exaggeration that new books are a luxury, the possession of which is confined to the wealthy class, and that they are placed by their price altogether beyond the reach of the great bulk of the people" (*Rep.* 211). Though he shied away from a full endorsement of the royalty system on the basis of "the present state of public opinion," he recommended that it be "kept in view as the object of future reforms," and went on to rehearse its many advantages—

for both authors and readers, the domestic and the international scene—over the extant monopoly system (*Rep.* 212).

Mallet's analysis distinguishes itself as one of the Commission's few extended meditations on the underlying principles of copyright. Witnesses in favor of monopoly copyright had tended to deflect criticism by invoking commercial conventions or by making traditionalist appeals to the author's absolute property rights. Proponents of royalties had been more interested in the founding assumptions of copyright, but too often had used them as mere stepping stones on the way to their own garbled proposals. By separating the absolute property rights model from the incentive model and subjecting both to the litmus test of the "public interest," Mallet exposed the failures of the current law and the inadequacy of the Commission's recommendations for reform. Even more dramatically, he deployed a singular form of analysis—a hybrid that combined prominent traits of radical free trade and neoclassical economics. He followed Jevons in regarding the value of all commodities as a function not of labor but of supply and demand—that is, of scarcity. But he differed from Jevons in applying a similar sort of rule to *property:* in place of the Lockean model that had underwritten copyright law from its inception, Mallet proposed to limit property rights to natural conditions of scarcity. Of course, such a proposal raises as many questions as it purports to answer; for example, what guarantees the just distribution even of a more limited form of property? What criteria divide "limited" from "unlimited" resources or "natural" from "artificial" scarcities? Is not innovation a scarce enough commodity to merit at least provisional property rights? For all that it begs these questions, though, Mallet's Report provides a pole star seldom glimpsed by either Jevons or the "divine right of authordom" faction of the Copyright Commission. In going beyond the inherent solipsisms of Jevons's hedonic calculus, he had insisted that models of value and property be explicitly accountable to the public interest rather than to loose monads of idiosyncratic desire.

The minority statements appended to the Commission's Report were not the only postmortem analyses. In the wake of the report, articles by Commissioner Froude and witness Farrer appeared almost simultaneously in *The Edinburgh Review* and *The Fortnightly Review,* respectively. As a disciple of Carlyle and a believer in history as a chronicle of individual heroic gestures, Froude had been a scourge of the anti-copyright witnesses during the hearings and unreservedly defended the Commission's final Report. But where the Report had deliberately watered down its account of the monopoly-royalty debate, Froude, in his explosive retelling, represented the Commission as a kind of governmental conflagration—one enkindled by conspiratorial socialist economists from the Board of Trade but fought bravely back by his fellow men of sense and genius. He also couched the copyright debate in loaded ecclesiastical terms, portraying Trevelyan, Macfie, Farrer, and Mallet as sanctimonious emissaries from the Vatican of laissez-faire economism:

> The movement against copyright has originated with, and been carried on by, two or three speculative gentlemen in a Government department, who cannot reconcile the existing book trade with the orthodox theory of the nature of *value*.... Political economy has become a sacred science. An economic heresy is not a mistake, but a crime, and 'monopoly' is as frightful in the eyes of the Board of Trade, the official guardians of orthodox doctrine, as the denial of the real presence was to the Council of Trent.... Parliament will consider a causeless disturbance of an important business a greater evil than an economic inconsistency, and will surely hesitate before they gratuitously exasperate the whole body of the literary profession.[54]

Spencer had trumped the free trade positions of Macfie and others with his "freer-trade" argument, challenging the laissez-faire orthodoxy to purify itself in his own image. Froude, instead, took a heterodox stance, casting the anti-copyright party as Roman Catholic prelates forcing their Church dogma on Protestant "heretics."[55] Eccentric literary genius, in other words, was being assailed by doctrinaire bureaucratic meddlers who could see no difference between "the marketable merit of a book" and "the marketable merit of a piece of calico or a sample of sugar."[56] This last snub was aimed at the papacy of free trade: Cobden had been a calico printer, Macfie a sugar refiner.

As for the complaint that the monopoly system enshrined expensive first editions, Froude thought it nearly unworthy of rebuttal. The Board of Trade's obsession with "fresh" literature for the middle and working classes, he implied, was a category error conflating bread and books; truly valuable books would never grow stale, and in fact required the passage of time and slow digestion by elite critics to be certified as valuable. The masses were better off protected by such a filtration system than overstimulated by a constant flood of cheap first editions:

> Free countries do not tolerate a censorship of the press, because no one can be trusted to exercise it. Yet who would not approve a censorship which would really divide the good from the bad? And the close period of copyright answers the purpose of censorship more effective than was ever enforced by civil or ecclesiastical tribunal. It allows a time for public opinion to weigh the merits of each new contribution to its art or to its thought. If at the end of the period it continues in demand, it is thus proved to be really valuable; and then, and not till then, it is passed on to become the property of the nation.... The best writings of each generation are gathered by a natural selection out of the contemporary rubbish.

The "public opinion" that would weigh the merits of new books, of course, was limited to those who could afford to purchase new books or to borrow them from circulating libraries—certainly a restricted conception of the "public." That "public" would then play benevolent censor to the "nation" at large. Froude scoffed at Trevelyan's notion that literature would exert a stronger social influence "if all classes—upper, middle, and lower—could participate in a common interest and discuss [contemporary books] together." Such a leveling gesture would gum up the mechanism of cultural Darwinism—the process of putatively "natural" selection by an elite "public" that refreshed and refurbished the cultural genome. "Better for the people, better for every one of us whose stomach is not seasoned by antidotes, to read books whose worth has been tested, than to devour every new dainty."[57] It was Froude's last word on the copyright issue, as he was soon to become an even busier man. In 1881, Carlyle would die, leaving Froude as his sole literary executor.

Farrer's *Fortnightly* article "The Principle of Copyright" had begun as a written supplement to his testimony to the Commission and was cited by Mallet in his dissenting Report. Where Farrer's spoken evidence had dwelt largely on the practical matter of copyright reform, his article burrowed down to "the conflicting principles which lie at the bottom of the subject." Oddly, though, he chose not to write the bulk of the article in his own voice, instead presenting long summaries of the perpetual copyright and anti-copyright views in quotation marks and leaving the reader to "draw his own conclusion." The strategy is a strange mix of staged objectivity and candid bias: having presented the discussion as a "disinterested" debate, Farrer admits to treating the anti-copyright view more fully because it is less often heard, its opponents (authors and publishers) tending to control the means of literary dissemination. More subtly, Farrer's rhetorical ventriloquism embodies the anarchist view of discourse articulated by its own anti-copyright voice:

> Facts once collected are admitted to be the property of the world. Conclusions, thoughts, ideas, cannot be so controlled and charged for. Unlike physical products of labour, they are capable of unlimited extension. Nay, they derive their value from the number of other minds which receive and are affected by them. Laws which are applicable to objects of consumption have no application to knowledge, thoughts, and feelings.
>
> "'Tracera-t-on des bornes à cette consommation intellectuelle, qui se nomme la publicité. Une idée qui est consommée ne disparaît pas encore au coup; elle grandit, au contraire, elle se fortifie, elle s'étend à la fois et dans le temps, et dans l'espace. Donnez-lui le monde pour consommateur, elle deviendra inépuisable comme la nature et immortelle comme Dieu.'"
>
> ["'Let us trace the boundaries of this intellectual consumption, which is called publicity. An idea that is consumed does not then suddenly disappear; on the contrary, it expands, it becomes stronger, it extends itself all at once both in time and in space. Give it the world for consumer, and it will become inexhaustible like nature and immortal like God.'"][58]

To support his notion of a free economy of ideas, Farrer quotes a book by the French socialist Louis Blanc entitled *Organisation du travail* (1839), a book that had helped ignite the February Revolution of 1848 by advocating the formation of collectivist, state-supported "social-workshops." Blanc concluded the book with an invective against literary property regimes, which he saw as prostituting the author, infantilizing the reader, and degrading literature to a commercial speculation. But as a bitter opponent of laissez-faire economics, he argued for state-sponsored social libraries—the literary equivalent to the social-workshop—rather than free trade. Farrer's citation of Blanc not only helps explain the cries of "socialist" or "communistic" proclivities within the Board of Trade, but illustrates the fundamental incompatibility between the stated aims of the antimonopolists and the free trade lexicon from which they built their arguments. Laissez-faire doctrine relied on the "invisible hand" posited by Adam Smith to translate individual self-interest into public weal; but both Macfie and Blanc had resorted to very visible hands—in the shape of a governmental royalty office or a state-supported social library—to foster the best literature and distribute it to the greatest number of citizens. Oscillating between free trade capitalism and state socialism, Farrer weakened the cases to be made for both. Having given voice to quite radical ideas, his article concluded much as his testimony did: by backing away from its own extreme impulses and proposing moderate changes to the extant monopoly form.

The antithetical views voiced by Farrer's article found a would-be synthesist in Matthew Arnold, whose 1880 *Fortnightly Review* article "Copyright" attempted to chart a sensible middle way between absolutism and abolition. For someone of his reputation, Arnold had said remarkably little to the Commissioners, beyond endorsing a term extension for the sake of the author's family. But his article suggests he had avidly followed the hearings, the Report, and the ensuing responses. Arnold began by praising Michel Lévy, George Sand's publisher, who had boldly introduced cheap first editions to France. Lévy's enterprise rejected Froude's distinction between books and bread: if the masses could develop the habit of reading, he predicted, it would not be long before "people shall ask for their book as impatiently as if it were a question of dinner when one is hungry." Arnold deplored the lack of such an attitude among British publishers and authors and criticized the circulating library system as "eccentric, artificial, and unsatisfactory in the highest degree." But his motivations were not limited to a school inspector's concern for the education of the masses; some reform of the literary marketplace, he added, was a necessary deterrent to messier, more "menacing" forms of change.

> If the system of our book-trade remains as it is, dissatisfaction, not loud and active at present,—I grant that to Mr. Froude,—will grow and stir more and more, and will certainly end by menacing, in spite of whatever conclusion the Royal Commission may now adopt and proclaim, the proprietary right of the author.... there will be an explosion of discontent likely enough to sweep

away copyright, and to destroy the author's benefit from his work by reducing it to some such illusory benefit as that offered by the royalty plan of Mr. Farrer.[59]

Keep the masses supplied with cheap books, he implied, and they will be less likely to abolish copyright forcibly. The notion of an anti-copyright coup may seem risible (though somewhat less so given the example of Louis Blanc), but it is not really the point: the imagined overthrow of the "proprietary right of the author" simply miniaturizes a more general fear of proletarian revolution. An uneducated, illiterate underclass would be harder to convince of the virtues of peaceable, incremental, parliamentary reform. Keep the masses supplied with cheap books, Arnold insinuated, and they will be less likely to revolt.

Counterposed in the article to the language of mass uprising—growing "dissatisfaction," "explosion of discontent," "sweeping away,"—is the Arnoldian doctrine of cultivation. Having betrayed an anxiety about violent change, Arnold switched the grounds of the debate from ethics to "delicacy" and from the domestic book trade to the international. By denying British authors copyright privileges, he claimed, lawmakers and consumers in the U.S. were not being "dishonest" so much as "indelicate," though "a finely touched nature" spurned both equally.

> Aristocracies, again, are brought up in elegance and refinement, and are taught to believe that art and letters go for much in making the beauty and grace of human life, and perhaps they do believe it. At any rate, they feel bound to show the disposition to treat the interests of artists and authors with delicacy; and shown it the aristocratic government and parliament of England have.... Still, on the whole, the spirit of the American community and government is the spirit, I suppose, of a middle-class society of our race; and this is not a spirit of delicacy.... As the great American community becomes more truly and thoroughly civilised, it will certainly learn to add to its many and great virtues the spirit of delicacy.

Though specifically aimed at the Philistine U.S., Arnold's charge of "indelicacy" also indicted anyone who questioned the "proprietary right of the author"—that is, the unlettered working class, governmental dissenters, and those free traders whose "worship of sharp bargains is fatal to delicacy."[60] For him, copyright was no mere commercial nicety but a key index of a people's sensitivity, cultivation, and aristocratic faith in "elegance and refinement," "art and letters," "beauty and grace." In essence, copyright was coextensive with the civilizing process—hence the refusal, thus far, of semi-civilized territories such as Canada, India, and the U.S. to enter into reciprocal copyright accords with Britain. The civilizing work of diplomacy and empire would not be done until it had produced a critical mass of delicacy—

and a critically delicate mass—whereupon the "proprietary right of the author" would become universal across the Anglophone world.

Yet Arnold's understanding of the "proprietary right" in question was not simplistic. Though he condemned the royalty system as unenforceable, he also dismissed the natural-rights advocates, particularly Huxley and Spencer, as deluded. "An author has no natural right to a property in his production," he wrote. "But then neither has he a natural right to anything whatever which he may produce or acquire." Echoing Trevelyan and Dicey (see note 39), he insisted that "property is the creation of law," and that all such creations must balance the individual's instincts against "the general advantage of the community."[61] For Arnold, the community's interest did not, as for Mallet, hinge on a distinction between natural and artificial scarcity but rather on difficulty of enforcement. Much as one might like to enjoy property in one's conversation, he observed, the pleasure yielded by such property could not justify the social costs of enforcing it. By the same token, perpetual copyright would be untenably difficult to secure. Even temporary copyright, Arnold admitted, was tricky to enforce, since any literary property was by nature "easy for others to appropriate." The appeal of temporary copyright was further diminished in Britain, where the monopoly form was complicit in a system that denied cheap books to the lower classes and thus imperiled the security of those very structures of cultivation copyright was designed to protect. Yet copyright was, after all, an indispensable mark of a civilized people. The logic of legal cost-benefit analysis and the ideological requirements of cultivation had reached an impasse.

Arnold's self-divided essay, in many ways, encapsulates the nineteenth-century legacy to the twentieth on the subject of intellectual property. In 1839, Arnold's father had begun his pro-Talfourd Bill petition by asserting that British common law "recognized the right of authors to a perpetual property in their own works," adding that a limited copyright "contrasts strangely with the absolutely unlimited term, during which the law recognizes a property in other things."[62] Though Huxley and a few other witnesses would agree with Thomas Arnold during the 1876–78 Royal Copyright Commission hearings, perpetual copyright was a dead issue by the end of the nineteenth century. So, as we have seen, was the notion of an alternative to fixed-term monopoly copyright. Between the two lay a muddle of conflicting ideas about the limited monopoly form that had survived a century of assaults from both sides. Proponents of the positivist–natural-right model of property (e.g., Huxley) saw copyright as an absolute entitlement and its limitation as a concession by the rightsholder to public opinion. Advocates of a functional-right model of property (e.g., Mallet) regarded the law as a bundle of rights granted by the state to encourage individual innovation for the collective good—in essence, as a tax levied on the public for the public weal and thus answerable to the criterion of distributive fairness. Meanwhile, if the Romantic rhetoric about original genius had become somewhat less grandiloquent, the convention of individual authorship still eclipsed collaborative models of invention and intersubjective understandings of meaning. Finally, there remained the sense that copyright was somehow characteristic of cultivated people, coupled with the half-awareness that cultivation is secured at a price, one usually paid by those least able to grasp—much less protest against—the inequities of the system that claimed to defend them. It was an ambivalent legacy indeed.

Afterlives of the Commission

I suggested at the beginning of this chapter that excavating the deeply contentious aspects of the 1876–78 Royal Copyright Commission might inform present-day debates about intellectual property law. How might this be so? To begin with, we need to recognize that the Commission was never entirely buried. Although forgotten or trivialized by most of the subsequent discourse on copyright, the dissenting views generated by the Commission have had their own quiet afterlife. Legislatively, circumscribed versions of the royalty system advocated by Macfie, Mallet, and others became law in the U.S. (1909) and Great Britain (1911), subjecting phonograph and player-piano recordings to a compulsory license system. A similar system was proposed in the U.S. in 1966 to legislate transmission rebroadcasts by TV cable companies but ultimately quashed by copyright holders; and a compulsory or statutory license now permits recording artists in the U.S. to "cover" musical compositions, once they have already been recorded, with the copyright holder's permission.[63] More important, Mallet's report in particular has helped to galvanize and sustain a counterdiscourse within law and economics to the reigning orthodoxy of monopoly copyright. In 1934, the economist Arnold Plant lavishly praised "the uniformly high quality of reasoning in Sir Louis Mallet's minority report" and admitted to sharing the Commissioner's skepticism as to whether monopoly copyright was necessary, effective, or defensible as an incentive to creation, even proposing that a Mallet-esque royalty scheme should supplant the long-monopoly form.[64] In 1967, Denis Thomas echoed Plant's skepticism in turn, asking "Does the ever-lengthening term of copyright protection enter [creators'] calculations very much, or indeed at all? Is it an inducement to give up one's means of livelihood and instead take up writing, painting, composing, or design?"[65] In 1970, a U.S. bill that eventually succeeded in extending copyright from a 56-year maximum to the length of the author's life plus 50 years precipitated Stephen Breyer's article "The Uneasy Case for Copyright." As his footnotes show, Breyer had read the Commission papers, including Mallet's dissenting Separate Report.[66] Breyer's critique of the natural-property-rights doctrine registered Mallet's strong influence:

> Since ideas are infinitely divisible, property rights are not needed to prevent congestion, interference, or strife. Nor does the fact that the book is the author's *creation* seem a sufficient reason for making it his *property*. We do not ordinarily create or modify property rights, nor even award compensation, solely on the basis of labor expended. . . . It is not apparent that the producer has any stronger claim to the surplus than the consumer or that the author's claim is any stronger than that of any other workers. . . . the case for copyright in books rests not upon proven need, but rather upon uncertainty as to what would happen if protection were removed.

The claim that "infinitely divisible" ideas require no property rights restates Mallet's assertion that property should preserve society only against conditions of "natural" scarcity; to create property in ideas and expression, then, would be to limit artificially what was naturally limitless. In the "social cost-benefit analysis" that followed the claim, Breyer used publishing statistics to destabilize the "incentive" theory of copyright. Copyright, he argued, was not needed to encourage authors to write and publishers to publish. The law tended to reward popular commercial works over those with "lasting social value"; since the government already funded two-thirds of the country's research and development work, why not have it finance all salutary works through subsidies, grants, and prizes? (The suggestion recalls Blanc and Macfie, and, for many respondents, raised the specter of a paternalist, even censorious, government.) Publishers need not fare badly in a post-copyright world either: a work's first publisher would have the advantage over potential copiers of its lead time and its prerogative of offering competitive cheap editions, and savings would be passed on to the consumer. Nonetheless, despite his motivating skepticisms, even Breyer could not quite recommend the abolition of copyright, and, in a loaded moment of allusion, dubbed the post-copyright world an "undiscover'd country" that "makes us rather bear those ills we have / Than fly to others that we know not of."[67]

How, then, might the Copyright Commission of 1876–78 inform the conditions and quandaries of millennial intellectual property law? The gaps between the two contexts are not only temporal but technological, conceptual, and lexical. Mallet, Macfie, and the other Commissioners of 1876–78 were arguing over the expressly material embodiments of intellectual property: first editions, deposit copies, colonial reprints, engravings, statues. Today the key terms belong to the digital revolution: RAM, reprography, user interface, "smart" copyright management information systems, noninfringing decompilation, anticircumvention, Clipper chips, mp3s, and the Digital Millennium Copyright Act. Yet by 1878, the Victorians had already witnessed epochal advances in information technologies. Machine-made paper, steam-driven presses, and lithography had appeared around 1800 and photography during the 1830s. Recorded sound was first heard in 1877 while the Commission sat, and moving pictures would follow ten years later, along with Monotype and Linotype.[68] Though the Commission had ostensibly gathered to update and consolidate a largely eighteenth-century, print-based copyright legacy, its participants shared the sense of also needing to lay foundations that could support coming technological advances. As Farrer presciently observed in his post-Commission article:

> Copyright [might] depend on the ease and cheapness with which the work can be reproduced. This seems to be a fruitful idea. The difficulty in applying it is that modern science tends to facilitate reproduction of all sorts of things, and that almost all subjects of copyright can be mechanically reproduced with more or less ease and cheapness. . . . printing a book, copying a photograph, photographing a drawing, engraving, chromolithography, copying a statue by machine, casts from a statue, are all mechanical modes of reproduction, more or less easy and cheap, which, according as they are more or less easy and cheap, more or less diminish the market value of the original.[69]

Sixty years before Walter Benjamin's essay "The Work of Art in the Age of Mechanical Reproduction," Farrer had come up with a commercial precursor to the erosion of "aura." In addition, the passage records Farrer's sense that copyright reform at the brink of technological change should perform a dual function: it needs both to provide a philosophical basis for all future forms of protection and to insist that future protection be implemented in ways appropriately specific to the new medium. In delineating this dual agenda, his motivating concern—and Mallet's, and Macfie's—was to keep the public interest uppermost in rationalizing private incentives and therefore to make lasting provisions for the public domain. It is this commitment to the public interest over the interests of rightsholders, combined with a belief in the renegotiability of even the most entrenched laws in the service of that public interest, that has been absent from much copyright legislation since the Commission and has helped produce the present maximalism.

Recent interventions in the intellectual property scene have shared Farrer's twofold demand for philosophical ground rules that protect the public domain and specific provisions for emerging media; one might say that such interventions embody the spirit of the dissenting Commissioners, even when they differ somewhat in ideological orientation. Among the most outspoken advocates of progressive intellectual property law reform along these lines is legal scholar James Boyle, who connects his advocacy to a critique of liberal legalism and state theory. Liberalism, he argues, harbors a central ambivalence in its conception of property, an ambivalence we have just seen was central to the 1876–78 Commission debates: on the one hand, property is an absolute right of dominion that fends off the incursions of the public; on the other, it is a negotiable bundle of entitlements balancing the owner's utility against the public's. Intellectual property law, Boyle writes, attempts "not only to clothe a newly invented Romantic author in robes of juridical protection, but to struggle with, mediate, or repress one of the central contradictions in the liberal world view."[70] The latter gesture relies on features associated with the Romantic author: genius, originality, and an idea/expression dichotomy. Genius not only recombines elements of the public domain but also creates something original. What it recombines are ideas; what it creates is expression. Thus, the convention that gives a property in expression but not in ideas is rationalized according to the Romantic creation-narrative; what seems like a "bundle" model of property is rooted in an "absolute" mythology. Furthermore, because originality makes authorial labor different in kind from manual labor, artists and inventors garner residual property rights in their creations, whereas other workers are denied such rights. In more baldly comparative terms, innovative labor is held to profit humanity *more* than merely productive labor and therefore to require special property incentives to keep the public well supplied with innovation. What Boyle calls the "stereotype" of the Romantic author, then, caulks the gap between "absolute" and "bundle" models of property, between the sovereign individual and the sovereignty of public good.[71]

As numerous critics of intellectual property orthodoxy have insisted, the Romantic-author paradigm within the law not only obscures the "bundle" model of property rights but can be terribly occlusive in its own right. What may seem like an elegant mediation between public goods and private incentives can often reward private entrepreneurial or corporate interests at devastating expense to public goods and the public good. One recent and well-known site of this phenomenon is Madagascar, home to 5 percent of the world's *Vinca rosea* species. Better known as the Madagascar or rosy periwinkle, this plant was first used by indigenous populations to treat diabetes. Learning of the treatment in the 1980s, the pharmaceutical company Ely Lilly tested the rosy periwinkle, developing the complex alkaloids the plant yielded into a treatment for childhood leukemia and a cure for Hodgkin's disease—together, a 100-million-dollar-a-year business.[72] But because of the structure of patent law, only the "transformative" energies of the Lilly researchers were rewarded with protection; the traditional ethnobotanical knowledge that led to the Lilly research was not. When Lilly began to cultivate and harvest the rosy periwinkle elsewhere, the unremunerated people of Madagascar destroyed their forests in order to grow subsistence crops. Boyle writes:

> Now *there's* a public goods problem. Precisely because they can find no place in a legal regime constructed around a vision of individual, transformative, original genius, the indigenous peoples are driven to deforestation or slash and burn farming. Who knows what other unique and potentially valuable plants disappear with the forest, what generations of pharmacological experience disappear as the indigenous culture is destroyed?[73]

Other examples of appropriations of indigenous bioknowledge and cultural lore abound. As with patents, so with copyrights and trademarks. In their work, Peter Jaszi and Martha Woodmansee list a number of successfully privatized appropriations from collective sources that intellectual property law does not recognize: East African motifs on mugs "© Smithsonian Institution"; the "Morning Mist Dream Catcher" copyrighted by "Pastime Industries, Inc. Hauppage, N.Y." and bearing the "INDIAN™" seal of approval; recordings of the Brazilian Suyá Indians used as background music in radio ads and television programs.[74] If, as Matthew Arnold implied in 1880, copyright is coextensive with the civilizing process, it has also proven to be a handy ally in the expropriating process. As Vandana Shiva, Rosemary Coombe, and others have pointed out, cases such as those involving the rosy periwinkle and the Morning Mist Dream Catcher amount to nothing less than state-licensed corporate neocolonialism.[75]

In the final pages of his book *Shamans, Software, and Spleens* (1996), Boyle makes several "moderate, reformist suggestions" for adjusting international property laws in the short term, while the society contemplates more extreme reforms. The copyright term, he proposes, should be shrunk to 20 years, "with a broadly defined fair use protection for journalistic, teaching, and parodic uses."[76] Software should be removed from patent and copyright rubrics and brought under a "sui generis" system of law more attentive to the peculiarities of the medium. A 10 percent tax should be levied on all pharmaceuticals developed as a result of ethnobotanical practices, and the revenues shared between the source community and an international biodiversity fund.[77] Intellectual property regimes should be audited by a General Accounting Office to ensure that they be properly calibrated intermediaries between private incentives and the public domain. Finally—and perhaps most radically—Boyle proposes that "Patents should be voidable at the instance of any party who can prove that an adequate return would have been provided merely by being first on the market, with the state paying the legal fees for successful suits."[78] By turning patents over to the public domain as soon as inventors had made profits large enough to keep them inventing, such a provision would result in a law more mindful of the public interest. It would take seriously a founding principle of Anglo-American intellectual property law: that patents and copyrights are not a "natural right," but a "social and economic rationale."[79] That rationale, like all property laws, should be a negotiable bundle of rights, vigilantly administered so that it encourages individual creation without overgarlanding it at the expense of public discourse and the public interest. Louis Mallet's suggestion that the duration of copyright shorten as its territory widened arose from a similar conviction: that a temporary monopoly should function as a fair but limited incentive, not as a state-sponsored lottery.

Even granting a certain homology between the late-nineteenth-century copyright scene and that of the present day, one may balk at taking contemporary cues from Victorian free traders, many of whom were men of power in the administration of empire. Charles Trevelyan's testimony, in particular, should stand as a cautionary tale about the potential complicity of intellectual property regimes—whether monopolistic or not—in imperial ones, or in the kind of corporate neocolonial project decried by Shiva and others. With free trade, one encounters a problem of translation. "Free trade" in our own moment has come to suggest "small government" conservatism, rather than a radical public-interest-minded critique of legal and economic conventions. But if the 1876–78 Commission debates teach us anything, it is that the rubric of free trade could shelter completely adverse viewpoints—from Spencer's reactionary social Darwinism to Mallet's more progressive and egalitarian agenda. (It was the Cobdenites, remember, who led the assault on the Corn Laws and the Taxes on Knowledge.) Presumably, James Boyle would find Louis Mallet's free trade affiliations less objectionable than the latter's faith in neoclassical economics—the basis of what is now a microeconomic model whose language of "consumer sovereignty" and "exogenous preferences" Boyle finds decisively limiting. Too often, that model fully or partially brackets out the conditions and agents of production: "Just as the market–natural right vision of property could be used to claim that workers were receiving exactly the proportion of social wealth to which they were entitled, so the authorship vision can be used—both rhetorically and theoretically—to obscure, undervalue, or simply ignore the contributions of 'sources.'"[80] Nonetheless, Boyle shares with Mallet not only a critique of the "natural rights vision of property" but an interest in redefining economic value itself—with an eye toward redistributing intellectual property, and thus wealth generally, to the excluded and exploited orders of human society. The latter gesture would critically overhaul, rather than enshrine, neoclassical economics: in place of a hedonic "consumer sovereignty" that eclipses the agents of production, it would install a "public sovereignty" that understands both individuals *and* communities as innovative producers.

Between them, the copyright critics of the late-nineteenth century and their turn-of-the-millennium counterparts supply a crucial corrective to present-day maximalist trends primarily underwritten by the logic of microeconomics and the funds of major corporations. When it comes to public goods problems, microeconomics says "let the market decide." Inventors who can't find backing to pay for patent searches and licensing fees must not have sufficiently worthwhile inventions. Writers, publishers, educators, and others who cannot afford high copyright royalties must lack the requisite demand for their work, whose deficient "social utility" is thereby confirmed. Traditional communities with shamanic cures have risked nothing in the global marketplace and should therefore gain nothing; their failure to develop and market their bioknowledge should not be sponsored by a tax on pharmaceutical companies. Clearly, this kind of free marketeering runs counter to both Mallet and Boyle; this is Spencerian "free trade," which sees the free market as a perfectly functioning hierarchy machine rather than as an equalizing force. Its present-day critics insist that such a view fails to internalize externalities—fails, that is, to account for the quiet but catastrophic depletions of the public domain and the public sphere by extreme privatization. They point out that those who most oppose state intervention in trade also require the most extensive state protections—ever-expanding intellectual property regimes, state-approved infringement-detection technologies, endless copyright, patent, and trademark litigation—for the commodified information in which they traffic. Having traced the legacy of the 1876–78 Copyright Commission, they might remark how easily property law becomes dissociated from its putative end—the protection and promotion of the collective weal—in the service of property for property's sake.

In thinking about how ideas and expressions circulate in a market society, we have been considering what economists call a public goods problem—one having to do with goods that are both undepletable (one person's use does not diminish the good for another's use) and nonexcludable (their benefits cannot be denied anyone). Classic examples of public goods include air, roads, and national defense, and the classic problem with public goods is how to encourage their production and protection given that they are not intrinsically scarce or privately owned. One solution to the problem is to let government provide and administer the public good, as in the case of roads and national defense. Another solution is to create an artificial scarcity in the good, or in some aspect of it, by creating exclusive private property rights. Copyright adopts this latter approach in relation to ideas, creating an artificial scarcity in expression in order to encourage the generation and dissemination of the new ideas incarnated in expression. The distinction copyright assumes between ideas and expression seems credible enough in relation to printed language, which "fixes" expression in a stable form whose ideational content might then be paraphrased in noninfringing language. But what happens to the idea/expression dichotomy, and to the public goods solution posed by copyright laws that rely on that dichotomy, when the expression is less stable, less permanent, and thus less susceptible to the artificial scarcity of a private property right? Where does talk fall along the idea/expression continuum? And is talk just a medium for the transmission of public goods (ideas and expressions), or might it be considered a public good in itself? In his 1880 article "Copyright," Matthew Arnold mused on the instability of talk in addressing the possibility of a copyright law in conversation:

> There is no property, people often say, in ideas uttered in conversation, in spoken words; and it is inferred that there ought to be no property in ideas and words when they are embodied in a book. But why is there no property in ideas uttered in conversation, and in spoken words, while there is property in ideas and words when they come in a book? A brilliant talker may very well have the instinct of ownership in his good sayings, and all the more if he must and

can only talk them and not write them. He might be glad of power to prevent the appropriation of them by other people, to fix the conditions on which alone the appropriation should be allowed, and to derive profit from allowing it.[81]

Although Arnold went on to discount the viability of conversational copyright, he cited a pragmatic rather than a conceptual or ethical obstacle: tracking spoken ideas and expression in order to secure the speaker's profits presented one with an "insuperable difficulty." That Arnold could entertain the notion of conversational copyright at all tells us something about the generally expansionist energies of the late-nineteenth-century copyright climate. That he found talk insuperably difficult to track tells us something about oral patterns of circulation, which present an inherent resistance to intellectual property forms reliant on sole and serial ownership and the commodification of expression. But what happens at the border between private intellectual property law and the public goods of oral discourse? What happens when "a brilliant talker," one who is perfectly able to write but possesses little instinct of private ownership, collides with the possessive individualism crystallized in a strong copyright regime? The next chapter considers these questions in relation to its central figure, the nineteenth century's most famous talker and plagiarist: Oscar Wilde.

[3]

Oscar Wilde: Literary Property, Orality, and Crimes of Writing

> What is copyright? It is not the right to ideas or to the form in which ideas are clothed. These, we all admit, are the exclusive property of him with whom they originate, so long as he chooses to retain them. He is, and ought to be, protected in the absolute and exclusive use of them, so long as he does not give them to the public. No one can compel him to publish them, and unless he publishes, any other person who may have obtained possession of them is, and ought to be, prevented from publishing them. No one, so far has the law been carried, may even publish a description of the unpublished book of another. And when the author has published, the actual book which he publishes is, and ought to be, his own chattel. Any one who takes it without his permission is guilty of theft. So far, a book stands on exactly the same footing as other property, and is, and ought to be, protected in the same way. It is here that copyright begins. Copyright is a right to prevent all other persons from imitating and reproducing that which the author has already given to the public.
> — T. H. Farrer, "The Principle of Copyright" (1878)

> I appropriate what is already mine, for once a thing is published it becomes public property.
> — Oscar Wilde

In 1878, the year in which the Royal Commission on Copyright submitted its Report, a young Irishman named Oscar Wilde, then in his fourth year at Magdalen College, Oxford, was awarded the Newdigate Prize for his poem *Ravenna*. On June 26, shortly after winning the award, Wilde recited parts of the poem by invitation at the Sheldonian Theatre before an audience that included the University's Vice-Chancellor; that same day, *Ravenna* was published as a pamphlet by Thomas Shrimpton & Son of Oxford, and offered for sale at 1s. 2d. Although not its author's first published poem, *Ravenna* was his first monograph. In the next few years, Wilde would become a celebrated poet, aesthete, and conversationalist and cause a sensation during a lecture tour of the U.S. In 1885, he would embark on the most productive decade of his dazzling literary career, publishing a wide array of reviews, articles, essays, tales, aphorisms, poems and poems-in-prose, plays, and a novel. During that career, his extravagant and generous habits would be supported partly by proceeds from this literary work, his ownership of which was guaranteed by the monopoly copyright regime that had survived the Board of Trade's assault during the Royal Commission. He would carefully husband his literary property rights in his publications, on at least one occasion negotiating with a publisher to retain his copyright in a tale set to appear in the magazine.[1] He would even, in 1884, become an unwitting poster boy for photographic copyright in the U.S.[2] In an 1886 review of *Low Down* by Two Tramps, he claimed he was "sorry to see that that disregard of the rights of property which always characterises the able-bodied vagrant is extended by our tramps from the defensible pilfering from hen-roosts to the indefensible pilfering from poets . . . bad as poultry-snatching is, plagiarism is worse."[3] Years later, after his trial and his imprisonment for sodomy, writing from Reading Prison of his recent bankruptcy proceedings, Wilde would mention among the losses that most grieved him the sale of his copyrights in his published works and plays.[4]

Glimpsed at these isolated moments, Wilde seems an exemplary citizen of the nascent copyright state, one who lived contentedly on proceeds from the literary property he had won by original creative labor. Even in lamenting the loss of his copyrights, he appears to prize them as something more than a means of securing profits—as an authorial birthright, as the property form the writer most properly and inalienably owned and whose forfeit most wounded the writerly soul. But as ever with Wilde, the truth is more complex. In addition to the generative transgressions for which Wilde is now better known—of stodgy middle-class aesthetics, of the moralizing Philistine press, of repressive sexual norms and the laws that enforced them—Wilde was also a transgressor of literary property orthodoxy and was seen by his contemporaries as such. Certainly he profited from intellectual property law and could be vigilant in collecting his writerly debts: his deathbed letters chiefly concerned royalties owed him for *Mr. and Mrs. Daventry*, a play whose scenario he had sold to its writer, Frank Harris. Yet the financially straitened Wilde had also sold options on the same scenario to at least five other unknowing parties, flouting the very notion of serial and exclusive property in ideas even as he profited by it.[5] Nor was this his only breach of the conventions of literary property. Over the course of his literary career, Wilde was repeatedly and publicly charged with plagiarism. More significantly, he actually practiced it, in one case—the Chatterton notes, to which I will return—purloining the bulk of a lecture transcript from two other writers. He boasted to Max Beerbohm, "Of course I plagiarise. It is the privilege of the appreciative man. I never read Flaubert's *Tentation de St. Antoine* without signing my name at the end of it. *Que voulez-vous?* All the best Hundred Books bear my signature in this manner."[6] Wilde's rhetorical and practical disregard for private literary property has led his grandson Merlin Holland to posit, with perhaps equal parts reverence and discomfort, a Wildean "communism of language and ideas," a kind of intellectual collectivism that stands in stark opposition to the logic of copyright law, with its individualist incentive of exclusive rights.[7]

At least in part, the collectivism Holland identifies was a corollary of Wilde's professed socialism—his contention, as he put it in his 1891 essay "The Soul of Man under Socialism," that "converting private property into public wealth, and substituting cooperation for competition, will restore society to its proper condition of a thoroughly healthy organism, and insure the material well-being of each member of the community."[8] As a number of recent studies have shown, Wilde's socialism had a complicated intellectual and political provenance. But among its many sources was his Irish cultural inheritance, and particularly the oral dimensions of that inheritance. As an Irishman, Wilde grew up in what Deirdre Toomey has called "the most oral culture in Western Europe, a culture which retained primary orality as well as oral/writing *diglossia* well into the twentieth century."[9] Such a formulation may tread near a kind of essentialism: even in the nineteenth century not all Irish were great talkers, nor all great talkers Irish. But whether or not one regards Wilde's orality as specifically and intrinsically Irish, he did spend his youth steeped in fabulous talk. The genteel intellectual circles in which Wilde's family moved were coteries of spectacular conversation, the most celebrated talker in the room often being Wilde's mother, Speranza. Of course, her Merrion Square salons were hardly the domain of "primary orality," an orality to which writing is alien. But Wilde did encounter varieties of primary orality through his father, whom he accompanied on archaeological and folklore-gathering expeditions in rural Ireland. There he also witnessed not only the wonders of talk circulated and dispersed, but the losses incurred when talk was annexed, set down, owned, and sold. For William Wilde was not only an avid collector and publisher of Irish folklore, but one acquainted with the potential damage wrought by his own undertaking. In his preface to his collection of *Irish Popular Superstitions* (1852), he had written:

> These legendary tales and Popular Superstitions have now become the history of the past—a portion of the traits and characteristics of other days. Will their recital revive their practice? No! Nothing contributes more to uproot superstitious rites and forms than to print them; to make them known to the many instead of leaving them hidden among, and secretly practised by the few.[10]

William Wilde knew that the massive rural depopulation brought about by the Famine, coupled with the spread of education and the decay of the Irish language, threatened to eradicate the oral traditions of the Irish agricultural classes.[11] Those vanishing traditions needed chroniclers, and he was glad to be one. But he also recognized that while publishing orally circulated narratives, cures, and charms might preserve them for the sake of posterity, it did a permanent violence to the conditions of oral transmission that were among their defining characteristics. Those conditions included plurality (the proliferation of variant tales without a single "official version"), mutability (tailoring retellings to suit the audience), and a kind of communal ownership in which information could circulate and proliferate unfettered by private literary property forms. Stories could also operate in place of more orthodox coin. Charles Gavan Duffy in *Young Ireland* (1881) described the function of oral narratives not only in rural community-building but in exchange:

> By the fireside on a winter night, at fairs and markets, the old legends and traditions were a favorite recreation. The wandering harpers and pipers kept them alive; the itinerant school-master taught them with more unction than the rudiments. Nurses and seamstresses, the tailor who carried his lapboard and shears from house to house, and from district to district, the pedlar who came from the capital with shawls and ribbons, the tinker who paid for his supper with a song and a story, were always ready with tales of the wars and the persecution.[12]

In cash-poor rural communities, narrative could be a more binding currency than money—one that was fungible but not privately ownable. In the spirit of "the tinker who paid for his supper with a song and a story," William Wilde accepted legends, superstitions, proverbs, and folk cures from his rural patients in place of monetary fees; while patients told their tales to the physician, an amanuensis would write them down. But transcription and publication not only calcified a plural, mutable narrative into a single telling; they also brought under the rubric of private accumulation (the sole authorship and copyright of Sir William Robert Wills Wilde) material whose value had originally dwelt in its circulation and in its status as the property of a community. To record such material was to preserve it, but it was also to "uproot" and "embalm" it. Whether the embalmer merely conserved what was already dead or actually aided in the killing was open for debate.

To learn about orality from within literacy, however, is also to learn a certain discourse about orality, that discourse by which literate culture imagines *primary* orality as also *prior*—as the egg or Eden of spontaneity, collectivity, and authenticity from which literate culture has emerged or fallen. Such a discourse informs some of Wilde's remarks about orality: he has Gilbert say in "The Critic as Artist" that "When Milton became blind he composed, as everyone should compose, with the voice purely, and so the pipe or reed of earlier days became that mighty many-stopped organ whose rich reverberant music has all the stateliness of Homeric verse.... Yes: writing has done much harm to writers. We must return to the voice.... As it now is, we cannot do so."[13] Yet for all his paeans to Homeric verse, Wilde also knew that oral epic was not a space of conversational spontaneity, tending as it did to create opportunities for improvisation only within elaborate codes and structures—metrical constraints, mnemonic devices, standardized epithets, inventories, recursive architecture—that one might identify as writerly *avant la lettre*. Even if Wilde's work does not go so far as to make orality a hallucination of writing, it recognizes at least that "primary orality" is in part a construction by literate culture of its other, and therefore not revivable in practice. Instead, his more formally transgressive writings, and his career generally, suggest that to import the forms of primary orality into typographical England does less to ventilate literate culture than to translate orality into terms that literacy can recognize—sustained circulation into plagiarism, a reservoir of proven formulas into self-plagiarism, a cento of innovations, renovations, and appropriations into private literary property. Rather than naively imagine orality as a tonic to writing, as nature to writing's artifice, or as authenticity to the travesty of type, Wilde recognized that the longing for orality as origin, nature, or authentic prehistory may be the most characteristic thing about print culture, which thrives by manufacturing origins and measuring its distance from them in order, alternately, to wound or worship itself. His writing both embodies and inflicts an ache for the forms of orality while elaborately demonstrating their irrecuperability, even their unknowability: we must return to the voice, yet as it now is, we cannot do so.

It is especially fitting, then, that Wilde left many contemporaries who felt with Robert Ross that his "personality and conversation were far more wonderful than anything he wrote, so that his written works give only a pale reflection of his power. Perhaps that is so, and of course it will be impossible to reproduce what is gone for ever. I am not alas a Boswell."[14] Yeats implied that Wilde's writing was only successful when he played Boswell to his own Johnson: "Only when he spoke, or when his writing was the mirror of his speech, or in some simple fairytale, had he words exact enough to hold a subtle ear.... [H]is plays and dialogues have what merit they possess from being now an imitation, now a record, of his talk."[15] For both Ross and Yeats, the oral Wilde was the irretrievable and thus idealized origin from which his writings derived and usually declined, activating a longing for the lost voice. Other memorialists attributed his propensities for talk, along with his other alterities, to a Celtic naiveté they found enchantingly "foreign." William Ward, a friend of Wilde's at Magdalen College, remembered

> How brilliant and radiant he could be! How playful and charming! ... I daresay we were a little dazzled by his directness and surprised by the unexpected angle from which he looked at things. There was something foreign to us, and

inconsequential, in his modes of thought, just as there was a suspicion of a brogue in his pronunciation, and an unfamiliar turn in his phrasing. His qualities were not ordinary and we, his intimate friends, did not judge him by the ordinary standards.[16]

Wilde himself occasionally deployed the racial stereotype of the indolent, profligate Irishman, writing in *De Profundis* that "the virtues of prudence and thrift were not in my own nature or my own race," and ascribing his weakness for Alfred Douglas to his own "proverbial good-nature and Celtic laziness."[17] To the extent poetry required industry, Wilde conceded that the Irish failed in it, but with redemptive bravado: "We Irish are too poetical to be poets; we are a nation of brilliant failures, but we are the greatest talkers since the Greeks."[18]

The elegant levity of that formulation masks the persistence and seriousness of Wilde's stance toward the oral/written interface, its legal and economic ramifications, and its capacity to structure social exchange. I want to suggest that Wilde is better understood as a self-conscious practitioner of a resuscitated "orality" than as a naive or indolent Irish writer who happened to talk well and commit the odd plagiarism. Thus, his acts and celebrations of literary appropriation occurred across the cultural rift they simultaneously mapped, demonstrating how the normal operations of primary oral transmission become "literary crimes" in a private print culture. Toomey describes the clash between the two:

> [The] cardinal sins of literacy are the cardinal virtues of orality. Originality in an oral culture consists not in inventing an absolutely new story but in stitching together the familiar in a manner suitable to a particular audience, or by introducing new elements into an old story. The persistent charge against Wilde of plagiary would seem oxymoronic in an oral culture. Wilde's tendency to start from the very familiar or traditional in his oral tales—something already given and known, the Bible, Fairy Tales, is again fully characteristic of orality.[19]

For many, "stitching together the familiar in a manner suitable to a particular audience" will never be more than a euphemism for plagiarism. But rather than attempting to whitewash the stigma of Wilde's plagiarism from within the logic of print culture, Toomey demonstrates the contingency of plagiarism's stigma on the finite cultural logic not just of literacy but of private literary property, bestowing a potentially critical function on a practice that is usually deemed criminal. Pursuing the implications of such a critical function, I will argue that by embodying and disseminating the "cardinal virtues of orality" within a culture of literacy, Wilde contributed during his career to a counterdiscourse within private print culture, one that deplored the monopolistic, individualist incentives of copyright and looked to other discursive practices for a more collectivist alternative. We should remember here that plagiarism is an ethical transgression rather than a legal one, and that the plagiarist only infringes copyright when the purloined text is protected by copyright and the plagiarism published. Plagiarists, in other words, are not ipso facto critics of intellectual property law. Wilde's plagiarism, however, was one element in a whole constellation of habits, gestures, attitudes, and proclivities that coherently opposed the privatizing of imaginative expression. Though Wilde may never actually have violated intellectual property law, his life and work were a standing critique of copyright's ethical and philosophical bases—its view of expression as property rather than as social matrix, its narrowly mechanistic understanding of human motivation, its dedication to a possessive individualist model of the self.

Wilde's rehabilitated orality comes into sharpest focus with the reciprocity of his exchanges: though generous in his appropriations of published literary property, Wilde tended to be equally generous (the *Daventry* case is an exception) in allowing others to pilfer and profit by his ideas. Because writing, as he claimed, bored him, his listeners often reaped the profits for tales he never bothered to publish; as Pearson affirms, "countless stories of his invention have been published under other men's names and hundreds of his sayings have brightened other men's books"—not always identified as Wilde's, and seldom to his financial advantage.[20] Some dozen writers are known to have recorded Wilde's unwritten stories, and a handful more—including Frank Harris, George Moore, Arthur Symons, and Evelyn Waugh—published Wilde's oral tales as their own.[21] When one absconder confessed he had published a Wilde tale under his own name, Wilde's response was revealingly mild: "Stealing my story was the act of a gentleman, but not telling me you had stolen it was to ignore the claims of friendship."[22] Since he regarded published material as "public property," unpublished oral tales were the more appropriable for being the stuff of a communal experience—so long as an oral acknowledgment of the appropriation was made. Wilde not only plagiarized, but created a community of plagiarists; by scattering his literary ideas and expressions around him for others to seize freely, he united writers in theft. In doing so, he endowed a private print culture with the dynamics of an idealized oral culture: stories received as gifts were passed on as gifts; narratives branched in abundant retellings, limning a community through circulation rather than reinforcing private ownership through accumulation. In such a community, narrative seldom came to rest in an individual trove; instead, it was passed along from hand to hand in a lively parody of private literary property.

The emphasis here on the dynamics of orality is crucial. Not one to abjure print entirely for bardic recitation, Wilde returned to the voice in his writings by reproducing oral transmission patterns rather than spontaneous vocal cadences, allowing the dynamics of primary orality to occupy and restructure the space of writing. The texts that host this *geste*—I will discuss the Chatterton manuscript and "The Portrait of Mr. W. H." at length, but one might add "The Sphinx without a Secret" (1887) and *The Picture of*

Dorian Gray (1890), among others—set up informational economies that mimic the dynamics of private intellectual property law, extravagantly calcifying ideas, expressions, beliefs, and theories so that they circulate like objects, from one lone possessor to the next.[23] To these satirical models of the literary marketplace under copyright, Wilde's texts supply their phonocentric, collectivist alternatives through negative example, and often through form as well: ambiguous genres disrupt the reading protocols of literary culture, and transgressive compositional methods (e.g., a plagiarism that, if published, would have infringed copyrighted texts) disrupt the ethical and legal codes that protect private literary property. Thus the ghost of orality lodges in the commodified house of literary culture. This Wildean haunting finds its most dramatic expression in his Chatterton lecture notes of 1886, a text whose genre is as ambiguous as its compositional method is transgressive: the notes are a pastiche of clippings and handwriting seemingly intended for both oral delivery and eventual publication, and they plagiarize page upon page from other writers' books. The next section of this chapter reads the Chatterton manuscript not as the product of simple indolence or journeyman's haste, but as a self-conscious and thoroughgoing meditation on the ideologies embedded in dominant concepts of literary crime and literary property—as an intervention whose plagiarized form supplies the punch line to the joke its content tells about forgery.[24] After mapping the interplay between forgery and plagiarism in the Chatterton notes, I turn to a discussion of "The Portrait of Mr. W. H." (1889), reading that story as a literary property parable that revisits the transgressive gestures of the Chatterton manuscript, but with the difference that it more overtly theorizes and licenses the earlier text's appropriations according to a heterodox, fundamentally oral model of circulation and valuation—and for a less occulted audience. Where the Chatterton manuscript conflates the signature traits of literary with oral culture, "Mr. W. H." collapses theory into theater, travestying copyright's power to commodify not just expression but, in extreme circumstances, ideas and belief. Both texts conscripted the figure of Thomas Chatterton to a sustained assault on the indwelling logic and ideology of private intellectual property, just as both were being powerfully—and perhaps irreversibly—consecrated in law and in the marketplace. The chapter concludes with a brief consideration of *De Profundis*, Wilde's long prison letter, whose argument transfigures its author's bankruptcy and imprisonment into the renunciatory grace of a public domain, and whose radical intertextuality models freer circulations of affect and sympathy.

Wildean Stolentelling

By the time Wilde was composing his lecture notes in the mid-1880s, Thomas Chatterton had been the subject of a century's worth of encomia

The Copywrights

and special pleading; to invoke him, then, was to participate in a tradition of reimagining Chatterton according to one's agenda. Coleridge had made him a sort of patron saint of neglected and martyred geniuses in his 1794 "Monody on the Death of Chatterton"; Wordsworth enduringly dubbed him "the marvellous Boy, / The sleepless soul that perished in his pride" in "Resolution and Independence" (1807); and Keats's 1815 "Sonnet to Chatterton" followed suit.[25] In 1856, Henry Wallis exhibited his celebrated painting *The Death of Chatterton,* which sensationally fixed its subject in the Victorian imagination as an eroticized male ephebe, *déshabillé* and exquisite even in death—a figure that resonates in the beautiful, self-slain Cyril Graham of Wilde's "Mr. W. H." By 1880, the Romantic fascination and affiliation with Chatterton had enshrined the poet as Romanticism's key precursor. That year, Dante Gabriel Rossetti wrote to Hall Caine that "Not to know Chatterton is to be ignorant of the *true* day-spring of modern romantic poetry," a view Wilde would ventriloquize in his lecture shortly before concluding it with an untitled (and unattributed) Rossetti sonnet that likened Chatterton to Shakespeare and Milton.[26] Even nearer to Wilde's rhetorical trajectory was an unsigned *Foreign Quarterly Review* essay published in 1842, since attributed to Robert Browning. The essay opened with a cursory review of a book by one Richard Henry Wilde (no relation) on Tasso, but quickly swerved into an extended discussion of Chatterton. Coleridge, Keats, Wordsworth, Shelley, and Rossetti had praised the boy-poet without overt reference to his famous forgeries, seeming rather to insist on his authentication by heaven and on his status as *"true* day-spring." Browning, by contrast, addressed Chatterton's forgery directly, if only to acquit him of lasting blame on the basis of financial necessity: referring to the poet's occasional habit of making centos from appropriated language, he wrote "There is never theft for theft's sake in Chatterton."[27] Wilde would adopt Browning's strategies of distortion and special pleading on behalf of the young forger, but with a further twist: instead of excusing Chatterton's forgeries, he celebrated them as a theft for art's sake.[28] Tellingly, the formulation also applies to Wilde's purloined lecture. Like the Romantic poets, Wilde had appropriated Chatterton as a personal ancestor, as the founder of the artistic kleptocracy to which he imagined himself the heir. Insofar as the forger is always "inventing his own inheritance," as Susan Stewart puts it, Chatterton had originated a kind of genealogy, though one that was only transmissible by a perpetual rewriting of origins.[29] In conscripting Chatterton, his legatees reenacted the fictionality of origins even while embodying a longing for their legitimacy.

Wilde lectured at least once on the "marvellous boy," on November 24, 1886, to an audience of 800 at London's Birkbeck College.[30] The talk was part of a failed campaign by Wilde and Herbert Horne, editor of the *Century Guild Hobby Horse,* to build a Chatterton monument at the poet's school in Bristol. Wilde's lecture was slated for publication in the *Hobby*

Horse, which announced in October 1886 that "Mr. Oscar Wilde's article on Chatterton has been unavoidably postponed until the January number." But the article never appeared. No contemporary reactions to the talk seem to exist, but Wilde's lecture notes have survived in manuscript.[31] As with the later essay "Pen, Pencil, and Poison," the narrative traced by the notes is part biography, part aesthetic theory, part special pleading. They are also a meditation on genius, authenticity, originality, authorial identity, and literary property, revealing as much about Wilde's own self-fashioning as they do about Chatterton. Bafflingly, though, they remain unpublished, even in a scholarly edition. That the notes exist only in manuscript form may result from the fact, embarrassing to many Wildeans, that they are not purely manuscript: outnumbering the pages of Wilde's cursive are dozens of printed pages cut bodily out of two books on Chatterton—Daniel Wilson's *Chatterton: A Biographical Study* (1869) and David Masson's *Chatterton: A Story of the Year 1770* (1874)—and pasted into Wilde's notebook. Such clippings might be pardoned as overzealous scrapbook-keeping, but Wilde has done more than cut and paste: he has struck out irrelevant or awkward passages, added occasional words, and written transitions between Wilson's and Masson's biographical work to build a smooth narrative of purloined texts. These glaring and protracted plagiarisms have elicited several reactions from Wilde scholars. Richard Ellmann is silent on the subject of the cuttings, whereas Rodney Shewan describes Wilde's script as "augmented by clippings from printed biographies," suggesting the notes were "intended to form the basis of the article announced for the October number of the *Hobby Horse.*"[32] But Merlin Holland admits that "whatever the proposed destination for the piece, [Wilde] was clearly going to use several thousand words of someone else's research in his piece," and finds Wilde's methods "profoundly disturbing."[33]

Part of what disturbs about the Chatterton manuscript is that it pleads both innocent and guilty to charges of plagiarism, by turns concealing and confessing its own illicit mode of production. A long opening paragraph tantalizingly names "the contortions that precede artistic production," but forbears to mention Chatterton's forgeries, sliding to a biographical generalism. Typically coy, Wilde beckons his listeners forward by warning them away, admonishing that "it is almost better for us not to search too curiously into the details of the artist's life" even as he prepares to lay Chatterton bare. The warning enticement serves for Wilde as well: to read on is to see Wilde's literary transgressions laid bare, and thereby to confront a central aspect of his work.

> The contortions that precede artistic production are so constantly treated as qualities of work[s] of art that one is sometimes tempted to wish that all art were anonymous. For every true artist, even [t]he portrait painter or dramatist, be his work absolutely objective in presentation, still reveals himself in his

manner. Even abstract forms such as music and colour have much to tell us about the nature of him who fashions them, and take the place of the biographer. Indeed in some cases it is almost better for us not to search too curiously into the details of the artist's life—the *uncompleteness* of Keats' life for instance blinds many of his critics to the *perfection* of his song—and it is well on the whole that we know so little about Shakespeare. [Quotes Matthew Arnold's sonnet to Shakespeare.]

Yet there are cases where the nature of the artist is so bound up with the nature of the man, that art criticism must take account of history and physiology in order to understand the work of art. And this is specially so in the case of Chatterton—without a full comprehension of his life the secret of his literature is not revealed—and so in going over the details of the life of this marvellous boy I do so not to mar the perfect joy and loveliness of his song by any overemphasis of the tragedy of his death, but simply to enable us to understand the curious form he used, and to appreciate an art that to many may seem an anachronism.[34]

The "curious form" Chatterton used was not just antiquarianism, but forgery: during his brief literary career, the boy from Bristol wrote numerous poems, romances, and genealogies, passing them off as the work of a fictional fifteenth-century monk named Thomas Rowley. At the level of self-revelation, Wilde's lecture will also "enable us to understand" its own "curious form"—plagiarism. What forgery and plagiarism share is the crime of misattribution, a manipulation of the tie between authorial identity and property: the forger annexes another's name to his own text, the plagiarist annexes another's text to his own name. In other ways, these twin violations are importantly separate: forgery is a sin against authentic identity, plagiarism a sin against originality. But the forger's mismatch of property and identity clears discursive space for the plagiarist's mirror-image crime. While he addressed the one, Wilde was both committing and theorizing the other.

Western intellectual property law holds that the bond between author and text is natural, essential, and inimitable; by marking a text with a singular stylistic thumbprint, the author earns and asserts ownership of the text. The opening paragraph of Wilde's Chatterton lecture rehearses this argument in order to assail it: "every true artist . . . reveals himself in his manner," while his works "tell us about the nature of him who fashions them, and take the place of the biographer." Because the manner proceeds unmediated from the man, all art is biography. But here Wilde begins to equivocate, one moment denouncing the frequent conflation of art with artist by wishing "that all art were anonymous," the next arguing that Chatterton's art cannot be understood apart from the artist. The equivocations continue throughout the manuscript, with Wilde alternately marveling at Chatterton's ventriloquisms and detecting moments when his true voice can be heard within the forgeries: at one moment, a "sly touch of humour betrays the modern Rowley's hand" [79]. Is style, then, an essential or an accidental property of the individual writer? Wilde's waffling registers a rhetorical rather than an intellectual uncertainty: how best to justify Chatterton's forgeries—by contextualizing them within the poet's life narrative, or by launching a theoretical assault on the iron bond between authorial identity and property?

As usual Wilde does both, grafting Wilson's and Masson's biographical material onto his own more theoretical passages, so that he may both narrate and exonerate Chatterton's forgeries. Environment figures highly in the Wilde-Masson-Wilson account, as it did in Browning's 1842 essay. As the nephew of the local sexton, the future forger was exposed at an early age to a trove of medieval documents—registers, accounts, title deeds to church property—kept in the muniment room of Bristol's Church of the Blessed Mary of Redcliffe. During his life, Thomas Chatterton Sr. had pilfered these parchments to use as binding papers in the school where he was master; after his death, his son made them his playthings, and exposure to the papers awoke in him a kind of de facto neoclassicism. "In all probability," Wilson writes in one of the clippings, "Chatterton's first efforts with the pen and pencil were scrawled in the margins of deeds in imitation of characters engrossed in the time of the Plantagenets" (27–29). Later, money troubles led Chatterton to try profiting by his penchant for mimicry. Wilde and Wilson recount how the boy—always the inventor of inheritances, whether for himself or for others—forged a patent of nobility connecting a local pewterer, Mr. Burgum, to the noble De Bergham family.[35] Wilde decriminalizes the forgery by calling it "a brilliant if somewhat daring act of imagination" (57) even as he links the crime to Chatterton's poverty. He contracts this ambivalence from Wilson, who does not know how to parse Chatterton's mixture of authenticity and fakery, innocence and criminality:

> It was with Chatterton's heraldry as with his antique prose and verse: a vein of earnestness is inextricably blended with what, in other respects, appears as palpable fraud. We are reminded of the boy and the visionary dreamer, in the midst of his most elaborate fictions, till it becomes a puzzle to determine how much of self-deception and of actual belief were blended with the humour of the jest. (61)[36]

The Burgum scam's financial motivations reappear in Chatterton's grandest deception, his attempt to sell several "Thomas Rowley" manuscripts to Horace Walpole. The forgery was nearly bought, in both senses, until a friend of Walpole's cast doubt on the authenticity of a sample, precipitating Chatterton's confession. As a nameless, penniless adolescent from Bristol, the young poet lacked the allure of his fifteenth-century avatar, and Walpole spurned him.[37] Borrowing antique glamour or a noble title had been the only way to overcome the stigmata of youth, poverty, and anonymity; unmasked, Chatterton succumbed first to his debts, and eventually to suicide.

The most extraordinary aspect of Wilde's Chatterton lecture is not the simple fact of its plagiarisms, but the uncanny way it absorbs its interpolations. By excising a few archaisms from Wilson's and Masson's prose ("improved their lear together" becomes "were educated" [65]), much as Chatterton had added them ("forletten," "mitches," "chyrche-glebe") to his own, Wilde produced a prose cento whose style is believably "Wildean" throughout. That none of his listeners seems to have recognized Wilde's plagiarisms further illustrates the lesson of both the lecture notes and Chatterton's life: that the essentialist notion of individual style has more to do with readerly expectations than with authorial self-identity. Uncanny, too, is the way the Wilson and Masson clippings work preposterously as a gloss on the very text they help constitute—as if Wilde chose to clip-and-save only those passages that spoke to his activity of plagiarizing. Thus Wilson's account of the primal scene of Chatterton's literary crimes—his imitating medieval characters in the margins of ancient church parchments—not only exposes the mingled root systems of forgery and plagiarism, but doubles as an account of Wilde's own appropriations, his own transgressive neoclassicism. The Burgum pedigree swindle, the story of a fakery that claims to authenticate, holds the mirror up to Wilde's plagiarisms, a thievery that claims to originate. And Chatterton's libelous will, which Wilde clipped from both Masson's and Wilson's texts, echoes the Burgum forgery by satirizing orthodox transmissions of property. Instead of bequeathing his material property (he had none), Chatterton wills his personal properties—mostly unappreciated virtues—to his heirs, berating them in the process. Thus his modesty is to be divided between Mr. Burgum and "any young lady who can prove, without blushing, that she wants that valuable commodity," while he leaves "to Bristol all my spirit and disinterestedness, parcels of goods unknown on her quays since the days of Canning and Rowley" (109). Chatterton's humility, religion, powers of utterance, free thinking, moderation, abstinence, and generosity are disposed of in like fashion, and the will ends with a satire not only on inheritance but on the very nature of material and literary property:

> I leave Mr. Clayfield the sincerest thanks my gratitude can give; and I will and direct that, whatever any person may think the pleasure of reading my works worth they immediately pay their own valuation to him, since it is then become a lawful debt to me, and to him as my executor in this case.... I leave all my debts, the whole not five pounds, to the payment of the charitable and generous Chamber of Bristol, on penalty, if refused, to hinder every member from a good dinner by appearing in the form of a bailiff. If, in defiance of this terrible spectre, they obstinately persist in refusing to discharge my debts, let my two creditors apply to the supporters of the Bill of Rights. (109–11)

By facetiously investing Mr. Clayfield with the posthumous proceeds from his literary work, Chatterton thumbs his nose at both copyright law and the unwritten laws of authenticity that doomed him to anonymity during his lifetime. Having caricatured the concept of transmissible literary property, he goes on to bequeath his debts—a sort of antiproperty—as if they were properly heritable.

In a sense, Wilde is the heir apparent to Chatterton's negative legacy: the debts bequeathed by the forger are precisely what the plagiarist inherits, since Wilde's lecture is a tissue of ill-gotten and unpaid literary debt. But Wilde is Chatterton's intellectual heir in a more general sense as well. Toward the end of the lecture, he argues (this time apparently in his "own" words, though with Chattertonian echoes) that writers inherit *only* debt from their testators, and that English Romanticism itself is therefore a legacy of debts, even a legacy of theft:

> All great artists have personality as well as perfection in their manner.
> What seems technical is really spiritual—lyrical octosyllabic movement Scott stole [from] Coleridge. Coleridge got [from] Chatterton what Coleridge claimed as a new principle in poetry—the anapestic variations in correspondence with some transition in the nature of the imagery or passion—was in reality Chatterton's—influence of Chatterton seen in Coleridge's Kubla Khan and Christabel[,] and Keats' Eve of St. Agnes— . . . continuity of English poetry—Chaucer—Spenser—Chatterton—Coleridge—Keats—Tennyson—Morris. (155–59)

Wilde had opened the lecture by describing Chatterton in the orthodox terms of literary filiation and originality, as "the father of the Romantic movement in literature, the precursor of Blake, Coleridge and Keats, the greatest poet of his time" (9). But in closing it, he transvalues the English Romantic tradition from a patrilineage into a litany of theft: Scott stole from Coleridge who stole from Chatterton; their thefts, in turn, begot Keats and Tennyson and Morris. No longer a genealogy of original geniuses, Romanticism is what a plagiarist (Coleridge, whose plagiarisms were well known by Wilde's time) filched from a forger—much as the lecture itself is what a plagiarist stole *about* a forger. Moreover, these thefts of seemingly "technical" operations like the "lyrical octosyllabic movement" are transformed into the essence of literary identity. Wilde suggests that "spirit," the writer's inalienable "manner" or "personality" and the basis of private literary property, is a byword for spoils, a hot property. Thus, writers do not so much possess or exude originality as arrogate it to themselves by effacing illicit origins, claiming to own most what they most owe—a paradox borne out by Wilde's own copious plagiarisms in the Chatterton manuscript.

The astonishing conclusion to Wilde's lecture notes begins by trumpeting what the introduction had only murmured in euphemism: Chatterton's forgery. By pardoning the poet's literary crimes on aesthetic grounds, Wilde arrived at his most extreme formulation to date of the vaunted ethical/aesthetic divide. For this reason, the lecture's closing is the hatchery for ideas that would suffuse later works like "Pen, Pencil, and Poison" and "The Portrait of Mr. W. H.":

The Copywrights

> Was he [a] mere forger with literary powers or a great artist? The latter is the right view. Chatterton may not have had the moral conscience which is truth to fact—but he had the artistic conscience which is truth to Beauty. He had the artist's yearning to represent and if perfect representation seemed to him to demand forgery he needs must forge. Still this forgery came from the desire of artistic self-effacement.
>
> He was the pure artist—that is to say his aim was not to reveal himself but to give pleasure—an artist of the type of Shakespeare and Homer—as opposed to Shelley or Petrarch or Wordsworth. (149–51)[38]

Replace "forgery" with "plagiarism" and the star turn of the Chatterton manuscript becomes a self-justification: if perfect representation seems to Wilde to demand plagiarism, he needs must plagiarize, though the forger's "self-effacement" becomes self-aggrandizement in the plagiarist. "Perfect representation," importantly, is anchored not in the artist's accurate self-portraiture but in the necessity of "giving pleasure"—a pleasure that seems to justify even plagiarism. Wilde continues:

> He was essentially a dramatist and claimed for the artist freedom of mood. He saw the realm of the imagination differed from the realm of fact. He loved to let his intellect play—to separate the artist from the man—this explains his extraordinary versatility. He could write polished lines like Pope, satire like Churchill, Philippics like Tu[ll]ius, fiction like Smollet—Gray, Collins, Macpherson's Ossian. Also his statements that "He is a poor author who cannot write on both sides" and this curious note found in his papers—"In a dispute concerning the character of David, it was argued that he must be a holy man from the strain of piety that breathes through his whole works—Being of a contrary opinion and knowing that a great genius can affect anything, endeavoured in the foregoing poems to represent an enthusiastic Methodist." (151–53)

In a gesture later anatomized by "The Portrait of Mr. W. H.," Wilde's Chatterton lecture pursues its thesis—that Chatterton's works are incomprehensible outside his biography—only to dissuade itself in the end. Having set out to assert the identity between the artist and his art, it concludes by sundering the two, insisting that true art conceals, rather than reveals, the artist. "Great genius" is not the self-identity of an original personality but a perfect ventriloquism—an "extraordinary versatility" that "can affect anything," from scathing urban satire to bucolic odes to the famous forgeries of Macpherson.[39] Scorning self-identity, geniuses "write on both sides" by throwing their voices into other personas, endowing David with the voice of an "enthusiastic Methodist." By extension, genius is the ability not only to throw one's own voice but to appropriate others' voices as both Wilde and Coleridge did—a notion that would restore to plagiarism the identity of a cardinal virtue, an identity it could only possess in a culture without the

[104]

revered figure of lone genius, a code of attribution, or copyright's possessive individualism.[40]

In the end, both celebrations and excoriations of the Chatterton manuscript must be mitigated partly by uncertainty: we will probably never know whether Wilde lectured directly from the notes, nor whether he intended to publish the lecture in the outrageous form in which it survives, although it is hard to believe he would have courted extensive plagiarism charges so blatantly in a print medium. For some, Wilde's plagiarisms are less objectionable given that he never claimed credit for them in print, as if the exclusively oral context of the text's transmission lessened the stigma incurred by its mode of composition. And certainly, as I pointed out earlier, the unpublished status of the manuscript means that its commissions of plagiarism never had the chance to become copyright infringements as well. But the hybrid status of the Chatterton manuscript makes it more durably problematic than such simple pardons allow. Stranded in the middle territory between the privacy of the writing desk and the publicity of print, between its oral delivery and its textually complex materiality, the Chatterton manuscript is a conflationary space where the ethics of orality and literacy contaminate one another. Without doubt, the lecture's exclusively oral delivery makes its textual appropriations appear less transgressive.[41] Yet the oral scene of the lecture's transmission seems reciprocally tainted by the appropriative mode of the text's composition. Moreover, although the transcript's appropriations may arise out of an oral practice, they can only be discerned as textual traces: Wilde's plagiarisms are plainly visible on the page but inaudible in talk, reminding us that orality hardly recognizes even verbatim appropriation *as* appropriation. What the manuscript seems to work at illustrating is the affinity—even the identity—between writing and the potential criminalization of discourse. One name for this affinity is copyright, which connects authors to their writings not only to protect those writings against criminal misappropriation, but to hold the author accountable for writings that may themselves be criminal, or at the very least transgressive of supralegal ethical and professional codes. By pardoning Chatterton's ethical transgressions on aesthetic grounds, the manuscript attempts to extend itself the same pardon, yearning through its form—its cardinal oral virtues of unembarrassed appropriation, adaptation, recirculation, and its uncopyrighted status—for a precriminalized state of discourse.

That yearning, though, is ultimately solipsistic: as far as we know, Wilde alone of his contemporaries both heard and read the manuscript, and was alone privy to its agonistic games. The hybrid nature of the Chatterton manuscript makes it a text with an original audience of one, a private joke at which only a future public could laugh, and then only with discomfort. Since even that joke would have vanished with its publication in the *Century Guild Hobbyhorse,* Wilde salvaged what the manuscript achieved in its formal transgressions and made it the theme of his story, "The Portrait of Mr. W.

H.," which appeared in the July 1889 issue of *Blackwood's Magazine*. Despite its much larger audience, however, "Mr. W. H." did not abandon the Chatterton lecture's solipsistic tendencies altogether, but instead demonstrated solipsism to be the residue left by the waning of belief under empiricism, and by the withering of uncommodified circulation under copyright.

A Parable of Intellectual Property

As "The Portrait of Mr. W. H." begins, the narrator and his older friend, Erskine, are discussing literary forgeries in terms that reprise the Chatterton lecture notes: the forger's criminality is muted in the name of "perfect representation" and self-realization, and ethics are insistently winnowed from aesthetics.

> I know we had a long discussion about Macpherson, Ireland, and Chatterton, and that with regard to the last I insisted that his so-called forgeries were merely the result of an artistic desire for perfect representation; that we had no right to quarrel with an artist for the conditions under which he chooses to present his work; and that all Art being to a certain degree a mode of acting, an attempt to realise one's own personality on some imaginative plane out of reach of the trammelling accidents and limitations of real life, to censure an artist for a forgery was to confuse an ethical with an aesthetical problem.[42]

Art being "a mode of acting," "Mr. W. H." sets out not only to rehearse the preoccupations of Wilde's Chatterton lecture but to perform them in the theater of theory. Whereas more traditional criticism soberly analyzes and theorizes, "Mr. W. H." *stages* analysis and theory in the theater of fiction, framing a "scientific" narrative (objective observation that revises a hypothesis to fit evidence) within an "aesthetic" one (subjective creation that disfigures evidence to fit hypothesis). In the process, the truth-claims of science and criticism are shown to be contingent on something at once less empirical and less moral: "the artistic conscience which is truth to Beauty," the aesthetic truth Wilde had used to license Chatterton's literary forgeries. At the same time, Wilde's text coyly avoids identifying which frame—science or art—is finally outermost. By depicting quixotic characters in the act of concocting, transmitting, and dismissing a plausible literary theory, the tale removes generic and discursive markers crucial to interpretation, casting its readers into heuristic quicksand. Contemporary reviews of the piece registered its readers' puzzlement at its ambiguous status. The *Tablet* remarked that "Mr. W. H." had "stopped short . . . of the true criticism," but also wondered tentatively, "is Mr. Wilde joking?" In the *Westminster Review*, Cecil W. Franklyn displayed his immunity to Wilde's humor by chiding the piece for its fancifulness: "And the wide eye of conjecture may roll, in divine frenzy, over the ample Shakespearean fields, without fearing any let or hindrance in the form of the dead wall of certainty."[43] Rather than tolerating Wilde's *mise-en-abîme* concentrisms of art ("the wide eye of conjecture") and science ("the dead wall of certainty"), Franklyn condemned "Mr. W. H." for infecting science with whimsy. In missing the tale's central joke, he also missed its graver insinuation that art and science, like authenticity and falsity, are equally matters of convention and thus the playthings of ideology. Remove the conventional generic signals and they become both indistinguishable and subject to manipulation.

But the point of Wilde's experiment in amphibian genre, ultimately, is not to merge science and art, but to plead their separation: if science traffics in the provable, art should be impervious to proof or rationalization. The seemingly impermeable barrier Wilde erected between ethics and aesthetics serves the similar purpose of protecting art from the normalizing gestures of "good conduct." As he would later write in "A Few Maxims for the Instruction of the Over-Educated," "What is abnormal in life stands in normal relations to Art. It is the only thing in life that stands in normal relations to Art."[44] To escape being the vassal of public opinion, art needed a preserve of its own. Still, the barrier between ethics and aesthetics was itself a canny forgery, for Wilde had insisted in the Chatterton manuscript that the subversive and imaginative power of art forgery lay specifically in its willingness to commit ethical transgressions—especially transgressions of the ethics of private property. Passing a fake off as original relativized the notion of authenticity, the basis of indwelling value in artistic property. By making free with social codes that governed not only ideas of authenticity but the transmission of authority and property (say, in the case of a forged check or will), the forger menaced the basic infrastructures of a property-based society. As a parable about forgery, "The Portrait of Mr. W. H." is necessarily a parable about property as well.

Following their discussion of famous literary forgeries, Erskine asks the narrator, "What would you say about a young man who had a strange theory about a certain work of art, believed in his theory, and committed a forgery in order to prove it?" (1). The young man in Erskine's story is an old school friend, Cyril Graham, an orphan raised by his maternal grandfather, Lord Crediton. In the dawn of their friendship, Cyril is an "effeminate" (3) boy-actor who plays Shakespeare's lead female roles at Eton and Trinity. After leaving school and the stage, Cyril develops a theory about Shakespeare's sonnets: the mysterious "Mr. W. H.," "Onlie Begetter" and sole dedicatee of the poems, was a beautiful boy-actor named Willie Hughes who became "the keystone of [Shakespeare's] dramatic power" (15)—the lover and muse for whom he wrote parts such as Juliet, Rosalind, and Cleopatra. But Erskine is skeptical. As the theory relies heavily on clues within the sonnets—their wordplay on "Will" and "Hews," the poet's references to a fair young man who inspires him—it lacks the "independent evidence" to prove it more than a narcissistic fantasy of Cyril's. Determined to convince Erskine at any cost, Cyril commissions a portrait of Willie Hughes holding a volume of the sonnets, passing it off as an authentic discovery. Erskine is converted, and for a blissful three months the two men "go over each poem line by line, till we had settled every difficulty of text or meaning" (9). But when Erskine accidentally discovers the forgery and denounces the theory, Cyril shoots himself to prove his unswerving fidelity to it, having (perversely) willed Erskine the forged portrait as a plea for credence. A self-slain forger and boy-beauty, Cyril is a latter-day Chatterton.

Erskine remains unconvinced, but his tale converts the narrator, who spends months combing through the sonnets and scouring archives for traces of a historical Willie Hughes. As the evidence mounts, the researcher merges with the research, dissolving the scientific myth of objectivity: "Every day I seemed to be discovering something new, and Willie Hughes became to me a kind of spiritual presence, an ever-dominant personality" (14–15). Yet just after he mails his incontestable findings in a letter to Erskine, the narrator's belief ebbs entirely, and he renounces the theory as an idle fancy. When the two men meet, Erskine announces that he has now been won back over to the theory and departs for Germany to establish that Willie Hughes "had been the first to have brought to Germany the seed of the new culture"— that he was the "Onlie Begetter" of German Romanticism (17). Two years later the narrator receives a letter from Erskine, who announces his plan to repeat Cyril's suicide in the name of Willie Hughes. The narrator rushes to Germany only to discover Erskine's suicide, too, was a forgery: his friend has died of consumption—and bequeathed him the forged portrait. His friends are convinced the portrait is authentic; "I have never cared to tell them its true history," he concludes, "but sometimes, when I look at it, I think there is really a great deal to be said for the Willie Hughes theory of Shakespeare's Sonnets" (21).

If "Mr. W. H." is indeed a parable about property, then the portrait of Willie Hughes would seem to emblematize material property in general— that which is tangible, ownable, and transferable. In a sense, Wilde's tale does nothing more than trace the portrait's production and circulation, calling special attention to the moments when it changes hands through inheritance. Commissioned by Cyril, it passes from him to Erskine, who describes it as "the only legacy I ever received in my life" (2). After Erskine's death, his mother gives it to the narrator, saying, "When George was dying he begged me to give you this" (21). Like most alienable material property, the portrait is owned by one party at a time, bequeathed by one to the next, and fully surrendered by the person whose hands it leaves. Its materiality is foregrounded, too: the only physical object described at length by the narrator, it is also the sole piece of material evidence—albeit forged—for Cyril's theory.[45]

But the capacity to be owned and exchanged is not exclusive to material property in "Mr. W. H." As pivotal as the portrait-inheritance scenes are, the true medium of accumulation and transmission in the tale is a nonmaterial one: *belief.* Like the Willie Hughes portrait, belief in Cyril's theory of the sonnets can only be held serially, never simultaneously; it is transferred from Cyril to Erskine to the narrator to Erskine and finally—if tentatively—back to the narrator.[46] That the narrator loses his faith just after mailing his evidence to Erskine confirms the tie between credence and material property. "I put into the letter all my enthusiasm," he writes, with unwitting literalism; "I put into the letter all my faith" (18). Faith and enthusiasm, it turns out, behave exactly like alienable material property: once put into the post, they pass like belongings from one owner to the next.[47] The scene of the narrator's apostasy is central to the tale's meditation on property, since it characterizes belief as a limited quantity that exhausts itself through expenditure:

> It seemed to me that I had given away my capacity for belief in the Willie Hughes theory of the Sonnets, that something had gone out of me, as it were, and that I was perfectly indifferent to the whole subject. . . . Perhaps, by finding perfect expression for a passion, I had exhausted the passion itself. Emotional forces, like the forces of physical life, have their positive limitations. Perhaps the mere effort to convert any one to a theory involves some form of renunciation of the power of credence. (18–19)

Most striking here is the narrator's sense that belief is "some*thing*" that can be accumulated, given away, transferred, "exhausted." Circulating like an object or finite substance, belief belongs to a closed economy where "emotional forces, like the forces of physical life, have their positive limitations," and where poor husbandry can lead to depletion. According to such a dogma of parsimony, belief is the scarce money of the mind.

As a parable about ideal property that behaves like material property, "Mr. W. H." is also a parable about intellectual property. In the age of patents and copyrights, expression and ideas (like belief in Wilde's tale) can circulate like physical property: they are transferable, salable, inheritable, legislated, privately owned. The Frenchman Charles Coquelin had condemned patent law's reification of ideas along just these lines in his 1873 *Dictionnaire de l'économie politique,* impugning

> that strange confusion of thought which puts on the same level an invention . . . the peculiar characteristic of which is that it can be disseminated through many minds and can be exploited in a hundred different places at the same time—with a material object, necessarily circumscribed, which, because it cannot be divided, can only be possessed by one man and which cannot be usefully exploited except where it is.[48]

Intellectual property law stipulates that a person may copyright another person's work so long as she does something of her "own" to it. Thus, translators, abridgers, annotators, and anthologists may copyright their work. In Wilde's tale, each theorist "owns" (both possesses and professes) the Willie Hughes hypothesis only while he is adding to the work of a forerunner: Cyril revises Tyrwhitt (the eighteenth-century scholar who first proposed a boy-actor as addressee of the Sonnets), the narrator revises Cyril, and Erskine presumably revises the narrator. Tellingly, each man *professes* his belief in the theory only as long as he *possesses* it; the moment he transfers the theory to another person, he can no longer own it in either sense. Such a reading points out the human costs of subjecting beliefs, expression, and ideas to the paradigms of private property. At no point in the tale does a community of the faithful—or even a confraternity of the faithless—clearly exist; even the blissful three months shared by Erskine and Cyril are blighted, in retrospect, by Cyril's knowledge that his co-religionist's belief rests on a forged piece of evidence. Instead, the conversion of one person is always the result of another's apostasy, possession the result of surrender. The lesson is that ideas and expressions that are privately held cannot be held in common.

If "Mr. W. H." warns against the commodification of art and belief, what does it hold out as an alternative? When Wilde referred to the tale, he played up its focus on belief. "You must believe in Willy Hughes," he told Helena Sickert, "I almost do myself."[49] Though belief is in peril of being commodified into fact, it is also the only tonic to that process of commodification—hence Wilde's injunction, "You must believe." The tale's embrace of credence and credulity is embedded not only in its thematics, but in a name. Cyril's grandfather and guardian, Lord Crediton, may be the sole character in the story who remains credulous: "To the present day Lord Crediton is under the impression that [Cyril's suicide] was accidental" (10). The tie here between *credit* and *credence,* though, goes beyond a shared root in the Latin *credere,* "to believe": in Wilde's view, both belief and borrowing are forms of protest against private property. In the 1891 version of *The Picture of Dorian Gray,* when Lord Henry Wotton is offered money by his rich Uncle George (a kind of Lord Creditor), he declines, saying "But I don't want money. It is only people who pay their bills who want that, Uncle George, and I never pay mine. Credit is the capital of the younger son, and one lives charmingly upon it."[50] Credit, for Wilde, stands in opposition to both thrift and inheritance, the cornerstones of individual property that embody its scarcity and its transferability; credit is a sort of fissure in individual property that leads back to communal property. So long as ideas, expressions, or beliefs can be owned as private property, they will circulate like private property; thus, "A truth ceases to be true when more than one person believes in it."[51] By contrast, ideas and beliefs untrammeled by intellectual property forms might be the matrix of community—as in the oral traditions of the nonliterate rural Irish, where narratives were neither privatized nor slain in the name of absolute verity.

That credulity might outlast the assault of empiricism and commodification is the message of the tale's ending. Looking at the forged portrait that was the evidential lynchpin in Cyril's "romantic theory" (19), the narrator nonetheless thinks "there is really a great deal to be said for the Willie Hughes theory of Shakespeare's Sonnets" (21). If the portrait disproves the theory on the level of fact, it authenticates it on the level of art and belief; having been ejected from the realm of empiricism, the "romantic theory" has taken root in its proper soil, that of fable and founding myth. Like the Willie Hughes theory it seems to advance, "The Portrait of Mr. W. H." had an afterlife beyond its initial publication, though an ironic one: instead of adopting its antiempiricist stance, the tale's disciples sought more "independent evidence" for the historical Willie Hughes. In dissuading itself of its own "real" viability, "Mr. W. H." had converted several of its readers, chief among them Lord Alfred Douglas, who called the theory "so good and so ingenious that it is a thousand pities [Wilde] did not write it and put it forth as a theory and nothing else."[52] Douglas fervently pursued the theory and in 1933 published his *True History of Shakespeare's Sonnets*. Samuel Butler was also enough persuaded by "Mr. W. H." to devote years to the theory, although he never acknowledged Wilde's influence. A more ambivalent convert was James Joyce, whose "Scylla and Charybdis" chapter in *Ulysses* both mentions Wilde's tale and reprises it more cynically: Stephen Dedalus, young littérateur, spins an elaborate psychobiographic theory of Shakespeare that unconverts the theorist without converting any of his listeners. And in 1942, as William Cohen reports, reference to a William Hewes, a shoemaker's apprentice connected to Marlowe's company, was discovered in the Canterbury archives; life, it seemed, had obligingly imitated Wilde's art.[53]

Insolvent Creditor

Eight years after the first publication of "The Portrait of Mr. W. H.," Wilde wrote what may be the most extraordinary of all his works from solitary confinement in Reading Prison. Painstakingly drafted, emended, and recopied during the early months of 1897, Wilde's long letter to his lover, Lord Alfred Douglas, did not appear in print until February 1905, over four years after Wilde's death. When he was released from prison, Wilde had given it to Robert Ross for copying, and in another letter named the piece *Epistola: In Carcere et Vinculis;* but the posthumous Methuen & Co. imprint bore the title *De Profundis*, one suggested to Ross by E. V. Lucas, a director at Methuen. Ross altered Wilde's text in more substantive ways as well: the 1905 *De Profundis* was a heavily expurgated version of the letter that omitted a number of long and potentially libelous passages castigating Douglas and his father, the Marquess of Queensberry, as well as any clear indications as to the letter's addressee. The day after publication, Lucas reviewed the posthumous volume for the *Times Literary Supplement*. While conceding that Wilde's letter realized "the terrible conditions under which it was written," Lucas questioned Wilde's sincerity in terms that recall the fakeries of Chatterton and Cyril Graham: "This is not sorrow, but its dextrously constructed counterfeit.... Oscar Wilde, however he may have begun life, grew to be incapable of deliberately telling the truth about himself or anything else." Lucas went on to belittle the author of *De Profundis* according to the popular image of Wilde as a wasteful and criminal genius—a "witty and irresponsible Irishman" whose "genius lay in lawlessness," a "hand-to-mouth intellect" who aspired to laurels beyond the reach of his gift for light foolery. Oddly, having given *De Profundis* its solemn title, Lucas implied Wilde was unworthy of it: if the letter was a cry from the depths, it was the disingenuous cry of a poseur whom even prison could not reform. Lucas's stance was echoed in later notices, which tended either to laud or to excoriate Wilde for remaining quintessentially Wildean despite his incarceration. Max Beerbohm was among the celebrants: "Oscar Wilde was immutable. The fineness of the book as a personal document is in the revelation of a character so strong that no force of circumstance could change it, or even modify it. In prison Oscar Wilde was still himself." George Bernard Shaw proclaimed in the *Neue Freie Presse* that "no other Irishman has yet produced as masterful a comedy as *De Profundis*," and wrote to Ross that "the unquenchable spirit of the man is magnificent: he maintains his position and puts society squalidly in the wrong—rubs into them every insult and humiliation he endured—comes out the same man he went in—with stupendous success."[54]

But despite its reviewers' claims that Wilde had remained immutable and unreformed even in prison, *De Profundis* did contain signs of a change in Wilde's ethics and aesthetics, a change that seemed to register Wilde's solitary imprisonment and hard labor. In "The Soul of Man under Socialism," Wilde had rejected a Christian Individualism that "could be realised only through pain or in solitude," on the basis that "All sympathy is fine, but sympathy with suffering is the least fine mode.... Pain is not the ultimate mode of perfection. It is merely provisional and a protest."[55] *De Profundis* reversed that verdict: "I now see that sorrow, being the supreme emotion of which man is capable, is at once the type and test of all great Art.... behind Sorrow there is always Sorrow. Pain, unlike Pleasure, wears no mask." Having preached the truth of masks in *Intentions* and elsewhere, he now seemed to abjure them, announcing that "Truth in Art is the unity of a thing with itself." Where he had mounted a career-long attack on utilitarianism and Philistinism by celebrating the uselessness and unnaturalness of art, he appeared now to embrace the uses of nature: "It seems to me that we all look at Nature too much and live with her too little.... We call ourselves a utilitarian age, and we do not know the uses of a single thing." The letter also seemed to renounce the less abstract transgressions Wilde had glamorized in his pre-prison days, such as defaulted debtorship and plagiarism. In its uncut version, Wilde's former toasts to credit as "the capital of the younger son" gave way to a soberer proposition: "For every single thing that is done someone has to pay." It is the refrain whose repetition was meant to chasten Bosie:

> Your one idea of life, your one philosophy, if you are to be credited with a philosophy, was that whatever you did was to be paid for by someone else: I don't mean merely in the financial sense—that was simply the practical application of your philosophy of everyday life—but in the broadest, fullest sense of transferred responsibility.... The fact is that you were, and are I suppose still, a typical sentimentalist. For a sentimentalist is simply one who desires to have the luxury of an emotion without paying for it.... You think that one can have one's emotions for nothing. One cannot. Even the finest and the most self-sacrificing emotions have to be paid for. Strangely enough, that is what makes them fine. The intellectual and emotional life of ordinary people is a very contemptible affair. Just as they borrow their ideas from a sort of circulating library of thought—the *Zeitgeist* of an age that has no soul—and send them back soiled at the end of the week, so they always try to get their emotions on credit, and refuse to pay the bill when it comes in.

For Wilde, this new emphasis on the repayment of financial and experiential debts, with its stark denunciation of credit, was a radical swerve. Its corollary—that "in the strangely simple economy of the world people only get what they give"—would have been unrecognizable to the Wilde of "Phrases and Philosophies for the Use of the Young," who remarked that "It is only by not paying one's bills that one can hope to live in the memory of the commercial classes."[56] His condemnation of those who "borrow their ideas from a sort of circulating library of thought" seemed similarly to depart from the youthful Wilde's boast that plagiarism was "the privilege of the appreciative man." By repudiating debtorship and intellectual appropriation, Wilde seemed to forsake his profligate and purloining selves, and with them his critique of thrift and private property.

Still, the gravity and lyrical outrage of the letter, along with its focus on "Christ as precursor of the Romantic movement in life," can exaggerate its discontinuities with Wilde's earlier writing. In many ways *De Profundis* deepens, extends, and completes gestures in its author's pre-prison work rather than abandoning them. Although the letter excoriates the defaulting debtor, it goes on to transvalue bankruptcy into an enviable and generalized state of grace, a state in which the bankrupt can apprehend connections to other people in ways impossible for the propertied subject. In effect, *De Profundis* alchemizes bankruptcy into a spiritual precondition for humility and sympathetic identification with others' sorrow. Moreover, the letter's apparent devaluation of intellectual debtorship and intertextual passion belies its massive accrual of intellectual debt, its own considerable intertextuality. Having reimagined bankruptcy as a renunciatory condition that fosters intersubjectivity, Wilde's letter invites the intellectual debtor into that state of receivership, making intertextuality and intersubjectivity the axes of a communal, unpropertied matrix—a public domain.

In Reading Prison, Wilde had good reasons for appearing, at least, to denounce debtorship. Regenia Gagnier has argued that writing *De Profundis* enabled Wilde to combat the squalor, solitude, and unproductive labor of prison.[57] But prison was not the only disaster to befall Wilde between his literary triumphs of the early nineties and his reproachful letter to Bosie; there was also his bankruptcy. Having lost his libel action against Queensberry, Wilde was liable for his opponent's court costs. Douglas had initially promised to pay these costs if Wilde lost, but his family had recanted. Other creditors appeared with bills, and eventually an execution was put on Wilde's house and his possessions sold at auction; as he wrote to Bosie, "it was to pay for some gifts of mine to you that the bailiffs had entered the home where you had so often dined." In one of the letter's painful enumerations, Wilde lists the most cherished belongings he lost in the bankruptcy auction:

> My Burne-Jones drawings: my Whistler drawings: my Monticelli: my Simeon Solomons: my china: my Library with its collection of presentation volumes from almost every poet of my time, from Hugo to Whitman, from Swinburne to Mallarmé, from Morris to Verlaine; with its beautifully bound editions of my father's and mother's works; its wonderful array of college and school prizes, its *éditions de luxe*.

Several months into his sentence, Wilde had to appear twice in public Bankruptcy Court hearings, where he was declared officially bankrupt and his estate put into receivership. He writes, "Step by step with the Bankruptcy Receiver I had to go over every item of my life. It was horrible." Judging by *De Profundis*'s obsessive treatment of the bankruptcy, the event figured as prominently in Wilde's thoughts as his imprisonment did, underwriting the letter's fixation with detailed retrospection and inventory: "each detail that accompanied each dreadful moment I am forced to recall: there is nothing that happened in those ill-starred years that I cannot recreate in that chamber of the brain which is set apart for grief or for despair." Echoing its primal scene—Wilde's "horrible" session with the bankruptcy receiver—the text teems with lists of lost things: money misspent on lavish meals and hotels and gambling, literary projects hijacked by Bosie's demands and interruptions, weeks wasted in violent scenes, genius squandered in overindulgence and folly:

> The Law has taken from me not merely all that I have, my books, furniture, pictures, my copyright in my published works, my copyright in my plays, everything in fact from *The Happy Prince* and *Lady Windermere's Fan* down to the staircarpets and door-scraper of my house, but also all that I am ever going to have. My interest in my marriage-settlement, for instance, was sold. . . . My interest in our Irish estate, entailed on me by my own father, will I suppose have to go next.[58]

No longer an occasion for antinomian bons mots, bankruptcy was the curtain that crashed down on the Wildean comedy of inexhaustible credit. Wilde might have been lecturing an earlier, more careless incarnation of himself when he chided Bosie, "You seem to be under the impression that Bankruptcy is a convenient means by which a man can avoid paying his debts, a 'score off his creditors' in fact. It is quite the other way. It is the method ... by which the Law by the confiscation of all his property forces him to pay every one of his debts."[59]

But Wilde does more here than lecture Bosie and himself on "the virtues of thrift and economy"; despite his claim that "Love does not traffic in a marketplace, nor use a huckster's scales," *De Profundis* is in effect a long IOU from Wilde to the man on whom he had spent no less than everything—"my life, my genius, my position, my name in history." In this sense, debtorship is not just a topic in *De Profundis* but its governing metaphor: for the benefit of his defaulted lover, Wilde enumerated the "thousand unpaid debts of gratitude you owed me." In the process, he converted himself from an insolvent debtor into an insistent creditor, chastising Bosie for not "making some slight return to me for all the love and affection and kindness and generosity and care I had shown you," and more materially for refusing to save Wilde from bankruptcy by paying Queensberry's court costs. Bosie had tapped him out like a line of credit; by tallying the champagnes and pâtés and jeweled sleeve-links he had bought for Bosie, Wilde played bankruptcy receiver this time to his emotionally insolvent lover, repeating his own grim proceedings with a difference. He also reversed his position as a criminal with a debt to society, saying that society "shuns those whom it has punished, just as people shun a creditor whose debt they cannot pay."[60] But Wilde was not seeking anything as pedestrian as repayment. Instead, he imaginatively reshaped himself as a creditor in order to claim the creditor's Christ-like prerogative: to forgive his debtors.

Not surprisingly, *De Profundis* is Wilde's most ambivalent text, oscillating between vituperation and forgiveness, self-abnegation and self-glorification, rebuke and manifesto, romance and finance, Bosie and Christ. But the letter is also transformative, and it numbers Wilde's losses in order to fashion a new ethics and aesthetics of loss—hence its emphasis on pain, sorrow, and self-surrender as the new "Truth in Art." Wilde's losses included his freedom, his reputation, even his right to see his children; but the letter returns most frequently to his lost property, finally turning propertylessness into a condition of grace. In the noon of his acclaim, Wilde had used his financial and literary debts to critique the "demoralising" "nuisance" of private property, but those debts had always kept the taint of misappropriation about them. Now that the law had taken away "not merely all that I have ... but all I am ever going to have," he set forth a new renunciatory ideal, an ethos of self-purgation. He had adumbrated it in "The Soul of Man under Socialism," which represented Christ as needing "neither property nor health; he is a God realising his perfection through pain."[61] The Christ of *De Profundis* taught, similarly, that "one only realises one's soul by getting rid of all alien passions, all acquired culture, and all external possessions be they good or evil." In such an ascetic state, only one property remained to *be* realized: humility, which Wilde found "hidden away in my nature, like a treasure in a field." He deemed it his "ultimate discovery.... Of all things it is the strangest. One cannot give it away, and another may not give it to one. One cannot acquire it, except by surrendering everything that one has. It is only when one has lost all things, that one knows that one possesses it."[62] Unlike alienable property as "The Portrait of Mr. W. H." had satirized it, humility was not susceptible to exchange, transmission, inheritance, or accumulation; it was, to the contrary, inseparable from disinheritance and bankruptcy. It was the sole inalienable property of the insolvent debtor.

Notwithstanding the letter's newfound interest in exceptions over type, Wilde generalized his insolvency into a universal condition: "And what is true of the bankrupt is true of everyone else in life. For every single thing that is done someone has to pay." In reflecting on his own life after property, he imagined a human community of the bankrupt and dispossessed, one where "there was no difference at all between the lives of others and one's own life." Part of recognizing this contiguity of all lives lay in cherishing one's obligations to others—one's debts of gratitude. Wilde recounted how, as he passed in handcuffs from prison to bankruptcy court, Robert Ross had been there to raise his hat; the gesture reminded him of a saint's kneeling to wash the feet of the poor. "I store it in the treasury-house of my heart. I keep it there as a secret debt that I am glad to think I can never possibly repay."[63] In a community of the bankrupt, debts of gratitude—here a byword for "humility"—were all that one could own, all that was worth owning. To be a miser of those debts was to treasure human interdependence above an independence rooted in private possession.

The Wilde of *De Profundis* carried his renunciatory ethos into the aesthetic, and specifically textual, realm as well. In a rare (and strange) comment on his own literary style, he claimed to abjure all exaggeration, rhetoric, and "surplusage" in the letter's stylistic economy, once again implying that "Truth in Art is the unity of a thing with itself"—in this case, the unity of an intention with its expression:

> As for the corrections and *errata*, I have made them in order that my words should be an absolute expression of my thoughts, and err neither through surplusage nor through being inadequate. Language requires to be tuned like a violin; and just as too many or too few vibrations in the voice of the singer or the trembling of the string will make the note false, so too much or too little in words will spoil the message. As it stands, at any rate, my letter has its definite meaning behind every phrase. There is in it nothing of rhetoric.

It was not for nothing, Wilde added, that he had made himself "Miser of sound and syllable, no less / Than Midas of his coinage" (the verse quotation is from Keats's "Sonnet on the Sonnet"). This vaunted exactitude in literary bookkeeping explains why Wilde's letter is so hard on literary and intellectual debtorship, proclaiming that ordinary people "borrow their ideas from a sort of circulating library of thought," and that "Most people are other people. Their thoughts are some-one else's opinions, their life a mimicry, their passions a quotation."[64] But Wilde's new renunciatory ethos also rejected the conditions of private ownership that made for miserliness. Thus, despite its quarrel with quotation, *De Profundis* makes free with literary property. Wilde's claim to a new economy of language, with its rejection of "surplusage," is itself an unattributed paraphrase from a book Wilde had reviewed in 1890, Pater's essay on "Style" in *Appreciations*:

> Self-restraint, a skillful economy of means, *ascêsis*, that too has a beauty of its own; and for the reader supposed there will be an aesthetic satisfaction in that frugal closeness of style which makes the most of a word, in the exaction from every sentence of a precise relief, in the just spacing out of word to thought, in the logically filled space connected always with the delightful sense of difficulty overcome. . . . Say what you have to say, what you have a will to say, in the simplest, the most direct and exact manner possible, with no surplusage.[65]

So many of the passions annunciated by *De Profundis* are themselves quotations and allusions and paraphrases—not just from Pater but from the Bible, Euripides, Dante, Shakespeare, Goethe, Wordsworth, Arnold, Renan, and others—that its invectives against quotation seem disingenuous. Even the central aphorism, "a sentimentalist is simply one who desires to have the luxury of an emotion without paying for it," which the *Dictionary of Cynical Quotations* still attributes to Wilde, is a reworded epigram from another of Wilde's favorite texts, Meredith's *The Ordeal of Richard Feverel* (1859): "Sentimentalists are they who seek to enjoy Reality, without incurring the Immense Debtorship for a thing done."[66] If the letter's deep intertextuality reveals anything, it is that all passion may indeed be a quotation, and furthermore that the citationality of passion may be the main source of its power.

Having imagined a life after property, the ascetic Wilde went on to imagine a life after intellectual property; he had, after all, forfeited not only his physical belongings in bankruptcy, but his copyrights as well. In such an afterlife, implying that all passion is quotation was simply nodding to the innate intertextuality of a community of the dispossessed, one where "there was no difference at all between the lives of others and one's own life." Strangely, because of the conditions of material, social, intellectual, and archival deprivation in which it was written, *De Profundis* escapes the taint of plagiarism or misappropriation despite its extensive and generally unacknowledged borrowings. Penned by an incarcerated bankrupt, it raises the question of how any system of attribution or copyright could signify for such a subject, one who lived in the aftermath of property's vanishing. By imagining a discourse that outlasts its property form and passes on to a collective space, the letter strangely borrows the procedural narrative of copyright and elevates it to a spiritual level. At the same time, it remakes bankruptcy in the image of an Elysianized public domain, a space in which ideas and expressions are stripped of their temporary incarnations as property to circulate freely, in the same uncommodified condition literacy attributes, at least, to oral discourse. That condition of orality, which Wilde's memorialists would describe as the irrecuperable origin of Wilde's genius, is constructed here as its longed-for terminus. Conceived in such a terminal space, Wilde's *Epistola: In Carcere et Vinculis* is a postscript to his literary life: a writing after writing, a discourse that is post-property, post-copyright, post-genius.

As soon as he had finished his long letter to Bosie, Wilde named Robert Ross as his literary executor in the event of his death, putting him in "complete control over my plays, books and papers," adding that "the deficit that their sale will produce may be lodged to the credit of Cyril and Vyvyan," Wilde's sons.[67] For "deficit," Wilde had probably intended "profit," though the slip is suggestive of the letter's transformative operations, its reimagining of receivership as a new order of human receptivity. In the end, however, Wilde's deficits were literally to his credit. In an irony Wilde might have winced at or winked at, the posthumous sales of the 1905 *De Profundis* were what finally delivered the Wilde Estate from bankruptcy.[68]

Having died in 1900, Wilde remained in his grave in only the most literal sense; over the course of the twentieth century, he would return again and again—as text and testimony from beyond the grave, as renovated reputation, as spin-off, as ghost, as harbinger, and finally as icon. Wilde's early status as cultural revenant owed partly to the posthumous publication of *De Profundis:* shorn of its more personal passages, it seemed less a letter than a testament, one dispatched not from prison but from the sepulcher. Through much of the century, the manuscript of Wilde's letter to Bosie would exist in a strange relation of displacement with both Wilde's body and his post-mortem copyrights. In 1909, Robert Ross deposited the manuscript of the letter in the British Museum on the condition that it be kept from the public for a term of 50 years—that is, until January 1, 1960. Thus the manuscript was installed in a narrative seemingly borrowed from copyright: an exclusive right would protect the work for a set term whose lapse, long after the death of its author, would release the text to public access. Locked away in the vaults of the British Museum, the unique document invited association with Wilde's buried physical remains, and the promise of the letter's eventual release from secrecy and return to the public sphere seemed to promise a similar resurrection of its author's body. On one occasion, the contractual mausoleum that contained *De Profundis* was even unsealed prematurely, and the manuscript brought forth as evidence in a way that seemed to perform such a resurrection. In 1912, Alfred Douglas brought a libel suit against Arthur Ransome's *Oscar Wilde: A Critical Study*, which Douglas felt had actionably misrepresented the nature of his relationship with Wilde. But thanks to Ross, who had helped Ransome in writing the book and was still the executor of Wilde's literary remains, the manuscript of *De Profundis* was exhumed from the British Museum, and its unpublished sections were read aloud in court both to demonstrate the erotic nature of the Douglas-Wilde attachment and to acquit Ransome of the libel charge. Through the surrogate body of the manuscript, Wilde seemed to have returned to the juridical scene of his own downfall, bearing posthumous witness to his transgressive and enduring love for Bosie and chiding his lover anew for renouncing that love.

Wilde was again resurrected in the courtroom during the 1918 libel trial against Noel Pemberton Billing, the publisher of the right-wing journal the *Imperialist*. Under the heading "The Cult of the Clitoris," Billing had insinuated that dancer Maud Allan, then appearing as the lead in a dance version of Wilde's *Salomé*, was compromising the British Imperial war effort by encouraging the spread of lasciviousness and homosexuality, vices that made British government and military officials vulnerable to blackmail by German agents. The ensuing trial, which ended by acquitting Billing of libel, sat in judgment of Wilde's life and legacy as much as of Allan's dancing, leading Robert Ross to describe it as "kicking the corpse of Wilde."[69] But there were other forms of return as well, in the publication of Wilde biographies and memoirs, in collected and complete editions of his writings, and in adaptive works such as Richard Strauss's opera *Salome*, which debuted in Dresden in 1905, the same year *De Profundis* was published. There were revivals of Wilde's plays and, later, film versions of the tales and plays, of *Dorian Gray*, and of Wilde's life. During the last quarter of the twentieth century, Wilde returned in new political incarnations as well: he was conscripted as an icon, variously, for Utopian socialism and gay liberation movements and rehabilitated as a homosexual martyr to straight hegemony and as a contrary angel of incipient gay culture and identity. Perhaps most recently, he has been reclaimed as an Irish writer, talker, and intellectual by members of the Irish Studies community and stands risen from the grave of adoptive Englishness. Even the Wilde-as-revenant trope had itself entered the mass-media discourse about Wilde. In 1998, two years before the centenary of Wilde's death, Walter Kirn of *Time* magazine heralded the writer's "multimedia postmortem comeback" in a slew of new plays, films, publications, websites, and exhibitions, adding that Wilde seemed likely to become "the aesthete's Elvis" on the grounds that "both the King of Rock and the King of Epigram have been resurrected as secular saints."[70]

The Copywrights

In 1905, the German American writer G. S. Viereck reported a rumor that Wilde was not dead but in hiding, waiting to make a spectacular return when public opinion became more hospitable, and it was not until months after causing an international stir with these reports that Viereck owned up to having concocted the rumors himself. His 1907 thriller, *The House of the Vampire,* figures prominently in the next chapter of this book.[71] Like Viereck's Wilde hoax, the novel indulges in the fantasy of Wilde's return, in this case through its undead aesthete-protagonist, a vampire who sucks unrealized ideas for artistic creations, rather than blood, from his victims. I argue that Viereck's novel and the 1909 play based on it, in their central conceit of thought-vampirism, constitute Wildean meditations on intellectual property regimes that cause expression and ideas to circulate like objects. But if both the figure of Wilde and certain Wildean literary gestures have been conjured in Viereck's work, it is toward the explicitly non-Wildean end of legitimating the violent appropriation of ideas by Great Men, an appropriation which the Great reciprocate by hewing a path to the future, even if they must cut through lesser humans in order to do so. And yet despite its extreme individualist orientation, Viereck's *Vampire* story engages the fundamental dichotomies of copyright closely enough to set in motion a critique both of those dichotomies and of its own proto-fascist vitalism. Before turning to Viereck's vampire texts, however, the chapter develops a more recent context—the emotionally charged discussions surrounding the 1998 Sonny Bono Copyright Term Extension Act—in which to think about the extralegal functions of copyright law. Postmortem copyright, I suggest there, is not only a legal regime that balances private economic incentives and public discourse, but a space in the cultural imaginary that is haunted by the authors whose literary remains and legacies it enables to persist after death in a reverent stasis. Copyright is now, and was partly engineered to be, a province of ghosts—a space where the absent enjoy an amplified presence through the capacity of the law to memorialize them, and where the return of revenants like Wilde is incarnated in the surrogate body of a property form that endures after death. It is, moreover, a spectral domain whose fundamental oppositions—idea versus expression, genius versus plagiarist, appropriation versus creation—are haunted by their own terrible contingency.

[4]

The Reign of the Dead:
Hauntologies of Postmortem Copyright

> SON of my buried Son, while thus thy hand
> Is clasping mine, it saddens me to think
> How Want may press thee down, and with thee sink
> Thy children left unfit, through vain demand
> Of culture, even to feel or understand
> My simplest Lay that to their memory
> May cling;—hard fate! which haply need not be
> Did Justice mould the statutes of the Land.
> A Book time-cherished and an honoured name
> Are high rewards; but bound they Nature's claim
> Or Reason's? No—hopes spun in timid line
> From out the bosom of a modest home
> Extend through unambitious years to come,
> My careless Little-one, for thee and thine!
> —WILLIAM WORDSWORTH, "A Poet to His Grandchild" (1838)

One of the most influential pieces of U.S. copyright legislation in recent years has been the Sonny Bono Copyright Term Extension Act (CTEA), which became law on October 27, 1998. Under the Bono Act, the already substantial copyright terms established by the 1976 Copyright Act were extended by an additional 20 years. Works created on or after January 1, 1978, are now protected for the duration of the author's life plus 70 years, while anonymous works, pseudonymous works, and "works for hire" created by or for corporations are shielded for 95 years from publication or 120 years from their date of creation, whichever is shorter. And all works published and copyrighted between 1923 and 1978 are protected for 95 years regardless of their mode of authorship. The public domain has been nearly frozen: almost nothing will enter it until 2019, when the copyright protection in works published in 1923 will finally lapse, 95 years after it began.

Proponents of the Bono Act made several sorts of arguments. The term extensions, they said, would harmonize U.S. law with European Union copyright terms, which had been set in 1993 at author's life plus 70 years.[1] They would help stimulate investment by rightsholders in the preservation, restoration, and dissemination of more durably lucrative intellectual properties. They would improve copyright's incentive for creative people by allowing at least two generations of an author's heirs to defend and benefit from that person's intellectual property. And the longer postmortem term would adjust for the longer life expectancy of those heirs as a result of improvements in medical knowledge and technology, ensuring they would be able to fully enjoy the fruits of the creative estates their forebears had labored to win for them. Opponents of the Bono Act warned that the rhetoric of individual incentives and inheritable intellectual property estates, however tempting, masked the more relevant function of the act: to prolong the life of valuable corporate-held copyrights. They pointed out that intellectual property giants such as Time-Warner and Disney had made major campaign contributions to the act's sponsors in the House and Senate as well as soft money contributions to the National Republican Senatorial Committee.[2] And they warned that repeated extensions to copyright terms could eventually result in the extinction of the public domain altogether. But critics of the extension were hampered not only by corporate lobbying power and public apathy but by unlucky timing: the final version of the unobtrusively packaged bill reached the Senate floor shortly after the delivery of the Starr Report and was passed by voice vote in the House, while the nation's attention was occupied with the Lewinsky scandal. The day before his impeachment hearings began in the Senate, President Clinton signed the Bono Bill quietly into law.

Naming the Copyright Term Extension Bill after the late Congressman Sonny Bono, a former singer-songwriter who had been killed in a skiing accident, was both a rhetorically brilliant and a philosophically revealing tactic on the part of the bill's backers. It emphasized not only the postmortem aspect of copyright law, whose duration is measured from the date of the author's death, but the long-standing tradition of glorifying postmortem copyright as an estate authors may bequeath to their heirs. The bill's supporters put substantial star power behind their deployment of this tradition: during Senate and House hearings on the proposed legislation, Bob Dylan, Quincy Jones, Alan Menken, Carlos Santana, Henri Mancini's widow, and Arnold Schoenberg's grandson all testified in support of a term extension that would prolong the duration of intellectual property estates. But perhaps most effectively, the name of the Bono Act dressed commerce in the more dignified and seemingly disinterested garb of commemoration. On the day the act passed in the House, Sonny's widow and political successor, Congresswoman Mary Bono, said:

> Actually, Sonny wanted the term of copyright protection to last forever. I am informed by staff that such a change would violate the Constitution. I invite all of you to work with me to strengthen our copyright laws in all of the ways available to us. As you know, there is also [Motion Picture Artist Association President] Jack Valenti's proposal for a term to last forever less one day. Perhaps the Committee may look at that next Congress.[3]

Bono's remark performed a canny act of ventriloquism, making endorsement of the high-stakes legislation seem to issue from the commercially neutral realm of the Hereafter. As the putative last wish of the dearly departed, copyright became coterminous with memory: to extend it would be to revere the deceased Sonny Bono and cultural luminaries like him, whereas to limit it would be to desecrate the memory of the dead. Intellectual property was elevated to the status of a memento mori—a glorious legal mausoleum—and the public domain implicitly vilified as the annihilation of memory in the horror of anonymous burial. Mary Bono had been informed that the Constitution explicitly forbade perpetual copyright, giving Congress the authority "to promote the progress of science and useful arts, by securing for *limited* times to authors and inventors the exclusive right to their prospective writings and discoveries."[4] Having invoked the authority of the dead and the rhetoric of sacred commemoration, however, the Congresswoman deplored the Constitutional provision for a limited copyright and patent regime as an inconvenient and worldly obstacle to her holy cause. And like all crusaders she looked hopefully to the next horizon: a future term extension that, by fulfilling the letter of the Constitution but clearly violating its spirit, would approach the asymptote of eternal life, lasting "forever less one day."

Although both proponents and opponents of the Bono Act used predictably extreme language in arguing their cases, the particular nodes around which their language clustered demonstrate the high imaginative and affective stakes of copyright and the public domain. Supporters of the act represented the public domain not only as the grave of memory but as a space of scandalously legalized theft, one in which authors' heirs would be prematurely stripped of their rightful legacies and forced to see their forebears' unprotected works appropriated and potentially mutilated by unscrupulous, profiteering strangers. In his testimony before the Senate Committee on the Judiciary, songwriter Patrick Alger lamented that creators ever had to relinquish their property: "The notion of public domain is a troublesome one for creators, because we are the only property owners who are required to give up our property after a certain time."[5] The grandson of composer Arnold Schoenberg quoted his grandfather's opinion that the public domain amounted to licensed piracy: "The copyright law was considered up to now as forbidding pirates to steal an author's property before a maximum of 56 years after its registration. After this time every pirate could use it freely, making great profits without letting the real owner 'participate' in the profits of his property."[6] Mary Rodgers, the president of a lobbying organization called AmSong, Inc., put it the most succinctly: "I wish, in a way, the public domain didn't exist at all."[7] For Rodgers, Alger, Bono, and other advocates of perpetual copyright, each term extension constituted an incremental victory of memory over annihilation, reverent inheritance over legalized vandalism: though the body dies, the creative legacy lives on in an afterlife lengthening toward eternity.

For the act's opponents, however, the extension of postmortem copyright was not a heavenly afterlife for creative legacies but a form of legal undeath, a means by which the vitality of dead creators is narrowly and unnaturally protracted at the expense of the living. They pointed out that a rich public domain not only increases the general accessibility of works but also provides source material essential for fresh creation; whereas extending an already long copyright term impoverishes the public domain in order to fortify private estates that too often "protect" works by restricting their circulation and censoring their use. They argued that shorter terms would in fact bestow a better afterlife on dead creators, enabling their work to live on in a more meaningful and generative way: not as a private enclosure providing revenue for a few descendants or corporate shareholders, but as a legacy enjoyed and renewed by the whole culture. For its more extreme critics, long postmortem copyright is nothing short of a licensed vampirism of the public domain, one in which an individualist mythology—the straitened lone creator bequeathing a legacy to reverent heirs—is carefully mobilized by corporations who often purchase copyrights from artists or their legatees, and who are the chief sponsors and beneficiaries of term extension.

As we have seen, the legislative discourse of copyright conventionally pivots around a question of balanced exchange: what variety and duration of right will provide creators with incentive sufficient to induce them to publish their works but not so extensive that it will have a chilling effect on the public domain it aims to promote? There is a dark twin to this rationalist discourse, however, one that belongs to the procedural margins of copyright but is central to the law's imaginative operations. For although it may seem prosaic in its technicalities, copyright law has no less a cultural function than to determine and police the border between the living and the dead. Its peripheral discourse addresses a whole range of the law's secondary characteristics: the illicit or unbalanced appropriations the law can permit and the generative ones it can prohibit, its links to commemoration and consecration, its intimate ties to the death of the author, and its vaunted conquest of death through its power to confer one or another kind of afterlife on creations and creators. But although the copyright in a work currently insists on its conquest of death by explicitly outliving the work's creator, it has not always done so. The first copyright statutes in both Britain and the U.S. granted a temporary monopoly lasting a maximum of 28 years from publication—a term independent of the duration of the author's life, and short enough that many writers lived to see their earlier works enter the public domain. Yet even in the first century of copyright, the law justified the limited duration of its protection by reference to the mortality of authors. In September 1789, Thomas Jefferson wrote to James Madison that the term of copyright should be grounded in "The principle, that the earth belongs to the living, and not to the dead." Jefferson had used actuarial mortality tables to work out the optimal term for copyright, which he felt should last one generation, or about 19 years (the 1790 Copyright Act allowed instead for 14 years, with the possibility of renewal for an additional 14). By ensuring that copyrights in works did not outlive their creators, such a term would obey his view that "the earth belongs in usufruct to the living."[8]

Strange as it may sound, copyright has become increasingly death-oriented since Jefferson's day. In 1814 a British act extended copyright protection until the author's death if he or she outlived the 28-year term, and in 1842 the term was extended to 42 years or the length of the author's life plus 7 years, whichever was longer. In the U.S., copyright has moved more slowly, but no less surely, toward a long postmortem term: beginning with a maximum term of 28 years in 1790, the period increased to 42 years in 1831, to 56 years in 1909, to author's life plus 50 years in 1976. Today in the U.K. and the U.S., as well as in the European Union, the copyright term for works by individuals is life plus 70 years. The history of Anglo-American copyright, then, is in part the story of how a comparatively brief monopoly grew into an estate that outlives its creator by the length of a lifetime and seems to be making a bid for perpetuity, for immortality—in other words, for the status of tangible property. And as the life span of copyright has overtaken that of its most immediate beneficiary—the work's creator—it has become the site for debates not only about the optimal balance between individual incentives and public goods but about cultural memory, the sanctity of the dead, and the longevity of their intentions and legacies. As a result, both the advocates and the critics of perpetual copyright have come to sound increasingly like theologians or spiritual mediums, debating the nature of death's domain and its dominion, in turn, over the living. For instance, because the Sonny Bono Term Extension Act's proponents had dedicated their work to the living memory of the dead, those who have questioned the act's constitutionality since its passage have ended up insisting on the irrevocable deadness of the dead. Deceased creative people, they point out, have for obvious reasons finished creating and are therefore beyond the pale of a retroactive incentive in the form of copyright term extension. Law professor Lawrence Lessig represented the plaintiff in *Eldred v. Ashcroft* (formerly *Eldred v. Reno*), the first of several cases attacking the Bono Act's constitutionality.

[125]

Bono also violates the Constitution, Lessig says, because it flunks the copyright clause's "incentive" requirement. Since you can't give an incentive to a corpse—and the new law extended protection retroactively, to works created by authors now dead—it fails the litmus test. "The Supreme Court has consistently said the primary purpose of copyright is not to give authors some particular benefit, but to protect the public domain," says Lessig. "Extensions can't be retroactive, because the Constitution gives Congress the right to grant exclusive rights only if those rights create incentives to produce more speech. Extending these benefits retroactively doesn't serve any purposes the copyright clause was designed for."[9]

Understandably resistant to the powerful memento mori rhetoric of the act's proponents, Lessig and his collaborators have attempted to shift the argument to the less emotionally charged question of copyright's constitutional aims, which are clearly oriented around the protection and fructification of the public domain for the sake of the living, rather than the safeguarding of authorial property, legacy, and memory. Yet the commemorative and consecrative powers Lessig and others attempt to downplay are precisely the attributes that have steadily raised the metaphysical stakes of copyright over the last 250 years.

Sonny Bono was not the first prominent advocate of perpetual copyright, although he may have been the first to promote it from beyond the grave. No less a figure than William Wordsworth was preoccupied with extending the term of copyright, ideally to perpetuity, and for reasons that transcended monetary profits: as Susan Eilenberg has put it, "he addressed the government as if it had jurisdiction over the border between the dead and the living and could repair by legal means the damage death wreaks upon human bonds."[10] As of 1814, a work's copyright in Britain ended, in most cases, with the life of its author. Because the author's life and literary estate were coterminous, the writer seemed to die twice in one death, leaving behind two bodies—a physical corpse and a literary corpus—that might be desecrated. As Thomas Hood put it in a petition to Parliament on term extension, "when your petitioner shall be dead and buried, he might with as much propriety and decency have his body snatched as his literary remains."[11] Although the expiration of the literary estate with the body adhered to Jefferson's dictum that the earth belongs in usufruct to the living, it horrified Wordsworth, as did the law's implication that the public domain should thrive in direct proportion as authors died, practically feasting on their corpses. So brief a copyright term, he argued, rewarded writers only for recognition during their lifetimes and therefore encouraged ephemeral hacks rather than writers likely to produce works of enduring genius. In his Preface to his 1815 collected *Poems*, Wordsworth had placed himself among those original visionaries who wrote less for the living than for the unborn, attempting to create the taste by which their works would one day be enjoyed. Although it could not remunerate such writers after death, a postmortem copyright term would compensate them with the knowledge that their heirs, at least, would profit by work whose contemporaries had been unequipped to appreciate it. By thus relieving "men of letters from the thralldom of being forced to court the living generation," postmortem copyright would constitute a bridge between the dead and the unborn, all but bypassing the living whose rights of usufruct had so concerned Jefferson.[12]

In an 1819 letter, however, Wordsworth went farther, implying that copyright reform *could* compensate the dead. In the letter, Wordsworth explained his reasons for refusing to help fund a monument to the poet Robert Burns. Writers of genius, he wrote, did not require stone monuments, because their literary works were their monuments. But the durability of those works could be ensured through a legal memorialization: "towards departed Genius, exerted in the fine Arts and more especially in Poetry, I humbly think, in the present state of things, the sense of obligation to it may more satisfactorily be expressed by means pointing directly to the general benefit of Literature."[13] The copyright reform to which Wordsworth obliquely refers (as "means pointing directly to the general benefit of Literature") is offered here not as an incentive to living writers but as a gesture of retroactive reward, commemoration, and even appeasement to "departed Genius." As Eilenberg writes, "Represented thus, the money that copyright produces loses its materialistic associations and becomes spiritualized, after a fashion: offered to the dead, it comes to resemble an oblation." Despite Lessig's recent complaint that you can't give an incentive to a corpse, Wordsworth's position demonstrates that the pro-Bono rhetoric of posthumous commemoration through term extension has a long prehistory in the metaphysical discourse surrounding copyright. The effect of that rhetoric over the last two centuries has been to shift the debate over copyright's duration from its original grounding in "incentive" to the more affective, magical category of "commemoration." If this process has also shrunken and deconsecrated the public domain, it has made these incursions seem a small price to pay for the metaphysical gains they underwrite. After all, a term extension appears to ask little enough of the public domain—nothing beyond a little more patience—and in return, it claims to fortify copyright's power over desecration, forgetting, and death. It was during Wordsworth's lifetime, and due in no small part to his efforts, that British copyright law began to vanquish death by levying a higher tax on the public domain: though the 1842 Copyright Act provided neither perpetual protection nor the term of life plus 60 years that supporters like Wordsworth had sought, it did institute the first explicitly postmortem copyright term of author's life plus 7 years. But for Wordsworth, 7 years was too narrow a ledge from which to make the leap to literary immortality. He arranged that his masterpiece *The Prelude* not be fully published until after his death, in part so that its copyrights would more substantially outlive him.[14] Having relinquished his physical body, the dead author would return in the legal body provided by posthumous copyright.

The Copywrights

As the appeals of Wordsworth and the Bono supporters illustrate, Anglo-American copyright has drifted from incentive toward consecration, from promoting the public domain to fortifying individual and corporate estates, by way of a series of strange conflations. In both appeals, the distinction between the duration of an author's intellectual property estate and the longevity of that person's cultural legacy is collapsed, with the resulting insinuation that a culture is incapable of remembering, treasuring, and consecrating work whose copyright has ended. It is easy enough to think of writers, composers, and artists whose cultural legacies have flourished long after their copyrights have lapsed, to say nothing of those who remain canonical despite having lived and produced before copyright law existed. Conversely, copyright protection provides no guarantee of consecration: the vast majority of creative people are forgotten by the culture at large long before their works join the public domain. But a postmortem copyright term fires the imagination of creative people, who, because of the Western cultural preoccupation with individual artistic "immortality," tend already to be driven in part by the hope of producing a lasting cultural legacy. The conflation of cultural and proprietary legacies is compelling, too, for those who stand to benefit financially from the prolongation of both legacies and from their protracted symbiosis: the cultural legacy sustains a demand for the work protected by the copyright estate, while the high prices and restricted access maintained by the estate can increase the elite glamour and apparent vitality of the cultural legacy.

The more haunting conflation, however, is that of copyright's life expectancy with the author's. In part, this gesture simply extends the conventional fantasy of immortality-through-works: because postmortem copyright terms ensure the integrity and restricted access of my works after my death, I will "live on" more palpably through them. But the inheritability of a postmortem copyright estate also confers an attenuated life-after-death on the creator, much as the intentions expressed in a will can outlive the testator, continuing to produce change in a world the deceased has left. In creating copyrightable works, as in making a will, I participate through the prosthesis of the law in a future I will not corporeally experience. In this respect, postmortem copyright gives authors the virtual experience of being undead before they are dead, of holding proleptic sway over the living from beyond a grave they have not yet gone to. Copyright may or may not contribute to the "immortality" of an author after death; its more important and preposterous function is to make the author feel immortal before death. Yet we should also observe that copyright, as long as it remains a *temporary* monopoly, confers a strictly limited immortality on the author, less a conquest of death than a deferral of it. Although literary property law allows the author to return in a manner after death, the authorial revenant is undead, not immortal; like the undead, it can finally die, in this case into the public domain. In its limited duration, intellectual property is signally unlike most tangible property forms, which can be privately owned, exchanged, and bequeathed indefinitely. One might expect tangible property, then, to contain or stand in for its creator's immortality, since its status as property is eternal; certainly this is one logic of monuments. But to be eternally property is also, in the majority of cases, to be eternally a material object. It is the very temporariness of intangible property that sets it apart from the property status of objects, making it seem more akin to the human creator whose mortality and spiritual aspects it shares. Intangible property can stand in as a surrogate for its creator because it is similarly mortal and possesses a similarly dematerialized essence. Yet paradoxically, that kinship also gives rise to the desire, at least among advocates of perpetual copyright, to immortalize intangible property in the place of its mortal creator—to assert Sonny Bono's cultural immortality, for instance, by making his copyright estate eternal. If literary property law helps construct the boundary between ideality and materiality, mortality and immortality, it is also caught between those states, pulled in the direction of immortality because it is mortal, and toward materiality because it is ideal.

Copyright, then, presides over last things, last wishes, and the possibility of a life, or legacy, at least, that outlasts death. Given its increasingly eschatological function since Wordsworth's time, one is hardly surprised to find the cultural discourses surrounding copyright evolving a necromantic vocabulary—reanimated corpses, ghosts, revenants, vampires, resurrections—that requires its own spectral science or *hauntology*, to use a term coined by Jacques Derrida in his *Specters of Marx* (1995). A portmanteau combining "haunting" and "ontology," Derrida's notion of hauntology recognizes the inadequacy of conventional ontological dyads (being versus not-being, presence versus absence) in thinking about specters, those liminal figures that, as Warren Montag puts it, were "never alive enough to die, never present enough to become absent. What exists between presence and absence that prevents the nonpresent from simply disappearing?"[15] Derrida develops a hauntological reading not only of Marx's spectral presence in the work of his heirs and detractors but of spectrality in Marx's own work, even positing a hysteron proteron haunting of the pure concept of use value by exchange value: "Just as there is no pure use, there is no *use value* which the possibility of exchange and commerce . . . has not in advance inscribed in an *out-of-use*—an excessive signification that cannot be reduced to the useless." Reciprocally, he adds, exchange value is "likewise inscribed and exceeded by a promise of a gift beyond exchange."[16] The notion that use value and exchange value contaminate one another in such a way has suggestive implications for the construction of the oral/written interface, some of which I have addressed above in relation to Wilde. And it prompts us to consider both how the legal division between copyrighted work and work in the public domain might map onto the categories of exchange value and use value, and how that mapping would be complicated by the mutual hauntings of gift by commodity, commodity by gift. The public domain, we might hazard, haunts copyright through the category of fair use, which gives the commodity a foreglimpse of its eventual death into a public gift economy. Copyright, reciprocally, haunts the public domain through the possibility that unprotected works might continue to function as scarce, embattled, commodified resources in cultural-capital economies long after they have themselves ceased to be private intellectual property.

Derrida's notion of hauntology opens out, ultimately, into a messianic political orientation that regards the present as haunted not only by the past (historicity) but by traces of a future that is unforeseeable because it will stand in a relation of radical discontinuity with the present; this messianism he has described subsequently as a "waiting without expectation" that strains toward "the coming of an eminently real, concrete event, that is, to the most irreducibly heterogeneous otherness."[17] In the present context, however, I do not attempt to engage Derrida's concept of hauntology, or its wide range of implications, in full. Instead, I borrow the notion of hauntology toward a more circumscribed end: to question the artificial clarity of copyright's ontological and legal metaphysical bases, and to suggest how generative the underlying muddiness has been of fantasy, anxiety, and misappropriation in literary texts I read as reflecting on intellectual property. Copyright would seem to belong to a fairly straightforward legal ontology: a creation either is or is not sufficiently original to garner copyright protection; it either is protected or resides in the public domain; the particular objects of copyright protection are expressions, not ideas; protected expressions circulate as private property, whereas ideas and unprotected expressions circulate as public property. But we have already seen how such binarisms, as appealing as they are to the legislative need for categorization, can do a violence to the inherently complex and ambiguous objects they govern. In addition, these dyads often fail to maintain even their theoretical discreteness: the conceptual firewalls copyright law erects between "idea" and "expression," or between "original" and "derivative" work, can seem laughably porous even before they are applied to particular cases. By insisting on the distinctness and purity of artificially separated realms, literary property law attempts to banish, or even deny the existence of, the figures and texts that regularly walk through its walls. In its panicky, trumped-up claims to ideological closure and ontological immunity to such haunting, copyright *is* an exorcism. But strangely, the more the law has attempted to legislate the border between the dead and the living, the more recourse its advocates have had to the same transgressive and liminal figures the law seeks internally to lay. A hauntological reading of copyright should address the frequent appearance of ghosts, vampires, revenants, and the undead in the figurative discourses—both critical and celebratory—surrounding literary property law. But it must go on to tie that figural repertoire into the categories and deep structures of the law, asking how the spectral operations of haunting, oblation, exorcism, consecration, and contamination might speak to the socioeconomic and cultural work of copyright law. Such a reading should also see the ways the law constructs, polices, and sometimes breaches the border between the living and the dead as symptomatic of its manipulations of other categories, other thresholds.

In attempting a hauntological reading of copyright and its spectral presence in the literary imaginary of late modernity, the central part of this chapter looks at two texts from the first decade of the twentieth century, a period during which Western copyright law was abandoning shorter terms that ran from a work's publication date, and adopting terms tied to the length of the author's life. In 1909, the U.S. copyright term was extended to a flat maximum of 56 years from publication (not officially a postmortem term, though long enough to outlive many or even most authors), while most other European countries were in the process of instituting explicitly postmortem terms (Germany adopted a term of author's life plus 50 years in 1908, and Britain did likewise in 1911). As it crossed the threshold of the author's death, copyright was itself in a transitional state, and its liminality registers in this chapter's cardinal texts. These will be unfamiliar to most readers: George Sylvester Viereck's novel *The House of the Vampire* (1907), and its spin-off play, *The Vampire* (1909), which Viereck co-authored with Edgar Allan Woolf. What novel and play exhibit is, firstly, a preoccupation with how literary language (both expression and ideas) originates, circulates, and is celebrated or forgotten; and secondly, a sense that the first question cannot be addressed without opening the border between the living and the dead. Though neither play nor novel names copyright overtly, both texts are attuned to the rhetoric, dynamics, and problematics of literary property law, as contemporary reviewers recognized. But because both *Vampire* texts are exempt from the demands of statutory clarity and simplicity, they are able to meditate more fully than the law does—if also more cryptically—on the darker and more ambiguous questions raised by copyright. Among these questions: what is really the role of appropriation in creation? Where should its limits be set? Does the law's stated motivation of promoting the public domain mask a deeper commitment to great individuals' appropriations from the mass? Does it, by contrast, attempt to domesticate what is in fact the violent process by which a hungry, undiscerning mass devours and dismembers its fragile individual luminaries? Which is the more menacing, the intellectual property owner who will rob the public in order to achieve life after death, or the omnivorous public domain that is the terminus of property, the black hole down which creation, expression, ideas, property, and even memory disappear?

These questions are structurally central to *The House of the Vampire*. Viereck's literary thriller celebrates plagiarism as a form of spiritual vampirism, narrating a string of artistic expropriations and ultimately absolving and subsuming them into an extremely objectionable Great Man theory of history. In *Our Vampires, Ourselves,* one of the few recent critical investigations to address Viereck's novel, Nina Auerbach contends that Viereck's vampire-protagonist "exposes the cannibalistic violation within Carlylean myths of heroic individualism."[18] Although such a critique can be discerned among the novel's cross-currents, it is crucial to note that Viereck endorsed—and later became famous for endorsing—a politics that combined "cannibalistic violation" with heroic individualism. Fascinated by "the Great" in his youth, Viereck went on to become a defender of Hitler during the thirties and a pro-Nazi propagandist in the U.S. during World War II; in 1941 he was convicted for violating the Foreign Agent's Registration Act and spent the next six years in prison. Even early in his life, Viereck's political views were as extreme as his later political acts were influential, so much so that his literary output, when it is read at all, tends now to be read exclusively for the political symptoms it exhibits.[19] Though it would be absurd to claim that the Nazism of Viereck's middle years is perfectly and unequivocally legible in his first novel, to sever *The House of the Vampire* utterly from its author's subsequent acts would be to miss the ways in which the book incubates a gesture its author would later make in full: an aestheticized, knowing surrender to the totalitarian personality.

I recognize that to read a book such as *The House of the Vampire* in relation to literary property law runs a double risk: one can appear to claim either that copyright is the Archimedean fulcrum of fascism, or that the text's meditations on literary property may be meaningfully quarantined from its proto-fascist valences. My intention here is to take a route between these extremes by suggesting that, although copyright may not have a straightforwardly deterministic tie to mass-politics, the construction of individual versus mass intellectual property rights (e.g., copyright versus the public domain) does have political ramifications: it not only affects the circulation of power/knowledge but also models other social relations between individual and mass. I will, in addition, make an uncomfortable but necessary point that takes us back to the question of hauntology: that revolutionary spirits can, and often do, haunt radically conservative demesnes in ways that vex supposedly stable oppositions, including that of revolutionary versus reactionary. In Viereck's novel, these phenomena of haunting and contamination occur when certain elements of a collectivist critique of intellectual property are made to drive a politically reactionary plot. In a broader context, the temporary nature of intellectual property haunts a general property regime whose norm is perpetual. During the late nineteenth century, copyright and patent law were sometimes referred to as "communistic" in orientation, even as they were becoming indispensable property forms in capitalist economies and would subsequently become major legal bulwarks of capitalism in the information age. As long as it remains a temporary form, intangible property will, in some measure, haunt the hegemony of perpetual, tangible property.

The Reign of the Dead

Absorbing Genius

George Sylvester Viereck burst on the New York literary scene at the age of twenty-two with *Nineveh and Other Poems* (1907), a collection of verse that won its author the reputation of boy-genius. Viereck's first novel, *The House of the Vampire*, was published the same year and aimed to capitalize on the sensation caused by *Nineveh*. Although its title suggests a descent from *Carmilla* or *Dracula*, the novel exudes the "subtle perfume" (its favorite phrase) of Wilde rather than the more pungent neo-gothic vapors of Le Fanu or Stoker. Its central figure, the American literary lion Reginald Clarke, might be a second coming of Wilde: the narrator describes him as a man destined to be "remembered in New York drawing-rooms as the man who had brought to perfection the art of talking. Even to dine with him was a liberal education" (4). Clarke occupies luxurious rooms on Riverside Drive, where he writes amid a veritable warehouse of Wildean icons: "A satyr on the mantelpiece whispered obscene secrets into the ears of Saint Cecilia. The argent limbs of Antinous brushed against the garments of Mona Lisa." Bristling with sphinxes and fauns, Clarke's studio also houses images of the great creators and conquerors: busts of Shakespeare and Balzac, "a picture of Napoleon facing the image of the Crucified" (19). Into this super-decadent setting Clarke introduces his latest prodigy, the young poet Ernest Fielding, who has come to live with his mentor. Getting his first glimpse of Clarke's salon, Ernest is surprised to find that every *tchotchke* in the place—a Chinese mandarin, a Hindu monkey-god—has appeared in one of his host's literary works. Clarke soon explains this phenomenon: "A man's genius is commensurate with his ability of absorbing from life the elements essential to artistic completion.... Re-creation, infinitely more wonderful than mere calling into existence, is the prerogative of the poet" (23–24). Wilde, in a former life, had drafted a similar claim: "It is only the unimaginative who ever invents. The true artist is known by the use he makes of what he annexes, and he annexes everything."[20]

It soon becomes clear to the reader (though not, strangely, to Ernest) that Clarke's genius absorbs more than coffee-table curios into his re-creative work. Walkham, a sculptor friend, tells Ernest that he is suddenly unable to complete his latest work-in-progress, his "original conception" and "motive" for the statue having vanished "as if a breeze had carried it away." But when he hears Clarke reading from his own new work—an epic about the French Revolution—Walkham just as suddenly recovers his idea; exultant, he beams to Clarke, "your prose suggested to me, by its rhythmic flow, something which, at first indefinite, crystallised finally into my lost conception of Narcissus" (26, 28). And no sooner does the sculptor's inspiration revive than Clarke's withers, so completely that he abandons his epic. "Poetry in the writing," Clarke explains to Ernest, "is like red hot glass before the master-blower has fashioned it into birds and trees and strange fantastic shapes.

A draught, caused by the opening of a door, may distort it" (50). Clarke's likening nascent poetry to blown glass is crucial here. In the world of Viereck's novel, artistic ideas and inspirations behave in much the way that theories do in Wilde's "The Portrait of Mr. W. H."—like material objects, alienable, capable only of singular and serial ownership, susceptible of exchange, appropriation, depletion, and loss. In other words, ideas obey some unwritten bylaw of the conservation of mass. As Walkham says, "Nothing is ever lost in the spiritual universe" (26).

As the months of his apprenticeship wear on, Ernest begins to experience this intangible conservation firsthand. His time with Clarke, strangely, has coincided with a long creative dry spell. Finally, during an outing with his friend Jack, he conceives an idea for a play, "a brilliant weft of swift desire—heavy, perfumed, Oriental—interwoven with bits of gruesome tenderness" (47). He composes the play feverishly in his mind, stringing "pearl on pearl, line on line, without entrusting a word to paper" (unwritten words, again, have congealed as objects), yet puzzling over the sense that "his thoughts seemed strangely evanescent; they seemed to run away from him whenever he attempted to seize them" (49). Those runaway thoughts, it turns out, have fled straight to Reginald Clarke's pen. Just when he feels ready to write his play, Ernest attends a reading of his host's newest dramatic masterpiece and is chilled to hear his "own" words coming out of Clarke's mouth. Somehow, the elder writer has plagiarized Ernest's entire *unwritten* play—itself a perfect alloy of *Hamlet* and *Salomé,* complete with a "sombre-hearted Prince," an adulterous mother-Queen, and a veiled princess who kisses her father's decapitated head (63). On hearing the charge, Clarke reassures Ernest that he has simply become neuraesthenic from overwork and prescribes a vacation for his young disciple. Installed in an Atlantic City resort, Ernest meets and befriends Ethel Brandenbourg, a painter and former lover of Clarke's, abandoned by him when her creative wellsprings ran dry. As he falls in love with Ethel, Ernest is inspired again—this time to write a novel, *Leontina.* Yet when he returns to Clarke's chambers, exhaustion again prevents him from actually writing the work; even his dreams about *Leontina* are infiltrated by ghoulish footpads, and he wakes unrested. But because of his mentor's charisma, he rebuffs his other friends: "by a strange metamorphosis, all his affection for Ethel and Jack went out for the time being to Reginald Clarke" (95). Love, too, can be siphoned from one body to another according to the novel's law of affective transfusion.

Moved to intervene by her growing affections for Ernest, Ethel corners her former lover at a soirée and demands that he explain his powers of fascination and appropriation. In honor of their dead love, Clarke obliges: he was born, he tells her, with "unlimited absorptive capacities," and with the power not only of "absorbing the special virtues of other people" but of rejecting "every element that is harmful or inessential to the completion of my self" (113). He possesses a super-genius, that is, for both consumption and selection—an insatiable appetite governed by impeccable taste. Ethel is stunned, believing him only because she has been his victim and dubbing him a "vampire-soul." Clarke objects to the vampire moniker, and attempts to exonerate himself and his appropriative powers in what Viereck took to be the novel's central passage:

> "In every age . . . there are giants who attain to a greatness which by natural growth no men could ever have reached. . . . They are the chosen. Carpenter's sons they are, who have laid down the Law of a World for millenniums to come; or simple Corsicans, before whose eagle eye have quaked the kingdoms of the earth. But to accomplish their mission they need a will of iron and the wit of a hundred men. And from the iron they take the strength, and from a hundred men's brains they absorb their wisdom. Divine missionaries, they appear in all departments of life. In their hand is gathered today the gold of the world. Mighty potentates of peace and war, they unlock new seas and from distant continents lift the bars. Single-handed, they accomplish what nations dared not hope; with Titan strides they scale the stars and succeed where millions fail. In art they live, the makers of new periods, the dreamers of new styles. They make themselves the vocal sun glasses of God. Homer and Shakespeare, Hugo and Balzac—they concentrate the dispersed rays of a thousand lesser luminaries in one singing flame that, like a giant torch, lights up humanity's path." (117–18)

Beneath this absorptive-charismatic theory of history lies a simple determinism: already "one of the master-figures of the age," Clarke cannot rest in his appropriations because "We are all slaves, wire-pulled marionettes: You, Ernest, I. There is no freedom on the face of the earth nor above. The tiger that tears a lamb is not free, I am not free, you are not free" (124–25). Ethel goes to Ernest with her newfound illumination, describing Clarke as a vampire, in the novel's only explicit dilation on the undead:

> "They are beings, not always wholly evil, whom every night some mysterious impulse leads to steal into unguarded bedchambers, to suck the blood of the sleepers and then, having waxed strong on the life of their victims, cautiously to retreat. Thence comes it that their lips are very red. It is even said that they can find no rest in the grave, but return to their former haunts long after they are believed to be dead. Those whom they visit, however, pine away for no apparent reason. The physicians shake their wise heads and speak of consumption. But sometimes, ancient chronicles assure us, the people's suspicions were aroused, and under the leadership of a good priest they went in solemn procession to the graves of the persons suspected. And on opening the tombs it was found that their coffins had rotted away and the flowers in their hair were black. But their bodies were white and whole; through no empty sockets crept the vermin, and their sucking lips were still moist with a little blood. . . . The world is overcoming the shallow skepticism of the nineteenth century. Life has become once more wonderful and very mysterious. But it also seems that, with the miracles of the old days, their terrors, their nightmares and their monsters have come back in a modern guise." (144–46)

Ernest protests that vampires were only a medieval superstition and could hardly exist "in this great city, in the shadow of the Flatiron Building," asking incredulously "How can a man suck from another man's brain a thing as intangible, as quintessential as thought?" But Ethel (apparently) demolishes his skepticism by exclaiming "Ah, you forget, thought is more real than blood!" (147–48). The implication: that thought obeys the same zero-sum logic—closed economy, scarcity, reciprocity in exchange, transfusion, and appropriation—as blood. A search of Clarke's writing desk yields proof of her theory: a near-finished manuscript of what was to have been Ernest's *Leontina,* set down in Clarke's "foreign hand," and therefore lost to its true author (164).

Finally alerted to his host's methods, Ernest resolves to lie awake and catch Clarke at his nocturnal brain-burglary. But twice he falls asleep, dreaming of a ghostly hand thumbing through the pages of his mind. The second time, "by a superhuman effort," he rouses himself just in time to discover Clarke leaving his bedroom through a secret panel; he confronts his mentor, charging him as "an embezzler of the mind, strutting through life in borrowed and stolen plumes" (177, 182). Clarke counters by reprising his speech to Ethel, identifying himself as the latest incarnation of the master-spirit, a transhistorical titan who forges the future from the pig-iron of lesser souls:

> "I am a light-bearer. I tread the high hills of mankind . . . I point the way to the future. I light up the abysses of the past. Were not my stature gigantic, how could I hold the torch in all men's sight? The very souls that I tread underfoot realise, as their dying gaze follows me, the possibilities with which the future is big. . . . Eternally secure, I carry the essence of what is cosmic . . . of what is divine . . . I am Homer . . . Goethe . . . Shakespeare . . . I am an embodiment of the same force of which Alexander, Caesar, Confucius and the Christos were also embodiments . . . None so strong as to resist me." (184–85; original ellipses)

When Ernest assails him physically, Clarke retaliates by draining everything that remains in the ephebe's soul—will, feeling, judgment, memory, fear—like so much wine from a skin. Ethel, arriving breathlessly to rescue her young lover, sees a humanoid form stumble out of Clarke's house, "a dull and brutish thing, hideously transformed, without a vestige of a mind," a babbling animal "Without a present and without a past" (189–90). The thought-vampire's next victim, Ernest's friend Jack, passes this bestial remnant on his way up Clarke's stairs, and the cycle begins again.

I have intimated that Viereck's later political attraction to totalitarian personalities can be seen stirring in *The House of the Vampire,* particularly in its glamorization of the Great Man as the vampire-consumer of lesser beings' intellectual vitality. This is not to deny the presence in the novel of certain countercurrents to its celebrations of violent appropriation. The *Vampire*'s strange central premise—that ideas and expressions circulate like objects—might itself be scavenged from Wilde's "The Portrait of Mr. W. H.," which, I argued, mounted a critical parody of copyright law by recasting belief in the mold of material property. After all, that logic of copyright is what allows Clarke to take full credit for Ernest's works simply by beating him to the writing desk; the same logic demands that Ernest attempt to steal back Clarke's manuscript of *Leontina* rather than simply write down his own.[21] In a rare moment of unclouded sympathy, a narratorial voice in the *Vampire,* speaking on Ernest's behalf through free indirect speech, expresses the novel's otherwise latent outrage at Clarke's appropriations, the consumer culture that underwrites them, and the laws that protect them: "Was Reginald to enjoy the fruit of other men's labour unpunished? Was he to continue growing into the mightiest literary factor of the century by preying on his betters? Abel, Walkham, Ethel, he, Jack, were they all to be the victims of this insatiable monster?" (178).

The novel's—and Viereck's—main response to these questions, however, turns out to be a resounding, almost unambivalent Yes. Though the *Vampire* has elements of a cautionary tale (the concluding scene, for example, where Clarke gruesomely decants Ernest's soul), its affective and persuasive energies are massed behind the thought-vampire rather than against him. If at times he appears monstrous, Reginald Clarke is still more fascinating, sending the narrator into raptures of description: "As he stood there he resembled more than anything a beautiful tiger-cat, a wonderful thing of strength and will-power, indomitable and insatiate" (159). For Clarke, an unflinching vitalist, strength and willpower are their own justification, the more so if they shape the world's future. He says of his victims, "Their strength is taken from them, but the spirit of humanity, as embodied in us, triumphantly marches on" (119). Since these indispensable overmen thrive by a kind of human sacrifice, the victims of that sacrifice must find their consolation in having fed the march of greatness—in being absorbed into the very tissues of the world-spirit's titans. Viereck, for his part, left little doubt as to his own sympathies with the absorptive theory of genius articulated in the *Vampire;* his published remarks on the subject are essentially indistinguishable from Clarke's:

> You've heard of the "great American novel"? Well, I've written it.... It's something entirely new in fiction. The hero is a vampire. In every age there have been great men—and they became great by absorbing the work of other men. For instance, Shakespeare, a great genius, took the plots of less known writers and transformed them by his genius into gems of true art and poetry. Today John Rockefeller, by his great genius, has acquired material wealth by absorbing smaller capitalists. These vampires, like a sun glass, gather the rays of others and give them forth with concentrated power. The hero of my book is a poet—he absorbs the poetry of others and gives it forth with greater power.[22]

> The vampire mind appears in all branches of life. Rockefeller possesses the genius of absorbing gold even as Napoleon possessed the genius of absorbing power. The founders of the great world-religions have never been what is commonly known as original thinkers. Messiahs have come and gone and the same message has been reiterated again and again in the flights of the eons. Thus the founder of Christian Science has followed merely in the steps of comparatively recent mystics and her philosophic system is brazenly copied from the writings of the obscure Phineas P. Quinby.[23]
>
> My Vampire is the Overman of Nietzsche. He is justified in pilfering other men's brains. It is a unique figure in the literature and drama of the world. I have taken the individual and made him stand for a type.[24]

By 1907, Shakespeare's source-plundering was hardly news. What remains chilling here, though, is the slide from Shakespeare's plot-stealing to clearly nonliterary appropriations—Rockefeller's absorption of capital, Napoleon's of power—as if thefts of storylines (which tend, even under the copyright laws instituted generations after Shakespeare's death, to be treated as public domain material) were on a plane with *coups d'état,* violent annexations, and corporate takeovers.[25] Eerier still is Viereck's saying that his vampire-overman is "justified" in his appropriations, without so much as a "because"; vitalism, again, poses as its own justification.

The House of the Vampire fared badly among reviewers, several of whom condemned the book as a clumsy rehash of *The Picture of Dorian Gray.*[26] Still, like many a revenant novel, *The House of the Vampire* rose from the grave of critical condemnation to enjoy an afterlife on the stage. Viereck was helped in revamping the book by a college friend named Edgar Allen Woolf.[27] The play, retitled simply *The Vampire,* opened at the Schubert Theater in New York on January 18, 1909.[28] While hardly the "Sensation of the Season" one paper claimed it to be, *The Vampire* did provoke a storm of critical responses, many of which recognized and engaged the play's meditations about the nature of genius, originality, and, in particular, literary property. The most common critical reaction to the play was simple incredulity, inspired in particular by its representations of brain-burglary: "You cannot throw open the window and yell 'Thief!' to a man who has merely what he thinks you thought that you thought. It is too subtle. It is too intangible. And there is no redress." No one could steal the "linked gems of your mentality, like so much sausage," went the critical refrain—though with a telling note of anxiety—because thoughts did not circulate like things:[29]

> It would appear to the casual observer that ideas differ from money in that when a thief steals a purse its owner has it no longer, while a thief may steal an idea and still leave it in the possession of the owner. But this was not the theory upon which Edgar Allen Woolf and George Sylvester Viereck worked. Their proposition resolved into this: 'If you steal a man's idea, he no longer has

it.' Not only that, but the victim of this burglary of the brain begins to suffer from anaemic imagination. His creative powers decline, little by little, until he finds himself wholly impotent for further work.

> Up to yesterday afternoon I was, I confess, unaware that a thought was like a stilton cheese, a streetcar transfer, or a glass of beer, and that its appropriation by somebody correlated as a loss by somebody else.... [the protagonist's] brain is burglarized. He can't finish his novel. Can you build a wall if somebody is always stealing bricks?[30]

Jefferson, like other early skeptics about intellectual property law, had likened the transmission of ideas to the passing of a flame from candle to candle: "He who receives an idea from me," he wrote, "receives instruction himself without lessening mine; as he who lights his taper at mine, receives light without darkening me."[31] In other words, Jefferson identified ideas as public goods, susceptible to equal access and nonrival consumption by all potential consumers. Viereck's and Woolf's detractors complained that *The Vampire* treated ideas as if they were no longer flame-like, but congealed—not shared out in kindling proliferations so much as lost or seized, stilton-like, by self-interested individuals. Their complaint was a little reductive: what gets stolen in *The Vampire,* as in *The House of the Vampire,* are not only the disembodied ideas for books and poems but often the fully composed, if previously unwritten, texts themselves—in other words, expression in addition to ideas, form in addition to content. (I will return to the texts' construction of this idea/expression dichotomy below.) But they rightly drew attention to the play's bizarrely closed informational economy, wherein only one person at a time could possess expression, draining it from another to whom it was then lost. That closed economy brings us much nearer to copyright, which confers sole and serial ownership, if not on expression *tout court,* then on its reproducibility and sale.

A paean to righteous appropriation, *The Vampire* attracted a small group of intellectual property claimants who attacked Viereck and Woolf for the same kinds of creative seizure the play had anatomized and celebrated; if Viereck's vampire had built a legend by feasting on minor poets, these claimants would feast now on *The Vampire*. No sooner had the play opened than one Arthur Stringer began accusing its authors of plagiarism. The plot of *The Vampire,* he contended, had been lifted from his 1903 novel *The Silver Poppy,* originally titled *The Yellow Vampire.* Like the Viereck-Woolf play, *The Silver Poppy* "is the story of an author who stole fame, who appropriated the ideas of others and prospered on them, until the final discovery came about." Stringer directed readers to pages 199–202 of his novel to see "how the idea of the vampire seizing on and draining the vitality of its victim was there made use of by me." Viereck's riposte was suitably pseudo-Wildean in tone, yet stamped with his trademark assertion of the overman's right to appropriate:

The Copywrights

> I am really sorry the charge is not true, because in that case it would be conclusive proof that my theory of thought absorption is true. Even if I had absorbed ideas from works of an inferior quality I still would feel justified in using them, but, unfortunately, I have not done anything of the kind. In fact, the theory of the absorptive powers of genius is not new by any means, and it has been ably treated by a number of writers. What, then, is remarkable about it if it should be true in my case, although I know it is not? As a result of these charges ... I find myself in the curious position of writing about a human vampire while I am charged with being such a vampire myself. It is both amusing and uncanny.[32]

The reply remakes accusation into aggrandizement, belatedness into strength, and Viereck himself into a bashful, bemused sort of thought-vampire. Still, Viereck was less insouciant than he seemed, launching a $100,000 libel suit against Stringer, who went to the slaughter-bench of Viereck's self-promotion with a knowing sigh: "the very thing that play needs is good advertising, and I suppose this suit will give it to them."[33] If *The Vampire* fattened on such scandals, it remained well fed throughout its run. Another viewer charged that the play had been translated and plagiarized from an (unspecified) overseas source.[34] Eventually even the name of the play came under attack for alleged copyright infringement. A playwright named Maurice Lyons said he had submitted a play of the same name to the Schubert Theater, only to have the manuscript returned to him. Claiming to have copyrighted the title in 1907 (then as now a legal impossibility), he sought a court's restraining order against the theater.[35] Another plaintiff, the Japanese actress Madame Fuji-ko, declared copyright ownership in the names *The Vampire, The Vampire Cat,* and *The Vampire Cat of Nobishuma;* she too insisted she had sent a synopsis of her play (itself an adaptation from a Japanese legend) to the Schubert with no response beyond Viereck's appropriation of the title.[36] The theater dismissed both claims as absurd and in time the various suits, like the play, sank from public view.

Colorful as these complaints may be, their enduring interest lies in their contiguity with the play's central interests, as if *The Vampire* had spawned hostile lawsuits in the brackish waters of its theme. Viewed in a broader context, however, the miasma of infringement claims might seem a product less of a site-specific contagion than of changes in the contemporary legal arena. In the U.S., the years 1905 through 1909 saw the first major overhaul of domestic copyright law since the Act of 1870, and the same newspapers that reviewed *The House of the Vampire* and its stage spin-off made note of concurrent debates about the duration, extent, nature, and administration of copyright protection, particularly in relation to emerging media such as film, recorded music, and piano rolls. Without ever mentioning the word "copyright," Viereck's novel and play had tapped into a vein of contemporary discourse about both the power and the limits of intellectual property law. Skeptics could interpret *The Vampire* as a cautionary tale about the appropriations and erasures licensed by a law that treated ideas and expressions like objects, while supporters could cry out that even copyright failed to protect one against all forms of intellectual theft—the crepuscular kinds against which "there is no redress."

The Vampire and Hauntologies of Copyright

Brad Sherman and Lionel Bently have memorably described literary property as capable of being "stolen through a pane of glass and carried off by the eye without being found on a person."[37] Possessed of a ghostly anessence, susceptible to such dematerialized forms of theft, literary property often attracts a similarly spectral metaphysics, one that can shift the discussion away from standard legal and proprietary terms and toward the paranormal. *The Vampire*'s advocates defended it not on the basis of its ideal property models but for its psychological ground-breaking. During a special matinee for the literati, the poet Edwin Markham rose from a stage box to salute the playwrights' "real achievement in opening a new psychic problem."[38] Soon critical response was swamped by the sexier lexicon of parapsychology—telepathy, mesmerism, hypnotism, clairvoyance, thought-transference—and the questions of intellectual property became subordinated to the shadowy, more sensational realm of the paranormal. The New Haven *Register* provided a whole roster of mind experts to ratify its praise for *The Vampire*, claiming the play was "in keeping with such noted psychologists as Fournier d'Albe, Sir Oliver Lodge, Sir William Crooks, and Professor Hugo Munsterberg of Harvard. It was Fournier d'Albe who recently advanced the theory that the soul is a tangible substance and can even be photographed."[39] The play's celebrants hardly questioned its central premise about the circulation of expression: if the soul had now been captured in silver nitrate, then who would doubt that ideas and their linguistic incarnations could ossify into objects, be stolen like sausages or exchanged like cheese? This turn toward the paranormal, however, was less an abandonment of the play's meditations on literary property than an attempt to think them in terms that seemed better suited to a singularly intangible and disincarnate property form.

Returning to *The House of the Vampire*, I want to consider how the discourse of the paranormal and, in particular, the ghostly, might take us deeper into the novel's symptomatology of intellectual property law, rather than leading us away from it. Such a consideration must revolve around Reginald Clarke, the center of the novel's reflections on undeath, anessence, literary property, and their confluences. Clarke's ambiguous ontological status—is he protagonist or antagonist? living or undead? vampire or mesmerist? light-bearer or creature of darkness? revenant from the remote past or prophet of a future pregnant with possibilities?—may seem a mere inconsistency in Viereck's novel, but it works to enhance the character's spectrality and liminality such that his afterimage outlasts the more forgettable aspects of the text. As its chief figure of ghostly contamination and transgression, Clarke tropes a whole range of hauntological conflations in the novel's thinking about the nature of intellectual creation, circulation, appropriation, and property. In him, the conventionally distinct figures of producer and consumer, author and reader, creator and copier are made to interpenetrate one another almost to the point of merging. Similar gestures of opposition, conflation, and collapse characterize the novel's imaginative treatment of copyright's grounding dichotomies: idea versus expression, originality versus appropriation, authorial rights versus public benefit, protection versus free speech. In performing these gestures, *The House of the Vampire* does more than wishfully enact conflationary gestures on the legal and cultural metaphysics of copyright; instead, it registers the transitional state of contemporary copyright law, exposing the conceptual instabilities and incoherences in both the law and its repertoire of ancillary mythologies.

As we saw in this book's first chapter, Edward Young's productivist Romanticism imagined that authors did their most original work when they minimized their inputs and influences. Even in less extreme formulations than Young's, Romanticism tended to situate literary value in the scene of production rather than in the scene of consumption. Wordsworth's notion that truly original writers created the taste by which they would eventually be enjoyed may have been oriented toward a future generation of reader-consumers, but the real work of their delayed consumption was to validate the scene of production, and in particular the austere choices of genius to forgo present sales in the hope of a higher, more enduring future acclaim. Despite its genuflections to genius, however, *The House of the Vampire* exhibits the marginalist hedonics of William Stanley Jevons rather than the Romantic productivism of Young or Wordsworth. In fact, few novels of the period so vividly tie literary to economic neoclassicism. Insofar as Clarke dominates the novel, the *Vampire* is a portrait of the neoclassical author, which is to say, of the author as insatiable consumer. For consumption is Clarke's primary work, and his literary output depends with almost comic exactitude on his intake. Lest its readers reject Clarke's absorptive mode of authorship as a mere aberration, the *Vampire* tirelessly insists on a transhistorical, transcultural genealogy of vampire-geniuses—an ever-expanding lineage that includes Homer, Confucius, Caesar, Christ, Shakespeare, Goethe, Napoleon, Balzac, Rockefeller. These Major Authors of history and culture, according to Clarke, conquered not through their originality but through absorption, appropriation, and recombination. Hardly sui generis, genius and vitalism are now functions of intellectual feeding. As in the writings of the plagiarism apologists, digestion becomes a figural crux in such a model. Ernest, whom Reginald will eventually crush "as a magnificent carnivorous flower might close its glorious petals upon a fly" (126), blames his mysterious sense of depletion on bad bowels, since "The stomach is the source of all evil." Reginald's reply sparks one of the novel's most suggestive, if bizarre, exchanges:

> "It is also the source of all good. The Greeks made it the seat of the soul. I have always claimed that the most important item in a great poet's biography is an exact reproduction of his menu."
> "True, a man who eats a heavy beefsteak for breakfast in the morning is incapable of writing a sonnet in the afternoon."
> "Yes," Reginald added, "we are what we eat and what our forefathers have eaten before us. I ascribe the staleness of American poetry to the griddle-cakes of our Puritan ancestors. I am sorry we cannot go deeper into the subject at present. But I have an invitation to dinner where I shall study, experimentally, the influence of French sauces on my versification." (128)

The gustatory talk, of course, screens Clarke's more taboo hunger for ideas, forms, and inspirations: for brain food. And in keeping with its marginalist nature, Clarke's absorptive hunger even displays a principle of falling marginal utility: during their revelatory chat, he tells Ethel, "I cared less for you every day, and when I had absorbed all of you that my growth required, you were to me as one dead, as a stranger you were" (123). As Jevons and other marginalist economists had posited, the satisfaction of appetite transforms it by degrees into revulsion, and a new hunger must be created, then sated; the craving to consume resituates and repeats itself literally ad nauseam.

But as much as Reginald Clarke models the neoclassical author-as-consumer, he stands in at the same time for the public, to which neoclassical thought attributed the same insatiability. Though the novel insists repeatedly that "vampire-souls" such as Clarke differ in kind from the "lesser souls" they plunder, its universalization of insatiability works against that typology, putting authors on the same hedonic plane as their readers. Such a gesture also flies in the face of Romantic typologies that set genius apart, though with the different rationale that geniuses were original, visionary, exempt from the public's tendency toward immediate and facile self-gratification. In copyright discourse roughly contemporary with Viereck's novel, the typological distinction between author and public was breaking down too, and along similarly Jevonsian lines. In his *Seven Lectures on the Law and History of Copyright in Books* (1899), Augustine Birrell complained that "the question of copyright has, in these latter days, with so many other things, descended into the marketplace, and joined the wrangle of contending interests and rival greedinesses." With patronage dead and mass literacy increasing, he observed, the rising financial stakes in the literary marketplace were fueling authorial greed:

> Up to a recent date there is abundant evidence to show that authors' profits have, with few exceptions, been small, and this general smallness had an influence upon their position and governed their ideas. But now there exists, and

The Copywrights

every day its swollen ranks are recruited, a great, greedy, ill-informed, tasteless public, chiefly composed of people under middle age, who are anxious to be amused, and, so far as is consistent with amusement, to be instructed by means of books, magazines, newspapers, plays, and pictures. To gain and retain the ear of this public even for a decade, to tickle their fancy, to win their confidence, is (to a prolific writer) to make a fortune, and at no time in the world's history was the spending of a fortune so easy and so agreeable as in the England of today. Half-a-dozen really popular novels (and every novel is not popular that seemeth so), a couple of successful long-running plays, will put their authors in possession of a sum of money more than equalling in amount the slow accumulations of thirty years of a laborious and successful professional life.... Indifference to the money honestly produced by the sale of books has never been a general characteristic of the British author, who for the most part has always taken whatever he can get. Shakespeare and Milton were paid the market-price of their labour.... Carlyle, Dickens, Thackeray, Miss Brontë, George Eliot, Tennyson, and Browning were honest men and women who, though they did not exactly write for money, took as much money as they thought they could get for what they had written.[40]

Birrell's disdain for a "great, greedy, ill-informed, tasteless public" is nothing new; more striking is his ultimate refusal to distinguish between writers who catered to that public and writers who refused to do so. Wordsworth had staked his reputation on that distinction and on his membership in the latter group, but for Birrell all writers are equally susceptible to financial temptation in a market hungry for fortune-making blockbusters. In fact, it is hard to tell which he imagines to be the greedier lot, the reading public or the writers whose primary ambition seems to be the acquisition of a fortune that is, after all, "so easy and so agreeable" to spend in turn-of-the-century England. In Birrell's scenario, literary culture is powered by the anticipation of pleasurable expenditure, and authors are primarily consumers for whom literary production is secondary, a means to the end of spending a literary fortune. Nor does he limit authorial insatiability to the contemporary scene; instead, he discerns it retroactively in all the canonical British writers since Shakespeare. For Birrell, readers and writers—even "great" ones—were not distinct types but identically constituted subjects who differed only in taking separate routes toward the single end of pleasurable consumption.

Like Viereck's novel, Birrell's commentary is symptomatic of the transitional status of Anglo-American copyright during the late nineteenth and early twentieth centuries. The law, as we have seen, was turning from a relatively brief set term to a longer postmortem one; its affinities were shifting away from the public domain toward the copyright holder, away from its origins in a public benefits rationale toward a partial regrounding in author's natural rights; and it was registering the newly dominant paradigms of neoclassical economics. These last helped transform the conceptual bases of copyright: no longer even attempting to be an elegant system of mutual benefit for author, bookseller, and public, copyright acted as referee in a market of "contending interests and rival greedinesses." It negotiated a standoff—one that has, if the Bono Act debates are any indication, both calcified and intensified during the last century—between two sumptuary, desiring, identically insatiable but opposed forces: the authors who wanted to extract as much from previous authors and from the public as possible, and the public who wanted to extract as much pleasure as possible for the least possible expense. In such a standoff, each camp regards itself as righteous but imperiled, its opponent as menacingly, inhumanly voracious. From the public's vantage, authors would survive by dominating in death over the living through postmortem copyrights; from the rightsholder's stance, the public would thrive by being the premature grave of authorial property and memory, absorbing into its domain those things which should be kept separate, limited in their accessibility, sacrosanct in their integrity.

Copyright holds the vampire-author and the vampire-public in an uneasy mutual check. In Viereck's novel, Reginald Clarke embodies this stalemate by standing in at once for maximalist copyright and its violation. On the one hand, he is a proleptic incarnation of Mary Bono's adversary: the Napster generation that sees every text as abandonware, the hungry public that annihilates individual creative achievement. As the reader who would thus consume the writer's vital essence even before that writer's death, he is both the agent of forgetting and the unmarked grave of memory. On the other hand, Clarke is emblematic of the author in strong copyright regimes: the celebrated individual who flourishes at the expense of the very public that is the true but unacknowledged origin of his creations. Clarke's victims, in such a reading, are not the authors robbed by a piratical public, but a public looted by ruthless author-plagiarists. As public, Clarke steals from the Romantic genius; as author, he achieves his status as Romantic genius by stealing from the public. Both readings preserve the notion that works of art possess a "true" origin, which they locate in Clarke's victims and show to be effaced and forgotten through the thought-vampire's appropriations. That both readings are not only plausible but mutually constitutive allegorizes the way in which the neoclassical logic of copyright constructs author and reading public as interchangeably voracious adversaries.

There is a sense in Viereck's novel that even when copyright law is properly obeyed and calibrated, it operates on a zero-sum principle, subjecting not only thought and expression but the utility of authors and readers to a closed economy modeled on the human circulatory system. (The publisher, significantly, drops out of the scheme entirely; Viereck's novel reflects the law's rhetorical foregrounding of authors over their publishers, even though the latter often held the copyright in works.) As Ronald Bettig and other Marxist critics of copyright have pointed out, this zero-sum principle forms another anchor point in neoclassical economic accounts of intellectual property law.[41] It is legible, for example, in Stanley Besen's assertion that intellectual property law should strike an ideal balance between creators and consumers by providing "protection to the point where the value of the additional knowledge created equals the reduction in the value of the usefulness of the knowledge created by the restriction."[42] Although the rhetoric of the balanced equation here may seem to promise an optimal and even just outcome, it would produce such a balance using the blunt quantitative tools of utility-maximization and positivist cost-benefit analyses. Moreover, such accounts cannot easily comprehend deviations from a core assumption of neoclassical economics: that "economic actors pursue their own material well-being as best they can, given the constraints imposed by markets and ultimately by property law."[43] As Bettig notes, other incentives to creation (e.g., donation, persuasion, love of learning, work ethic) get bracketed as "non-market" attributes, as do forms of informational value which exceed the cost and price of the information (e.g., production of wisdom, reduction of conflict, promotion of democracy); and neoclassical economics seldom attempts to internalize even these positive "externalities."[44]

Yet while Viereck's novel reproduces this closed economy in its psychic registers, it plays havoc with it in another sense—by complicating the key opposition between readers and writers, the parties whose utilities the law must optimally balance. In its violent way, the novel makes a point not unlike that of the Victorian centonists and plagiarism apologists: that writing is impossible without anterior acts of reading, that creators are always already copyists in some degree. It also implies, at least, the reverse: that readers are always already authors. Though a more elusive point, it holds true to the extent that the public domain authorizes copyright; that readers make authorship financially remunerative and possess the power of canonizing authors; and that readers and readerly communities not only consume meaning, but are essential to its production and dissemination. The violence of the appropriative acts the *Vampire* texts describe owes, at least in part, to the closed informational economy the texts inherit from copyright, an economy that prescriptively constructs author and public as adversaries in a zero-sum game, transforming into property, and thus into the medium of opposition, information that might more generatively be treated as a freely circulating constituent or catalyst of human welfare. In this respect, *The House of the Vampire* replicates certain conceptual bases of copyright in order to demonstrate (albeit in an extreme and allegorized case) the kinds of violence, commodification, and fruitless opposition those bases can subtend. Though in other ways the novel's conflation of author and public makes both seem indistinguishably self-interested, the same conflation raises the possibility that author and public might be regarded as co-participants in the production of meaning, and thus as co-beneficiaries, rather than adversaries, in the protection or liberation of expression by law.

Another dichotomy equally central to copyright and Viereck's novel is that between ideas and their expression. Though this dichotomy was not explicitly stated in the earliest copyright statutes, it has since become a crucial distinction in determining what the law does and does not protect: copyright protects a work's expression—the particular sequence of signifiers of which it is constituted—and not the facts and ideas expressed by the work. The uses of such a distinction seem clear enough: it divides published work into private and public aspects, securing property rights in the reproduction and sale of specific linguistic embodiments of ideas, while allowing the ideas themselves to be freely appropriated, transmitted, and transformed by readers. Indeed, according to a public benefits rationale for copyright, the law's protection of expression is a means to the end of fructifying public discourse by inciting the introduction, circulation, and recombination of ideas in the public sphere. In practice, however, the idea/expression dyad reproduces the metaphysics and thus the attendant problems of more familiar dualisms such as form versus content, manner versus matter, mind versus body. The idea/expression dichotomy assumes, for instance, that ideas are fundamentally paraphrasable—that they have a discrete, uncompromised existence outside their linguistic incarnations and maintain a transmissibility independent of specific formulations—and that therefore the monopoly in particular embodiments of an idea will not prevent that idea's circulating free of its protected articulations.

This might be true in starker cases of factual reportage or propositional ideas, but more ambiguous examples abound, "literary" language being perhaps foremost among them. In legal metaphysics, characters, situations, and plots tend to be construed as the ideal, and therefore unprotected, content of literary works.[45] But are these attributes of literary texts held to be their truly essential ones, those whose free circulation it is most important to ensure for the sake of public discourse and free speech? Quite to the contrary, the attributes of a text conventionally held to determine its literariness, and thus the bulk of its cultural value, tend to be those *least* dissociable from their expressions, tend to be forms of apprehension as expression, and through expression—in other words, those aspects of a text that *are* protected by copyright. Bereft of their expressive embodiments, a literary text's "ideas" can seem a sad assemblage of commonplaces, stock characters, and shopworn plots, just the sort of *scènes à faire* Shakespeare is praised for having transformed into masterpieces by his genius—*for expression.* (Ironically, Viereck's novel was impugned by critics as stylistically vacuous and therefore insufficiently literary, as possessing "only" an idea—that is, "only" something susceptible of free public appropriation—and not a very credible one at that. The critic who wrote "It is a pity that some such vampire did not steal Mr. Viereck's idea before he spoiled it" was writing legal nonsense: according to the law's categorical stipulations, ideas cannot be stolen, as they are not eligible for private property status under copyright.) By allowing only the most perfunctory aspects of a literary work to remain public property while privatizing what are arguably its most essential attributes, copyright cleaves to the idea/expression dichotomy but reverses the supposed priorities of its public benefits rationale.

Literary texts do not present the only problematic case for the idea/expression dichotomy. Fiona Macmillan Patfield writes that "in some cases the relationship between content and form is so close that protecting the form or expression can result in a monopoly over information or ideas." As an example, Patfield cites copyright protection in data tables and compilations that have been organized in such a way that no other form of presentation is meaningful or possible. In the 1984 case *BBC v. Time Out,* an English court's decision to uphold the plaintiff's copyright in television listings effectively gave it a monopoly on the information those listings contained; the BBC's monopoly on the form of the list became, from the standpoint of its competitors, tantamount to a monopoly on its content, on the "ideas" the listings "expressed."[46] Though little in the way of public discourse may seem to be at stake in a monopoly on television listings, more dramatic failures of the idea/expression dichotomy can privatize information to the point of imperiling the very thing that must determine the limits of copyright: free speech.[47] In still more recent cases, the idea/expression dichotomy has allowed copyright owners to enjoin others from using their intellectual properties—often through sampling and other creative means of appropriation—for purposes of parody and critique, despite fair use provisions defending precisely those purposes. Such cases constitute a defense of private intellectual property rights at the expense of free speech, a phenomenon legal scholars have begun to call private (as opposed to state) censorship. In such cases, the idea/expression dichotomy again licenses a reversal of the priorities of the public benefits rationale that supposedly grounds Anglo-American copyright.

Though the cases to which I have referred postdate Viereck's novel and play, these texts both activate and problematize the idea/expression dichotomy in their brain-burglary premises, as was clear in the critical responses they drew: recall one reviewer's complaint that thoughts cannot be stolen, as they are in *The Vampire,* like streetcar transfers or stilton cheeses. But the status of what gets stolen in the play and novel is less clear than such reviews make it seem. Early in the novel, the sculptor Walkham reports that he has lost his inspiration to work on a statue of Narcissus "as if a breeze had carried it away," only to recognize that lost inspiration in Clarke's new epic of the French Revolution: "So your prose suggested to me, by its rhythmic flow, something which, at first indefinite, crystallised finally into my lost conception of Narcissus" (26–28). Transferred from sculpture to prose, the "motive" or "conception" at issue is clearly an idea rather than its expression. But when Clarke reads aloud the play he has stolen from Ernest, the theft recognized by the latter is no longer a matter of inspiration, or of character and plot and situation, but of expression: "This was more than mere coincidence. This was plagiarism. . . . Ernest listened to the words of his own play coming from the older man's mouth" (59, 62). That Ernest had composed the play in his head but never written it down, however, muddies the idea/expression divide, which presupposes the ethereality of ideas against the materiality of expression: Ernest's ideas had been bodied forth in words, but the words had not yet been incarnated in script or print. Clarke's frequent transgressions of the barrier between the ethereal and the material—his ability to dematerialize and pass through barricaded doors, to rifle through thoughts as if leafing through pages, to steal the unwritten as if it were written—trope the novel's general hauntological contamination of the idea/expression divide that is so ontologically fundamental to copyright. This gesture of contamination does not so much inflict instability on the idea/expression dichotomy as reflect the instability that dichotomy already harbors. And it gives the lie to two of copyright's most cherished assumptions: that ideas, which copyright exempts from private property status, can never be stolen or monopolized; and, conversely, that expression possesses a stable materiality that makes it straightforwardly susceptible to theft and capable of protection. The borderline case the novel and play dramatize, the case of unwritten expression that is nonetheless vulnerable to theft, seems exceptional, even paranormal. But it possesses an ontological instability that may, despite the law's reliance on the clear separation between ideas and expression, characterize copyright's general case.

Critics of Viereck and Woolf's play complained not only that its vampire could steal thoughts, but that, once he did so, his victims no longer possessed them; once Ernest's unwritten expressions have been lifted, not even the ideas those expressions manifested remain to him. I have suggested that this closed intellectual economy participates in a critical parody of the neoclassical economic rationale for copyright as a détente between opposed groups, the creators and the public. But insofar as it celebrates this zero-sum economy, the novel also articulates its withdrawal, and its author's withdrawal, from the liberal-democratic state in whose free market (in goods, services, and ideas) neoclassical economics finds its ideal environment. For such a state, the free flow of information is conceived as vital to the democratic operations of debate, exchange, coalition, and decision, so that citizens are both maximally informed and discursively free to contest the powers of the state. An early figuration of this free flow of information, the Jeffersonian image of the candle flame, posits a collective economy of inexhaustible plenitude, unobstructed access, and limitless reproducibility as a sort of oasis from the legally defended properties and scarcities of the free market:

> That ideas should freely spread from one to another over the globe, for the moral and mutual instruction of man, and improvement of his condition, seems to have been peculiarly and benevolently designed by nature, when she made them, like fire, expansible over all space, without lessening their density at any point, and like the air in which we breathe, move, and have our physical being, incapable of confinement or exclusive appropriation.[48]

Since the donor loses nothing by enkindling the recipient's wick, everyone stands to gain by circulation, by mass-illumination. Viereck's scarcity model, by contrast, allots only a limited amount of candlepower to the dark world. As a rare resource, it must be annexed by a vitalist elite, by those illuminati who "concentrate the dispersed rays of a thousand lesser luminaries in one singing flame that, like a giant torch, lights up humanity's path" (118). Though *The House of the Vampire* partly parodies the commodification of expression and ideas, it more often capitalizes on that commodification in evolving its conservative mythologies: yes, expression and ideas ought to be sprung from the private hoards of the "rank and file," but only to be more freely absorbed by the overmen. It is here that the novel's intellectual property thematics dovetail with, and even centrally articulate, its absorptive theory of history and its proleptically totalitarian affinities. Both novel and play are concerned not with safeguarding a public domain or discourse but with demonstrating economic and legal means by which these might be foreclosed, as well as mythological means by which their foreclosure could be legitimated and even glamorized. Indeed, the totalitarian regime whose advocate Viereck would eventually become relied on practices akin to the closed intellectual economy of his novel and play—practices whereby ideas contrary to those endorsed by the state could be monopolized, stigmatized, impounded, and effectively removed from circulation.

Yet despite their totalitarian tendencies, the *Vampire* texts also exposed the ways in which Anglo-American intellectual property law in the early years of the twentieth century was beginning to fail the liberal-democratic ideal it supposedly served. There are many reasons for this failure, a failure I have described as a gradual reversal of the priorities of the public benefits rationale in favor of stronger intellectual property regimes. James Boyle has described one particularly compelling reason, which has to do with the dual, and often conflicted, roles information plays in the free market and how the grounds of that opposition have shifted during the twentieth century. We might characterize these two roles as infrastructural and commercial. As a structural precondition of the perfect market imagined by neoclassical economics, "perfect information" must be equally and simultaneously accessible to all; but as a commodity within the circuits of the same free market, information tends toward privatization and other limitations on access that increase its value.[49] Unfortunately, neither economic analysis nor legislative policy has developed an adequate means to harmonize these roles, or even to distinguish consistently between cases to which one rather than the other applies. The result, coeval with the flourishing of informational corporate capitalism in developed democratic states, has been a slide toward commodifying information. The fortunes made in the growing information economy have financed massive lobbying power and helped underwrite a legislative and judicial climate of copyright maximalism. Simultaneously, the consolidation of media organs into conglomerates has obstructed perfect information, despite the fact that the acceleration and wider dissemination of communications technology have created the potential for a more efficient, free, and accessible exchange of ideas.

The increasing circumscription of public discourse by corporate private property rights has led a number of legal philosophers and scholars to call for a more flexible regime of intellectual property rights and, indeed, of private property rights in general, not in the name of the free market ideal of perfect information but as embracing a more dialogic conception of democracy *as* public discourse. Building on work by Owen Fiss and Alan Hutchinson, Rosemary Coombe imagines such a regime retiring the reductive laissez-faire conception of free speech as an individual right to be free from state constraint, and instead reconceiving free speech as promoting "the conditions for the maximum participation of all people in the ongoing negotiation of the social good." Where current liberal applications of free speech tend to favor the wealthy and powerful by constructing the public sphere as a free market, the alternate model would attempt to counteract the monopoly on effective free speech by concentrated wealth, even to the extent of curtailing corporate private property rights to promote the free speech of dissenting, subaltern social actors.

> In this scenario, private property rights are not understood either as preexisting or as standing in isolation from or in opposition to public rights to speech. Rather, it is recognized that we must collectively negotiate the appropriate combination of state involvement and abstention necessary to facilitate dialogue in all circumstances. . . . No longer a domain of absolute private rights to exclusive enjoyment in which one is free from government interference, property would have to be recognized as a diverse package of privileges and responsibilities that serve social aspirations for democratic experience.[50]

Coombe describes private intellectual property as renegotiable because it must be subordinate to democratic society's promotion and protection of dissenting discourse; in her scenario, any private intellectual property rights that impede the free speech of the underrepresented should be subject to mitigation. It is just such a flexible, radically democratic conception of intellectual property that the *Vampire* texts, with their scorn of weakness and alterity and their disregard for freedoms of speech and expression, make unimaginable in their ideological registers. But in their hauntologies of the dualisms basic to strong intellectual property rights—idea versus expression, public versus private, reader versus author, consumer versus producer—Viereck's novel and play anticipate a later, more systematic critique that looks to recover the dissenting input of those social actors submerged in a free market society—the "lesser souls" whose annihilation Viereck so chillingly naturalizes.

I have argued that the radically conservative *Vampire* texts are, in effect, haunted by a radical democratic critique not only of totalitarian informational economies but of the strong intellectual property tendencies liberal democracies were beginning to exhibit. Fascinatingly, late-nineteenth-century writers on intellectual property law had begun to see copyright itself as haunted by affinities to political philosophies that differed from that of liberal-democratic capitalism—not by totalitarian philosophies but by radically collectivist ones that now sound uncannily like those of Fiss, Hutchinson, Coombe, and other progressive critics of intellectual property orthodoxy. The English barrister Thomas Scrutton ended his treatise on *The Laws of Copyright* (1883), which he wrote in the aftermath of the 1876–78 Royal Commission, with the following admonitory meditation on copyright's collectivist bases:

> And the whole of this discussion has tended to shew the "communistic" character of the Law of Copyright. Literary and artistic productions are treated as property, but that property is created in, and limited by, the interests of the community. Strictly dealt with, it should be limited until further limitation defeats its own end. The term of protection is to be made long enough to induce the best authors to produce the best classes of works, and in strictness should be no longer. But if, as often happens, it appears unjust to popular opinion that an author should lose the fruits of his labour during his lifetime, or, as in some cases, that his immediate descendants should suffer, an arbitrary term is suggested, without reference to the value of particular works, but ensuring that at least all literary property shall last till no one will be specially grieved by its abolition.
>
> This is of course nothing else than reversion of a man's property to the community on his death, a system which was one of the first steps by which individual property was carved out of the property of the community, and which is one of the suggestions of Communism or Socialism at the present day. I do not point this out as an objection to the system, for I think it the right one, but rather that its true character may be seen. For discussions of the Laws of Literary and Artistic Property have been so fruitful both in arguments from analogy and in arguments which, if analogically applied, would lead to results startling and unwelcome to those who put them forward, that it is important that the principles on which the law rests should be clearly grasped. By all means let it be acknowledged that literary property is a creation of the State, and that the State in creating it may impose conditions and limitations, even though the acknowledgement is used as the basis for a suggestion that no book should obtain copyright unless it has a good index! But let us remember that the position is applicable to all kinds of property. Limit in the interests of the State the duration of property in books, if you like, but recognize that the same arguments may be used to limit the duration of property in land, the power of bequest at death, and the devolution of the property of an intestate. And above all, a caution which is most necessary in arguing the matter, and dealing with questions of so-called "justice," "right," and "utility," let us be careful that we understand what we mean by these terms, for though such an investigation may be tedious to our lofty intellects, perhaps even fatal to our pet arguments, it will certainly result in greater clearness and brevity, and less idle declamation.[51]

Scrutton's conclusion, we should remember, partly refers to Herbert Spencer's complaint during his Commission testimony that Louis Mallet's royalty proposal was "communistic" in "equalising the advantages of wealth and poverty." But Scrutton goes beyond Spencer in observing the collectivist nature not of a proposed royalty scheme but of the provisions for a temporary monopoly already extant in copyright. For Scrutton, copyright foregrounded what is functionally true of all property but often drowned out by the rhetoric of natural rights: that property is a creation of the state rather than an absolute right that antedates and subordinates other rights and interests, and that as a state-created right it is subject to adjustments in the "interests of the community." Though Scrutton likely makes the point in order to quarantine copyright's "communistic character" from other property forms, he raises the possibility that the same character could seep beyond its limits, becoming "applicable to all kinds of property."

The seepage of copyright's communistic attributes to other property forms seems less likely in the present, when those attributes seem more circumscribed than ever. As the Bono Act illustrates, a specter is haunting limited copyright—the specter of perpetual copyright, which, like all ghosts, issues from the past but may also act as harbinger of things to come. This revenant has its origin in the mid-eighteenth century, when a series of British legal cases culminating in *Millar v. Taylor* (1769) found that the common-law right of perpetual literary property overrode the temporary term granted by the Statue of Anne. That decision was itself overturned in 1774, and Augustine Birrell proclaimed in 1899 that "Perpetual copyright is dead. Nobody cares about it any longer."[52] Nonetheless, despite that emphatic coroner's report, perpetual copyright has since found—and continues to find—powerful, persuasive, and well-financed advocates. At the same time, though, we might take a cue from Scrutton and see copyright as engaged in a reciprocal haunting. A specter is haunting perpetual private property—the specter of copyright. As long as it remains temporally bounded, copyright will help constitute a partly, if increasingly trivially, "communistic" oasis within a private property regime that is almost uniformly perpetual, and within a judicial climate where the interests of private property regularly infringe on those of free speech, freedom of expression, and the public domain. It remains to be seen whether that exception will be closed down in compliance with the dominant model, or opened up and applied to other forms of collectivized property. We might add that this is always the case with the spectral: that it remains to be seen.

Postmortem Copyright and the Work of Mourning

Having dealt at some length now with problems of anessence and contamination in certain of copyright's ontological categories, I want to return to the spectral attribute with which this chapter began—undeath—in order to consider how copyright might work to lay rather than to harbor the dead author as revenant. As we have seen elsewhere in this book, copyright law tends to get discussed according to narratives about the safeguarding of the author's rights, estate, and memory; the provision of socioeconomic incentives for the fructification of the public domain; and the balancing of those incentives against consumption, future creation, and freedom of speech and expression. But as the rhetoric of the Bono Act's supporters attests, copyright participates in another narrative, one that has received little explicit critical attention: that of mourning. I have suggested that bounded postmortem copyright terms extend the limited lifespan of the writer by effectively replicating it—by providing, through legal surrogation, a sort of second body that ultimately proves as mortal as the first. But that bounded postmortem term is additionally—even principally—directed at the individuals and the society that survive the deceased, working to delineate a kind of mourning period. During periods of mourning in a great variety of cultures, the bereaved engage in rituals of commemoration, gestures of self-denial, and outward displays—the trappings and the suits of woe—that signify their condition to the community. The deceased is kept more present than absent, whether through the performance of commemorative acts, the deferred interment of the corpse, the refusal to disturb the personal effects of the deceased, or moratoria on levity and self-indulgence that might disrespect or offend the lingering spirits of the dead. But the period of mourning does end; everyday routines are resumed, the widow or widower might pair again, and the full range of generative and progenerative work is again embraced. There is a renewal of investment in the present and its denizens; emphasis returns to the living, and the possessions and resources of the deceased are transferred to their usufruct. This does not mean that the dead are forgotten, or even that, as Freud claimed, the mourners totally and finally withdraw their libidinal investments in the deceased, becoming fully detached from the lost love object; but it does attempt to ensure that the dead do not eclipse or dominate the living.[53]

Now that it explicitly survives the author-owner, copyright plays a role in the work of personal and collective mourning: it establishes a limited period of commemoration during which the dead remain present despite their absence, spectrally exerting their influence through copyright estates that provide, in most cases, for living descendants and beneficiaries. The postmortem term reproduces the logic and the seasons of mourning, too, ultimately encouraging a reinvestment in the living by restricting the more concentrated forms of commemoration and mortification to a limited period. As the duration of postmortem copyright lengthens, however, so does the duration of the mourning period it limns, and eventually the law sponsors an interminable mourning that strives to maintain ties with the lost loved one at the expense of a reinvestment in the living, particularly at the expense of the public domain whose mortification it prolongs and prolongs. Postmortem term extension sets in motion a feedback loop, a seemingly insatiable appetite for further term extension: the longer the term, the worthier the dead become of mourning, such that their increased worthiness can be honored only by further extending the period of mourning. Instead of facilitating a reinvestment in the living, the protracted grieving period licensed by long postmortem copyright hypercathects the lost object; the more inimitable and indomitable the dead appear, the more inconsolable are their survivors, the more inviolable their estates. In this emerging grief-culture of copyright, it is now hard to imagine a shortening of the term that would not be perceived as both an insult to living authors and an assault on the sanctity of the dead—a simultaneous violation of creativity and the sacred precincts of memory, legacy, and mourning.

Against such a predisposition, one might point out that dead authors are no more inevitably desecrated or annihilated when their works join the public domain than the deceased is forgotten once the period of mourning ends; that commemoration simply changes in shape and intensity after grief has done its work; and that a circumscribed mourning period, like the terminable mourning of bounded copyright, can lead not toward forgetting but toward continuing. The maximalist alloy of commemoration and commerce, however, is a strong one. Mary Bono has wished for a copyright term lasting "forever less one day." Such a term may be nonsensical, but its nonsense is that of the hysterically bereaved—and, one should add, of the financially well-endowed: in Bono's remark, the griefwork of a limited copyright has been transfigured into a bid for immortalization through interminable mourning, an inconsolable state that harmonizes with the maximization of revenues from intellectual property holdings extended, like the memory of the dead, toward perpetuity.

This is not entirely to denigrate the work copyright law has come to perform in relation to mourning, however little that work may have occurred to the framers of the first copyright statutes. Much as mourners dedicate the personal space and effects of the deceased as a museum or shrine, the law can preserve the works of dead authors in what appears to be an undisturbed sanctity and integrity, beyond the reaches of a public supposedly eager to seize, dismember, disfigure, and desecrate them. The absence of such a preservation now seems a horrifying prospect. In fact, part of what most disturbs about *The House of the Vampire* is that such mourning seems unimaginable in its world. Having rewritten forcible appropriation, evacuation, and death as "natural" processes in the life span of the World Spirit, Viereck's novel cannot conceive of loss because it only values human subjects as the carriers of what it truly prizes: ideas, expression, and inspiration as world-making energy. Because the vampire-soul drains, preserves, and transmits all that is valuable in its victims, nothing worthy of mourning is lost, and what is sacrificed—the human husk wrung of its ideational nectar—is beneath grief. Yet as Viereck's novel and play strangely comprehend through their ambiguities, the opposite extreme—the interminable mourning of unlimited copyright—is equally objectionable, equally vampiric: having immortalized the dead author through a perpetual intellectual property regime, it cannot comprehend the attendant annihilation of the public domain as a loss worth mourning. Instead, the grief-stricken culture of copyright maximalism wishes annihilation on the public domain, exhibiting the vampire-hunter's remorseless animus against an undead foe that will make earth hellish if it is not consigned to hell. As we have seen in the *Vampire* texts and the hearings for the Sonny Bono Copyright Term Extension Act, the desperate oppositional vocabulary of living versus undead, memory versus annihilation, heaven versus hell, has become the lingua franca of a debate whose stakes, for many of its participants, are nothing less than eschatological.

To the host of specters that haunt copyright, recent harmonizations of the law on both sides of the Atlantic have added yet another revenant: that of copyright resurrected from the grave of the public domain through the legal necromancy of term extension. A 1994 GATT agreement incorporated into the U.S. copyright code revived the expired copyrights in certain foreign works; and though the Bono Act did not restore public domain works to copyright, its 20-year extension did provide an elixir of youth to nearly expired copyrights.[54] More dramatically, fully retroactive term extensions in the European Union and Britain restored the copyright in all works that had fallen into the public domain during the 20 years prior to harmonization.[55] James Joyce, the central figure of the next chapter, was among the authors whose lapsed copyrights were revived and extended. Joyce died in 1941, and his works had entered the public domain in Britain and the European Union on January 1, 1992, in accordance with the 50-year postmortem term then in place. The new legislation returned Joyce's works to copyright until the end of 2011 in Britain and the E.U.[56] Though some of the European legislation granted "reliance party" exemptions on permissions and royalties to parties with "substantial" plans to publish or adapt public domain works that were subsequently returned to copyright, the keyword "substantial" was left to the courts to define in litigation and has provided rightsholding plaintiffs and their lawyers with an entrée.

The James Joyce Estate, whose sole beneficiary is the author's grandson Stephen Joyce, has chosen to take such an approach, either refusing permissions or demanding above-market royalties for adaptations and publications, even those that were in the works before the retroactive term extensions gave the Estate a new lease on life. Since 1995, the Joyce Estate has forbidden the publication of new print and digital editions of Joyce's work, prevented or exorbitantly charged for public readings, translations, and inclusions of excerpts within anthologies, and enjoined the performance of numerous musical adaptations.[57] In 1998 the Estate even sued the sponsors of a nonprofit round-the-world reading of *Ulysses* that had been webcast on Bloomsday of that year.[58] An advocate of copyright harmonization and term extension ("I do not see why I should renounce my rights"), Stephen Joyce has claimed that he acts only out of respect for the dead and concern for the works' integrity: "What is most important for me is to protect the spirit and the letter of my grandfather and to defend his writings and struggles."[59] Thus, in demanding that composer Mario Borciani withdraw his musical adaptation *Molly Bloom: A Musical Dream* from the Edinburgh Fringe Festival in July 2000, the Joyce Estate explained, "you propose to treat the Molly Bloom Monologue as if it were a circus act or a jazz element in a jam session. This was clearly not the intention of the author. Therefore we must refuse you permission."[60]

In other cases, however, the rationale for the Joyce Estate's denials of permission has seemed more capricious. In May 2000, the Estate refused to grant 23-year-old Irish composer David Fennessy permission to use 18 words from *Finnegans Wake* ("As we there are where are we are we there from tomittot to teetootomtotalitarian. Tea tea too oo") in a three-and-a-half-minute choral composition that had been commissioned by Lyric FM for European radio broadcast. Stephen Joyce complained that Fennessy had misspelled the title of his grandfather's work and that the words from the *Wake* were insufficiently distinguishable on the demo recording. But the decisive reason for the Estate's refusal of permission was a matter of taste: Joyce wrote, "To put it politely, mildly my wife and I don't like your music."[61] The sheer number of permissions requests the Joyce Estate receives for republication and quotation, for readings and translations, and for film, musical, and stage adaptations illustrates the extent to which Joyce's work continues to inspire artists, attract fans, precipitate fresh creation and criticism—in other words, the extent to which it is *living* work. The vitality of Joyce's work 60 years after its author's decease would seem the best possible form of commemoration a creative person could desire—something approaching, perhaps, the longed-for "immortality" an enduring cultural legacy is supposed to bestow on a dead author. Such a legacy is primarily cherished, sustained, marketed, consumed, reevaluated, and regenerated by a public in whose affective domain, at least, it has clearly come to reside. One might even argue that Joyce's work has become an important enough part of its readers' heritage—of the preexisting cultural discourse they inherit—that its continued susceptibility to private censorship approaches an infringement on their rights of free speech and freedom of expression. For Stephen Joyce, however, a portion of that public seeks to deform, debase, mishandle, and misappropriate the works and memory of his grandfather. Luckily for him, the windfall of 20-year copyright extension has given the Joyce Estate the legal means by which to continue policing and enjoining these abuses, prolonging the period of mourning during which the dead must be reverenced, their spirits placated by oblation, their bodies preserved from decay, their belongings maintained in dusty but life-like constellations, their intentions divined, deployed, and defended. One might expect the intentions of the dead to be among the first things to slip beyond the mourner's reach, but this is not the case with Stephen Joyce. The grandson often visits his famous grandfather's tomb in the Flüntern cemetery at Zurich, not just to remember James Joyce in his absence but to commune with his ghostly presence: "I speak to him, he answers me."[62]

[5]

James Joyce, Copywright: Modernist Literary Property Metadiscourse

> Really it is not I who am writing this crazy book. It is you, and you, and you, and that man over there, and that girl at the next table.
> — JOYCE to EUGENE JOLAS, speaking about *Finnegans Wake*

> A work belongs to its author by virtue of a natural right, and thus the courts ought to protect an author against the mutilation and publication of his work just as he is protected against the ill use someone might make of his name.
> — JOYCE, "Communication sur le Droit Moral des Écrivains" (1937)

James Joyce's stance on originality, literary crime, and literary property refused any foolish consistency. In discussing and defending his work, Joyce oscillated between embracing collective authorship and wrapping himself in the mystique and privileges of the individual genius. Though he claimed *Finnegans Wake* was being written by all humanity, it must be the first work of imaginative fiction in which an author complains about the copyright status of one of his previous works: the *Wake* reminds us that *Ulysses*, because of its alleged obscenity, was "not protected by copriright in the United Stars of Ourania."[1] In 1937 Joyce took time off from writing the supposedly collectivist *Wake* to appear before the Paris Club of PEN International, where he defended the "Moral Right of Writers" to own, control, and protect the integrity of their works and name. His major works, similarly, swing from plundering the treasury of the archive to fortifying themselves against spoliation: if *Ulysses* borrows voraciously from hundreds of precursor texts, its intertextual debts seem paradoxically central to the text's self-presentation as inimitably singular, unassailably original, even worthy of its sly self-nomination as "Ireland's national epic."[2] This Joycean antinomy—between a collectivist model of intertextuality and a possessive individualist, natural-rights model of authorial property—has attracted a variety of critical responses. For the most part, these have tended toward two kinds of conclusion: one that tells us something about Joyce (that he wanted to have it both ways, that he was a fair-weather critic of the bourgeoisie, that he was a tactically super-subtle critic of the bourgeoisie), the other something about language (that originality is a hallucination of intertextuality, that literary capital is a mosaic of literary debts).[3] Without contesting the validity of either kind of conclusion, this chapter makes a different sort of suggestion: that the tension in Joyce's life and work between collective and individual models of literary property is symptomatic of a particular moment in the history of copyright law and the markets it limned—a moment characterized by copyright's connection to state censorship, and by the law's infiltration into literary texts as an emerging metadiscourse.

Earlier chapters of this book have shown that between 1840 and the beginning of World War I, British and U.S. copyright laws were naturalized as an indispensable feature of the legal and cultural landscape. Having entered the nineteenth century as a medley of contradictory and site-specific statutes, the laws of literary property in the U.K. underwent a series of reforms, arriving in the early twentieth century as a standardized and streamlined code implemented by a bureaucracy of professional clerks.[4] In the U.S., the Constitutional mandate "To promote the progress of science and useful arts, by securing for limited times to authors and inventors the exclusive right to their respective writings and discoveries" had been massively elaborated through statute and precedent.[5] Despite vocal protests, particularly from free trade radicals in Britain, copyright had also extended its temporal and spatial domain, protecting a broader range of compositions and creations for longer terms and, thanks to new international agreements, across a growing number of borders.

To gain protection from this legal apparatus, however, writers had to comply with its procedural requirements by displaying copyright notices on every published copy of the text, submitting deposit copies of their work to a centralized office within a set term from the date of publication, and registering a claim of copyright there. Although the U.S. Copyright Act of 1909 made copyright in a work independent of its deposit and registration, these remained a precondition to bringing a suit for infringement and were therefore essential to securing a legally defensible copyright claim.[6] The same Act also stipulated that in order to secure U.S. copyright, English-language books first published in foreign countries had to be first deposited in their foreign imprints, then reset and printed in the U.S., and finally deposited and registered in their domestic imprints, all within a period of several months from their first publication abroad.⁷ This meant that any books U.S. publishers refused to print—whether for moral reasons or out of commercial concerns that the book would be declared obscene by federal law and "excluded from the mails"—were also prevented from being deposited or registered in time to garner legally defensible copyright protection. Thus, at the time *Ulysses* was published, the newly refined and extensive U.S. copyright code interlocked with obscenity laws to compound the power of state censorship, effectively punishing the writers of transgressive books by denying their work any status as intellectual property, and thus any chance of making legal profits in the U.S. Only writers willing to expurgate the obscene passages from their books—or, better still, to write inoffensively enough from the start that printers and publishers wouldn't balk at bringing out their work—could hope to keep their copyrights and their profits. By making copyright procedurally conditional on literary decency, U.S. intellectual property law exerted not just a protective but a disciplinary influence on literary production and literary culture. In essence, the protective, prohibitive, and policing functions of the copyright/censorship nexus were coordinated operations of a single regime. One would be surprised to find that such a regime had *not* left its imprimatur on the works themselves.

The last dozen years or so have seen a surge of interest among Joyce scholars in how the exigencies of copyright and censorship in the U.S. helped shape *Ulysses'* composition, revision, publication, circulation, reception, and reputation. There is now a growing body of work on the New York Court of Special Sessions decision that halted the book's 1918–21 serialization in the *Little Review* and severely impaired its chances for copyright status in the U.S.; on Samuel Roth's pirated serialization, which took advantage of the book's lack of U.S. copyright, and the ensuing International Protest and legal injunctions Joyce secured against Roth; on the eventual lifting of the obscenity ruling in the U.S. and the consequent reinstatement of the book's American copyright; and on the hopelessly complex status of its U.S. copyright in the present day.⁸ Regarding this last question, Robert Spoo has recently argued that owing to *Ulysses'* U.S. publication history—and particularly to its early legal status as obscene and therefore essentially uncopyrightable—most editions of *Ulysses* are in fact no longer under copyright in the country where Joyce's novel first began to appear in serialized form.⁹ Though I am both persuaded by and sympathetic to Spoo's argument, my primary aim here is not to rehearse further the details of the literary property regime under which *Ulysses* was written and published, but rather to demonstrate that this regime has left its imprint on more than the novel's copyright page—that it is legible in both thematic and structural elements of the text itself.¹⁰ As I indicated above, I read *Ulysses* in this context as an extreme case that supports a more general claim, one already suggested by my readings of Wilde's work and Viereck's *Vampire* texts: that since the inception of copyright law in the early eighteenth century, a growing number of texts (both literary and nonliterary) register a deepening self-awareness about their status as intellectual property.

Treating Joyce's *Ulysses* as a symptomatic case may seem perverse: despite T. S. Eliot's claim that subsequent fictions must adopt its "mythical method," *Ulysses* is most often celebrated for its singularity rather than for its inauguration of a school or perpetuation of a type.[11] Moreover, Joyce's novel was singular in a period when singularity was at an aesthetic premium: interwar literary modernism produced a rich variety of works that insisted loudly on their uniqueness, works whose writers staged a break not only with what they constructed as nineteenth-century convention but with their own earlier work. However, this portrait of "Modernism" as an aesthetic of singularity and discontinuity is one that attends both too credulously and too exclusively to the literary texts themselves, tending to omit consideration of the larger social and institutional matrices in which the works were caught up, in mixed relations of protest, complicity, genuflection, and prostration. A number of critical reevaluations of interwar modernisms have lately taken a more skeptical view of the rhetoric of discontinuity in modernist self-presentation, excavating relations of continuity between "high" modernist texts and concurrent developments in commercial and consumer culture, structures of corporate capitalism, scientific and technological discourse, mass-production, mass-politics, and metropolitan and anti-colonial nationalism.[12] This chapter participates in that general project of recontextualization, illustrating the high degree to which a cardinal text of interwar modernism was enmeshed—both commercially and thematically, and by turns symbiotically and antagonistically—in intellectual property law. In Joyce's *Ulysses* one finds an illustrative tension between the book's singularity and a complex of copyright and obscenity laws designed to apply uniformly to all texts, laws that were becoming more extensive and finely reticulated during the decades in which modernist writers were making their conspicuous gestures of formal rupture.

Ulysses disqualified itself for U.S. copyright because of its supposedly extreme violations of decency, but its fate made legible an alliance between copyright and censorship to which all texts were subject, and to which others would fall prey. Yet Joyce's novel had begun its ruminations on the question of literary property long before it fell afoul of U.S. copyright law. This chapter traces a metadiscourse on literary property in *Ulysses* that gets incubated in early chapters and emerges full-blown in the book's fourteenth episode, "Oxen of the Sun," which Joyce completed in the summer of 1920—after several issues of the *Little Review* containing earlier episodes had been confiscated and burned, but well before the book's U.S. serialization was suppressed for good in early 1921.[13] By dwelling on the intellectual property law regime that would first vilify and only later help protect

James Joyce, Copywright

it, *Ulysses* exhibits advance symptoms of a metadiscursive preoccupation that would not fully manifest itself in the culture until later on, with the rash of postmodern works that have overtly engaged and often directly antagonized copyright law and its new alliances with private censorship. The chapter concludes, then, with the observation that the dominance of intellectual property law is an often overlooked condition of postmodernity, and that the critical response elicited by this dominance across a wide spectrum of postmodern cultural production is anticipated by Joyce's novel.

Although I will have occasion here to refer to a number of Continental copyright doctrines (French, German, Spanish), I will be discussing *Ulysses'* ruminations on literary property primarily as they relate to the procedural narratives and legal metaphysics of Anglo-American copyright law. This may seem an odd move, given that *Ulysses* was uncopyrightable in the U.S. between 1921 and 1934, banned in England, and first fully published in France, a country whose *droit d'auteur* doctrine separates it in several important ways from the limited-monopoly copy-privilege granted by Anglo-American law.[14] Nonetheless, Anglo-American copyright was the system Joyce knew best and under which he had published the majority of his works before *Ulysses*.[15] However much it may have benefited Joyce, Anglo-American copyright more spectacularly bedeviled him, as the *Wake*'s animus against it reveals—an animus that is merely a residue of *Ulysses'* deeper, if less explicit, engagement with monopoly copyright. By publishing the stigmatized *Ulysses* in France, where he was living at the time, Joyce found refuge in a culture whose copyright/censorship complex would countenance his book's publication and protection. But much as its author had left both Dublin and Ireland without leaving them behind, *Ulysses* is marked by its sustained backward gaze toward the literary property regime it could no longer call home.

Copyright Metadiscourse

How, then, might *Ulysses* be understood as conversant with its status as intellectual property? The word "copyright" appears exactly once between the covers of the first edition, but that appearance is in the properly external space of the book's copyright notice: "*Copyright by James Joyce.*" Moreover, intellectual or *intangible* property law seems remote from the occupations and preoccupations of the book's characters: Stephen Dedalus may be an indifferent teacher, an aspiring poet and literary theorist, and a praiser of his own future, but he is no booklegger or Copyright Registry clerk. At several points in *Ulysses*, however, Stephen does participate in exchanges that raise the question of financial recompense for future literary works and by implication the question of whether he would retain, forfeit,

[163]

or sell his property rights in them. On hearing his hydrophobic excuse for bathing only once a month ("All Ireland is washed by the gulfstream"), Haines informs Stephen,

> —I intend to make a collection of your sayings if you will let me. . . .
> —Would I make any money by it? Stephen asked.
>   Haines laughed and, as he took his soft grey hat from the holdfast of the hammock, said:
> —I don't know, I'm sure. (U 1.477–93)

What is principally on display here, of course, is the English Haines's ethnographic condescension in gathering what he takes to be authentically Irish utterances, using the varnish of permission to gloss over appropriations that resonate with the imperialism of his father's business of "selling jalap to Zulus" (U 1.156). But this brief passage not only satirizes the colonizer's quest to appropriate an authentic colonial expression or creation; it also gestures at the intellectual property regime that makes such appropriations legally legitimate and economically attractive. Among the borders copyright patrols is the one that divides oral and written language: although written expression is obviously copyrightable, oral expression is not generally held to be so. Thus the enterprising writer, having transcribed and published the speech of others, possesses intangible property rights in an expression whose original value dwelt in an oral context of expenditure and free circulation. The word "Usurper" that ends the "Telemakhos" chapter suggests not only Mulligan's demand that Stephen give him the key to the Martello tower but Haines's would-be usurpation of Stephen's oral, and therefore legally appropriable, epigrams (U 1.744).

Yet we should also note that, true to its contradictory tendencies, *Ulysses* engages in the very practice it appears to critique here, collecting oral expressions (Joyce was famous for jotting down other people's utterances and interpolating them in his fiction) under the sole copyright of its author. It could hardly fail to do so, since any text that transcribes spoken language annexes that oral discourse as private literary property. To link Joyce and Haines through appropriations across the oral/written interface is not necessarily to accuse Joyce of hypocrisy, nor to elide the difference between transcriptive texts that exploit or exoticize colonial subjects and texts that seek to celebrate, defend, or constructively critique them. It is, however, to observe that copyright law *does* elide such differences, endorsing written appropriation of oral discourse regardless of the transcriber's agenda or the context of appropriation. Like any legal code, copyright can replicate dominant power relations as much in what it permits as in what it prohibits, and this fact helps explain the radical ambivalence of a text that finds itself the beneficiary of appropriative gestures legally indistinct from the ones it deplores. In that word "Usurper," then, *Ulysses* not only charges its villains but also recognizes its own methods as reflected in the cracked lookingglass of the law.

Later on, Haines will miss Stephen's meditation on literature and property in "Scylla and Charybdis" because he has gone off in search of a still more authentically Irish cultural offering, a copy of Douglas Hyde's *Love Songs of Connacht*. Meanwhile, holding court in the National Library, Stephen is put in the uncomfortable position of having to say whether he believes his own psychobiographical theory about Shakespeare. His response triggers one of the chapter's several self-recursive moments, this one specifically constellated around the question of property and profit in writing:

> —You are a delusion, said roundly John Eglinton to Stephen. You have brought us all this way to show us a French triangle. Do you believe your own theory?
> —No, Stephen said promptly.
> —Are you going to write it? Mr Best asked. You ought to make it a dialogue, don't you know, like the Platonic dialogues Wilde wrote.
> John Eclecticon doubly smiled.
> —Well, in that case, he said, I don't see why you should expect payment for it since you don't believe in it yourself. . . . you are the only contributor to *Dana* who asks for pieces of silver. Then I don't know about the next number. Fred Ryan wants space for an article on economics.
> Fraidrine. Two pieces of silver he lent me. Tide you over. Economics.
> —For a guinea, Stephen said, you can publish this interview. (*U* 9.1064–85)

This passage not only raises the general theme of recompense for writing but identifies itself, and by extension the whole of "Scylla and Charybdis," as both potential and manifest intellectual property. Stephen offers to sell the journal *Dana* his rights in the interview, under a sort of "work-for-hire" copyright provision. (It is worth remembering here that the U.S. copyrights in the serialized portions of *Ulysses* were held, not by Joyce, but by the *Little Review*'s founder and co-editor Margaret Anderson.)[16] More importantly, his offer—which, we note, is ignored—is made in the context of the Library episode, itself a Platonic or Wildean dialogue of the kind Richard Best suggests that Stephen write. In depicting what is in multiple ways the scene of its own genesis, the episode calls attention both to its status as the embellished transcript of an actual conversation and to the fact that this written status also garners property rights and even profits for its author. All these operations are starkly juxtaposed to the chapter's topical figure, Shakespeare, who wrote under pre-copyright conditions of patronage, acquiring the bulk of his income by the nonliterary occupations Stephen lists: "a capitalist shareholder, a bill promoter, a tithefarmer . . . a cornjobber and moneylender" (*U* 9.711–12, 9.742–43). Eglinton's remarks about "economics," then, are not incidental but central to this moment of self-reflexivity, in which the text insists on how, in the post-Shakespearean era of statutory copyright, its status as property secures its profitability. At the same time, the references in "Scylla and Charybdis" to Shakespeare's patrons remind us of another antinomy surrounding the text's composition: despite Joyce's insistence on his authorial rights in *Ulysses,* the book was written under a resuscitated Renaissance system of patronage, a system that historically antedated both statutory copyright and the notion of authorial rights Joyce was to invoke in 1927 against Samuel Roth's piracy.[17] The episode's ambivalences about paternity (is it essential or merely a "legal fiction"?) might ask a similar question about literary patronage, while its meditations on the relationship between literature and economics pit the fact of financial incentives against the man-of-genius myth of spontaneous authorship. Among its other mappings, the episode charts *Ulysses'* bizarre itinerary between two historically discrete regimes of authorial inducement: the Scylla of patronage and the Charybdis of copyright.

In the discussion of "Oxen of the Sun" that follows shortly, we will see a particular relationship between language and the body built into the episode's architecture, which pairs a chronological parody of English prose styles with the physical processes of evolution, gestation, and parturition. This pairing may appear to have little enough to do with literary property, until we recall that the postmortem copyright terms widely implemented during the years in which Joyce conceived and wrote *Ulysses* had made literary property's duration depend on the longevity of the authorial body, whose terminal lifespan they thereby foregrounded. The expulsion of baby from womb toward the end of "Oxen," then, also tropes the expulsion of written expression, at the end of its copyright term, from a property form tied to the body of the author. Much as the laboring mother in "Oxen" exerts an influence on the episode's stylistic games despite remaining unseen, the authorial body in postmortem copyright holds sway over the literary estate despite having vanished in death. Before developing this reading of "Oxen" further, however, I want to delve for a moment back into *Finnegans Wake,* which as we have seen contains a less-coded metadiscourse about literary property, one that links copyright's itinerary to another form of expulsion. Among the "Mamafesta" titles in I.iv, we find "Cowpoyride by Twelve Acre Terriss in the Unique Estates of Amessican" (*FW* 105.35–36); and in the "Shem" chapter, shortly after a dog-Latin recipe for excretory ink, we are told "he shall produce nichthemerically from his unheavenly body a no uncertain quantity of obscene matter not protected by copriright in the United Stars of Ourania or bedeed or bedood and bedang and bedung to him" (*FW* 185.29–32).

The fusion in these passages of copyright with cowpies and *kopros* (Greek for "dung"), the linking of the U.S. with urine ("Ourania") and the toilet

("Amessican" likening America to a messy can), constitute, on the face of things, nothing more than Joyce's complaint about the de facto uncopyrightability of *Ulysses* in the U.S. as a result of the 1921 obscenity ruling and his subsequent refusal to expurgate the book for a copyrightable edition. If we read this connection between copyright and bodily excretion back into *Ulysses,* however, we discover a more systematic meditation on literary property than these one-liners in the *Wake* suggest. Enthroned in the jakes at the end of "Calypso," Bloom reads Philip Beaufoy's story "Matcham's Masterstroke" and then wipes himself with it, in a recognition not only that the writing is excremental but that writing and reading are part of a cycle of production and consumption that is homologous with ingestion, digestion, and excretion.[18] In "Aeolus" Myles Crawford notices the corner Stephen has torn off Deasy's letter in order to jot down what turns out to be a poem highly derivative of Douglas Hyde; in asking "Who tore it? Was he short taken?" (*U* 7.521), Crawford insinuates that someone has (justifiably) done with Deasy's letter what Bloom did with his copy of *Titbits*. Later, in the phantasmagoria of "Circe," Crawford answers a telephone, "Hello. *Freeman's Urinal* and *Weekly Arsewipe* here," only moments before Beaufoy appears in person to accuse Bloom of being "A plagiarist. A soapy sneak masquerading as a *littérateur*" (*U* 15.811–23). Here ingestion and excretion are linked not just to reading and writing but more specifically to the production and misappropriation of expression. Back in the "Lestrygonians" episode, Bloom had already conflated ingestion, cognition, and intellectual property when he thought, "never know whose thoughts you're chewing" (*U* 8.717–18). This constellation of phrases and associations demonstrates the extent to which the interior of the body—be it brain or intestine—is a site of anxiety and liminality when it comes to ownership. How much does the mind have to alter a thought for that thought to cease being a foreign body, a purloined property, and become one's own? Or a string of more pungent questions: when you're eating someone else's food, when does it technically become yours? When it becomes feces? And how long do you own your feces? At what point in the process of departing from you do they cease to be yours? In the last decade of the twentieth century, plaintiffs sued for intellectual property rights in their internal organs and genetic information; how long can it be before someone files to retain the rights to a fecal patent?[19]

In a sense, the duration and codification of copyright law attempt to impose an imaginary clarity on the murky, messy, transgressive process by which a culture ingests, digests, expels, composts, and recycles expressions and ideas. In doing so, the law quotes some of the peristaltic dynamics of the body's digestive process. The body transforms the initially private property of food into the public property of sewage, at the same time transporting it from the private spaces of cupboard, kitchen, and mouth to the public domain of the sewer. As if parodying this bodily process, copyright law privatizes intellectual property within a temporary-monopoly form before allowing it to join the public domain. As long as a text remains "in the system" of copyright, its identity as property and thus as commodity is legally guaranteed; when it exits that system at its nether end, it putatively leaves an exchange economy for the gift economy of the public domain—always a fecal gift economy—where it fertilizes future creation, either by enabling the publication of cheap royalty-free editions, or, particularly in an age of pastiche and sampling, by providing freely available source materials for upcoming generations of creators. If the U.S. gets described as a giant jakes in the *Wake*, it is because its obscenity laws had condemned *Ulysses* to enter the public domain there immediately, to become an undigested fecal gift without having first taken a 56-year-long cowpoyride as a legally protected property and commodity. The book's potty-mouth had sent it on a quick trip to the sewer of the U.S. public domain, where its obscene status meant it could not be legally obtained by the public. Doubly stigmatized, *Ulysses* spent a dozen years in the dual hell of a public domain that was not really public, as a property neither profitable to its author nor legally accessible to its readers.

Surely this fact helps to explain Joyce's ambivalence toward the public domain, which because of the copyright/obscenity nexus was not the eventual destination of a protected *Ulysses* but the punitive space of public censure where it bore its stigma of obscenity. As long as it lasted, that stigma could only worsen: the novel's contraband status, coupled with the ongoing demand sustained by its international reputation, put it regularly in the warehouses of bookleggers, the catalogues of pornographers, and the suitcases of smugglers. Such dodgy company, in turn, seemed to ratify the book's obscenity anew. To rescue *Ulysses* from obscenity would mean rescuing it from the contraband public domain where the censor had cast it and restoring it to the state-created, state-approved grace of literary property. And yet as much as Joyce himself deplored its premature consignment to the public domain, *Ulysses* had already imagined the public domain as its inevitable, proper, even longed-for terminus.

"Oxen of the Sun": Coming to Terms

In a letter to his friend Frank Budgen, Joyce joked that for the "Nausicaa" chapter of *Ulysses* he had invented a "specially new fizzing style (Patent No 7728 S.P. E.P. B.P. L.P.)."[20] The word "new" was less a claim to radical stylistic originality than a gesture toward several of the genres parodied by "Nausicaa"—namely, women's magazines and advertisements for women's fashion and beauty aids—which depended heavily on the rhetoric of newness. But it is in "Oxen of the Sun," the episode immediately following "Nausicaa," that the parodic energies of *Ulysses* reach their greatest intensity and variety. And despite the patent-worthy style of "Nausicaa," Joyceans have seen "Oxen" as the episode that has the most to do with intellectual property, though there has been little elaboration on the nature of that connection. Critical hunches about the episode's relation to copyright arise from several of its major attributes: its chronology of English prose parodies, its explicit interest in discourses of biological and textual reproduction, and its implicit interest in property. John Gordon writes, for instance, that in "Oxen," "the growth of English prose is from homogeneity to heterogeneity, paralleling the evolution of literature from its ancient communal form to modern ideas of originality and copyright."[21] Mark Osteen echoes Gordon in observing that only the more recent (i.e., post-Elizabethan) stylists parodied by the episode would have considered themselves "authors—owners—in the modern sense," and adds that "Oxen" might be read as a self-portrait of its author as "a plunderer of copyrights."[22] In both cases, copyright is numbered among the modern conditions of authorship invoked by the episode's chronological form but ends up playing only a minor role in the subsequent analysis. And of the many narratives critics have identified in the compacted strata of "Oxen"—everything from gestation and parturition to faunal and political evolution, nation-birthing, literary stylistic development, spiritual and interplanetary journeys—the legal narrative of copyright has been conspicuously absent.

The absence of a systematic discussion of copyright in critical accounts of "Oxen of the Sun" will not have troubled many readers of a text that is multilayered enough without it, and in whose known layers such weighty subjects are already plainly at issue. In undertaking a discussion of copyright's relevance for "Oxen," then, I want to show that the subject of literary property is not only raised and engaged deeply by the text but that it implicates a number of the episode's better-known discourses, particularly those centered around paternity, parody, and the gendered reproductive metaphysics of form versus content. In 1949, the poet and critic A. M. Klein glossed a sentence in the episode's "Dickens" parody with a tantalizing formulation: "The right of paternity is copyright."[23] The remark partly alludes to moments in "Oxen" that address Stephen Dedalus's status as an author and owner: Stephen lies that he has received money "for a song which he writ" (*U* 14.287) when in fact it is only the remains of his teaching salary; perhaps sensing the lie, his friend Lynch later tells him he will better deserve the laurels he puts on in jest when "something more, and greatly more, than a capful of light odes can call your genius father" (*U* 14.1119). We even learn in the episode's final pages that Stephen's earlier telegram to Mulligan was not original but a "Mummer's wire. Cribbed out of Meredith" (*U* 14.1486). If copyright is the right of paternity, then Stephen, like Hamlet, is too much in the son.

But Klein's somewhat cryptic gloss strikes at much more than these scattered passages, making copyright the ganglion where a number of the episode's central themes—property, writing, reproduction, the nature and privileges of paternity—intersect. In dilating on Klein's gloss here, I will suggest that "Oxen" does indeed identify copyright as a "right of paternity" but problematizes that identification as well. Concerned as it is with individual literary style, the control of biological and textual reproduction, the theft of sacred property, and the terminal chronologies of both gestation and literary tradition, "Oxen" not only implies copyright as a subject but is structurally determined by it in ways that only become clear by attending to the episode's composition. My analysis begins by showing that "Oxen" is interested not in plagiarizing the work of other writers but in testing the boundaries between fair use and infringement. The episode can ultimately be viewed as an encyclopedia of fair dealing and fair use, legal doctrines that were still evolving when *Ulysses* was published: "Oxen" asserts the legitimacy of mining works already in the public domain, of quoting copyrighted texts for purposes of criticism, and of transformative redeployments of copyrighted work under the rubric of parody. I identify three ways in which the episode engages copyright: by simultaneously inviting and deflecting infringement charges in its uses of source texts; by parodically replicating copyright's terminal narrative; and by ending with a chaotic portrait of the public domain in its mock-oral "tailpiece." After illustrating how the literary property metadiscourse in "Oxen" can complicate our understanding of stylistic "paternity," I will suggest that the episode's gendered and binary structure replicates the gendered metaphysics of copyright in order to comment critically upon that metaphysics, destabilizing the "paternity" trope it has seemed at pains to establish. At points along the way, I will argue that the episode performs a temporally limited copyright by insistently pairing its stylistic chronology with the narrative of gestation. Thus, the core narratives of "Oxen" involve the protection of a child and a text, respectively, whose viability postpartum is best served when their protective envelopment is brought to term.

The events of "Oxen of the Sun," so far as they can be discerned, seem straightforward enough: Leopold Bloom pays a call to the National Maternity Hospital on Holles Street to ask after his friend, Mina Purefoy, who has been in labor for three days and is finally about to give birth to a child. A nurse Bloom knows slightly invites him in out of a brewing storm, crosses herself after a lightning flash, and gives him a report on the laboring mother. Bloom then rather reluctantly joins up with a group of younger men—medical students, a local hanger-on named Lenehan, and Stephen Dedalus—carousing in a common room, lewdly joking and quarreling about topics touching on maternity, procreation, and parturition: contraception, abortion, birth chamber fatality, birth defects, fertility farms, the original mother, the Virgin birth, and mother Ireland. Soon the ranks are swelled by Buck Mulligan and his friend Alec Bannon, a young man who is wooing Milly Bloom but does not yet know the "stranger" in the room to be her father. All the while Mina Purefoy labors unseen in an upstairs room; with the exception of a loud thunderclap, her cries are the only sounds to pierce the male hubbub. Despite the nurses' appeals for more respectful behavior, the revelers become drunker and more lecherous, Bloom alone seeming inwardly to dissent from the misogyny of the conversation. When the birth of Mortimer Edward Purefoy is finally announced, the group decamps for Burke's public house for more drinks. There, Bannon discovers that Bloom is Milly's father and slinks away with Mulligan, who will meet Haines at the Westland Row station to catch the tram back to Sandycove and the tower to which the keyless Stephen has already decided he will not return tonight. After closing time the rest disperse, some chasing a fire truck in hopes of witnessing a blaze. Stephen and his friend Lynch head drunkenly toward a brothel in nighttown, with the still-sober Bloom tailing them out of fatherly concern for the young poet who, he has observed with regret, "lived riotously with those wastrels and murdered his goods with whores" (U 14.276).

To summarize the events of "Oxen" is a notoriously dicey business, however, because of the chapter's stylistic contortionism: most of the action in "Oxen" is related and refracted through a running chronology of English prose parodies, starting with a mocked-up alliterative Anglo-Saxon and ending with mimicries of Dickens, Newman, Pater, Ruskin, and Carlyle. The function of this parodic genealogy can appear harmonic, as if it offered a gestation of literary styles as a complement to the biological process of birthgiving that occasions the action, setting, and conversational topics of the chapter. But the relationship between style and event is ultimately more competitive than complementary. By pushing the birth of the Purefoy baby offstage, and by subordinating even its central events to the style in which it relates them, "Oxen" seems to stage the eclipse of matter by manner. At the same time, stylistic manner in "Oxen" borrows its gestation narrative from the very biological process it marginalizes: the episode's stylistic chronology falls into nine sections that total some forty paragraphs, the months and weeks, respectively, of human gestation. The prose parodies are studded, too, with sly references to embryological developments carefully keyed to the sequence and intervals of human intrauterine development. Moreover, the conflict "Oxen" stages between manner and matter is an explicitly gendered one: though Joyce's Gorman-Gilman schema for the chapter names "womb" as its organ, "mothers" as its symbol, and "embryonic development" as its technic, its foreground figures—both the medicals and the English prose writers whose styles describe their revels—are conspicuously male.[24] If maternity, birth, and female sexuality constitute the primary topics of discussion in "Oxen," they seem to do so in order that their status as "matter" may be underscored—matter in the sense of a primary but passive raw material awaiting the transformative and legislative energy of male-dominated "manner," which takes shape variously as literary style, biological and medical discourse, law, theology, politics, and drunken witticism.

I will return later to this apparent manner/matter binarism in the specific context of literary property law, but that context must first be established. After all, a mere summary of the episode's events gives little indication of its concern with property in general, to say nothing of intellectual property. From the perspective of copyright law, this makes some sense: the law usually treats a literary work's basic figures, themes, events, and *scènes à faire* as exempt from private ownership, an exemption mirrored by the absence of intellectual property discourse in these elements of "Oxen." But we can begin to close in on the presence of copyright in the episode by looking at its other elements. For starters, the title of "Oxen of the Sun" evinces some interest in property: it is the only one of *Ulysses'* eighteen chapter titles to contain a possessive.[25] The oxen in question are to be found in the episode's Homeric intertext, a sequence in the *Odyssey* that describes the theft and destruction by humans of divine property and the punishment that ensues. Having been warned by both Circe and Tiresias that the cattle grazing on Thrinakia island belong to the sun-god Helios, Odysseus makes his men swear not to tamper with the herd when they make landfall there. But weeks later, their boats grounded by storms and their shipboard stores exhausted, the men grow desperate; when Odysseus drowses off, they break their vow and kill the cattle, and their feast eventually earns them a Jovian thunderbolt and drowning. Their sins are disobedience, theft, and appetite: lacking Odyssean self-control, they violate the laws of property, hierarchy, and hospitality in order to placate their hunger.

When writing of "Oxen," Joyce emphasized reproductive crimes rather than the breach of property, command, or decorum, claiming that the episode addressed the "crime against fecundity committed by sterilizing the act of coition."[26] Yet it seems clear that the original Homeric crimes are still very much in play in "Oxen of the Sun," even if they have been meaningfully redistributed. In their irreverence and drunkenness, the male medicals reenact the disobedience, desecration, and transgressive appetites of Odysseus's men, even drawing a Homeric thunderclap in protest at their behavior. The breach of property, however, seems not to have been committed by the episode's characters but by its stylistic parodies, which aim to steal the souls of the writers they mimic. This apparent theft of style involves a transgressive consumption of its own, insofar as "Oxen" seems to have consumed its stylistic sources in order to abscond with them. Nor is the episode simply a repository of past sumptuary acts; it is the act of consumption itself, a writing that never strays from reading, insisting that readerly consumption is not just anterior to but practically constitutive of writerly production. By foregrounding stylistic appropriation, "Oxen" makes style the chapter's object of scrutiny, rather than its medium of scrutiny, alchemizing stylistic manner into subject matter. In thus performing a chronological mummery of styles, the episode challenges its reader to identify the "originals" it borrows and often burlesques—to place its textual offspring within their correct stylistic patrilineages, or to name the sacred cows that have been taken off. And though the mimicry of style is not itself a violation of copyright law, the intimation of theft in relation to canonical textual sources at least raises the subject of literary property and its possible violation.

Literary Larceny

Genetic studies of "Oxen" answer its summons to expose its origins, proceeding from the assumption that the episode's meaning inheres partly in the identity of its sources and in the ways those sources have been deployed. These studies also possess a forensic dimension that responds to the episode's seeming incrimination of its author as a literary rustler. They reveal that Joyce did not simply "have a good ear" for stylistic parody but fortified his mimicries by copying. In this respect, the chapter fulfills both definitions of *pastiche:* it is partly an imitation in the broad sense and partly a patchwork consisting of found materials. In preparing to write the episode, Joyce evidently quarried numerous words, phrases, and sentences from primary and secondary sources and copied them into his notesheets for the episode. During composition, he adapted the phrases he used to their new context in "Oxen," suturing the adapted phrases together with original material and other transformed borrowings into the completed text of the chapter. As the words and phrases on the notesheets went into the manuscript or were deemed unusable, they were crossed out. These compositional procedures—reading, excision, copying, alteration, collation, inventory, and cancellation—have led several commentators on "Oxen" to characterize its gestures not just as parody or even pastiche but simply as plagiarism. This verdict tends to be reached both casually and approvingly by critics who celebrate the episode's rejection of conventional models of literary ownership.[27] But as we have seen, plagiarism and copyright infringement are overlapping but nonidentical transgressions: the plagiarist who copies a public domain text may violate moral, professional, and institutional conventions but commits no infringement of copyright. Likewise, a person who reproduces and distributes parts of a copyrighted text without its author's permission may infringe copyright without committing plagiarism, so long as the text's authorship has been properly attributed. The only cases in which plagiarism occurs simultaneously with infringement are those in which a copyrighted text is both substantially reproduced and disseminated without permission *and* misattributed to the copyist. To understand whether "Oxen" is engaging the legal categories of copyright, the extralegal category of plagiarism, or both, we need to take a closer look at its composition and textual constitution.

The best way to approach the nature and extent of Joyce's literary recycling in "Oxen" is to work carefully through a passage from the episode with the help of source studies. The "Malory" paragraph that occurs early

The Copywrights

on in the episode has the advantage of brevity and is one of the more easily recognized of the earlier parodies, chiefly because of the care it appears to take with period vocabulary. Malory's work, which antedated statutory copyright, resided in the public domain when Joyce was writing "Oxen"; in one sense, then, copyright will drop out of the picture as we consider the passage. But in another sense, understanding how Joyce deployed source texts when there was no danger of infringement will give us a clearer idea of whether the game of "Oxen" is really plagiarism, or whether the episode is interested in courting other forms of transgression that may have more to do with copyright, particularly in later parodies whose source texts were still protected by the law. According to Janusko, the "Malory" parody is not only densely embedded with words, phrases, and mannerisms mined from Malory's work but is synoptic in its ambitions, attempting to convey "the essence of *Le Morte d'Arthur*" by sampling material from many of its best-known scenes.

> This meanwhile this good sister stood by the door and begged them at the reverence of Jesu our alther liege Lord to leave their wassailing for there was above one quick with child, a gentle dame, whose time hied fast. Sir Leopold heard on the upfloor cry on high and he wondered what cry that it was whether of child or woman and I marvel, said he, that it be not come or now. Meseems it dureth overlong. And he was ware and saw a franklin that hight Lenehan on that side the table that was older than any of the tother and for that they both were knights virtuous in the one emprise and eke by cause that he was elder he spoke to him full gently. But, said he, or it be long too she will bring forth by God His bounty and have joy of her childing for she hath waited marvellous long. And the franklin that had drunken said, Expecting each moment to be her next. Also he took the cup that stood tofore him for him needed never none asking nor desiring of him to drink and, Now drink, said he, fully delectably, and he quaffed as far as he might to their both's health for he was a passing good man of his lustiness. And sir Leopold that was the goodliest guest that ever sat in scholars' hall and that was the meekest man and the kindest that ever laid husbandly hand under hen and that was the very truest knight of the world one that ever did minion service to lady gentle pledged him courtly in the cup. Woman's woe with wonder pondering. (*U* 14.167–86)

Janusko tells us that the first two words, "This meanwhile," are the opening words of I.26 in Malory, the chapter in which young King Arthur, newly armed with the sword Excalibur and protected by its magic scabbard, is summoned to fight King Rience. A phrase from the Grail quest section of Malory, "Sir Galahad heard in the leaves cry on high," becomes "Sir Leopold heard on the upfloor cry on high." "Quaffed as far as he might" is adapted from Bedivere's throwing Excalibur "as far into the water as he might," and "Meseems it dureth overlong" echoes the wounded Arthur's subsequent remark to Bedivere, "Help me hence, for I dread me I have tarried over long," just before the king is borne away on a ship to Avalon. The longest adaptation in the paragraph—and one of the longest in all of "Oxen," one that seems to test the limits of legitimate borrowing and transformation—is based on Sir Ector's eulogy for the dead Lancelot, at the very end of the saga:

Malory, Le Morte d'Arthur, XXI.13	"Malory" parody in "Oxen"
And thou were the courteoust knight that ever bare shield; and thou were the truest friend to thy lover that ever bestrad hors. And thou were the truest lover of a sinful man that ever loved woman. And thou were the kindest man that ever struck with sword; and thou were the goodliest person that ever cam among press of knights. And thou were the meekest man and the gentlest that ever ate in hall among ladies. And thou were the sternest knight to thy mortal foe that ever put spear in the rest.	And sir Leopold that was the goodliest guest that ever sat in scholars' hall and that was the meekest man and the kindest that ever laid husbandly hand under hen and that was the very truest knight of the world one that ever did minion service to lady gentle pledged him courtly in the cup.

The Malory encomium is unquestionably the primary source text for Joyce's "Malory" parody, furnishing it with numerous rhetorical, syntactical, and lexical elements. The passages share not only the past-tense hyperbole of the eulogist but an additive syntax that exhibits an inventory of virtues within their various social contexts, as well as the words "hall," "ladies," "gentle," and a key cluster of superlative adjectives: "goodliest," "meekest," "kindest," "truest." One might say, after Burton's *Anatomy of Melancholy*, that Joyce has clearly larded his lean book with the fat of others' works.

But is the interlarding of found material in "Oxen" plagiarism? Certainly, Joyce's method of copying words, phrases, and passages out of books onto notesheets, then stitching them into his work after varying degrees of emendation, looks from a distance like the classic "cribbing" scenario. And juxtaposing Joyce's text with its putative source text in parallel columns—the general, if once again rather forensic practice in source studies, which I follow here—activates the suspicious hermeneutic of plagiarism-detection even before one arrives at a verdict. Yet, when read closely, the "Malory" parody, both in the parallel passages and as a whole, appears to achieve its effect less from what it baldly appropriates than from the comic distance it travels from its source material through ironic and occasionally bathetic transformations. The high, laudatory manner that the "Malory" paragraph inherits from its source text rings hilariously false when it stumbles into homeliness—as when it calls Bloom the kindest man "that ever laid husbandly hand under hen"—a phrase that it imports not from Malory but from the "Cyclops" episode, whose narrator remarks of Bloom, "Gob, he'd have a soft hand under a hen" (*U* 12.845). Malory's elegiac manner gets debased to the status of euphemism because of what the reader knows of Bloom: that he is neither a knight nor the latter-day equivalent of one; that he is no "truer" than the rest of us; and that he has just provided a rather less than chivalrous example of his vaunted "minion service to lady gentle" in "Nausicaa."

Other facts that lie beyond the high style's historical horizons are simply ignored: the parody gives no indication, save perhaps by omission, that Lenehan harbors ill will toward Bloom, who he believes has won money in a horse race on which he himself placed a losing bet. Yet while it generally remains within a plausibly historicized discourse and diction, the parody-style occasionally admits a howling anachronism. When Bloom makes a sympathetic remark about Mina Purefoy's long labor, Lenehan's wiseacre response—"Expecting each moment to be her next"—has not been rendered into a fifteenth-century mode; it is an untranslated Lenehanism like those in the *Dubliners* story "Two Gallants," or in the "Wandering Rocks" and "Cyclops" episodes of *Ulysses*. The paragraph's final alliterative fragment, "Woman's woe with wonder pondering," is equally out of place, suggesting an earlier idiom than Malory's, the alliterative Anglo-Saxon ("Before born babe bliss had. Within womb won he worship") from the episode's first pages (*U* 14.60). "Malory" even directly appropriates material from other writers, as if deliberately polluting the evident purity of its stylistic descent: "dureth" comes, according to analysis of Joyce's notesheets, not from Malory but from the fourteenth-century writer Mandeville, so that the phrase "dureth overlong" cross-pollinates the two writers' lexicons.[28] And Janusko identifies further borrowings from Wyclif, Fisher, Holinshed, North, Elyot, More, and Berners in the central paragraph of "Malory" parody.[29] Though Joyce has cribbed amply from Malory, the copied language does not provide a finished surface but an initial matrix that is subsequently transformed through adaptation, through the comic incommensurability of the archaic idiom with the 1904 events it struggles (or refuses) to represent, and through the presence of a host of competing "fathers." Copying is the primary goal neither of the passage nor of the episode, but simply a component in a more complex structure—a structure whose *topic* is copying.

The "Malory" parody in "Oxen" fairly indicates the nature and extent of the episode's textual recycling generally, perhaps even exceeding the average density of Joyce's transformative patchworking. And "transformative" is the crucial word: provided the "Malory" parody is typical of "Oxen" as a whole, we can conclude that Joyce transformed the episode's borrowings sufficiently to exonerate him of plagiarism. By contesting the plagiarism verdict here I do not aim to defend Joyce's writerly morals, but to insist on a more rigorous understanding of how "Oxen" does engage questions of literary property. This engagement is more critically attentive than plagiarism to what it transgresses, recognizing that plagiarism can violate the conventions of literary property without really questioning them. Along these lines, Joyce observed in the *Ulysses* notesheets that burglary constitutes "no attack on 'property.'"[30] In other words, the act of stealing ratifies the same convention of private property it seems to violate, at least to the extent that the theft is motivated by the thief's desire to obtain private property rights in the stolen object. In the context of literary property, such an observation would make plagiarism ancillary to, rather than critical of, the literary property form. Verbatim stealing confirms not only the value of the stolen literary property but the conventional axiom that its value inheres in its inimitableness, with the corollary that altering such a text, through paraphrase, condensation, or dilution, would depreciate it. Valuing the stolen text enough to purloin it, the plagiarist by definition fails to change it so drastically that it cannot be recognized as stolen. Plagiarism is both a depredation of a particular text and a genuflection to the literary property form, as it is simultaneously an aggrandizement and an inculpation of the copying self. By contrast, to achieve credible, recognizable parodies of individual styles without protracted verbatim appropriation—and, more outrageously, despite the use of anachronistic stylistic attributes, topics, and terms—is to flout the assumption that style is as idiosyncratic and as inimitable as a fingerprint, an assumption invoked as a rationale for copyright during its birth-century. Unlike the pirate who disregards the copyrights in particular texts, "Oxen" both mimics and critically engages copyright as a conceptual formation, and it does so, paradoxically, by both threatening and refusing to infringe.

Here we need to remember the reliance of early pro-copyright arguments on the notion of original and singular literary styles, the very notion "Oxen" takes pains both to exhibit and to interrogate. Style, according to these eighteenth-century arguments, was taken to be as unique as the human face and as immune to perfect impersonation. The English barrister Francis Hargrave published this *Argument in Defence of Literary Property* in 1774 as a meditation on *Donald v. Becket,* a case that established, according to Mark Rose, both "the statutory basis of copyright" and "the notion of the author's common-law right" in his or her work:

> The subject of the property is a written composition; and that one written composition may be distinguished from another, is a truth too evident to be much argued upon. Every man has a mode of combining and expressing his ideas peculiar to himself. The same doctrines, the same opinions, never come from two persons, or even from the same person at different times, cloathed wholly in the same language. A strong resemblance of stile, of sentiment, of plan and disposition, will be frequently found; but there is such an infinite variety in the modes of thinking and writing, as well in the extent and connection of ideas, as in the use and arrangement of words, that a literary work *really* original, like the human face, will always have some singularities, some lines, some features to characterize it, and to fix and establish its identity.[31]

As Rose points out, Hargrave's analogy between the original text and the human face "collapse[s] the category of the work into that of the author and his personality"; literary property is thus grounded on a "chain of deferrals"; its capacity to be owned is linked to its originality, which is linked to personality and eventually to the mythology of genius.[32] But even if that chain of deferrals begs a whole array of questions (How are texts and styles to be differentiated? What is meant by "*really* original"? What sort of person writes texts that fail to be "*really* original"?), the rhetorical thrust of the passage, at least, is clear: unique individuals produce unique texts in unique styles and thus should be the unique owners of those texts. Hargrave was helping transform the metaphysical basis of copyright law from a concession "for the Encouragement of Learning" into an individual's intrinsic right.[33]

The pastiche technique of "Oxen" constitutes part of the episode's literary property metadiscourse, challenging the Hargrave school's individualist view of the style/copyright rationale in part by appearing to imitate it. Coupled with its teleological birth-giving metaphor, the episode's imitation of great stylists seems to venerate Hargrave's high individualism; after all, the stylist who is arguably "born" after forty paragraphs of gestation is Carlyle, author of *On Heroes, Hero-Worship, and the Heroic in History* and "The Aristocracy of Talent." But when the property value of style springs from its inimitability—from an author's "mode of combining and expressing his ideas peculiar to himself"—then imitation erodes more than it adores. Still, a "faithful" imitation leaves intact the dyad of original versus copy, and within the Romantic logic of that dyad, imitators debase themselves more than the originals they parrot. One subversive strategy in "Oxen" is not merely to make copies but to make shoddy copies by mixing mannerisms, using words and allusions anachronistically, interbreeding authorial zones. That even imitations with the manifold authorial sources of "Malory" are adequate to suggest a unitary original illustrates the extent to which style's connection to authorial identity is a readerly prejudice rather than a unique writerly property. Neither reverencing nor robbing its originals by the perfect impersonation of plagiarism, the episode's conspicuously botched mimicries treat authorial personality as a borrowable prop rather than an essential property—as glove rather than thumbprint. Moreover, the extravagant citationality of "Oxen" insinuates that the great English and Anglo-Irish prose styles are not only borrowable but themselves borrowed. Again, these borrowings differ importantly from plagiarism: the notion that literary history is nothing more than traceable borrowings—a sequence of IOUs rather than a "chain of deferrals" anchored in genius—rejects Western traditions that view literary property as an estate won by the hermetic, self-made author. Ultimately, the episode critiques stylistic convention by its own extreme examples, so that anything that can be said of "Oxen" can be said of style in general. If "Oxen" is a "virtuoso performance," it insinuates that all style is performance. If its embryological and literary historical conceits seem gimmicky, it is in order that style itself can be unmasked as gimmick—and most importantly, as a gimmick that can be mimicked.

Seen this way, the structure of "Oxen" rounds critically on the genetic studies it seems to demand. If tracking the episode's sources to ground seems to answer its built-in dare, it also defies the deeper strategy of the text, which reconstitutes the dialectic of original and copy in order to destabilize it and the property form it underwrites. "Oxen" contains a double-dare: track the sources if you must, forget them if you can. Source studies of "Oxen" can reveal much about how Joyce shaped and strewed the material he borrowed; but they tend also to presuppose that the value of a copy inheres in the identity of the original and in the copy's fidelity to the original. Critics who note flaws in the chapter's ventriloquisms, then, condemn "Oxen" in the terms of the very poetics it attempts to challenge—a poetics that measures present writing by its repetitions of past masters. J. S. Atherton's contention, for instance, that Joyce executes a "perfect imitation of De Quincey's rhythms" but betrays "an air of perfunctoriness" in imitating Dickens assumes that faithful imitation is the point, and furthermore that it is possible—that a writer's style is both idiosyncratic and unified enough to be mimicked in a single paragraph.[34]

Parody

In other ways, too, source studies of "Oxen" have been necessary routes to the vista that reveals their own potential limitations. Though often grounded in the trope of unequivocal textual paternity, these studies have in fact vastly complicated the episode's paternity, which is not only multiple but heavily mediated by secondary sources. Joyce, it turns out, did not consult just primary texts but a series of anthologies as well, and may actually have begun by mining the anthologies; his own seemingly transgressive acts of excision, collation, and distortion echoed the similar but prior operations of anthologists. In addition to using George Saintsbury's *History of English Prose Rhythm* (1912) and what was then available of the *OED* (letters A through T), Joyce is known to have quarried and interpolated passages from at least three anthologies, all of which were published in England: William Peacock's *English Prose: Mandeville to Ruskin* (1903), A. F. Murison's *Selections from the Best English Authors (Beowulf to the Present Time)* (1907), and Annie Barnett and Lucie Dale's *Anthology of English Prose (1332 to 1740)* (1912). A significant amount of detective work has been done on the nature and extent of Joyce's use of material he found in these anthologies.[35] What has not been noted about these collections, however, is the degree to which their content was determined by considerations of copyright, and the resulting fact that "Oxen of the Sun" inherits aspects of its historical horizon from these considerations. Peacock made the problem explicit in the preface to his anthology: "Difficulties of copyright and considerations of space, added to the invidiousness of making selections from the more recent authors, have prevented the work from being carried much beyond the first half of the nineteenth century."[36] British copyright law in 1903, the year in which Peacock's *English Prose: Mandeville to Ruskin* appeared, protected works for 42 years from publication, or author's life plus 7 years, whichever was longer. With a single exception, all the writers included in Peacock's anthology had been dead at least 7 years by its publication in 1903, and most if not all of their works had entered the public domain. The exception, Ruskin, had died in 1900, and Peacock was able to reprint an extract from Ruskin's 1865 book *Sesame and Lilies* only with the permission of Ruskin's literary executors, whom he thanked in his preface. As Peacock's anthology was to be a part of Oxford's inexpensive "The World's Classics" series, paying royalties for the inclusion of numerous copyrighted works was not commercially feasible, with the result that *English Prose* foreshortens its canon.[37] The action of *Ulysses* is set only one year after the publication of Peacock's anthology, which Joyce appears to have mined more heavily than the other secondary sources. Fittingly, then, "Oxen" adopts the same authorial terminus as Peacock's book: though the episode's literary parodies end anachronistically with a "Carlyle" section that comes *after* parodies of younger writers (Macaulay, Huxley, Dickens, Newman, Pater, and Ruskin), Ruskin is the most recently deceased member of the chapter's pantheon. The so-called paternity of "Oxen" does not stop, then, at its primary or even secondary sources; it includes the conditions of copyright law that helped determine the endpoint of the style-canons the episode inherits from precursor anthologies.

Because the public domain is crucial as both a structuring concept and a textual resource in "Oxen of the Sun," its historical relationship to the concept of private literary property needs to be precisely articulated. Writing of the episode's engagement with the material and legal history of authorship, Osteen argues that "Everything preceding the 'Milton-Taylor-Hooker' passage is public domain, since the 'authors' of these passages would not have conceived of themselves as authors—owners—in the modern sense. The early sections are therefore a kind of public fund or freely circulating collective capital available to all linguistic laborers, rather than a series of signed investments."[38] Osteen's analysis reads the episode as a condensed history of Anglophone writing, as constituting a kind of timeline on which the Statute of Anne in 1710 marks the end of a pre-copyright era during which all works supposedly belonged to the public domain. We should note, however, that exclusive rights to "copy" existed as early as 1557—well before the Statute of Anne—in the form of registration through the Stationers' Company, a booksellers' and printers' guild that held a licensing monopoly. More important, the public domain did not antedate copyright during the early modern period; rather, the public domain was created by copyright law, which established that monopolies in the reproduction of a text were no longer perpetual, as they had been during the monopolistic heyday of the Stationers' Company, but strictly limited.[39] Thus, even works written long before the inception of copyright law can only be said to have "joined" the public domain as a result of the first copyright statute, which guaranteed the temporariness of monopolies in their reproduction. Insofar as it foregrounds the public domain status of some of its source texts, then, "Oxen" necessarily invokes the legacy and categories of copyright law and looks back through those categories at the pre-copyright past, rather than nostalgically evoking a collectivist era before copyright. Moreover, from a legal standpoint, much later source texts than those by Milton, Taylor, and Hooker had duly entered the public domain by the time *Ulysses* was published in 1922. Despite term extensions in Europe and the U.S. during the first decades of the twentieth century, only five of the writers parodied in "Oxen of the Sun" (Carlyle, Newman, Pater, Huxley, and Ruskin) remained under copyright by 1922; the rest had joined the public domain. The greater part of "Oxen," in fact, from its opening paragraphs all the way through the "Dickens" parody, mimicked the styles of public domain writers. In mining phrases from those authors' work in its chronology of parodies, the episode not only gestures toward the wealth of texts residing in the public domain, but demonstrates the sorts of creative reuses and transformations for which those public domain texts were freely available.

The bulk of "Oxen," by this reading, is a celebration of the public domain and its capacity to supply raw material toward fresh creation. Charles Dickens died in 1870, and his works had just entered the public domain in 1921 according to the 1911 British Copyright Act. As if in recognition of this new availability of Dickens's work, Joyce's "Dickens" parody appropriates near-verbatim material from chapter 53 of *David Copperfield* with unusual boldness: "a weary weary while," "with the old shake of her pretty head," "now she was very very happy," "it may never be again," even the Dickensian giveaway "Doady."[40] By adapting Dora's death chapter to a nativity scene, too, the passage tips its hat thematically to the birth of a literary corpus into the public domain with the termination of copyright, the author's second death. The remaining parodies, whose source texts had not joined the public domain in 1922, retreat from the boldness of "Dickens," taking smaller and less easily identified fragments from more diffuse sources and transforming them to a greater extent. Yet enough remains of the source expressions even in these final parodies to tread near minor infringement.[41] In addition, the majority of these appropriations have been quarried from anthologies rather than from primary texts (e.g., the "Carlyle" parody is taken primarily from Peacock and Murison), raising the possibility that "Oxen" infringes the anthologists' copyright in their selections of primary texts, even if it does not infringe the primary texts themselves. I want to suggest, however, that having raised such suspicions, "Oxen" mobilizes a defense against them by connecting parody—specifically, parody that appropriates material from its objects—to the public domain. In doing so, "Oxen" anticipates the special legal dispensation parody now enjoys under some copyright regimes, justifying its own appropriative parodies through a fair use defense no plaintiff in the early twentieth century had yet thought, or needed, to make. To put it another way, the emerging fair use defense for parody simply legitimates a longstanding practice within cultural production—the parodic practice of transformative redeployment.

To understand the episode's farsighted operations, we need to place *Ulysses* within the chronology of evolving fair dealing and fair use doctrines, a chronology that also tracks the gradual acceptance of parody as a form deserving a special copyright easement. Though Serjeant Talfourd had included a fair dealing clause in his original 1837 copyright bill, none was adopted in British law until the 1911 Act, which permitted "any fair dealing with the work for the purposes of private study, research, criticism, review or newspaper summary."[42] Fair use, the U.S. counterpart to fair dealing, was not codified until the 1976 Copyright Act, which allowed for "the fair use of a copyrighted work ... for purposes such as criticism, comment, news reporting, teaching (including multiple copies for classroom use), scholarship, or research."[43] French law now specifically exempts "parodies, caricatures, and pastiches" from copyright infringement, but neither the British nor the U.S. statutes specifically mention parody.[44] In fact, U.S. legal precedent seemed hardened against a fair use defense for parodies: in the 1950s, a split Supreme Court decision let stand a lower court ruling that Jack Benny's television parody of the movie *Gaslight* had infringed the original, and that Benny's fair use defense of his parody was illegitimate. Nonetheless, a recent U.S. decision has gone against that precedent, clearly legitimating parody, albeit within certain parameters, as a fair use of source material.[45] In *Campbell v. Acuff-Rose Music, Inc.* (1994), the Supreme Court exonerated the rap group 2 Live Crew's version of the Orbison/Dees song "Oh, Pretty Woman" of infringement charges, on the grounds that the group had not simply covered the original but parodied it, and therefore made a transformative use of the original.[46] The decision, in effect, established parody as a potential form of criticism or comment—forms of discourse the First Amendment cherishes—and therefore as a possible fair use of protected works, even when the parody is also a commercial venture.

There is a pleasant irony about the fair use defense for parodies that helps, in retrospect, to explain the transformational borrowings of "Oxen": whereas the reverent act of perfectly copying and disseminating a text can infringe its copyright, the irreverence of the parodist merits not only a fair use easement but copyright status of its own: 2 Live Crew's parodic "Pretty Woman" is a copyrighted work in its own right, as *Ulysses* is (arguably) also. The intent to ironize, ridicule, or even derogate aspects of an intellectual property, so long as that intent is carried out with the additional motives of criticism or comment, garners the parodist a degree of access to the object of parody that is denied the pious copyist. Of course, none of this goes against the commercial logic of copyright law: instead of cannibalizing the market for what it ridicules, a parody frequently increases the demand for its object, while fulfilling the requirement of originality through its often irreverent transformations and recontextualizations of that object. This is simply to say that parody may transform its object without breaching copyright, and that Anglo-American copyright law, at least, only demands reverence for its own permissions and interdictions, not generally respectful attitudes toward protected texts. "Oxen" goes at least this far. Through its discourses on property and theft, licit and illicit reproduction, the episode casts suspicion on its own modes of textual reproduction only to deploy what amounts to a fair use defense of its parodies *avant la lettre*, anticipating a time when such a defense would be necessary against attempts to curtail free speech and freedom of expression through copyright. It mounts this defense by borrowing just enough material, and transforming its borrowings just sufficiently, to assert the legitimacy and originality of imitative parody, along with the necessity that such parody not be shut down by intellectual property law. In effect, "Oxen" assumes that its parodic recontextualization of copyrighted material—its replication of that material with the sort of ironic difference we saw in the "Malory" and "Dickens" parodies—bestows an anticipatory public domain status on that material in the name of free speech, liberating it for creative and critical reuse.

In itself, this is no more than an attempt to carve out a legitimate space for parody using the immanent logic of copyright. But "Oxen" differs from most parodies in that it travesties not only its source texts but copyright itself. The episode achieves this parody of literary property laws by reproducing and transforming the terminal narrative of copyright in its own formal trajectory. "Oxen" ends as copyrights end: in the intellectual-property-less condition of orality. If the bulk of the episode's parodies embody the fresh creation that can result from a rich public domain and its anticipatory easements of copyright through fair use provisions, the episode ends with a still-more-suggestive model of public domain discourse. The last of the parodies, evidently of Carlyle's prose, describes the departure of the revelers from the lying-in hospital for Burke's pub. By the episode's embryological framework, gestation has ended; and the baby is finally born, even as the drunken company burst from their enclosure into the storm-rinsed Dublin night. Embryological development being a narrative of differentiation and individuation, one might expect the episode to conclude with an example of literary style at its most "developed," at its highest degree of complexity and eccentricity. Yet, strangely, the ten paragraphs that follow the "Carlyle" parody and bring "Oxen" to a close are a textual space not of specialized and hierarchical systems but of conflation and leveling, a jumble of utterances only partially traceable to their speakers and conversational contexts and certainly not affiliated with an individual writer's style. Instead of a biological rage to order, these paragraphs exemplify an informational rage to ordure, an entropic tendency toward a fecund but chaotic heterogeneity:

> All off for a buster, armstrong, hollering down the street. Bonafides. Where you slep las nigh? Timothy of the battered naggin. Like ole Billyo. Any brollies or gumboots in the fambly? Where the Henry Nevil's sawbones and ole clo? Sorra one o' me knows. Hurrah there, Dix! Forward to the ribbon counter. Where's Punch? All serene. Jay, look at the drunken minister coming out of the maternity hospital. *Benedicat vos omnipotens Deus, Pater et Filius.* A make, mister. The Denzille lane boys. Hell, blast ye! Scoot. Righto, Isaacs, shove em out of the bleeding limelight. Yous join uz, dear sir? No hentrusion in life. Lou heap good man. Allee samee dis bunch. En avant, mes enfants! Fire away number one on the gun. Burke's! Burke's! (*U* 14.1440–50)

In letters, Joyce described the parodies in "Oxen" as "enclosed between the headpiece and tailpiece of opposite chaos," and the chaotic "tailpiece" as "a frightful jumble of Pidgin English, nigger English, Cockney, Irish, Bowery slang and broken doggerel."[47] To Joyce's list, Atherton adds "French, Scottish, Yiddish, German, sixteenth-century English canting, pugilists' and motor-racing slang, together with scraps of Latin, Gaelic, mock Welsh-English . . . and 'Parlyaree,' the strolling players' jargon mainly derived from Italian."[48] Commentators on "Oxen" tend to agree that its counterintuitive climax abandons the domain of writerly style altogether, swerving from written to oral language. Hugh Kenner identifies orality with the newborn: "Partly it is the speech of 1904 that is born, emerging into the air after a long travail. . . . Spoken by a dozen voices simultaneously and picked up as if by an unseeing microphone, it is inelegant and nearly unintelligible."[49] Instead of a twentieth-century Ruskin or Carlyle, it is present-day talk—or, more accurately, a written performance of present-day talk—that gestates in what the episode constructs as the "womb" of written antiquity. Others have characterized the episode's chaotically oral conclusion as a discursive equivalent not to the baby but to the afterbirth: Richard Ellmann writes of "the placental outpouring at the end (it is the afterbirth as well as an ejaculative spray) which is an *aggiornamento* of style into contemporary slang."[50] Such a reading makes slang placental by identifying it as the dregs of what once nourished literary style; having begun as the essential supportive matrix of written language, orality ends as its expendable remainder.

Whatever sense we might make of Joyce's refusal to nominate a successor to Carlyle or Ruskin, the chapter's apparent swerve from written to oral bears crucially on the episode's meditations on literary property. As I remarked earlier of Wilde's conversation and Stephen Dedalus's epigrams, oral expression is not generally protected by intellectual property law. So the propertyless condition of orality which ends "Oxen" is not only the source from which a writer may annex literary property but also the eventual ter-

James Joyce, Copywright

minus of all copyrighted texts: the public domain to which oral utterance almost always belongs. In addition to its other developmental narratives, the chapter restages the way published language rides out the time on its copyright clock, to be delivered finally into the legal condition of orality. What gestates and is born, then, is not just oral slang or (as others have argued) Irish excess or *écriture féminine* or the modernist shoring of fragments against ruins; it is also the text as a public property. That the oral tailpiece is filled with quotations from written texts (everything from Swinburne to an evangelist's poster) actually strengthens its portrayal of the public domain, which consists not only of ideas, facts, and talk but of formerly protected texts. We might observe that these ten paragraphs of garbled, intoxicated speech and onomatopoeic burping and vomiting may not be an especially flattering portrait of the public domain. Nonetheless, this portrait enjoys pride of place in the episode, holding the Last End of literary property before the eyes of the authors whose shades the parodies summoned. That this portrait of orality is, after all, a written one constitutes a Joycean *ricorso:* from the ashes of dead copyrights arise new ones, the literary property that is *Ulysses* rising from a public domain enriched by a literary corpus the novel salutes and parodies, salutes through parody. By thus parodying the narrative of copyright, "Oxen" reverses the hierarchy between individual style and the public domain. In copyright's dominant cultural logic, style vitally safeguards the literary property of individual writers from the hell of public domain status. As "Oxen" demonstrates, however, we might rethink style not as a rampart that protects private property from public trespass but as part of the legal container that transports expression to its final destination—that is, as a delivery system of and to the public domain.

Binary

In noting the ways in which "Oxen" reverses the domination of substance by style, public domain by private property, we return to the question of the episode's binary structure. This clearly gendered structure—male manner versus female matter—invokes a complex of related dichotomies at the heart of Western metaphysics: mind/body, spiritual/physical, form/content, style/substance. The episode seems also to reproduce the dominant hierarchization of these pairs by privileging the abstract "male" elements over the concrete "female" ones: the idle male medicals over the laboring mother and nurses, the lounge over the birth chamber, style over event, and literary production over biological reproduction. By replicating these hierarchical binaries in its double context of physical and textual reproduction, "Oxen" acts out a trope central to patriarchal idealism, one that characterizes legitimate reproduction as a faithful "copying" or "printing" of the father's form by the maternal body. Some of the best-known formulations of this trope occur in the work of Shakespeare, who functions in *Ulysses* as a sort of patron saint of fathers, albeit often a parodic one.[51] *The Winter's Tale,* in its anxieties about adultery and illegitimacy, is rife with filial "copies" and "prints" of fathers: Paulina discerns in the infant Perdita, "Although the print be little, the whole matter / And copy of the father" (II.iii.948–99). Later a contrite Leontes says of Florizel, "Your mother was most true to wedlock, prince; / For she did print your royal father off, / Conceiving you" (V.i.123–25). Since a woman's reproductive fidelity to her husband is troped as "true" copying or printing, infidelity gets figured as counterfeiting. In *Cymbeline,* a key text for the "Scylla and Charybdis" episode of *Ulysses,* Posthumus bemoans "the woman's part" in contaminating his legitimacy:

> We are all bastards;
> And that most venerable man which I
> Did call my father was I know not where
> When I was stamp'd; some coiner with his tools
> Made me a counterfeit . . . Could I find out
> The woman's part in me! For there's no motion
> That tends to vice in man but I affirm
> It is the woman's part (II.v.2–22).[52]

Posthumus here anticipates Stephen Dedalus's statement that "Paternity may be a legal fiction" (*U* 9.844): by failing to be "true to wedlock," his mother allows an itinerant "coiner" to counterfeit her husband's legitimate stamp. Though Posthumus begins by blaming the man who "made me a counterfeit," he ends by blaming "the woman's part"—both the maternal role in reproduction and the part of himself that descends from his mother—as the source of his imagined illegitimacy. The "true copy" trope implies that all fault emanates from the woman's part in reproduction, the point at which the perfect transmission of her husband's form is incarnated with variable fidelity. By extension, a form of reproduction that could eliminate the faulty "woman's part," by means of either a faultless virgin mother (Christ born of Mary) or male parthenogenesis (Athena sprung motherless from the forehead of Zeus), would ensure a perfect printing off of heirs from the paternal original.[53] "Oxen" enacts the latter fantasy through its all-male chronology of prose parodies: male writers are begotten by, and in turn beget, only male writers. By pointedly excluding women writers from the episode's canon—even those few, such as Maria Edgeworth and Jane Austen, who appear in the anthologies he consulted—Joyce eliminated the "woman's part" altogether from the literary historical register of "Oxen," confining it to other aspects of the episode. Despite its designation as the "womb" or "uterus" or "matrix" of the novel, "Oxen" seems to incubate pure patrilineal form, unmixed with what Hamlet calls the "baser matter" of maternal influence.

Richard Ellmann writes of "Oxen of the Sun" that its "pastiches constitute a remarkable tribute to the literary tradition in English as the matrix out of which *Ulysses,* or any other work in this tongue, has to issue."⁵⁴ In celebrating the notion that Anglophone literary tradition acts as a "matrix" for new works in English, Ellmann is more comfortable than many writers on "Oxen" have been with its apparent annexation of female reproductive powers and figures to male literary production. Very much to the point, however, is his emphasis on the term "matrix" (see *U* 14.969). The term is Latin for "womb," with the earlier meanings "pregnant animal" and "female animal," and belongs to an etymological complex central to "Oxen": the cognates "maternal," "material," "matter," and "matrix," all of which descend from the Latin *mater,* "mother." Nonetheless, what "Oxen" seems to stage is not the neutral "issuing" of baby from womb, or of a new literary work from the "matrix" of the English tradition, but the appropriation of the womb's issue by male-dominated discourse. In Exodus 34, which I take to be a foundational text for "Oxen," the "one jealous God" of the Israelites declares: "All that openeth the matrix is mine; and every firstling among thy cattle, whether ox or sheep, that is male. But the firstling of an ass thou shalt redeem with a lamb: and if thou redeem him not, then shalt thou break his neck. All the firstborn of thy sons thou shalt redeem." The maternal matrix may be the indispensable source of new life, but in a patriarchal culture it has no rights of property in its issue. Male issue is immediately subsumed to transactions between men and a male deity: men sacrifice firstborn male animals, fathers redeem their firstborn sons by sacrificing male animals in their place. Female issue is also appropriated, principally to transactions among men, and eventually repeats the generative acts of the matrix. The divine claim to own "all that openeth the matrix" occurs, as "Oxen" does, in the context of exclusively male writing: Moses, faithful copyist of God's mandates, has returned to Mount Sinai to receive the commandments a second time, having destroyed the first set in his rage at seeing the Israelites worshiping a golden calf—"whoring after" pagan idols, as Yahweh puts it, in an expression that links the proliferation of false gods to female sexual promiscuity, both violations of commandments issued by "the one jealous God." As before, Moses has hewn the stone tablets on which he will write the commandments at God's dictation: law is the divine imprimatur upon raw materials prepared by human hands. And yet Exodus 34 significantly describes the *second* scene of the commandments' transmission, and, by foregrounding the annihilation of the original tablets, insists on the belatedness of writing, on the law's status as copy even though it issues both times from God. "Oxen" inherits from the passage a narrative of male succession rooted in fidelity to a unique figure (the "one jealous God" who authors the law, and the author as origin of an inimitable style) but made anxious by a reliance both on potentially error-prone copying and on the generative powers of a "matrix" it can neither control nor do without.

These tensions in "Oxen of the Sun" between matter and manner, between a generative matrix and the patrilineal appropriations of its issue, contribute to the episode's meditations on Anglo-American copyright law, which, as we saw in the previous chapter, harbors its own versions of these binarisms: the idea/expression dichotomy that determines which attributes of a work it does and does not protect. Aspects of a work that qualify as "expression" the law protects by granting the holder a temporary monopoly in their reproduction, distribution, adaptation, public performance, and public display. Aspects falling into the category of "ideas" are not protected by copyright law and belong to the public domain where they are available to all. So far this sounds as if the idea/expression dichotomy addressed only the ontological status and destination of works, but it addresses their origin as well. The law recognizes that at least some components of a work will be drawn from the common stock rather than invented ex nihilo. When only the ideas that comprise a work are drawn from elsewhere, the new ("original") expressions in which those ideas are encoded receive copyright protection. But extant expressions copied into a new work do not become the intellectual property of the copyist; they constitute a hole, as it were, in the fabric of the new work's copyright. Passages that *Ulysses* directly quotes from other works, whether those sources are copyrighted or public domain works, are not copyrighted anew in their Joycean context. Thus, I can reproduce, disseminate, sell, and display pages of verbatim quotations "from" *Ulysses,* so long as they are themselves quotations from antecedent texts— for example, Stephen's suggestive telegram, which is taken bodily from Meredith's *The Ordeal of Richard Feverel,* and seems obliquely to comment on its own complex literary property status: "The sentimentalist is he who would enjoy without incurring the immense debtorship for a thing done." I can copy reams of such quotations without infringing *Ulysses'* copyright, however much I may infringe that of its source texts. Copyright's idea/expression dichotomy forms nothing less than the boundary between private property and public domain, or between one person's private literary property and another's.

"Oxen" raises the stakes of copyright's seemingly genderless categories by restoring them to the explicitly gendered metaphysics out of which they spring. But it does more: having reasserted the gendering of the idea/expression dichotomy, it proceeds to radically destabilize it. The text makes this process all the more dramatic by at first seeming to provide optimal conditions in which ideas might be distinguished from their expressions. After all, the episode's central joke, and its central violence, is the incompatibility of its matter with its manner—the conspicuous gulf, for instance, between a chivalrous style and the bawdy, modern conversations it is made to record. Whatever laughter or discomfort this incompatibility elicits from the reader, it at least seems to guarantee a legible distinction between form and content; how else could the reader know to laugh or writhe? However, despite its seeming insistence on the distinction between form and content, the structure of "Oxen" thinks their utter conflation. If ideas are meaningfully discrete from their expressions, then the ideational contents of "Oxen"—its "actual" events, facts, utterances, topics, arguments—should be recuperable from what copyright discourse calls their expressive "fixation." Having laughed or shuddered, the reader should then be able to reverse the stylistic operations of filtration, elaboration, transcoding, circumlocution, and euphemism, retrieving the naked content that has been so distortively incarnated in the episode's language. But no one who has wrestled at length with "Oxen" would affirm that this is possible with even a provisional certainty. Much as one may make informed guesses as to what "actually" happens or is said, language that seems simply to refract the episode's events and utterances turns out to be irreducibly constitutive of both. And while the often grotesque incommensurateness of style with substance certainly implies the presence of a substance, it does so only by a kind of negative space: our laughter or discomfort arises not from the spectacle of stylistic bias or blindness acting on ontologically prior facts and ideas, but from our sense that these disembodied ideas and facts are at best rough deductions from formal premises, at worst the belated hallucinations of expression. By performing this collapse, "Oxen" enacts a deep skepticism about copyright's notion that ideas and facts are anterior to their particular expressions, and thus separable, yielding to paraphrase, transmissible without either disfigurement or infringement.

This skepticism gets replicated at the level of the chapter's patchworked composition, which further demonstrates the porosity of the membrane copyright puts between form and content. Here again, one might expect the idea/expression dichotomy to be, if anything, clearly reflected in the episode's evidently binary treatment of manner and matter, private and public property: "manner" would comprise those elements susceptible of private ownership, and "matter" those that circulate publicly; the latter would receive the imprint of the former. Yet, as we have amply seen, manner is the matter and style the primary substance in "Oxen": having invoked the conventional grounding of private literary property in style through its parody-chronology, the episode works to habilitate the recirculation of style as public property by exhibiting the many ways *expression* can belong to the public domain, whether by antedating copyright, by reaching the end of its term, or through the circuits of fair use, critique, and parody. Where the patriarchal idealism I discussed above affiliates substance with the passive, unpropertied "woman's part" in the creation and reproduction of meaning, "Oxen" insists on the material status of the male literary styles it parodically replicates, both by detaching them from the literary property form and by making them bear the imprimatur of the physical process of gestation that structures the episode. And by taking not only the ideas but the expressive aspects of precursor texts as its "matrix" or "source material," the episode articulates a wish, at least, that public domain status be the general rather than the exceptional case not only for ideas but for expression as well. This wish is repeated, finally, in the episode's terminal swerve to a simulated orality, which stages the birth of private literary expression not from but into the matrix of the public domain. By both beginning and ending with a portrait of the public domain, "Oxen" rejects the notion that "all that openeth the matrix" could belong, in any final sense, to patriarchal idealism or to the literary property form it underwrites. If the episode does not entirely separate the public domain from its gendering as female, its figural appropriation of the womb, or its stereotyping as a feminized gift economy, it at least upsets the domination of this complex by its masculinized counterpart, the pattern that shapes and controls the matter.

In this sense, "Oxen" may be a more faithful copy of copyright than I have been suggesting. Anglo-American copyright, at least in early statutory and constitutional formulations, also reverses the dominance of matter by pattern. As an "Act for the Encouragement for Learning" (Britain) and a mandate "To promote the progress of science and useful arts" (U.S.), the inaugural copyright statutes valorized ideas over expression as the vital stuff of public discourse, so vital in fact as to justify the creation of a temporary monopoly in expression in order to promote the generation and circulation of ideas. Though expression may seem to be elevated as the subject of private property, its privatization is a means to a dual end: the generation of ideas and the generation of expression that eventually attains the public property status of ideas when the temporary monopoly in its reproduction ends. In the U.S., a "merger doctrine" in case law even holds that when ideas cannot be extricated from their expression, then the private property in the expression is trumped by the importance of keeping the ideas public property.[55] But although the merger doctrine has sometimes succeeded in preventing the privatization of certain "useful" ideas, it is not generally applied to the less obviously useful realm of literature. Although in Western aesthetics imaginative literature is often taken to be that writing whose content is least extricable from its form, courts have tended to construe the "ideas" in literary texts narrowly—as their plots, morals, situations, and the common generic elements that make up their *scènes à faire*.

By this standard, the ideas of "Oxen" would be a plot summary appended, perhaps, by a description of its multilayered structure and complex composition. But the episode demonstrates the inadequacy of just such a standard by its extravagant conflations and crossings of manner with matter, and by its sustained challenge to the notion that ideas could be thinkable "outside" of syntax, diction, and style. This challenge illustrates a legally entrenched discrimination between literature and more "useful" works: where ideas and expression merge in "useful" genres, the public domain status of the ideas trumps the private monopoly in their expression. However, where ideas and expression merge in literary texts, the reverse happens: the private property in expression trumps the public domain status of the ideas. One might object that a literary text like "Oxen" by its nature contains none of the sorts of "useful" ideas or facts whose public domain status the idea/expression dichotomy is concerned to guarantee; that no crucial empirical data or indispensable terms of public discourse are removed from circulation by the copyright in its expression. But ironically, copyright's long drift toward increased private rights has applied its disposition toward literary texts to all intellectual properties, increasingly allowing private expression to trump public property in ideas, and with diminishing exceptions. As I have argued elsewhere in this book, the law's initial prioritization of public discourse over private property has been slowly reversed over generations of copyright maximalism; the withering of the public domain means that pattern now dominates over matter in priority as well as property. "Oxen," we could say, is a faithful copy of early copyright but a counterfeit of the late-modern and postmodern regime; in the latter role, it is a deliberately botched replica, one that differs in parodic, ironic, and admonitory ways from what it duplicates.

Ulysses and Postmodernity

"Oxen of the Sun" has been a cardinal text among theorists of postmodern cultural production, for whom the episode anticipates both the ubiquity and the peculiarly neutral affect of parody in postmodern forms. Fredric Jameson has called "Oxen" the "most obvious realization" of *pastiche,* a term I have so far used to describe the episode's peculiar synthesis of imitation and transformative appropriation.[56] Jameson, however, describes pastiche not just as a formal technique of mimicry or appropriation, but as a particular disposition on the part of mimicry toward its object—an attitude of decentered and often humorless neutrality, which for Jameson is symptomatic of the social and linguistic fragmentations that characterize postmodernity. Replacing the more centered, normative operations of parody when those operations become impossible, Jamesonian pastiche is a mimicry that does not assume the existence of a "normal language" or "ordinary speech" from which its object ridiculously or outrageously deviates:

> Pastiche is, like parody, the imitation of a peculiar or unique, idiosyncratic style, the wearing of a linguistic mask, speech in a dead language. But it is a neutral practice of such mimicry, without any of parody's ulterior motives, amputated of the satiric impulse, devoid of laughter and of any conviction that alongside the abnormal tongue you have momentarily borrowed, some healthy linguistic normality still exists. Pastiche is thus blank parody, a statue with blind eyeballs: it is to parody what that other interesting and historically original thing, the practice of blank irony, is to what Wayne Booth calls the "stable ironies" of the eighteenth century.

The Copywrights

Though Jameson reads the transition from modernism to postmodernism in pastiche's eclipse of parody, he cites "Oxen" as one of several high-modernist texts in which pastiche has already become the dominant mode of mimicry. Linda Hutcheon distinguishes differently between pastiche and parody, dividing them according to trajectory rather than epoch: parody seeks "differentiation in its relationship to its model," whereas pastiche "operates more by similarity and correspondence." Nonetheless, in defining parody broadly as "imitation characterized by ironic inversion, not always at the expense of the parodied text" and as a "bitextual synthesis," Hutcheon also acknowledges that parody need not ridicule or even criticize its object, and that the value-neutral parody becomes the dominant parodic form in postmodernity. "Oxen of the Sun," she maintains, is "a most obvious example" of a parody that contains or co-opts pastiche, framing the genuflective repetitions of pastiche within a more broadly parodic environment that ironically underscores the difference between copy and original.[57]

Clearly, the literary mimicries of "Oxen" refuse to deliver, or even dream of, anything like the "normal language" Jameson claims parody must assume as a baseline from which to measure the eccentricity of what it ridicules. Nor could one describe the polyglot, at points nearly impenetrable, heterogeneity of the mock-oral tailpiece as "ordinary speech": it is as far from a 1904 lingua franca as the Anglo-Saxon parody that begins the episode. But the copyright metadiscourses of "Oxen"—its deconstruction of inimitable style as the basis for private literary property, its advance deployment of fair use defenses of its appropriations, its terminal narrative, its oral terminus, and its serious play with the manner/matter dichotomy—do suggest a point of commonality for postmodernity's otherwise dispersive idioms: namely, the increasingly unified regime of intellectual property law that governs the obscurest professional idiolect and the most hermetic literary style. The growth of this regime has been driven by some of the same phenomena that for Jameson characterize multinational capitalism: "New types of consumption; planned obsolescence; an ever more rapid rhythm of fashion and styling changes; the penetration of advertising, television, and the media generally to a hitherto unparalleled degree throughout society."[58] In addition to their frequently discussed social, economic, and perceptual effects, these phenomena underwrite a shift in emphasis from tangible to intangible properties, increasing the value and legal protection of properties in texts, images, designs, compositions, trademarks, trade secrets, slogans, jingles, look-and-feel, and celebrity. The growing stakes of intangible property forms in postmodernity have powered an expansion in the legal protection of those forms, as Rosemary Coombe notes:

> The judicial inclination to recognize more and more intangible interests as forms of property corresponds to the high period of postmodernity (from about 1970). Rights to control intangibles, usually signifying texts of one form

or another, were increasingly affirmed on the grounds of unjust enrichment (Thou shalt not reap where thou has not sown) and the need to provide incentives to creators to produce cultural valuables.[59]

This expansionism in intellectual property law seems, in turn, to have catalyzed a reaction in postmodern cultural production, where the frequency, intensity, and audacity of parodic forms have increased in apparent proportion to the growing dominion of intellectual property law.[60] Whether this proportional flourishing of parody/pastiche with intellectual property law demonstrates copy-culture's growing protest against the dominance of copyright, or its parasitic relationship to a legal regime whose deep logic it replicates despite its oppositional rhetoric, is a question posed, rather than answered, by the literary property metadiscourses of "Oxen." But the episode does offer copyright, along with its twin and foil, the public domain, as the matrices that organize and unify an otherwise decentered array of styles, rhetorical horizons, and worldviews.

That an otherwise fragmented social and discursive landscape should be united through intellectual property law gives one little enough to celebrate: observing it, one notes the hardening of a carapace whose innards have simultaneously withered away. But however chilling this notion is, the possibility that intellectual property law may be causally, rather than coevally or coincidentally, related to the withering of a critical public discourse and the public interest is far more chilling. Cyberlaw scholar and activist Pamela Samuelson has lately made just such an argument, warning that the postmodern copyright climate, despite occasional ventilations such as the *Campbell v. Acuff-Rose* parody decision, is eerily re-creating pre-copyright conditions such as de facto monopolistic perpetual ownership and a complicity between intellectual property law and censorship. Samuelson cites the recent consolidations of copyrights in media conglomerates, the deterioration through case law of most fair use provisions, the supplanting of author's rights by shareholder's rights, and the increased criminalization of copyright infringement as evidence that copyright law in postmodernity has begun to drift from its constitutional anchorage in the public interest and freedom of expression, and back toward the repressive, censorious, and monopolistic functions of Renaissance copy privileges.[61] If this is indeed the case, then Joyce's novel, with its aggressive celebrations of the public domain and its proleptic assertions of fair use, begins to look less like a prophecy or precursor of unbounded postmodern discursive forms and more like an unrealized, outmoded utopia.

As a way of testing Samuelson's hypothesis about the repressive drift of copyright in postmodernity, I would like to conclude this chapter with a thought experiment that imagines how *Ulysses* and its reception would have differed if the book had first appeared under an early-twenty-first-century copyright and publishing regime rather than under the interwar copyright conditions that marked its actual publication. I recognize this experiment, in addition to imagining extreme cases of private censorship, presupposes the existence of an immanent and transhistorical textual content that can be given an alternate form by stamping it with a different period's legal conditions, and that it thereby relies on a binarism I have suggested the novel works to problematize. Nonetheless, I think such an experiment can underscore the ways in which *Ulysses* both suffered and flourished as a result of the intellectual property environment in which it was written and published, as well as illustrating the climate changes that have occurred in the global copyright ecology since the 1920s. So let us imagine that as *Ulysses* is first published in 1922, copyright has a postmortem term of 70 years in most countries; the U.S. has ratified the Berne Convention on international copyright; the Agreement on Trade-Related Aspects of Intellectual Property Rights has stressed rightsholder sovereignty over national authority to limit copyright protection and thereby weakened fair use at the international level; *Campbell v. Acuff-Rose* has made parody a potential form of fair use in the U.S., where state censorship has declined but private censorship is on the rise; and the rise of the "information age" has significantly raised the financial stakes of copyright, increasing rightsholders' incentives, entitlements, and readiness to litigate in defense of their intellectual property.

First we should note the many ways in which our anachronistic version of Joyce's novel might improve on the original: because the U.S. obscenity/copyright loophole has been closed, this *Ulysses* has not been stigmatized as obscene and therefore exempt from copyright in the U.S., and there will be no Samuel Roth to capitalize on the novel's unprotected status. Because the book will no longer invite state censorship on obscenity grounds, printers and publishers are unafraid to be associated with it: instead of being banned, smuggled, or impounded, this *Ulysses* will be brought out simultaneously in all the major markets by major publishers. Having been typed by English-speaking rather than French-speaking typists, as well as thoroughly proofread, it will bear no prefatory request from Sylvia Beach, as the actual first edition of *Ulysses* did, for "*the reader's indulgence for typographical errors unavoidable in the exceptional circumstances.*" There will be no welter of competing "corrected" editions down the line and no critical debate about which of them is the least deplorable. Thus, a whole sector of the present Joyce industry will have had no occasion to come into being; but we can console ourselves a little that Joyce, in our thought experiment, will likely be better remunerated and regarded for a novel whose publication will have caused him less grief.

But let us compare the text of our hypothetical *Ulysses* with the historical one. The first 1922 Shakespeare and Company imprint of *Ulysses* bore the following statement on its copyright page:

James Joyce, Copywright

> *Tous droits de reproduction, de traduction
> et d'adaptation réservés pour tous les pays y compris la Russie.
> Copyright by James Joyce.*[62]

Written in two languages, French and English, the statement not only looks ahead to the polyglot nature of the text at large but also lays claim to two cultures of copyright: the limited-monopoly privilege of the Anglo-American regime under which *Ulysses* first appeared in serial form, and the natural law *droit d'auteur* doctrine of Continental copyright under which it was first published in full. Turning back the Greek-blue cover of our imaginary *Ulysses,* however, we find a very different sort of notice: a litany of highly specific assertions, warnings, and prohibitions, including an extremely conservative corporate interpretation of fair use doctrine that expressly limits textual reproduction to brief passages for purposes of review:

> Copyright © by James Joyce
>
> All rights reserved. No part of this book may be reproduced in any form or by any electronic or mechanical means, including information storage and retrieval systems, without prior permission in writing from the publisher, except by a reviewer who may quote brief passages in a review. Any members of educational institutions wishing to photocopy part or all of the work for classroom use, or publishers who would like to obtain permission to include the work in an anthology, should send their inquiries to the publisher.
>
> CAUTION: *Ulysses* is fully protected under the copyright laws of the United States, Canada, United Kingdom, and all British Commonwealth countries, and all countries covered by the International Union, the Pan-American Copyright Convention, and the Universal Copyright Convention. All rights, including motion picture, recitation, public reading, radio broadcasting, television, video or sound taping, all other forms of mechanical or electronic reproduction, such as information storage and retrieval systems and photocopying, and rights of translation into foreign languages, are strictly reserved.
>
> The moral rights of the author have been asserted.
>
> You must not circulate this book in any other binding or cover, and you must impose this same condition on any acquirer.[63]

Following this cluster of No Trespassing signs, with their barely concealed aggression and implied threats of prosecution, is a standard claim to the work's status as fiction—a prophylaxis against possible libel suits, and one that runs hilariously against the grain of Joyce's pervasive use of the names of actual people, locales, institutions, and businesses in the text of *Ulysses:*

The Copywrights

This is a work of fiction. Names, characters, places, and incidents either are the product of the author's imagination or are used fictitiously, and any resemblance to actual persons, living or dead, events, or locales is entirely coincidental and not intended by the author.

Finally, we find, in minuscule type, *twenty-five pages* of "Acknowledgments" of permission to reprint previously published material. If the above copyright statements bristled with the publisher's implied will to litigate, these Acknowledgments testify to a corresponding care on the part of the author and publisher to obtain permission for the book's reproduction of copyrighted material, as if by demonstrating a scrupulous recognition for other intellectual properties they could prove their desert of the same high degree of copyright protection. Here are a few sample entries:

> Grateful acknowledgment is made to the following for the permission to reprint previously published material:
>
> *Avery Morris Co., Ltd.:* Excerpted lyrics from "Love's Old Sweet Song" by G. Clifton Bingham, copyright © 1884 Avery Morris Co., Ltd., all rights for the U.S. and Canada administered by Colgems-EMI Inc.
>
> *Dr. Oliver St. John Gogarty:* Excerpted text from unpublished manuscript "The Song of the Cheerful (but Slightly Sarcastic) Jesus," copyright © 1904 by Dr. Oliver St. John Gogarty. Printed by permission of Dr. Oliver St. John Gogarty.
>
> *Gill & Son Publisher and T. Fisher Unwin:* Excerpted text from *The Love Songs of Connacht: Being the Fourth Chapter of the Songs of Connacht*, copyright © 1893 by Douglas Hyde. Reprinted by permission of Gill & Son Publishers, Dublin and T. Fisher Unwin, London, on behalf of Douglas Hyde.
>
> *Felix Culpepper Group, Ltd.:* Excerpted text from *The Ordeal of Richard Feverel* by George Meredith, copyright © 1859 by George Meredith. Reprinted by permission of the Felix Culpepper Group, Ltd., London, on behalf of the Estate of George Meredith.
>
> *T. Fisher Unwin and William Butler Yeats:* Excerpt of "Who Goes with Fergus Now?" from *The Countess Cathleen* by William Butler Yeats, copyright © 1892 by William Butler Yeats. Reprinted by permission of T. Fisher Unwin, London, and William Butler Yeats.[64]

And so on, for every copyrighted text of which *Ulysses* reproduces even a small portion. The acquisition and recording of copyright permissions for each of these quotations may seem a slight matter, a simple assertion of having played by the rules. But these permissions—so common in the copyright pages or endpapers of novels today as to be practically beneath notice—

speak eloquently of an intellectual property regime that admits of no minima beyond which a text may be reproduced without permission. They set a standard by which the reprinting text (here, our hypothetical *Ulysses*) expects to be treated in its turn, a standard that recognizes the smallest reuse of material as a potential infringement and reduces fair use to the quotation of brief passages for review. It is difficult to imagine that *Ulysses,* had it been written and published under such a regime, would have made nearly as extensive use of its protected source texts or of the unpublished writings (e.g., the youthful Gogarty's doggerel) of others.

Flipping ahead to "Oxen of the Sun" in our imaginary version of Joyce's novel, we find the episode greatly altered, in part as a result of the differences copyright has made to its secondary source texts. Instead of ending with Ruskin, the turn-of-the-century anthologies from which "Oxen" has been largely mined conclude with the major author whose work has most recently fallen into the public domain: Charles Lamb (1775–1834), whose copyrights have lapsed as of January 1, 1905, according to the 70-year postmortem term. "For considerations of copyright," Peacock's anthology will have omitted writers dead for fewer than 70 years, among them De Quincey, Macaulay, Landor, Dickens, Carlyle, Newman, Pater, Huxley, and Ruskin. "Oxen" will either have ended its parodies accordingly early or resorted to vaguer, less extensive imitations. Even if U.S. law might have permitted its appropriative parodies as a result of the *Campbell v. Acuff-Rose* decision, this *Ulysses* could still fall afoul of other monopoly-copyright regimes—e.g., British, Japanese, or Canadian—that do not make similar fair use provisions for parody. And in Continental countries whose intellectual property law regimes descend partly from natural law, Joyce's parodies might be thought to violate the semi-sacred *droit d'auteur.* In France, a parody that intends to harm the original author's work, or to be insulting or slanderous, transgresses even the specific fair dealing provisions for parody and pastiche, while in Spain the *droit d'auteur* empowers the author to restrain "any distortion, modification, or alteration . . . that is likely to prejudice his legitimate interests or threaten his reputation."[65] In the 1927 protest he staged against Samuel Roth's pirated serialization of *Ulysses,* Joyce used the rhetoric of the *droit d'auteur* to decry Roth's "appropriation and mutilation" of his property; his 1937 statement to the PEN Club on "le Droit Moral des Écrivains" did likewise. But under the current, more stringent provisions of that regime, Joyce's own work might have been viewed as illegally appropriating and mutilating the works of others, targeting their reputations, and making an actionable "ill use" of their names.

But what if Joyce had, in characteristic fashion, refused to alter *Ulysses* in accordance with a more overdetermined intellectual property climate and insisted on publishing the novel as it stands? Let us imagine that advance review copies of the *Ulysses* we know have been obtained by the estates of protected authors parodied by Joyce's novel. No longer bereft of its copyrights in 1921, the Dickens Estate in our thought experiment now holds them for seventy years postmortem—in other words, until 1941, the year in which Joyce himself will die. Offended by the way the appropriative "Dickens" parody in "Oxen" appears to belittle Dickens's writing, and doubly offended by Joyce's having named two of the Purefoy brood, Charley and Mary, after Dickens's children, the Estate complains that *Ulysses* will negatively impact demand for Dickens's work and threatens to sue for copyright infringement. Wily lawyers employed by Dickens's heirs make clear that even if the British law finds in favor of Joyce, they will litigate in *droit d'auteur* countries where both writers' works have been published, claiming that *Ulysses* seeks to harm, insult, and slander Dickens's work and reputation. Other interested literary estates—those of Macaulay, Carlyle, Pater, and Ruskin—follow suit in threatening legal action. Oliver St. John Gogarty joins the fray of naysayers, writing to refuse Joyce permission to quote his "Song of the Cheerful (but Slightly Sarcastic) Jesus," "Medical Dick and Medical Davy," and other unpublished verse in *Ulysses*.

Joyce's publishers, though they believe in the quality and potential importance of *Ulysses*, are concerned that even without the costs of copyright litigation the book may scarcely repay their investment in it—after all, a book of this length already suffers reduced profit margins through its high material outlays, and its combination of costliness and obscurity may deter buyers. Reluctant to risk expensive international lawsuits in order to be bellwethers for the parody/fair use defense and the potential fair use in reprinting unpublished material, the book's publishers in non-U.S. countries ask Joyce to alter his parodies of protected authors so that they are both less appropriative and less identifiable. They also stipulate that he remove several hundred lines' worth of quotations from protected material whose rightsholders are demanding prohibitively high licensing fees. Our hypothetical Joyce refuses to comply, and when his publishers renege on their contracts, he finds himself in a situation not unlike that of the historical Joyce in 1921, driven by an adverse legal and moral climate to publish the book under substandard conditions outside the countries where the book would likely have found its primary readership. But there is a key distinction between the real Joyce and our anachronistic clone, one that measures the distance between 1922 and 2002: the real Joyce was hamstrung by the judgment that his book was unprintably obscene and only subsequently by copyright laws that interlocked with the obscenity ruling. The Joyce of our thought experiment, by contrast, suffers not from the stigma of obscenity but from copyright regimes that regard even the minimal appropriation and parody of private intellectual property as a far worse crime.

Conclusion: Copyright, Trauma, and the Work of Mourning

Luckily, James Joyce did *not* have to write and attempt to publish *Ulysses* under a turn-of-the-millennium intellectual property regime, as I imagined at the end of the previous chapter. Yet it is partly in the name of canonical writers such as Joyce, their cultural legacies, and their heirs and estates that the law has become so much more extensive during the last half-century. The result is that present-day artists have to work under maximalist or "thick" copyright constraints that were unknown to the very precursors in whose name the new constraints have been instituted. Not enough people are struck by this killing irony or chilled by the way living artists' creative latitude has been reduced in order to grant retroactive incentives to the dead. Of course, the thickening of copyright does not benefit the dead alone; extensions to copyright terms and protections can also benefit living authors, whose incentives to create are supposedly increased in proportion as their postmortem literary estates are expanded. But those same living writers and creators also lose by such extensions, which decrease the public domain from which they may draw materials for their work. One might object that only a very few contemporary artists depend on borrowings from public domain material or on fair use redeployments of copyrighted works. One might add that such artists tend to occupy rarefied experimental fringes and should not be the determining cases for intellectual property laws whose highest-stakes participants are the creators of more-mainstream works distributed by mass-media conglomerates. But such objections vastly underestimate the extent to which even mainstream cultural production depends increasingly, in an age of samples, digests, remakes, renditions, parodies, and pastiches, on the reuse of extant materials. Perhaps even more seriously, it assumes that the "stakes" of intellectual property law are only financial; that appropriative art is not political but "merely" aesthetic—merely concerned to console, divert, and entertain; and that its shutdown by thick copyright regimes would only result in the loss of expendable forms of diversion, rather than of indispensable forms of public discourse.

In combating these assumptions, advocates of "thinner," or less extensive, intellectual property regimes have ended up advocating, in addition, a reconception of the public sphere, such that public discourse crucial enough to require intellectual property easement would not be limited to the conventional noncommercial forms and public forums of explicitly "political" speech but would potentially include a much broader range of sites, genres, and dispositions of expression.[1] In this radicalized notion of democratic public discourse, the First Amendment would trump private intellectual property rights far more often, and more forcefully, than it does at present. For several reasons, the intellectual property form at the center of this reconception of the public sphere has not been copyright but the trademark. Perhaps more than any other intellectual property form, trademarks are susceptible to transformative redeployment. They are ubiquitous; self-contained; attached to commodities but also detachable from their contexts; designed for ease of recognition and therefore conducive to easily recognizable parody; and associated with group formation around consumerist categories (brand loyalty, in-group cool, brand-identified lifestyles) that themselves invite parody by excluded or dissenting subjects. In Rosemary Coombe's analysis, "The trademark is both a commodity with an exchange value in its own right and a sign that condenses a relationship between a signifier, a signified, and a referent (linking, for example, a logo, a lifestyle, and a product)."[2] Coombe goes on to cite Michael Warner's claim that "Nearly all of our pleasures come to us coded in some degree by the publicity of mass media. We have brandnames all over us." Thus, as Coombe paraphrases Warner, trademarks are in fact "constitutive parts of a public sphere, constructing a common discourse to bind the subject to the nation and its markets."[3] And as constitutive parts of a public sphere, those signifiers should not be overprivatized by the law.

But because dominant notions of the public sphere and political speech tend to exclude commercial discourse, trademarks are not generally recognized as potential units of public discourse whose appropriation might be worthy of free speech exemptions from private intellectual property law. As a result, trademark owners are legally able to control the circulation and signification of trademarks, which often start out as pieces of the public domain, in ways that are deleterious to freedom of speech. During the 1980s, the United States Olympic Committee (USOC) used trademark law to enjoin another organization from using the word "Olympic." San Francisco Arts and Athletics, a nonprofit organization, was sponsoring the Gay Olympic Games in order to "provide a healthy recreational alternative to a suppressed minority" and "educate the public at large towards a more reasonable characterization of gay men and women."[4] Though the USOC had raised no objections to uses of the word "Olympic" by the Youth Olympics or the Special

Olympics, it sought, in a clearly discriminatory fashion, to prevent the Gay Olympic Games from using its intellectual property. According to the Supreme Court, the salable glamour of the word "Olympic" was so much a product of the USOC's "own talents and energy, the end result of much time, energy and expense" that the word had become the Committee's exclusive domain.[5] Thus, an organization promoting the cultural visibility and legitimacy of a marginalized community was prevented by trademark law from using a word whose positive associations with both athletics and democracy surely antedated the efforts of its "owner," the USOC. One would think this now-infamous case clearly constituted a legalization of private censorship, but the public/private binarism inherent in intellectual property law makes the very phrase "private censorship" an oxymoron. Because the USOC is, as James Boyle puts it, "a *private* actor, and we are dealing here with *commercial* usage," this cannot, by definition, be a censorship issue: "There is no state action because we are in the private sphere—authors are not governments. There is no free speech issue because we are in the marketplace and not the polity."[6] Only Justice Brennan's dissenting opinion admitted the possibility of private censorship in finding that the USOC's dominion over even noncommercial uses of the term "Olympic" threatened freedom of speech.[7]

For all the attention trademark law has attracted, however, the present copyright law is no less hospitable to private censorship, or, in other words, the creation and enforcement of private intellectual property rights that infringe on the free speech of others. Copyright's most crucial and difficult task is to mediate between private intellectual property and free speech. But because of its connection to the life span of mortal authors and its creation of inheritable property rights, postmortem copyright activates a host of affective, highly personal, and sometimes transgenerational energies that are not obviously assimilated to the private property/free speech axis along which the law is usually debated. Before turning to a recent case in which copyright has been invoked to license private censorship, I want to look at some of these other affective force fields in which copyright so controversially sits and to consider how they might, after all, be related to the private property/free speech continuum in ways that can inform our thinking about the present legal regime. To do this, I will again appeal to meditations on copyright within a work of imaginative literature—this time, a much more recent work than those treated in the earlier chapters of this book, a Hugo Award-winning short story by Spider Robinson entitled "Melancholy Elephants."

In chapter 4, I argued that postmortem copyright has come to function as a kind of surrogate body for deceased writers, preventing the premature decay of a literary corpus into the public domain by legally incarnating authors' legacies in the private literary property "remains" of their estates. At moderate term-lengths, postmortem copyright can facilitate mourning by keeping an author's literary remains in a respectful stasis. But long postmortem copyright terms leave the paradigm of terminable mourning for that of interminable commemoration and canonization, even legal mummification and undeath, through the weird surrogation intellectual property affords. In extreme cases, as with the rhetoric accompanying the 1998 Sonny Bono Copyright Term Extension Act, postmortem copyright has been held to be coterminous with memory and the lapse of copyright to be a desecration or annihilation of memory. In the Bono hearings, we heard articulated a desire for copyright to last, if not forever, then "forever less one day," and a wish that the public domain did not exist, in the name of both the memory of the dead and the survivors' work of mourning. Read back through the lens of the 1998 Bono proceedings, Robinson's 1982 short story makes what now looks like a proleptic rejoinder to the Bono Act's dominant rhetoric, imagining a case in which thick copyright regimes exacerbate rather than alleviate mourning. The story revolves around a character who resembles Mary Bono in photo-negative, a widow in perpetual mourning not because copyright is too brief but because it is too extensive. Like Mary Bono, Robinson's protagonist is the widow of a songwriter—but a songwriter who, unlike Sonny Bono, was driven to suicide by thick copyright laws. And where Mary Bono sought to prolong copyright in honor of her deceased husband, Robinson's heroine attempts to appease her husband's unquiet spirit by fighting term extension so that other artists will not meet the same fate of seeing their new works shut down by oppressive intellectual property regimes.

"Melancholy Elephants" is a piece of proximate futurism set in the mid-twenty-first century, when the average human life span has increased to 120 years and the population to sixteen billion both on and off the planet. Technological advance has left much of humanity without conventional work, with the result that 54 percent of the population is entered on the tax rolls as artists. The dystopic elements of the story, however, are the result not of the usual sci-fi catastrophes—an apocalyptic war, say, or environmental or social collapse—but of the state of intellectual property law. In Robinson's depiction of the U.S. circa 2050, copyrights have come to be administered like patents: the Copyright Office applies a battery of computerized "originality tests" to candidate works and issues a copyright only to works that pass the test. This new rigor has produced dire results: two out of five new works submitted to the Music Division are deemed too derivative by the first computer search and thus unworthy of copyright; the per-capita rate of submissions to the Copyright Office has declined; and creative people, under the increased burden of having to prove their originality to a device with infallible memory and massive comparative powers, have become less productive, often destroying their own more derivative work in despair without even submitting it for consideration. Worse, as "Melancholy Elephants" opens, a bill is being considered that would extend copyright from a 50-year postmortem term to perpetuity, thereby realizing the dreams of Wordsworth, Southey, Mark Twain, and the Bonos.[8] The story follows Dorothy Martin, a lobbyist working on behalf of artists to prevent the passage of S. 4217896, on her visit to the palatial underground lair of a powerful U.S. senator, whom her organization has paid dearly for her to see.

One of the most noteworthy aspects of Robinson's story is that it posits a causal connection between copyright and personal and communal traumatization. Emphasizing the high stakes of the proposed copyright legislation, Martin begins her appeal to the Senator by telling him, "I believe that if S. '896 does pass, our species will suffer significant trauma." When the Senator eventually admits that he could not help her even if he were sympathetic to her cause, having already accepted a campaign contribution from another source in exchange for his promise to back the bill, Martin experiences a personal trauma, one in which her unmitigated grief over her husband's suicide and her failure to vindicate his death result in her desire to end her own life:

> All her panic and tension vanished, to be replaced by a sadness so great and so pervasive that for a moment she thought it might literally stop her heart.
> *Too late! Oh my darling, I was too late!*
> She realized bleakly that there were too many people in her life, too many responsibilities and entanglements. It would be a month before she could honourably suicide.⁹

Sensing Martin's devastation, the Senator tells her that the look on her face reminds him of the night his mother died, and, softening, invites her to make her case despite his prior commitment to support the bill, if only to satisfy his curiosity. Martin makes, in essence, a scarce-resource argument about cultural production, suggesting that fresh creation will decline even more dangerously if the raw materials of creation are interminably privatized. With human population, life span, and leisure time at unprecedented highs, more people are competing for a longer time for the raw materials of fresh creation. But with the "racial memory of our species" lengthening through writing, printing, and digital technology, and with copyright enforcing more extreme criteria of originality for new works, the available raw materials are shrinking in quantity even as demand for them intensifies. A perpetual copyright term, in Martin's analysis, would mean that no expression, once privatized, would ever become available for reuse in the cultural ecology; once expression becomes a nonrenewable resource, she opines, the cultural ecosystem will eventually collapse for lack of inputs.

However, the "significant trauma" Martin warned of earlier would not be even this "theoretical heat death of artistic expression," but rather the realization that it would precipitate: that artists are not inventors but merely discoverers of combinations of extant signs and stimuli. "To create implies infinite possibility, to discover implies finite possibility," she says. "As a species I think we will react poorly to having our noses rubbed in the fact that we are discoverers and not creators." Eventually, Martin illustrates the "psychic trauma" inflicted by such a disappointment by telling the story of her husband's death, following his realization that he was, after all, not a creator but only a discoverer.

> My husband wrote a song for me, on the occasion of our fortieth wedding anniversary. It was our love in music, unique and special and intimate, the most beautiful melody I ever heard in my life. It made him so happy to have written it. Of his last ten compositions he had burned five for being derivative, and the others had all failed copyright clearance. But this was fresh, special—he joked that my love for him had inspired him. The next day he submitted it for clearance, and learned that it had been a popular air during his early childhood, and had already been unsuccessfully submitted fourteen times since its original registration. A week later he burned all his manuscripts and working tapes and killed himself.

She ends her appeal to the Senator by insisting on the importance of forgetting to artistic discovery:

> Art is long, not infinite. 'The Magic goes away.' One day we will *use it up*—unless we can learn to recycle it like any other finite resource. . . . Senator, that bill has to fail, if I have to take you on to do it. Perhaps I can't win—but I'm going to fight you! A copyright must not be allowed to last more than fifty years—after which it should be flushed from the memory banks of the Copyright Office. We need selective voluntary amnesia if Discoverers of Art are to continue to work without psychic damage. Facts should be remembered—but dreams? . . . Dreams should be forgotten when we wake. Or one day we will find ourselves unable to sleep.

The Senator is persuaded by Martin's argument and agrees to help her even if his about-face on the bill ends his political career: "If you live long enough, . . . there is nothing new under the sun. . . . If you're lucky, you die sooner than that. I haven't heard a new dirty joke in fifty years. . . . I will kill S. 4217896." He and Martin part as allies and friends, with the Senator saying tenderly "we will comfort each other in our terrible knowledge" and Martin marveling that "it *is* better . . . shared."[10]

Certainly there is no shortage of objections one might raise to the account "Melancholy Elephants" gives of the legal metaphysics of copyright, its cultural ramifications, its similarities with nonrenewable natural resources, and the nature of artistic creation. To begin with, Robinson's story contains no discussion of fair use, though this omission may be symptomatic of the withering of fair use prior to possible turnaround decisions like *Feist Publications, Inc. v. Rural Telephone Service Co., Inc.* and *Campbell v. Acuff-Rose Music Inc.* during the early 1990s. It expends its polemical energies on a rather implausible version of the scarce-resource critique of copyright—the notion that the number of possible ideas and expressions is finite and in danger of being unsustainably harvested—rather than on the private censorship argument that has since proven more plausible and more urgent.[11] And perhaps most oddly, the story understands the Romantic notion of original genius to be illusory, but instead of replacing that illusion with a narrative more reflective of how people actually do create, it seeks to enlist the law in perpetuating the illusion of fresh creation ex nihilo. Artists, it argues, must be kept in a state of artificial innocence and earliness sustained by a "selective amnesia" that is in turn enabled by a limited copyright. And yet Martin's husband does not seem to have needed perpetual copyright to experience the trauma of his artistic indebtedness; the story, then, blames the specter of perpetual copyright for what it has already inflicted both by instituting a copyright regime that pre-screens works to establish their originality and by assuming the breakdown of the idea/expression dichotomy.[12] Finally, in imagining the "psychic trauma" artists would experience in learning that they were discoverers rather than inventors, the story vastly underestimates the extent to which many artists of Robinson's own and earlier generations (recall the Victorian plagiarism-apologists) not only understood invention in the original sense of *inventio,* or "coming upon" a preexistent object, but celebrated artistic "creation" as derivative, indebted, recombinant, recycled.

What saves "Melancholy Elephants" from being merely a dystopia erected on false premises, however, is its connection between thick copyright regimes, and mourning, melancholia, and "psychic trauma." This is not a connection one would expect to find in legal discourse, and it illustrates the capacity of imaginative literature to think about the social functions and repercussions of the law in ways not endogenous to the law. Nor is it a connection that gets fully developed in Dorothy Martin's plea to the Senator, which merely posits a traumatic disappointment among artists whose illusion of creation ex nihilo is shattered by a thick copyright system. But Martin herself experiences another sort of trauma that is more suggestive: the trauma of learning that one cannot placate the dead by changing the world ("*Too late! Oh my darling, I was too late!*"), and of being trapped in the self-abnegating condition of interminable mourning, the melancholic state named in the story's title. Martin's composer-husband is annihilated along with the Romantic mythology of radically original creation that copyright first encourages him to embrace and then catastrophically discredits. But his widow's experience raises questions about the role expression plays in the working-through of other traumas than the ones copyright might inflict, and thus about the role copyright plays in enabling or prohibiting expressive working-through that relies on the recirculation of protected texts. Dorothy Martin and Mary Bono are diametrically opposed in the relationship their mourning bears to perpetual copyright: Bono's requires it, whereas Martin's reviles it. But both do so to honor and placate the dead. One notes that in both cases, griefwork entails not creation ex nihilo but some prolonged relationship, whether reverent or irreverent, to extant texts. The work of mourning is explicitly not Romantic, in the sense that it has no need of radical originality or even the fantasy of radical originality. What it requires is sustained engagement with the found object of loss.

Robinson's story ends, curiously, with the formation of a posttraumatic community that is galvanized by its opposition to perpetual copyright: "We will comfort each other in our terrible knowledge . . . It *is* better . . . shared." By thus staging the opposition of communal mourning and perpetual copyright, the story implies something one might also conclude from Mary Bono's quest to commemorate her husband through copyright term extension: that the hypercathexis of postmortem intellectual property forms by the bereaved testifies to an absence in the culture of more communal, and more effective, kinds of mourning. However, when grief is expressed in a drive to extend the term of a temporally limited property form, it runs the risk of extending its own term toward the limitlessness of a melancholia that lasts "forever less one day." Worse still, as Robinson's story illustrates, such a drive to immortalize the deceased by extending copyright not only impoverishes the public domain of resources for future creation but can prolong and exacerbate the grief of others for whom transformative reuse is a highly effective mode of working-through.

Speaking of mourning here in connection with copyright law and the public discourse it supposedly fecundates may seem perverse, inasmuch as we tend to think of mourning as a private and apolitical process that occurs in a state of withdrawal from the public sphere. If we do so, however, it is not only because of the withering of communal forms of grieving but also because the work of mourning is accorded a marginal status in the conventional construction of the public sphere—the same marginal status, one might add, that is accorded to imaginative literature. The Bill of Rights grants no "Right to the unobstructed working-through of loss or trauma," and the very idea of such a right seems to exceed the proper latitude of state-guaranteed rights. But by opposing communal mourning and perpetual copyright, Robinson's story implies that effective mourning, particularly the kind devoted to the working-through of the "terrible knowledge" of communal trauma, is necessarily a public discourse and thus a form of expression important enough to the health of the democracy that it should not be infringed by excessive, private intellectual property regimes.

The lesson I take from "Melancholy Elephants" is not that we should wish for a "Right to unobstructed mourning," but rather that we should recognize mourning, literary expression, and mourning through literary expression as among the operations that occur within the public sphere, yet whose presence is inadequately recognized and accommodated there. But how might the public sphere better recognize and accommodate such operations without the state's making special provisions for them such as a "Right to unobstructed mourning"? Robinson's story suggests a way: the thinning of private intellectual property rights to clear a wider discursive bandwidth for a more broadly conceived public discourse, including but not limited to communal working-through. How would this facilitate, say, the work of mourning through literary expression? To consider this, one might construct a hypothetical case that merges the situations of Dorothy Martin and her husband—a case in which the working-through of a traumatic "terrible knowledge" involves an act of creative expression that derives from an extant text. Let us imagine a writer who belongs to a historically oppressed subaltern community, a descendant of the victims of a historical trauma—ethnic persecution and transportation, or enslavement, or genocide—whose aftereffects still pervade the culture to such an extent that certain traumatic symptoms are transmitted from one generation to the next. This writer seeks to participate in the communal working-through of the trauma by writing a book that appropriates aspects of an earlier work, one in which the violent and exploitive ideology of the dominant culture is nostalgically crystallized. If this earlier work has fallen into the public domain, there will be no legal obstacles to its transformative reuse by our hypothetical subaltern writer. However, if it is still under copyright, which is likely given both the long duration of the term and the relative recency of the trauma, we have a potential conflict between an arguably public act of expressive working-through on the one hand and private intellectual property rights on the other. A thin copyright regime will contain, at the very least, generous fair use provisions for parodic and critical appropriations from protected texts. These provisions signal to creative members of all communities, subaltern or not, that private intellectual property interests do not possess an inflexible sovereignty over transformative and critical expressions that derive from protected works. By contrast, a thick copyright regime will assert that even critical and transformative redeployments of the earlier work constitute an infringement of that work's copyright, and that the sovereignty of intellectual property trumps all potential reuses of that property, whether toward merely opportunistic commercial ends or the individual and collective working-through of historical trauma.

As abstract and rarefied as this hypothetical scenario may seem, it happens to describe the basic parameters of a real U.S. copyright case that has recently received international attention. The case concerns a book called *The Wind Done Gone*, a first novel by Nashville-based screenwriter and country music composer Alice Randall. Describing herself as being of mixed-race ancestry, possibly the descendant of a Confederate general and an African American slave, Randall first read Margaret Mitchell's 1936 bestseller *Gone With the Wind* when she was 12 years old. "There was something in the book that attracted and repelled me," she told a group of journalists. "Where were the mulattos on Tara? Where were the people in my family history?"[13] Her response, decades later, was to write a counter-novel to *Gone With the Wind* from the point of view of a mixed-race character, a gesture that attracted publicity long in advance of the summer 2001 release Houghton Mifflin had scheduled for the book. In essence, Randall's novel uses the framework of Mitchell's characters, plot, physical setting, and historical moment, but tells the story through the eyes of a character who does not appear in Mitchell's romance—Cynara Brown, or "Cinnamon," Scarlett O'Hara's half-sister and the daughter of the plantation's white owner and "Mammy," a slave who does appear in Mitchell's book.[14] Randall has remarked that she wanted to "redeem" Mitchell's classic by writing "an antidote to a text that has hurt generations of African Americans."[15] *The Wind Done Gone*'s redemptive strategy includes several devices for distancing readers from the focal characters of *Gone With the Wind*: Cynara refers to Scarlett as "Other," Rhett Butler as "R," and Ashley Wilkes as "Dreamy Gentleman"; even Tara, the plantation on which Mitchell's novel is partly set, is defamiliarized, becoming "Tata" in Cynara's narrative. *The Wind Done Gone* attempts to turn the affective geography of Mitchell's novel inside out: characters central in the original become marginal, whereas the African American figures who were bumbling and peripheral in *Gone With the Wind* occupy the complex center of Randall's story and sympathies.

Several months before the novel's publication date, however, lawyers acting for the Mitchell trusts filed for a temporary restraining order and preliminary injunction to halt its publication, alleging that Randall's book infringed Mitchell's copyright and calling *The Wind Done Gone* a "blatant and wholesale" theft of *Gone With the Wind*. As the hearing date approached, a number of well-known novelists, scholars, and entertainers—including Harper Lee, Pat Conroy, Ishmael Reed, Claude Brown, Rita Mae Brown, Tony Early, Yusef Komunyakaa, John Berendt, Henry Lewis Gates, Arthur M. Schlesinger Jr., Shelby Foote, Steve Earle, and Toni Morrison—wrote, signed petitions, and appeared publicly to defend Randall's book against the infringement charge.[16] According to Morrison, "What Miss Randall's book does is imagine and occupy narrative spaces and silences never once touched upon nor conceived of in Mrs. Mitchell's novel."[17] Morrison's remark attempted to make literary borrowing a means to original ends: Randall, she argued, had replicated aspects of Mitchell's novel in order to speak back to its skewed racial and gender politics and to the widely disseminated, stereotyped portrait it had painted of a romanticized ante-bellum South. Randall's statement was at once more personal and more historical than Morrison's, invoking her own racial identity and the historical traumas of slavery and enforced illiteracy her book sought to help redress: "Once upon a time in America, African Americans were forbidden by law to read and write. It saddens me and breaks my heart [that] there are those who would try to set up obstacles for a black woman to tell her story, and the story of her people, with words in writing. *Gone With the Wind* has enshrined a limited version of American history that continues to exert its power over the popular imagination. Part of literacy is responding to literature. I felt I had to take on Mitchell's novel directly. My book is an antidote to a text that has hurt generations of African Americans."[18]

In April 2001, U.S. District Judge Charles Pannell found for the Mitchell trusts and enjoined publication of Randall's novel, which he called an "unabated piracy" of Mitchell's book in that it appropriated not only the basic setting of *Gone With the Wind* but fifteen characters, several famous scenes, and some dialogue.[19] Lawyers defending Randall's book had invoked the parody/fair use defense legitimated by the U.S. Supreme Court in *Campbell v. Acuff-Rose Music, Inc.* (1994), arguing that *The Wind Done Gone* was not a commercially opportunistic sequel to *Gone With the Wind* but a politically motivated parody and critique of the earlier book and thus a form of "criticism" or "comment" permitted under fair use doctrine. The book's clear ideological oppositions to certain aspects of *Gone With the Wind* seemed, by the logic of the parody/fair use defense, to underscore its status as "criticism" and to reduce the likelihood of its being found uncritically derivative. But Pannell rejected the parody/fair use defense on the grounds that, in his opinion, the modest parodic, transformative, and critical elements of *The Wind Done Gone* were insufficient to justify its extensive borrowings.[20] He added that even if Randall's book were to be considered a parody, the object of its parodic critique was not *Gone With the Wind* in particular but slavery and racism generally, and that Randall had appropriated more of Mitchell's novel than was necessary to mount a general critique of slavery and racism.[21] The Court's decision in *Campbell v. Acuff-Rose,* recall, specified that a parody's source text and its primary target must be identical for the parody to be eligible for fair use status; a parody that reproduces aspects of a text it does not criticize infringes the copyright in that text. The parody/fair use defense, in other words, safeguards borrowing so long as it is used toward the democratically valuable ends of dissent, criticism, irreverence. In finding that *The Wind Done Gone* was not critical of *Gone With the Wind,* Pannell bizarrely failed to find in Randall's book the irreverent disposition toward Mitchell's that had partly led the Mitchell trusts to bring suit.

Having rejected the book's defensibility as critical parody, Pannell went on to emphasize the exclusive right of Mitchell's heirs to create or authorize a sequel to *Gone With the Wind.* In his analysis, Randall's "recitation of so much of the earlier work is overwhelming" to the point of constituting an unauthorized sequel. "When the reader of *Gone With the Wind* turns over the last page, he may wonder what becomes of Ms. Mitchell's beloved characters and their romantic, tragic, world. Ms. Randall has offered her vision of how to answer those unanswered questions. . . . The right to answer those questions and to write a sequel or other derivative work, however, legally belongs to Ms. Mitchell's heirs, not Ms. Randall."[22] U.S. copyright law defines a "derivative work" as one "based upon one or more preexisting works, such as a translation, musical arrangement, dramatization, fictionalization, motion-picture version, sound recording, art reproduction, abridgment, condensation, or any other form in which a work may be recast, transformed, or adapted."[23] The right to prepare and, by extension, to license derivative works is one of six exclusive rights the law gives rightsholders, the others being rights of reproduction, public distribution, performance, and display, and public performance of sound recordings by digital audio transmission.[24] The law does not specifically name "sequels" among derivative works, and one might argue that a sequel "derives" from an original work in a manner not adequately described as recasting, transformation, or adaptation. Nonetheless, case law has tended to accord sequels the status of derivative works, and the owners of the original work's copyright the exclusive right to create or license them.

The Mitchell trusts had utilized this right in the past to authorize a sequel, Alexandra Ripley's *Scarlett: The Sequel to Margaret Mitchell's Gone With the Wind* (1988), and were negotiating another authorized sequel at the time of the hearing. In addition, they had used their exclusive right in derivative works to establish certain ground rules for licensed sequels, constraints they likely regarded as protecting Mitchell's legacy from contaminative, or at least controversial, associations. According to novelist Pat Conroy, who considered writing a sequel to *Gone With the Wind* until he was informed of the ground rules, the trusts forbade sequels to depict interracial or homosexual sex.[25] Randall's novel depicts both. The trusts also stipulated that sequels not contain the death of Scarlett O'Hara. In *The Wind Done Gone*, Scarlett dies. From the trusts' perspective, the appearance of an unauthorized work both derived from and critically disposed to *Gone With the Wind* threatened to compromise the reputation of Mitchell's novel, possibly reducing commercial demand for it. *The Wind Done Gone*'s depictions of "transgressive" sex acts seemed to sully or even desecrate Mitchell's legacy further, turning her beloved classic into a bully pulpit for Randall's views on race and sexuality. And the death of Scarlett O'Hara in Randall's book might negatively affect the future of the *Gone With the Wind* authorized sequel franchise, or suggest that Mitchell's heroine, and by extension her legacy, were mortal. Finally, if *The Wind Done Gone* found its way into print, it might either be mistaken for an authorized sequel or suggest an indifference on the part of the Mitchell trusts to the *Gone With the Wind* sequel industry, and thereby weaken the viability of the trusts' future claims to authorize or prohibit derivative works.

Had the Mitchell trusts authorized Alice Randall's novel, they would have scored a double victory by asserting an ongoing interest in licensing derivative works while also showing a certain munificence in allowing a critical rejoinder to Mitchell's work to be published. Instead, the trusts' temporary legal victory occurred in the shadow of the negative publicity they garnered for enacting what their critics saw as the private censorship of a work that is unflattering to *Gone With the Wind*, and for having effectively silenced an

African American woman in the name of the cultural and intellectual property legacy of a white Southerner of privilege. But despite the price they may have paid for not doing so, it is difficult to imagine the Mitchell trusts' agreeing to authorize *The Wind Done Gone,* even if Randall's book had abided by the trusts' ground rules. Literary estates tend by their nature to be oriented around the commemoration and consecration of an author's work, and thus to be structurally disposed against encouraging work that might damage the reputation and commercial appeal of the author whose literary remains they exist to protect. Generally run either by an author's heirs or by passionate memorialist-advocates of an author's life and work, their chief business is the regulation, administration, and protection of an author's cultural legacy through intellectual property rights. When such estates are in the position to authorize lucrative derivative works, their commemorative function is complicated by a policing function with high financial stakes: the more vigilantly the legacy is policed through intellectual property law, the more revenue can be generated through the licensing of derivative works to sustain the work of commemoration and policing. Through a feedback loop, the purity of the cultural legacy, the financial health of the estate, and the surveillance of the intellectual property become mutually reinforcing. Thankfully, there are exceptions; but often the literary estates of well-known writers become so invested in strategies of legal and financial self-perpetuation that they grow distanced from the memory or intentions of the writers to whom they largely owe their existence, and from the most generous and generative deployments of those writers' legacies.

In the case of the Mitchell trusts, the drive to protect and commemorate Margaret Mitchell may have been more than usually acute for reasons connected not just with the financial stakes but with Mitchell's rather tragic life. Within months of its publication, *Gone With the Wind* had been hailed by the press as "more than a novel. It is a national event, a proverbial expression of deep instinct, a story that promises to found a kind of legend."[26] The book was awarded the Pulitzer Prize, and the 1939 film won a record ten Academy Awards. But Mitchell appears to have been finished, rather than launched, by the legendary status of her novel. In the wake of its success, she began suffering from the loss of her privacy and from a wide range of health problems; in 1949, at the age of 48, she was killed by a speeding taxi. *Gone With the Wind* constitutes Mitchell's entire mature literary output, and the book's copyright has borne the unusual compensatory and commemorative burden, for her legatees at least, of being the sole tangible legacy of the public acclaim that seems to have compromised her health even as it ensured her cultural immortality. Hal Clarke and Paul Anderson, the lawyers for the Mitchell trusts and friends of both Margaret Mitchell and her deceased brother, invoked the intentions of the dead in claiming that *The Wind Done Gone* was just the sort of derivative work the Mitchells would have wanted them to fight. According to Anderson, "Whether it was a legal obligation or not, we would want to keep our word to our friend."[27] One imagines that for Clarke and Anderson, the 1976 and 1998 Acts gave a welcome extension both to Mitchell's copyrights and to the consolatory function they perform in giving the trusts a means by which to safeguard her legacy. According to the copyright regime under which it appeared in 1936, *Gone With the Wind* would have entered the public domain at the end of 1992. The 1976 Act extended the work's copyright through the end of 2011. Now, thanks to the Bono Act, *Gone With the Wind*'s copyright and all the exclusive rights that comprise it will remain intact until the end of 2031.

But as I have suggested by juxtaposing the heroine of "Melancholy Elephants" with Mary Bono, in the affectively charged realm of copyright one person's consolation can prolong another's grief. For Mitchell's trustees, *Gone With the Wind* is a legacy whose integrity can be secured through its status as private property and whose unauthorized appropriation or adaptation might disquiet the ghost of its creator, or at least renew the grief of her survivors. For Alice Randall, however, the novel's status as private literary property does not lessen its enduring and quite public status in the national imaginary as a myth about compliant slaves, benevolent masters, and an Old South whose demise Scarlett's O'Hara famously deplores: "The more I see of emancipation, the more criminal I think it is. It's just ruined the darkies."[28] Defending Randall's book against the infringement charges, Wendy Strothman, an executive vice president and publisher at Houghton Mifflin, claimed "It is unconscionable to deny anyone to comment on a book that has taken on mythic status in American culture."[29] Strothman's remark parallels Warner's about trademarks in arguing that, despite being private intellectual property, Mitchell's novel is now a constitutive part of the public sphere, a status that should result in the mitigation of its copyright protection, at least for purposes of debate and dissent. The remark also implicitly redefines the public sphere, not as an idealized and exclusively factual realm but as one compounded of fact and myth, statistics and tropes, affect and argument, political, private, and commercial discourse.

Ironically, such a perspective takes the "mythic" status of *Gone With the Wind* more seriously than the guardians of its purity and private property status do: it comprehends that, for better or worse, Mitchell's novel does not have a totally separate ontological status in the national imaginary from slavery, racism, and the South during the Civil War and Reconstruction. Far from being "mere fiction" versus the "historical facts" of the period, Mitchell's novel has been a cornerstone text in a cultural mythology compounded of the two, using the "facts" of its historical backdrop to authorize a romance that has achieved a durability and intractability few "facts" ever attain—a kind of hyperfacticity. Binding its readers through its tempestuous romance plot to a pro-slavery South, the novel has contributed to a tolerance and even nostalgia for a sentimentalized period of exploitation and dehumanization— a nostalgia that is the more difficult to dislodge for being nursed by "mere fiction," supposedly the preserve of pure affect exempt from the demands of factual rigor, historiographic responsibility, or ethically defensible attitudes toward race and racism. In attempting to critique the legacy and ideology of *Gone With the Wind,* Randall recognized the power of contesting Mitchell's novel in the same "fictional" quarter of the public sphere where it held sway. Pannell's infringement decision, however, provided an object lesson in copyright's power to deepen a canonical text's entrenchment. Had it been upheld by higher courts, Mitchell's trustees would have succeeded in protecting what they thought to be her legacy by ensuring that *Gone With the Wind* spawned only adoring sequels. Randall and others would still have been able to critique Mitchell's novel through nonfictional analyses, which are not yet held to be "derivative works." But the most powerful, wide-reaching critique—one that, paradoxically, *must* derive from its object in order to meet it on the same generic field—would have been closed to them for thirty more years.

Happily for Alice Randall, Houghton Mifflin, and advocates of Randall's book and the fair use defense of parody, the preliminary injunction was overturned in May 2001 by the U.S. Court of Appeals in Atlanta, which adjudged Pannell's decision an "abuse of discretion in that it represents an unlawful prior restraint in violation of the First Amendment."[30] In its comprehensive opinion, the Eleventh Circuit affirmed the viability of the parody/fair use defense of *The Wind Done Gone,* questioned the likelihood that Randall's book would cannibalize the market for Mitchell's novel or its authorized sequels, and found that public interest and free speech values counseled against the issuance of an injunction.[31] Pannell's earlier approval of the injunction had touched off a national debate about the proper boundaries between free speech and copyright, and about how, in an enlarged conception of the public sphere, even a work of fiction criticizing another work of fiction might meaningfully comment on the historical atrocity of slavery. *The Wind Done Gone* even attracted corporate advocates. In the weeks before the Court of Appeals hearing, the raft of artists and academics who had defended Randall was joined by an impressive flotilla of media and technology companies, including the *New York Times,* the *Boston Globe,* the *Wall Street Journal,* the *Chicago Tribune,* the *Los Angeles Times,* the *Tampa Tribune,* Cable News Network, Cox Enterprises, Dow Jones & Company, and Microsoft. Though many of the supporting corporations were themselves intellectual property-rich, they nonetheless expressed concern over the court's "blocking publication of a potentially significant fiction that comments on the evils of slavery."[32] The friends-of-the-court briefs they filed in support of Randall testified, at least, that First Amendment advocacy could still outshine copyright defense as a corporate public relations gesture. Martin Garbus, a lawyer for the Mitchell trusts, complained that the Court of Appeals had caved in to the "political correctness" enforced by the media's endorsement of Randall's book, adding that "The racial issues—namely that Margaret

[213]

Mitchell's book is being attacked as racist and the fact that it is Randall, who is black, writing this—I think obscured the copyright issues."[33] But Randall celebrated the reversal, observing with pleasure that it had occurred on May 25, her protagonist's birthday: "And today is the day she will be free."[34]

By pronouncing Cinnamon Brown "free" with the lifting of the injunction, Randall was clearly referring to the exoneration of writer and book from the charge of infringement, with the result that the book and its characters were freed from the legal interdiction that prevented their release, or birth, into the world. But Randall's remark also intimated that the emancipation of *The Wind Done Gone* repeated, commemorated, and perhaps extended the emancipation of African Americans from slavery. That Cinnamon could be emancipated symbolically and legally—at once from slavery and from the jurisdiction of the Mitchell trusts—owes to a certain structural homology between slavery and copyright: like the slave, the literary character in an unauthorized derivative work is held to be the property of another person. In being released from the intellectual property holdings of the Mitchell trusts, Cinnamon troped not only Randall's release from the jurisdiction of that same estate but the author's public recognition as a legitimate copyright owner. By her own formulation, Randall was emancipated through the artistic self-ownership conferred by copyright; her freedom was not just a freedom *from* copyright (Mitchell's), but a freedom *to* copyright her own work. Thus we see the cultural power of copyright to bestow on writers, and particularly on writers who have successfully fought claims that their work was derivative, a sort of citizenship within the authorial polity.

But in its conflation of copyright and slavery, Randall's statement also takes us back to something Robinson's "Melancholy Elephants" seemed to insinuate: that copyright is not just a potential obstacle to the working-through of historical trauma but that it is, itself, a potential cause of trauma—or, equally, that it is a past cause of trauma, and one from which artistic creation is still in shock. This is not to suggest that copyright is a moral atrocity, let alone one equivalent to slavery. Nor would I align copyright with the "traumatic real," which James Berger describes as that which is "incommensurable with narrative and representation," or with the traumatic text, which is often confused with "some other discourse of the incommensurable—as a form of the sublime or the sacred."[35] And yet we have seen in this book how copyright has been increasingly conscripted to sacred functions such as mourning, commemorating, and even deifying creators; how it has been called upon to vanquish death by providing a legal body in which a dead author's spirit may persist; how it is taken to be the very bulwark of authorial personhood, and its violation the violation of a sacred right. We have seen how, at least within literary texts, copyright was for many years a taboo subject, as if it so forcefully determined a work's parameters that it could not be represented within that work. In what I have called the literary property metadiscourse of late modernity—the dawning self-consciousness of imaginative literature with respect to its status as intellectual property—we have perhaps seen the working-through, or perhaps merely the acting-out, of the massive impact copyright has had on the ways cultural discourse is produced, circulated, evaluated, and consumed. In our *Ulysses* thought-experiment, in Robinson's admonitory short story, and in the thankfully short-lived injunction against *The Wind Done Gone,* we have seen premonitions of the potentially catastrophic effect the law might have on fresh creation, and by extension on free speech and the public sphere, if it is permitted to thicken further. We can no longer deny the immensity of copyright's impact or the fact that its statutory codification in 1710 marked the advent of a new epoch. If scholars and artists are only beginning to understand the nature and extent of copyright's downstream influence on aesthetic criteria, on the construction of authorial incentives and entitlements, and on the global circulation of ideas, expression, and capital, it is because they remain inside copyright's influence, swayed by the putative object of study. The contemporary artworks that antagonize copyright and the scholarly studies that interrogate it participate in a deliberate and reasoned engagement with an overextended legal regime that may still be reined in. But because these oppositional works are launched from within cultural and academic markets where copyright not only dominates but partly predetermines the subject-positions and conditions of utterance, they cannot fully exit the thing about which they would speak. The counterdiscourse to strong copyright, in other words, is a symptomatic discourse.

Alice Randall's novel also belongs to a genre whose opposition is partly symptomatic of the traumatic thing it opposes: the genre of appropriative rejoinder (here, as before, I mean "appropriative" in the neutral sense of "making a thing one's own," without the common connotation of theft). It is a genre, moreover, that always achieves a part of its meaning in relation to intellectual property law. Months before the Mitchell trusts filed their infringement suit against it, *The Wind Done Gone* enjoyed advance buzz in *Newsweek* for its "Originality of Premise."[36] But the "originality" of the book's premise, at least, is strictly confined to its choice of source text and its particular angle of riposte. Randall's book belongs to a lengthening genealogy of works, many by subaltern writers, that reproduce aspects of a canonical text's architecture but rewrite that text from its margins for purposes of political protest, rejoinder, restitution, or the working-through of historical trauma. What Randall's novel does with Mitchell's is at least roughly analogous to what Jean Rhys's *Wide Sargasso Sea* (1966) does with Brontë's *Jane Eyre,* or J. M. Coetzee's *Foe* (1986) with Defoe's *Robinson Crusoe,* or John Gardner's *Grendel* (1989) with *Beowulf,* or Peter Carey's *Jack Maggs* (1998) with Dickens's *Great Expectations,* or Sena Jeter Naslund's *Ahab's Wife* (1999) with Melville's *Moby-Dick.* To circumscribe the "originality" of Randall's premise by affiliating it with such works, and even to attribute some of the readerly anticipation of *The Wind Done Gone* to its membership in this genre, is to impugn neither its value nor its originality of expression. It is, however, to situate it within a genre that is self-consciously engaged with problems of originality, replication, and cultural and literary property.

This genre of appropriative rejoinder from the margins asks to whom a text belongs, interrogating, among other things, the logic by which a work ideologically complicit in the historical subjugation of subaltern groups should remain unquestioningly celebrated or immune to powerful forms of criticism, parody, and reevaluation because of its status as private intellectual property. By repeating canonical works with critical differences, these rejoinders perform the reappropriation of a text by a character (and often by an author as well) whose dispossession and infantilization that text has helped naturalize. This gesture, in turn, stands in metonymically for the broader project of reopening historical narratives written by the victors and allowing the losers to rewrite them, possibly transforming the experience of loss into a belated aesthetic and moral strength. The strength such works can achieve is both knowingly belated and self-consciously intertextual because it understands the Romantic mythology of original creation ex nihilo as a form of conquest-narrative, one that ought not to be blithely embraced by the subjects of conquest, occupation, enslavement, and other multigenerational historical traumas. In their constitutive gestures of textual recirculation, *The Wind Done Gone* and its genre-mates recognize that this notion of a vacuum into which radically new things may come is a less tenable fantasy to those whose lives and works are violently and conspicuously predetermined by anterior structures of domination.

It has become almost reflexive for defenders of appropriative and transformative rejoinders to argue that literary "borrowing" of the order of Randall's is not just a newfangled postmodern trend but a long-standing creative practice whose genealogy can be traced to antiquity. Such arguments usually contain a list of appropriative classics, from the ancient Greeks to the present, thereby asserting the legitimacy of literary indebtedness while making Western literature seem unthinkably impoverished without "derivative" works. Several years before he was retained by the Mitchell trusts in their case against Randall, First Amendment lawyer Martin Garbus represented the publishing house Foxrock, Inc., in negotiations with Vladimir Nabokov's son Dmitri over a work supposedly derivative of *Lolita*. In celebrating the settlement of the case, Garbus noted:

> In *Agamemnon,* Aeschylus took characters and incidents (but not the whole story) from Homer, who took the incidents from history. The legend of Pygmalion became a play by George Bernard Shaw, which became the show *My Fair Lady.* If Homer's estate sued Aeschylus, or if Pygmalion's author sued Shaw, I would hope the ancient courts would allow the works. To take a mod-

ern example, Michael Cunningham's novel *The Hours*—this year's Pulitzer Prize winner for fiction and a work of unquestioned originality—pays homage to Virginia Woolf's *Mrs. Dalloway* and clearly refers to characters and incidents from that novel.[37]

Garbus's argument may be persuasive in general terms, but its hypothetical premise of "ancient courts" trying copyright infringement cases against not only Aeschylus but Shaw jokingly glosses over something crucial: that copyright law and the notions of original genius and illegal appropriation with which it is coeval are specifically modern formations that testify to a radical break with classical, medieval, and even early modern notions of authorship and intellectual property.[38] Part of what separates *Foe, Wide Sargasso Sea,* and other appropriative rejoinders from the works of Homer and Aeschylus is that the later texts were written, as were most of the works they engage, under modern intellectual property regimes that form part of the context for their appropriative and transformative gestures. One might say that copyright is one of the ineliminable contexts within which such works achieve their meaning.

Of course, *Foe, Wide Sargasso Sea, Jack Maggs,* and *Ahab's Wife* did not run the actual risk of infringement suits, as Defoe, Brontë, Dickens, and Melville had been dead long enough for their works to have entered the public domain. But the public domain status of their source texts is itself part of these texts' meaning, as I argued was the case with much of the "Oxen of the Sun" chapter of *Ulysses*. By engaging canonical texts whose copyrights have lapsed, appropriative rejoinders like Rhys's, Coetzee's, and Joyce's do one kind of work that the public domain exists to underwrite: the recirculation and dynamic reinterpretation of texts that have become part not just of the public domain but of the public sphere in its broadest sense. *The Wind Done Gone* performs the same work of reinterpreting a source text affiliated with historical domination, with the difference that its source text is not yet in the public domain. Whether or not one sympathizes with it, Randall's novel achieves part of its meaning by asserting that its project is more urgent than long postmortem copyright terms will permit, and by daring to provoke the very sort of infringement suit that was brought against it. In launching a parodic critique of race politics in *Gone With the Wind*, Randall had also, of necessity, launched a critique of the thick copyright regime that nearly put Mitchell's classic beyond the reach of such criticism for another generation. Judge Pannell's decision reveals something ugly about the thick copyright position, particularly when it deactivates the parody/fair use defense: namely, a structural bias toward maintaining canonical texts in unchallenged states of consecration. The reversal of Pannell's decision by the Court of Appeals is heartening and attests to both the vitality of First Amendment advocacy and the viability of the parody/fair use defense. In the face of the prevailing maximalism already embodied in U.S. and international law, however, it is a small countervailing force. The inevitable next wave of term and rights extension bills will seek to prolong the cultural privilege of canonical texts by deferring the legality, and thus the commercial viability, of critiques-in-kind. If copyright continues generally to thicken, it will, one imagines, further provoke the sense of urgency felt by critical parodists like Randall, and perhaps engender the richest *samizdat* literature ever to thrive in a free society.

The appearance of *Wide Sargasso Sea, Foe,* and other appropriative rejoinders is usually ascribed to the oppositional energies of anticolonial and postcolonial consciousness, feminism, and civil rights. But it is not incidental, I think, that this genre should have taken root during a period also notable for its intellectual property maximalism, and that the genre's constitutive works should articulate a challenge through their very form to the maximalist orthodoxy that makes not only texts but their sequels and spin-offs the intellectual property of a sole originator. If the oppositional energy of these works is directed at private intellectual property canons as well as at historical oppression and exploitation, we might posit a relationship between the two. Intellectual property maximalism may be one means by which its advocate-nations—most of them developed nations and former imperial powers—have compensated for the loss of territorial empires and the natural resources, forced or cheap labor, and captive markets that have historically attended them. Part of this compensation has been effected through the creation of a different order of spatial domain: the spread and "harmonization" of international copyright during the twentieth century has massively influenced the social production and meaning of space and extended the spatial influence of intellectual property-rich economies. But, as we have seen, the thickening of copyright during the same century also involved enlarging the rightsholder's imperium over time, granting extensive and exclusive ownership in the downstream effects of a work long after its author is dead. These expansionist moves, carried out in the names of creative individuals, have tended to expand the powers of estates and corporations even more dramatically. And because contemporary intellectual property regimes originated in developed Western nations and favor the modes of innovation and production dominant in those nations, the globalization of these same regimes has concentrated intellectual property-based wealth in the first world and maintained a neocolonial imbalance in the international flow of intellectual property, from the developing nations where much of it is harvested to the first-world nations where it is privatized, capitalized, transacted, and litigated.

The neocolonial uses of intellectual property law are most visible in patents, which enable multinationals to engage in, among other things, biopiracy—the appropriation of cures, seeds, spices, farming methods, cooking techniques, and other forms of cultural property developed collectively by traditional rural populations, which then, because of the individualist bias of the law, have no legal means by which to demand recompense for their expropriated communal intellectual property. Vandana Shiva and others have done pathbreaking work in exposing and protesting both corporate biopiracy and the legal metaphysics that make it possible; this is not the place to rehearse the details of their findings. But we have seen in the examples of the Joyce Estate and the Mitchell trusts how extensive postmortem copyright creates durable intellectual property demesnes whose trustees are endowed with substantial power to determine not only where the protected works will circulate but what degree of criticism, dissent, irreverence, and even adoring tribute will be permitted in a wide range of derivative works. Estates rely to a large extent on the public to determine the relevance and importance of protected works—in other words, the value of the estate—not just through consumption but through interpretation, debate, scholarship, fantasy, adaptation, distortion, and appropriation. But the estates are also empowered to dictate certain aspects of a work's afterlife, as well as to deny members of the public the right to express their responses in forms indebted to the same texts whose cultural vitality relies on the public's willingness to engage with them, enter into their worlds, and dissent from them. And these powers last a very, very long time. Though the situation brought about by strong copyright regimes is not exactly homologous with neocolonialist biopiracy, there are a number of disquieting similarities: in the power of both the literary estate and the multinational agribusiness to benefit from a collective to which it owes virtually nothing in return and to whom it can sell back the privatized fruits of public discourse; in the flourishing of private intellectual property industries through the evacuation of a public domain; in the unsustainable privatization of a commons whose former openness helped crucially to enrich and empower the advocates of its subsequent enclosure.

But we have also seen a certain coming-to-consciousness within literary communities and texts about copyright as a variously enabling, policing, and chilling force in both cultural production and the public discourse to which literature must be seen as belonging. We have discerned in the Anglo-American cento of the nineteenth century a readerly, or consumerist, model of authorship that performs a proleptic "fair use" of protected material for the sake not even of criticism or comment but of fresh creation. We saw how Victorian defenses of plagiarism and Oscar Wilde's commission of plagiarism engaged, through both argument and form, in a reevaluation of that literary offense, revealing the extent to which its transgressiveness is rooted in a productivist model of aesthetic value and in the private literary property conventions of a lettered culture. In Wilde's "The Portrait of Mr. W. H." and Viereck's *The House of the Vampire,* we saw the legal metaphysics of copyright—its creation of an alienable intellectual property and its idea/expression dichotomy, in particular—deployed at once centrally and skeptically in the plots of imaginative literature. The terminal narrative of copyright we found projected in Wilde's long prison letter onto a carceral aesthetics, and in Joyce's "Oxen of the Sun" onto a parodic chronology of English prose, in a textual environment that both capitalizes on and parodies copyright. And we saw in the earlier pages of this conclusion how copyright has become an implicit and explicit topic in an imaginative literature that has learned, in recent decades, to see the overextension of copyright as one of the traumatic preconditions of literary creation and subaltern working-through in postmodernity.

In describing the dawning self-consciousness of a literature in relation to its property status and the incubation of oppositional strategies by that literature, I have implied the growth of what one might call an anticolonialist discourse to intellectual property's colonization of the public sphere and the public domain. Such a formulation runs the risk of seeming to reduce the historical specificities of colonialism to a mere trope. This is certainly not my intention here, and I would point out that the structural homologies between colonialism and the thickening of copyright are compounded by emerging critiques of a corporate neocolonialism that is enabled by intellectual property law and is a direct legacy of more conventional forms of colonialism. Despite occasional hopeful decisions like *Campbell v. Acuff-Rose Music* and the recent Alice Randall case, something related is going on in the sector of the public sphere regulated by copyright: a legislative paternalism that says public discourse and the public domain must be further circumscribed—and for their own good. Against such paternalism, one observes that literary writers and their works are not just the passive subjects of copyright law, responding to its incentives and heeding its interdictions with equal docility. They are also symptoms of the legal regimes under whose incentives and prohibitions fresh creation occurs. And, as I have argued in this book, they should be seen as resources for present debates about intellectual property law, insofar as a number of these authors and texts have come to think, in ways that differ importantly from conventional legal discourse, about problems such as the law's core dichotomies, the extension of postmortem copyright toward what Peter Jaszi has called "perpetual copyright on the installment plan," and the consequences for democratic discourse of extreme textual privatization.[39] Attending to how intellectual property gets thought about *in* the imaginative works it governs will equip us to find a more generative balance in the law, to check shareholder and rightsholder sovereignty in favor of the diminished sovereignty of the public, and to rededicate the works—and the work—of our cultures to the usufruct of the living.

Appendix

A Collection of Nineteenth-Century Centos

1   ADDRESS
*Spoken to the Literary Friends assembled at Westfelton,
on Shakspeare's Birth-Day, 1814.
Formed from his Works.*

Kind friends, sweet friends, peace be unto this meeting,
Joy and fair time, health, and good wishes ever.
Now, worthy friends, the cause why we are met,
Is in celebration of the day that gave
Our matchless Shakspeare birth: and took him to
That undiscover'd country, from whose bourne
No traveller returns. He was in sooth
The most replenished sweet work of Nature,
Which from the prime creation e'er she fram'd;
And trained up within her own sweet court;
Where, being but young, he framed to the harp
Full many an English ditty lovely well.

Do not smile at me that I boast him off,
For ye shall find he will outstrip all praise,
And make it halt behind him:—'twere as well
To gild refined gold, to paint the lilly,
To throw a perfume on the violet,
To smoothe the ice, or add another hue
Unto the rainbow, or with taper-light
To seek the beauteous face of heaven to garnish.
Oh! he's above all praise: it were all one
That I should love a bright particular star,
And think to wed it, he is so above me:
In his bright radiance, and collateral light
Must I be comforted, not in his sphere.
Yet was he gentle: for who were below him
He us'd as creatures of another place,

    Notes to the centos will be found in the Notes section that follows this Appendix. Titled centos are keyed to the poem's number and title; untitled centos are keyed to the poem's number and first line.

And bow'd his eminent top to their low ranks,
Making them proud of his humility.

O thou divinest Nature! how thyself thou blazon'st
In this thy princely boy! he was as gentle
As zephyrs blowing below the violet
Not wagging its sweet head: and yet as rough,
His noble blood enchaf'd, as th' rudest wind
That by the top doth take the mountain pines
And make them stoop to th' vale. 'Tis wonderful,
That an invisible instinct should frame him
To poetry, unlearn'd; honour, untaught;
Civility, not seen in other; knowledge,
That wildly grew in him, yet yielded crops
As though it had been sown: for he could find
Tongues in the trees, books in the running brooks,
Sermons in stones, and good in every thing;
Holding as 'twere the mirror up to Nature,
Shewing Virtue her own feature, Scorn her image,
The very age and body of the time
Its form and pressure:—Hear but his Mirth,
Perforce you'd laugh, sans intermission,
An hour by the dial; for in his brain,
(Which then's as dry as the remainder biscuit
After a voyage), he hath strange places cramm'd
With observation, the which he vents
In mangled forms. In sooth a merrier man
Within the limit of becoming mirth
We cannot spend an hour's talk withal:
His eye begets occasion for his wit;
For every object that the one doth catch,
The other turns to a mirth-moving jest,
Which his fair pen (Conceit's expositor)
Delivers in such apt and gracious words,
That aged ears play truant at his tales,
And younger hearings are quite ravished.

So sweet and voluble is his discourse,
That hear him reason in Divinity,
And, all-admiring, with an inward wish
You would desire he had been made a prelate.
Hear him debate on Commonwealth affairs,
You'd say—it had been all-in-all his study.
List his discourse of War, and you shall hear
A fearful battle render'd you in music.
Turn him to any part of Poesy,
The Gordian knot of it will he unloose
Familiar as his garter; that when he speaks,
A still mute wonder lurketh in men's ears

To steal his sweet and honied sentences,
That not o'erstep the modesty of Nature,
Take them and cut them out in little stars,
They're thick inlaid with patines of bright gold,
And fall on us, like gentle dews from heav'n
Upon the plants beneath; they are twice blest,
They bless both him that gives, and him that takes.

Tho' Gentleness his soft enforcement be,
Yet he in fiction, in a dream of Passion,
Can force his soul so to his whole conceit,
That he can drown the very stage with tears,
And cleave the general ear with horrid speech,
Make mad the guilty, and appal the free,
Confound the ignorant, and amaze indeed
The very faculties of eyes and ears.

He can call spirits from the vasty deep,
Make church-yards yawn, and shew the sheeted ghosts
Revisiting the glimpses of the moon,
Making night horrible, and tales unfold
That harrow up the soul, and freeze the blood
To hear them squeal and gibber.—

      He is Fancy's midwife,
Ruling at will, by his so potent art,
The elves of hills, brooks, standing lakes, and groves,
That do by moonshine, green sour ringlets make,
Whereof the ewe not bites; that dew-drops seek,
And hang a pearl in ev'ry cowslip's ear,
While sweet the moonlight sleeps upon the bank
And tips with silver all the fruit-tree tops.

He's of Imagination all compact,
For aye his eye, in a fine phrenzy rolling,
Doth glance from heav'n to earth, from earth to heav'n,
And as Imagination bodies forth
The forms of things unknown, his ready pen
Turns them to shapes, and gives to airy nothings
A local habitation and a name.

Oh! what a noble piece of work was he,
In faculty, in reason infinite!
Express and admirable, like an angel!
A combination and a form indeed
Where every god did seem to set his seal.

Heav'n has him now.—Yet let our idolat'rous fancy
Still sanctify his reliques; and this day
Stand aye distinguish'd in the calendar
To the last syllable of recorded time.

And from his fair and unpolluted grave
May violets spring.—With sweetest fairest flowers,
While proud pied April, drest in all his trim,
And Summer lasts, and I live here, Sweet William,
We'll strew thy grave. Carnations and streaked gilliflowers,
Hot lavender, mints, savoury, marjoram,
The freckled cowslip, burnet, and green clover;
The marigold, that goes to bed with 'Sun,
And with him rises weeping. Daffodils,
That come before the swallow dares, and take
The winds of March with beauty: violets dim,
But sweeter than the lids of Juno's eyes,
Or Cytheraea's breath: pale primroses
That die unmarried, ere they can behold
Bright Phoebus in his strength. Bold oxslips, and
The crown Imperial: lillies of all kinds,
The flower-de-lis being one.—And then we'll all
Ring Fancy's knell, with concord of sweet sounds,
And true-love showers.—

  Sweets to the sweet, farewell!
For if we take him but for all in all,
We ne'er shall look upon his like again.

2   ODE TO THE HUMAN HEART

  Blind Thamyris, and blind Mæonides,
   Pursue the triumph and partake the gale!
  Drop tears as fast as the Arabian trees,
   To point a moral or adorn a tale.*

  Full many a gem of purest ray serene,
   Thoughts that do often lie too deep for tears,
  Like angels' visits, few and far between,
   Deck the long vista of departed years.

  Man never is, but always to be bless'd;
   The tenth transmitter of a foolish face,
  Like Aaron's serpent, swallows up the rest,
   And makes a sunshine in the shady place.

  For man the hermit sigh'd, till woman smiled,
   To waft a feather or to drown a fly,
  (In wit a man, simplicity a child,)
   With silent finger pointing to the sky.

  But fools rush in where angels fear to tread,
   Far out amid the melancholy main;
  As when a vulture on Imaus bred,
   Dies of a rose in aromatic pain.

A Collection of Nineteenth-Century Centos

Music hath charms to soothe the savage breast,
    Look on her face, and you'll forget them all;
Some mute inglorious Milton here may rest,
    A hero perish, or a sparrow fall.

My way of life is fall'n into the sere;
    I stood in Venice on the Bridge of Sighs,
Like a rich jewel in an Ethiop's ear,
    Who sees through all things with his half-shut eyes.

Oh! for a lodge in some vast wilderness!
    Full many a flower is born to blush unseen,
Fine by degrees and beautifully less,
    And die ere man can say 'Long live the Queen.'

*The printer's devil had taken upon himself to make the following addition to these lines:—

Blind Thamyris, and blind Mæonides,	(*Something like Milton*).
Pursue the triumph and partake the gale!	(*Rather like Pope*).
Drop tears as fast as the Arabian trees,	(*Why, this is Shakspeare*).
To point a moral or adorn a tale.	(*Oh! it's Dr. Johnson*).

To the succeeding lines the same authority had added in succession the names of Gray, Wordsworth, Campbell, and so on throughout the poem. What does he mean? Does he mean to say he has ever met with any one of these lines *before*?

3   [UNTITLED]

    When lovely woman stoops to folly,
        And finds too late that men betray,
    There's such a charm in melancholy,
        I would not if I could be gay.

4   [UNTITLED]

    There's a beauty for ever unchangingly bright
        For coming events cast their shadows before;
    Oh! think not my spirits are always as light,
        Like ocean-weeds cast on the surf-beaten shore.

5   "ON LIFE, ET CETERA"

Know then this truth, enough for man to know:
Be thou as chaste as ice, as pure as snow,
Who would be free themselves must strike the blow.
Retreating lightly with a lovely fear
From grave to gay, from lively to severe,

The Copywrights

    To err is human, to forgive divine,
    And wretches hang that jurymen may dine
    Like quills upon the fretful porcupine.
    All are but parts of one stupendous whole,
    The feast of reason and the flow of soul.

    We ne'er shall look upon his like again,
    For panting time toils after him in vain,
    And drags at each remove a lengthening chain;
    Allures to brighter worlds, and leads the way
    With sweet, reluctant, amorous delay!

6   [UNTITLED]

    'Tis distance lends enchantment to the view,
    It was the sweetest flower that ever grew.

7   [UNTITLED]

    'Twas Greece, but living Greece no more;
        Memorial frail of youthful years;
    He sat beside the cottage door;
        His was a grief too deep for tears.

8   [UNTITLED]

    The curfew tolls the knell of parting day,
        In every clime from Lapland to Japan;
    To fix one spark of beauty's heavenly ray—
        The proper study of mankind is man.

    Tell, for you can, what is it to be wise,
        Sweet Auburn, loveliest village of the plain;
    'The Man of Ross!' each lisping babe replies,
        And drags, at each remove, a lengthening chain.

    Ah! who can tell how hard it is to climb,
        Far as the solar walk or milky way?
    Procrastination is the thief of time,
        Let Hercules himself do what he may.

    'Tis education forms the common mind,
        The feast of reason and the flow of soul;
    I must be cruel only to be kind,
        And waft a sigh from Indus to the pole.

    Syphax! I joy to meet you thus alone,
        Where'er I roam, whatever lands I see;

A youth to fortune and to fame unknown,
   In maiden meditation fancy free.

Farewell! and wheresoe'er thy voice be tried,
   Why to yon mountain turns the gazing eye,
With spectacles on nose, and pouch on side,
   That teach the rustic moralist how to die.

Pity the sorrows of a poor old man,
   Whose beard descending swept his aged breast;
Laugh where we must, be candid where we can,
Man never is, but always to be blest.

9   [MOSAIC POETRY]

I only knew she came and went	*Lowell.*
Like troutlets in a pool;	*Hood.*
She was a phantom of delight,	*Wordsworth.*
And I was like a fool.	*Eastman.*
"One kiss, dear maid," I said and sighed,	*Coleridge.*
"Out of those lips unshorn."	*Longfellow.*
She shook her ringlets round her head,	*Stoddard.*
And laughed in merry scorn.	*Tennyson.*
Ring out, wild bells, to the wild sky	*Tennyson.*
You hear them, oh my heart?	*Alice Carey.*
'Tis twelve at night by the castle clock,	*Coleridge.*
Beloved, we must part!	*Alice Carey.*
"Come back! come back!" she cried in grief,	*Campbell.*
"My eyes are dim with tears—	*Bayard Taylor.*
How shall I live through all the days,	*Mrs. Osgood.*
All through a hundred years?"	*T. S. Perry.*
'Twas in the prime of summer time,	*Hood.*
She blessed me with her hand;	*Hoyt.*
We strayed together, deeply blest,	*Mrs. Edwards.*
Into the Dreaming Land.	*Cornwall.*
The laughing bridal roses blow,	*Patmore.*
To dress her dark brown hair;	*Bayard Taylor.*
No maiden may with her compare,	*Brailsford.*
Most beautiful, most rare!	*Read.*
I clasped it on her sweet cold hand,	*Browning.*
The precious golden link;	*Smith.*
I calmed her fears, and she was calm,	*Coleridge.*
"Drink, pretty creature, drink!"	*Wordsworth.*
And so I won my Genevieve,	*Coleridge.*
And walked in Paradise;	*Hervey.*

The Copywrights

The fairest thing that ever grew	*Wordsworth.*
Atween me and the skies.	*Osgood.*

10   **CENTO FROM POPE**

'Tis education forms the common mind;	*Moral Essays.*
A mighty maze! but not without a plan.	*Essay on Man.*
Ask of the learned the way? The learned are blind;	" "
The proper study of mankind is man.	" "
A little learning is a dangerous thing;	*Essay on Criticism.*
Some have at first for wits, then poets passed—	" "
See from each clime the learned their incense bring,	" "
For rising merit will buoy up at last.	" "
Tell (for you can) what is it to be wise.—	*Essay on Man.*
Virtue alone is happiness below;	" "
Honor and shame from no condition rise,	" "
And all our knowledge is ourselves to know.	" "
Who shall decide when doctors disagree?	*Moral Essays.*
One truth is clear, whatever is, is right.	*Essay on Man.*
Since men interpret texts, why should not we	*January and May.*
Read them by day and meditate by night?	*Essay on Criticism.*

11   **[UNTITLED]**

When first I met thee, warm and young,	*Moore.*
My heart I gave thee with my hand;	*Morris.*
My name was then a magic spell,	*Norton.*
Casting a dim religious light.	*Milton.*
But now, as we plod on our way,	*Percival.*
My heart no more with rapture swells;	*McNaughton.*
I would not, if I could, be gay,	*Rogers.*
When earth is filled with cold farewells!	*Patmore.*
The heath this night must be my bed,	*Scott.*
Ye vales, ye streams, ye groves, adieu!	*Pope.*
Farewell for aye, e'en love is dead,	*Procter.*
Would I could add, remembrance too!	*Byron.*

12   **LIFE**

1.—Why all this toil for triumphs of an hour?
2.—Life's a short summer, man a flower.
3.—By turns we catch the vital breath and die—
4.—The cradle and the tomb, alas! so nigh.

A Collection of Nineteenth-Century Centos

    5.—To be is better far than not to be,
    6.—Though all man's life may seem a tragedy.
    7.—But light cares speak when mighty griefs are dumb;
    8.—The bottom is but shallow whence they come.
    9.—Your fate is but the common fate of all,
  10.—Unmingled joys, here, to no man befall.
  11.—Nature to each allots his proper sphere,
  12.—Fortune makes folly her peculiar care.
  13.—Custom does not often reason overrule
  14.—And throw a cruel sunshine on a fool.
  15.—Live well, how long or short permit, to heaven;
  16.—They who forgive most, shall be most forgiven.
  17.—Sin may be clasped so close we cannot see its face—
  18.—Vile intercourse where virtue has not place.
  19.—Then keep each passion down, however dear,
  20.—Thou pendulum, betwixt a smile and tear;
  21.—Her sensual snares let faithless pleasure lay,
  22.—With craft and skill, to ruin and betray.
  23.—Soar not too high to fall, but stop to rise;
  24.—We masters grow of all that we despise.
  25.—Oh then renounce that impious self-esteem;
  26.—Riches have wings and grandeur is a dream.
  27.—Think not ambition wise, because 'tis brave,
  28.—The paths of glory lead but to the grave.
  29.—What is ambition? 'Tis a glorious cheat,
  30.—Only destructive to the brave and great.
  31.—What's all the gaudy glitter of a crown?
  32.—The way to bliss lies not on beds of down.
  33.—How long we live, not years but actions tell;
  34.—That man lives twice who lives the first life well.
  35.—Make then, while yet ye may, your God your friend,
  36.—Whom Christians worship, yet not comprehend.
  37.—The trust that's given guard, and to yourself be just;
  38.—For, live we how we can, yet die we must.

---

1. Young. 2. Dr. Johnson. 3. Pope. 4. Prior. 5. Sewell. 6. Spenser. 7. Daniel. 8. Sir Walter Raleigh. 9. Longfellow. 10. Southwell. 11. Congreve. 12. Churchill. 13. Rochester. 14. Armstrong. 15. Milton. 16. Bailey. 17. Trench. 18. Somerville. 19. Thomson. 20. Byron. 21. Smollett. 22. Crabbe. 23. Massinger. 24. Cowley. 25. Beattie. 26. Cowper. 27. Sir Walter Davenant. 28. Gray. 29. Willis. 30. Addison. 31. Dryden. 32. Francis Quarles. 33. Watkins. 34. Herrick. 35. William Mason. 36. Hill. 37. Dana. 38. Shakespeare.

13   THE POETS' "ESSAY ON MAN"

    1. What strange infatuation rules mankind,
    2. What different spheres to human bliss assigned;

The Copywrights

3. To loftier things your finer pulses burn,
4. If man would but his finer nature learn;
5. What several ways men to their calling have,
6. And grasp at life though sinking to the grave.

7. Ask what is human life? the sage replies,
8. Wealth, pomp, and honour are but empty toys;
9. We trudge, we travel, but from pain to pain,
10. Weak, timid landsmen, on life's stormy main;
11. We only toil who are the first of things,
12. From labour health, from health contentment springs.
13. Fame runs before us as the morning star,
14. How little do we know that which we are;
15. Let none then here his certain knowledge boast,
16. Of fleeting joys too certain to be lost;
17. For over all there hangs a cloud of fear,
18. All is but change and separation here.

19. To smooth life's passage o'er its stormy way,
20. Sum up at night what thou hast done by day;
21. Be rich in patience if thou in gudes be poor;
22. So many men do stoope to sight unsure;
23. Choose out the man to virtue best inclined,
24. Throw envy, folly, prejudice behind;
25. Defer not till to-morrow to be wise,
26. Wealth heaped on wealth, nor truth, nor safety buys;
27. Remembrance worketh with her busy train.
28. Care draw on care, woe comforts woe again;
29. On high estates huge heaps of care attend,
30. No joy so great but runneth to an end;
31. No hand applaud what honour shuns to hear,
32. Who casts off shame, should likewise cast off fear;
33. Grief haunts us down the precipice of years.
34. Virtue alone no dissolution fears;
35. Time loosely spent will not again be won,
36. What shall I do to be for ever known?

37. But now the wane of life comes darkly on,
38. After a thousand mazes overgone;
39. In this brief state of trouble and unrest,
40. Man never is, but always to be blest.
41. Time is the present hour, the past is fled,
42. O thou Futurity, our hope and dread.
43. How fading are the joys we dote upon,
44. Lo! while I speak the present moment's gone.

45. O Thou Eternal Arbiter of things,
46. How awful is the hour when conscience stings!
47. Conscience, stern arbiter in every breast,
48. The fluttering wish on wing that will not rest.

A Collection of Nineteenth-Century Centos

49. This above all,—To thine own self be true,
50. Learn to live well, that thou may'st die so too.
51. To those that list the world's gay scenes I leave,
52. Some ills we wish for, when we wish to live.

---

1. Chatterton. 2. Rogers. 3. Sprague. 4. Dana. 5. Ben Jonson. 6. Falconer. 7. Cowper. 8. Ferguson. 9. Quarles. 10. Burns. 11. Tennyson. 12. Beattie. 13. Dryden. 14. Byron. 15. Pomfret. 16. Waller. 17. Hood. 18. Steele. 19. Dwight. 20. Herbert. 21. Dunbar. 22. Whitney. 23. Rowe. 24. Langhorne. 25. Congreve. 26. Dr. Johnson. 27. Goldsmith. 28. Drayton. 29. Webster. 30. Southwell. 31. Thomson. 32. Sheridan Knowles. 33. Landor. 34. Edward Moore. 35. Greene. 36. Cowley. 37. Joanna Baillie. 38. Keats. 39. B. Barton. 40. Pope. 41. Marsden. 42. Elliott. 43. Blair. 44. Oldham. 45. Akenside. 46. Percival. 47. J. A. Hillhouse. 48. Mallet. 49. Shakespeare. 50. Sir J. Denham. 51. Spenser. 52. Young.

14   MARRIAGE

1. Marriage, if rightly understood,
   Gives to the tender and the good,
2. The eye, where pure affection beams,
   The tear, from tenderness that streams—
3. Whate'er a blooming world contains,
   That wings the air, that skims the plains.
4. Go search among your idle dreams,
   Your busy or your vain extremes,
   And find a life of equal bliss,
   Or own the next begun in this.
5. Cordial of life, thus marriage pours
   Her comfort on our heavier hours.
6. The hour that rolls for ever on,
   Tells us years must soon be gone—
7. Say, dost thou not at evening hour
   Feel some soft and secret power
   Gliding o'er thy yielding mind,
8. Nor leave one wretched thought behind?
9. Come press my lips and lie with me,
10. From avarice and ambition free;
11. Or say, what soft propitious hour,
    I best may choose to hail thy power!
12. Plain innocence, in white arrayed,
    Before us lifts her fearless head;
13. Whose yielding hearts and joining hands
    Find blessings twisted with our bands.
14. If these delights thy mind can move,
    Come live with me and be my love.

---

1. Cotton. 2. Logan. 3. Ogilvie. 4. Parnell. 5. Graves. 6. Dwight. 7. Langhorne. 8. Montgomery. 9. Kirke White. 10. Cowper. 11. Barbauld. 12. Thomson. 13. Watts. 14. Marlowe.

[231]

The Copywrights

15   [THE FATE OF THE GLORIOUS DEVIL]

1. A glorious devil, large in heart and brain,
2.   Doomed for a certain term to walk the night,
3. The world forsaking with a calm disdain,
4.   Majestic rises on the astonished sight.

5. Type of the wise who soar, but never roam—
6.   Mark how it mounts to man's imperial race!
7. High is his perch, but humble is his home,
8.   Fast anchored in the deep abyss of space.

9. And oft the craggy cliff he loved to climb,
10.   Where Punch and Scaramouch aloft are seen;
11. Where Science mounts in radiant car sublime,
12.   And twilight fairies tread the circled green.

13. And, borne aloft by the sustaining blast,
14.   Whom no man fully sees, and none can see;
15. 'Wildered and weary, sits him down at last,
16.   Beneath the shelter of an aged tree.

17. I will not stop to tell how far he fled,
18.   To view the smile of evening on the sea;
19. He tried to smile, and, half succeeding, said,
20.   'I smell a loller in the wind,' said he.

21. 'What if the lion in his rage I meet?'
22.   (The Muse interprets thus his tender thought.)
23. The scourge of Heaven! what terrors round him wait!
24.   From planet whirled to planet more remote.

25. Thence higher still, by countless steps conveyed,
26.   Remote from towns he ran his godly race;
27. He lectured every youth that round him played—
28.   The jostling tears ran down his honest face.

29. 'Another spring!' his heart exulting cries.
30.   Vain are his weapons, vainer is his force;
31. A milk-white lion of tremendous size
32.   Lays him along the snows a stiffened corpse.

33. The hay-cock rises, and the frequent rake
34.   Looks on the bleeding foe that made him bleed;
35. And the green lizard and the golden snake
36.   Pause at the bold irrevocable deed.

37. Will ye one transient ray of gladness dart,
38.   To bid the genial tear of pity flow?
39. By Heaven! I would rather coin my heart,
40.   Or Mr. Miller's, commonly called Joe!

1. Tennyson. 2. Shakespeare. 3. Thompson. 4. Taite. 5. Wordsworth. 6. Pope. 7. Grahame. 8. Cowper. 9. Beattie. 10. Rogers. 11. Hemans. 12. Collins. 13. Longfellow. 14. Prior. 15. Beattie. 16. Burns. 17. Wordsworth. 18. Hemans. 19. Crabbe. 20. Chaucer. 21. Collins. 22. Beattie. 23. Gray. 24. Campbell. 25. Bloomfield. 26. Goldsmith. 27. Rogers. 28. Burns. 29. Bloomfield. 30. Byron. 31. Falconer. 32. Thomson. 33. Joanna Baillie. 34. Byron. 35. Shelley. 36. Euripides. 37. Beattie. 38. Hemans. 39. Shakespeare. 40. Horace Smith.

16 [UNTITLED]

Breathes there a man with soul so dead,
Who never to himself hath said,
    Shoot folly as it flies?
Ah, more than tears of blood can tell,
Are in that word farewell, farewell;
    'Tis folly to be wise.

And what is Friendship but a name
That burns on Etna's breast of flame?
    Thus runs the world away.
Sweet is the ship that's under sail
To where yon taper points the vale
    With hospitable ray.

Drink to me only with thine eyes
Through cloudless climes and starry skies,
    My native land, good-night.
Adieu, adieu, my native shore;
'Tis Greece, but living Greece no more.
    Whatever is is right.

Oh, ever thus from childhood's hour,
Daughter of Jove, relentless power,
    In russet mantle clad.
The rocks and hollow mountains rung
While yet in early Greece she sung,
    I'm pleased, and yet I'm sad.

In sceptred pall come sweeping by,
O, thou, the nymph with placid eye,
    By Philip's warlike son;
And on the light fantastic toe
Thus hand-in-hand through life we'll go;
    Good-night to Marmion.

[233]

Notes

Introduction: Intellectual Property and Critique

1. These descriptions apply more precisely to Anglo-American copyright law than to Continental copyright regimes. To a much greater extent than British common law and U.S. constitutional law, the Continental civil-law tradition recognizes a *droit moral* or moral right—an authorial entitlement to control a work and to prevent others from altering it. In France this right is perpetual and therefore outlasts the finite term of copyright protection. The natural-rights doctrine of *droit moral*, in Raymond Sarraute's words, protects "the intimate bond that exists between a literary or artistic work and its author's personality." See Raymond Sarraute, "Current Theory on the Moral Right of Authors and Artists Under French Law," *American Journal of Comparative Law* 16 (1968): 465. Anglo-American law has at times recognized the existence of such a bond, as can be seen in the success authors have had in protecting their moral rights via rights of privacy/publicity and defamation and rights in derivative works; see the U.S. case *Gilliam v. American Broadcasting Cos., Inc.*, 538 F.2d 14 (2d Cir. 1976), in which the British comedy troupe Monty Python used copyright to defend the integrity of their programs against cutting to accommodate advertisement and censorship. However, Anglo-American law views the bond between work and authorial personality as alienable to a greater extent than does Continental law; thus, the artist who transfers the copyright in a work to a publisher or commissioner retains only limited rights in withdrawing it, preserving its integrity, being acknowledged as its creator (though see note 2, below, on the inalienable rights of attribution and integrity enjoyed by authors of visual works of art). See Michael P. Ryan, *Knowledge Diplomacy: Global Competition and the Politics of Intellectual Property* (Washington, D.C.: Brookings Institution Press, 1998), 63–65. Still, as Brad Sherman and Lionel Bently have recently argued, the differences between British intellectual property law and that of other legal communities is frequently exaggerated—often in order to claim that this "indigenous" or "vernacular" British canon is superior to those of other nations. See Brad Sherman and Lionel Bently, *The Making of Modern Intellectual Property Law: The British Experience* (Cambridge: Cambridge University Press, 1999), 212–15.

2. U.S. copyright law does endow authors of works of visual art with *inalienable* rights of attribution and integrity. Such authors have the right to claim authorship over their works, to prevent the use of their names in connection with works they did not create, and to prevent the use of their names in connection with distortions or mutilations of their works. Such authors also enjoy the right to "prevent any intentional distortion, mutilation, or other modification of that work which would be prejudicial to [their] honor or reputation," as well as the destruction of a work of recognized stature. See 17 U.S.C. § 106A(a) (1990). These rights last for the duration of the author's life. However, they should not be mistaken for copyrights. Unlike both the work itself and the copyright in the work, rights of attribution and integrity cannot be transferred to others.

3. U.S. copyright-term extensions since 1962 were as follows: 3 years to subsisting copy-

Notes to Pages 4–8

rights in 1962 (Pub. L. 87–668); 2 years to subsisting copyrights in 1965 (Pub. L. 89–142); 1 year to subsisting copyrights in 1967 (Pub. L. 90–141), 1968 (Pub. L. 90–416), 1969 (Pub. L. 91–147), 1970 (Pub. L. 91–555), and 1971 (Pub. L. 92–170); and 2 years to subsisting copyrights in 1972 (Pub. L. 92–566) and 1974 (Pub. L. 93–573); and 5 years to subsisting copyrights in 1976 (Pub. L. 105–298).

4. International law has recently resuscitated certain lapsed copyrights: Title V of the 1994 Uruguay Round Agreements Act restored the U.S. copyright in foreign works whose protection had lapsed due to "noncompliance with formalities imposed at any time by United States copyright law." If the World Intellectual Property Organization and the U.S. Congress adopt proposed legislation to create copyrights in databases, an effectively perpetual copyright will have been instituted: the 25-year copyright term for databases would be renewed every time new data were added to the database. See Siva Vaidhyanathan, *Copyrights and Copywrongs: The Rise of Intellectual Property and How It Threatens Creativity* (New York: New York University Press, 2001), 167.

5. The case, which I discuss at greater length in chapter 5, is *Campbell v. Acuff-Rose Music, Inc.,* 510 U.S. 569 (1994). In its ruling, the Supreme Court stated that even a for-profit parody might qualify as a fair use of the original it redeploys, as long as the parody comments critically in some way on the original. Though it broadened the purview of fair use, the ruling did not establish a blanket fair use exemption for all parodies, as subsequent cases have shown. In 1996, for instance, the U.S. Court of Appeals for the 9th Circuit upheld a federal district court injunction on behalf of Dr. Seuss Enterprises against a parody entitled *The Cat NOT in the Hat,* a book by "Dr. Juice" whose target was O. J. Simpson. The U.S. Court of Appeals ruled that the work failed to qualify as fair use under the *Campbell v. Acuff-Rose* precedent because its vehicle (Seuss's book) and its target (the Simpson case) were separate: "the substance and content of *The Cat in the Hat* is not conjured up by the focus on the Brown-Goldman murders or the O. J. Simpson trial." The Court's decision turned on a distinction in *Campbell v. Acuff-Rose* between "parody," which targets the text it mimics, and "satire," whose mimicry of a text is simply the means by which it assails another target; according to the Court's interpretation, *Campbell v. Acuff-Rose* only allows for the possibility of fair use in parodies, not in satires. See *Dr. Seuss Enterprises v. Penguin Books USA,* 109 F.3d 1394 (9th Cir.), *cert. dism'd* 521 U.S. 1146 (1997).

6. The statute that inaugurated British copyright law in 1710, widely known as the Statue of Anne, was actually entitled "An Act for the Encouragement of Learning, by Vesting the Copies of Printed Books in the Authors or Purchasers of such Copies, during the Times therein mentioned." See Harry Ransom, *The First Copyright Statute: An Essay on An Act for the Encouragement of Learning* (Austin: University of Texas Press, 1956).

7. Rosemary J. Coombe, *The Cultural Life of Intellectual Properties: Authorship, Appropriation, and the Law* (Durham: Duke University Press, 1998), 42, 77. The book's first chapter, "Objects of Property and Subjects of Politics," contains an excellent analysis of the political and philosophical costs of trademark maximalism.

8. See the case *Feist Publications, Inc. v. Rural Telephone Service,* 499 U.S. 340 (1991). The case is a rare exception to the general trend toward copyright maximalism in recent U.S. court decisions and legislation. However, it has proven an influential exception in subsequent cases and debates, largely precluding, at least for the present, copyright protection in databases (see note 4).

9. *Sheldon v. Metro-Goldwyn Pictures Corp.,* 81 F.2d 49 (2d Cir. 1936), *aff'd,* 309 U.S. 390 (1940).

10. In 1976, George Harrison's song "My Sweet Lord" was found to have infringed the copyright in Ronald Mack's "He's So Fine," as performed by The Chiffons. The court stated: "His subconscious knew it already had worked in a song his conscious did not remember. . . . That is, under the law, infringement of copyright, and is no less so even though subconsciously accomplished." See *Bright Tunes Music Corp. v. Harrisongs Music, Ltd.,* 420 F.Supp. 177 (1976).

11. William Wordsworth, "Preface to the Second Edition of *Lyrical Ballads,*" in *William Wordsworth: Selected Poems and Prefaces,* ed. Jack Stillinger (Boston: Houghton Mifflin Company, 1965), 453.

12. Richard Rorty, *Contingency, Irony, and Solidarity* (Cambridge: Cambridge University Press, 1989); see 44, 96.

13. Benjamin Kaplan, *An Unhurried View of Copyright* (New York: Columbia University Press, 1967), 117, 125. Kaplan writes, in an eloquent passage, "I conclude with the observation that when copyright has gone wrong in recent times, it has been by taking itself too seriously, by foolish assumptions about the amount of originality open to man as an artificer, by sanctimonious pretensions about the iniquities of imitation. I confess myself to be more worried about excessive than insufficient protection, and follow Voltaire in thinking that plagiarism, even at its worst, '*est assurément de tous les larcins le moins dangereux pour la société*'" (78). Both Mark Rose and Peter Jaszi (q.v., below) mention Kaplan as an indispensable precursor to their work on copyright.

14. Michel Foucault, "What Is an Author?" in *Textual Strategies*, ed. Josué Harari (Ithaca: Cornell University Press, 1979), 141.

15. At the same time, however, the essay has been read as dividing texts from authors entirely, as finalizing the author's deliquescence into a "function" of discourse. Whether or not such an interpretation misreads Foucault's essay is debatable. But I question this utter liquefaction of the author as much as I do the Romantic hypertrophy of original authorship. Such a gesture collapses into "discourse" the same "sociohistorical analysis" the essay elsewhere demands; it also utterly disregards the problems of individual agency and moral autonomy that are best addressed by that analysis. I would suggest that the meaning, ideology, and origins of a text should be neither limited to nor fully dissociated from the author, who must remain among the many conditions of a text's production, among the many figures that constrain its meaning, and among the many beneficiaries of its innovations. The biographical elements of the present study attempt to enact this suggestion by moving dialectically between the writing subject and other constraining figures of materiality, ideology, and signification. If authorship is not magnified as the sole source of innovation, meaning, and agency, neither is it dismissed as a barren convention or as a simple hallucination of discourse. The point, ultimately, is not to revile or defrock creative people but to find whether our reverences for them exact hidden tolls from less-visible subjects and whether those reverences serve occulted ends.

16. See Martha Woodmansee, "The Genius and the Copyright: Economic and Legal Conditions of the Emergence of the 'Author,'" *Eighteenth-Century Studies* 17 (1984): 425–48.

17. Mark Rose, *Authors and Owners: The Invention of Copyright* (Cambridge: Harvard University Press, 1993), 142.

18. See Peter Jaszi, "Toward a Theory of Copyright: The Metamorphoses of 'Authorship,'" *Duke Law Journal* (1991): 455–502, and "On the Author Effect: Contemporary Copyright and Collective Creativity," in Martha Woodmansee and Peter Jaszi, eds., *The Construction of Authorship: Textual Appropriation in Law and Literature* (Durham: Duke University Press, 1994): 29–56; James D. A. Boyle, *Shamans, Software, and Spleens: Law and the Construction of the Information Society* (Cambridge: Harvard University Press, 1996); Coombe, *Cultural Life of Intellectual Properties*.

19. On Wordsworth and copyright, see Paul M. Zall, "Wordsworth and the Copyright Act of 1842," *PMLA* 70 (1955): 132–44; Russell Noyes, "Wordsworth and the Copyright Act of 1842: Addendum," *PMLA* 76 (1961): 380–83; Susan Eilenberg, "Mortal Pages: Wordsworth and the Reform of Copyright," *English Literary History* 56 (1989): 351–74; Lee Erickson, *The Economy of Literary Form: English Literature and the Industrialization of Publishing, 1800–1850* (Baltimore: Johns Hopkins University Press, 1996), 60–69. On Dickens and international copyright, see Alexander Welsh, *From Copyright to Copperfield: The Identity of Dickens* (Cambridge: Harvard University Press, 1987), esp. 29–42; and Gerhard Joseph, "Charles Dickens, International Copyright, and the Discretionary Silence of *Martin Chuzzlewit*," in Woodmansee and Jaszi, eds., *Construction of Authorship*, 259–70.

20. Eilenberg mentions Wordsworth's hortatory sonnets in "Mortal Pages," 351. On Twain's pro-copyright manuscript, see Vaidhyanathan, *Copyrights and Copywrongs*, 69–78. Henry James's "An Animated Conversation," a colloquy on international copyright scripted for six characters and first published in *Scribner's Magazine* in 1889, has received comparatively little attention.

Notes to Pages 14–26

21. Sherman and Bently also note that histories of Anglo-American intellectual property law tend to leapfrog from the early eighteenth to the twentieth century. Such a narrative, they note, helps naturalize current conceptions of the law by implying an unbroken and unvexed continuity between the Statute of Anne in 1710 and the present. Histories of this kind overlook not only conceptual renovations of the law but also serious governmental and extra-governmental attempts, particularly during the latter half of the nineteenth century, to abolish both patents and copyrights altogether (see Sherman and Bently, *Making of Modern Intellectual Property Law,* 210).

22. Richard Terdiman, *Discourse/Counter-Discourse: The Theory and Practice of Symbolic Resistance in Nineteenth-Century France* (Ithaca: Cornell University Press, 1985), 61.

23. Ibid., 67–68.

24. Thomas Jefferson, Letter to James Madison (6 September 1789) in *The Portable Thomas Jefferson,* ed. Merrill D. Peterson (Harmondsworth: Penguin Books, 1977), 447.

25. See N. N. Feltes, *Literary Capital and the Late Victorian Novel* (Madison: University of Wisconsin Press, 1993); Margareta de Grazia, *Shakespeare Verbatim: The Reproduction of Authenticity and the 1790 Apparatus* (Oxford: Oxford University Press, 1991); and Chris R. Vanden Bossche, "The Value of Literature: Representations of Print Culture in the Copyright Debate of 1837–42," *Victorian Studies* 38 (1994): 41–68.

26. See Boyle, *Shamans, Software, and Spleens,* particularly chapters 3–5.

27. Coombe, *Cultural Life of Intellectual Properties,* 10.

28. Arnold Plant, "The Economic Aspects of Copyright in Books," *Economica* 1 (1934): 193.

29. Arnold Plant, "The Economic Theory Concerning Patents for Inventions," *Economica* 1 (1934): 51.

30. Stephen Breyer, "The Uneasy Case for Copyright: A Study of Copyright in Books, Photocopies, and Computer Programs," *Harvard Law Review* 84 (1970): 289, 350–51.

31. For examples, see, respectively, Tom G. Palmer, "Intellectual Property: A Non-Posnerian Law and Economics Approach," *Hamline Law Review* 12 (1989): 261–304; and Ronald V. Bettig, *Copyrighting Culture: The Political Economy of Intellectual Property* (Boulder: Westview Press, 1996).

32. See Martha Woodmansee and Mark Osteen, eds., *The New Economic Criticism: Studies at the Intersection of Literature and Economics* (London: Routledge, 1999).

33. Drucilla Cornell, "Toward a Modern/Postmodern Reconstruction of Ethics," *University of Pennsylvania Law Review* 133 (1985): 380.

34. Kaplan, *Unhurried View of Copyright,* 119–20.

1. Neoclassicisms: The Tectonics of Literary Value

1. Adam Smith, *An Inquiry into the Nature and Causes of the Wealth of Nations* (1776; rpt. New York: Prometheus Books, 1991), 35.

2. Robert L. Heilbroner, *Behind the Veil of Economics: Essays in the Worldly Philosophy* (New York: W. W. Norton, 1988), 106–7.

3. Smith, *Inquiry,* 39.

4. Kurt Heinzelman, *The Economics of the Imagination* (Amherst: University of Massachusetts Press, 1980), 10.

5. See Donald (Deirdre) McCloskey, *The Rhetoric of Economics* (Madison: University of Wisconsin Press, 1985) and *Knowledge and Persuasion in Economics* (Cambridge: Cambridge University Press, 1994); Arjo Klamer and Thomas C. Leonard, "So What's an Economic Metaphor?" in *Natural Images in Economic Thought: "Markets Read in Tooth and Claw,"* ed. P. Mirowski (Cambridge: Cambridge University Press, 1994).

6. E. F. Benson, "Plagiarism," *Nineteenth Century* 274 (1899): 977.

7. Francis Ysidro Edgeworth, *Mathematical Psychics: An Essay on the Application of Mathematics to the Moral Sciences* (London: C. Kegan Paul, 1881), 68, 74. Edgeworth continues: "Yet in the minds of many good men among the moderns and the wisest of the ancients, there appears a deeper sentiment in favour of aristocratical privilege—the privilege of man above brute, of civilised above savage, of birth, of talent, and of the male sex. This sentiment of right

has a ground of utilitarianism in supposed differences of *capacity*. Capacity for pleasure is a property of evolution, an essential attribute of civilisation. The grace of life, the charm of courtesy and courage, which once at least distinguished rank, rank not unreasonably received the means to enjoy and transmit. To lower classes was assigned the work of which they seemed most capable; the work of the higher classes being different in kind was not to be equated in severity. If we suppose that capacity for pleasure is an attribute of skill and talent; if we consider that production is an *unsymmetrical function* of manual and scientific labour; we may see a reason deeper than Economics may afford for the larger pay, though often more agreeable work, of the aristocracy of skill and talent. The aristocracy of sex is similarly grounded upon the supposed superior capacity of the man for happiness" (Edgeworth, *Mathematical Psychics*, 77–78; original emphasis).

8. Lewis Hyde, *The Gift: Imagination and the Erotic Life of Property* (New York: Random House, 1983), xi.

9. Howard Caygill, *Art of Judgement* (Oxford: Basil Blackwell, 1989), 85; John Guillory, *Cultural Capital: The Problem of Literary Canon Formation* (Chicago: University of Chicago Press, 1993), 302–3.

10. Adam Smith, *The Theory of Moral Sentiments*, ed. D. D. Raphael and A. L. MacFie (Indianapolis: Liberty Fund, 1982), 185, 181.

11. Smith, *Theory*, 179–80.

12. Smith, *Inquiry*, 36–37, 43.

13. Guillory, *Cultural Capital*, 315.

14. Adam Smith, *Lectures on Jurisprudence*, ed. R. L. Meek, D. D. Raphael, and P. G. Stein (Oxford: Oxford University Press, 1978), 83; original emphasis. Smith's view of art's relation to labor is complicated in *Wealth of Nations*, where he classifies artistic labor as unproductive labor, labor that is "unproductive of any value, and does not fix or realize itself in any permanent subject, or vendible commodity, which endures after that labour is past and for which an equal quantity of labour could afterwards be procured. . . . Like the declamation of the actor, the harangue of the orator, or the tune of the musician, the work of all of them perishes in the very instant of its production" (Smith, *Inquiry*, 271). By identifying artistic labor as unproductive, Smith anticipates Ricardo's bracketing of the scarce or unreproducible art object from other "vendible commodities."

15. John Locke, *Two Treatises of Government* (Cambridge University Press, 1963), 328–29, 338; original emphasis. Mark Rose notes that Locke recommended a copyright protection term of fifty to seventy years—much longer than the one-time renewable fourteen years originally granted by the Statute of Anne. See Mark Rose, *Authors and Owners: The Invention of Copyright* (Cambridge: Harvard University Press, 1993), 47.

16. Brad Sherman and Lionel Bently, *The Making of Modern Intellectual Property Law: The British Experience, 1760–1911* (Cambridge: Cambridge University Press, 1999), 23 n. 49.

17. William Enfield, *Observations on Literary Property* (London, 1776); reprinted in *The Literary Property Debate: Eight Tracts, 1774–1775*, ed. Stephen Parks (New York: Garland, 1974), 21.

18. *English Reports* 35: 1008–9; quoted in Benjamin Kaplan, *An Unhurried View of Copyright* (New York: Columbia University Press, 1967), 10.

19. *English Reports* 26: 489–91, 957.

20. Quoted in Kaplan, *Unhurried View of Copyright*, 17.

21. That Young wrote his celebration of originality at the urging of Samuel Richardson and with the novelist's collaboration is an irony many critics have noted. Walter Jackson Bate writes, "The conscience had taken another Trojan horse into the walls. . . . By the 1750s some of the least original minds of the time were beginning to prate constantly of 'originality.'" See Walter Jackson Bate, *The Burden of the Past and the English Poet* (Cambridge: Belknap Press of Harvard University Press, 1970), 105.

22. Edward Young, "Conjectures on Original Composition in a Letter to the Author of *Charles Grandison*," rpt. in Martin William Steincke, *Edward Young's "Conjectures on Original Composition" in England and Germany* (New York: F. C. Stechert, 1917), 45–46, 49. Elsewhere Young makes clear that genius is the paramount (if not sole) source of literary value: "By

the praise of genius we detract not from learning; we detract not from the value of gold by saying that a diamond has greater still. He who disregards learning, shows that he wants its aid; and he that overvalues it, shows that its aid has done him harm. Over-valued, indeed, it cannot be, if genius, as to composition, is valued more. Learning we thank, genius we revere; that gives us pleasure, this gives us rapture; that informs, this inspires, and is itself inspired; for genius is from heaven, learning from man: this sets us above the low and illiterate; that, above the learned and polite. Learning is borrowed knowledge; genius is knowledge innate, and quite our own" (Young, "Conjectures," 52).

23. Smith, *Theory,* 183.

24. Young, "Conjectures," 57.

25. Martha Woodmansee, *The Author, Art, and the Market: Rereading the History of Aesthetics* (New York: Columbia University Press, 1994), 39. See also M. H. Abrams, *The Mirror and the Lamp: Romantic Theory and the Critical Tradition* (New York: Oxford University Press, 1953), 198, for the influence of Young's concept of "vegetable genius" on the German Romantics.

26. Immanuel Kant, *Critique of Pure Judgment,* trans. J. H. Bernard (New York: Hafner Press, 1951), 150–51; original emphasis.

27. William Wordsworth, "Essay Supplementary to the Preface," *William Wordsworth: Selected Poems and Prefaces,* ed. Jack Stillinger (Boston: Houghton Mifflin, 1965), 477–79; original emphasis.

28. Chris R. Vanden Bossche, "The Value of Literature: Representations of Print Culture in the Copyright Debate of 1837–42," *Victorian Studies* 38 (1994): 50–51.

29. Thomas Babington Macaulay, *Prose and Poetry,* ed. G. Young (London: Rupert Hart-Davis, 1952), 731.

30. Vanden Bossche, "The Value of Literature," 47, 53.

31. In respect to modern copyright law, the labor theory of value survives among neither the defenders nor the detractors. Stephen Breyer's "The Uneasy Case for Copyright: A Study of Copyright in Books, Photocopies, and Computer Programs," *Harvard Law Review* 84 (1970), which attacked the foundations of intellectual property law, dismissed the labor theory of value along with the metaphysics of copyright. Breyer remarked that "We do not ordinarily create or modify property rights, nor even award compensation, solely on the basis of labor expended." After all, if "few workers receive salaries that approach the total value of what they produce," why should authors? In the final analysis, the disparity between the worker's salary and the value of the work was acceptable in that the savings were passed along to the consumer; see Paul Goldstein, *Copyright's Highway: From Gutenberg to the Celestial Jukebox* (New York: Hill & Wang, 1996), 23. In 1991, Breyer's future Supreme Court colleague Sandra Day O'Connor ruled that a Kansas telephone company could not copyright its white-page directory despite the labor involved in compiling the list. Although "it may seem unfair that much of the fruit of the compiler's labor may be used by others without compensation," O'Connor wrote that the decision was "neither unfair nor unfortunate"; copyright, in her view, should encourage and reward creativity, not mere "sweat of the brow" labor (Goldstein, *Copyright's Highway,* 213). The Romantic notion that literary labor is fundamentally different from manual labor in being "imaginative" rather than "mechanical" retains much currency.

32. David Ricardo, *The Principles of Political Economy and Taxation* (New York: Dutton, 1973), 6. Heinzelman cites a similar distinction between labor and valuation (though here it is "price" rather than "value") in Ruskin: "For remember always, that the price of a picture by a living artist never represents, never *can* represent, the quantity of labour or value in it." John Ruskin, *The Works of John Ruskin,* ed. E. T. Cook and Alexander Wederburn (London: G. Allen and Unwin, 1903–12), 16: 86.

33. Ricardo's point about unique statues and paintings clearly does *not* hold true, in most cases, for texts. Though rare manuscripts fall under the category of scarce and unreproducible artifacts, printed matter is fundamentally reproducible; literary properties demanded special legal protection *because of* their cheap reproducibility. The gap between unique artifacts and reproducible texts could be rhetorically bridged, though, if valuable texts were seen as the result of *innovation,* itself a scarce and unreproducible human quantity. This commodification of in-

novation was articulated during the Royal Copyright Commission debates of 1876–78. The same objections and recuperations were applied to inventions.

34. W. Stanley Jevons, *The Theory of Political Economy* (New York: Kelley, 1965), 38, 166; original emphasis.

35. Ibid., vii, xviii, xxxv, xxxvii–viii, xxxix.

36. F. J. Hudleston, "A Few Plagiarisms," *Tinsleys' Magazine* 253 (1889): 360.

37. For brevity's sake, I use the term "apologists" to denote the nineteenth- and early twentieth-century essayists—A. Mitchell, Andrew Lang, Fred Ford, F. J. Hudleston, W. H. Davenport Adams, William S. Walsh, E. F. Benson, Edward Wright, D. Hollis, and others—who defended or redefined plagiarism in their work. By grouping them under a single title, I do not wish to imply that this diverse group of writers constituted a discrete "movement" with a coherent and deliberate agenda; rather, they were scattered purveyors of an emerging critique of original genius and literary property, brought to their critique by disparate ideological motivations.

38. W. H. Davenport Adams, "Imitators and Plagiarists," *Gentleman's Magazine* (1892): 503.

39. A. Mitchell, "Plagiarism," *Knickerbocker* 43 (1854): 333.

40. Mitchell, "Plagiarism," 333. The digestive language also harks back to similar figurations in seventeenth- and eighteenth-century neoclassical defenses of imitation.

41. Fred Ford, "That 'Bugbear,' Plagiarism," *Writer: A Monthly Magazine to Interest and Help All Literary Workers* 2 (1888): 35.

42. Benson, "Plagiarism," 980–81.

43. William Sheppard Walsh, *Handy-Book of Literary Curiosities* (Philadelphia: J. B. Lippincott, 1892), 891–92. Proximately, "being Irish" here refers to William Henry Ireland, who forged several "recovered" Shakespeare plays during the 1790s; the larger question of what it means "to be Irish" with respect to literary property will be addressed in chapter 3, on Oscar Wilde. The ghost of Wilde may be detectable in Walsh's epigram about plagiarism's being only a venial offense unless it is found out. Wilde quipped often on the subject of plagiarism, and one remark of his acts as dark twin to Walsh's claim that the sources of ideas and expressions matter little compared to their effect on us. When an actress noted a resemblance between one of Wilde's scenes and a Scribe play, he confessed, "Taken bodily from it, dear lady. Why not? Nobody reads nowadays." See Richard Ellmann, *Oscar Wilde* (New York: Vintage Books, 1984), 375.

44. Sarah Bradford, *Disraeli* (New York: Stein and Day, 1982), 209; see Mitchell, "Plagiarism," 335.

45. Unsigned, "Plagiarism," *Leisure Hour: A Family Journal of Instruction and Recreation* 1162 (1874): 216.

46. Ralph Waldo Emerson, "Quotation and Originality," *Ralph Waldo Emerson*, ed. Richard Poirier (Oxford: Oxford University Press, 1990), 433.

47. Andrew Lang, "Literary Plagiarism," *Contemporary Review* (1887): 836; Jevons, *Theory of Political Economy*, 38.

48. Edward Wright, "The Art of Plagiarism," *Contemporary Review* 460 (1904): 514, 518.

49. Adams, "Imitators and Plagiarists," 623.

50. C. C. Bombaugh, *Gleanings from the Harvest-fields of Literature, Science and Art; A Melange of Excerpta, Curious, Humorous, and Instructive* (Baltimore: T. Newton Kurtz, 1860), 48. The book's title page identifies Bombaugh not as its author but as its "collator."

51. Ausonius's own *Nuptial Cento*, commissioned by Emperor Valentinian, was composed of lines from Virgil. Ausonius wrote that cento-making was "a task for memory only, which has to gather up scattered tags and fit these mangled scraps together into a whole, and so is more likely to provoke your laughter than your praise." Tony Augarde, *The Oxford Guide to Word Games* (Oxford: Oxford University Press, 1984), 138.

52. The mosaic poem printed in Bombaugh's *Gleanings* underscores the "traditional" nature of the cento by taking advantage of the vastly popular "literary ballad" quatrain. As George Dekker has pointed out to me, this form drew on an extremely limited domain of rhyme words, mostly monosyllabic, and was therefore particularly conducive to patchworking.

Notes to Pages 42–48

53. Bombaugh, *Gleanings*, 48–49.
54. Ibid., 4.
55. Frederick Saunders, *Mosaics, by the Author of Salad for the Solitary &c.* (London: Richard Bentley, 1859), 14, 15–17.
56. C. C. Bombaugh, *Gleanings from the Harvest-fields of Literature, Science and Art; A Melange of Excerpta, Curious, Humorous, and Instructive* (London: Griffith, Farran, Okeden & Welsh, 1890), v.
57. William T. Dobson, *Literary Frivolities, Fancies, Follies, and Frolics* (London: Chatto and Windus, 1880), 180, 188–89. I have reproduced the *People's Friend* cento, along with some fifteen other nineteenth-century secular centos, in this book's appendix.
58. In this respect, the Victorian cento prefigures present-day fanzine art, in which (predominantly female) fans appropriate and creatively rework characters, conceits, situations, and technologies from popular TV series (Star Trek has become the classic example) in fashioning their own pictorial and narrative self-expressions. Fanzine art has repeatedly provoked intellectual property suits through its appropriations and often oppositional redeployments of copyrighted characters, trademarked logos, and celebrity images. For recent scholarly work on fanzines, intellectual property, and popular cultural practice, see Henry Jenkins III, "Star Trek Rerun, Reread, Rewritten: Fan Writing as Textual Poaching," *Critical Studies in Mass Communication* 5 (1988); Constance Penley, "Brownian Motion: Women, Tactics, and Technology," in Constance Penley and Andrew Ross, eds., *Technoculture* (Minneapolis: University of Minnesota Press, 1991); Camille Bacon-Smith, *Enterprising Women: Television Fandom and the Creation of Popular Myth* (Philadelphia: University of Pennsylvania Press, 1992); and Rosemary J. Coombe, *The Cultural Life of Intellectual Properties: Authorship, Appropriation, and the Law* (Durham: Duke University Press, 1998), 117–29.
59. Although neither the cento nor the *Gleanings*-type volume is "fresh" in the Romantic sense of radically original, both meet copyright's more modest standards of originality or freshness insofar as they embody noninfringing creativity on the part of their compilers. Both genres belong to the category of works that are at once "derivative" of antecedent works *and* eligible for the copyright protection accorded "original" works. While none of these texts' verbatim inclusions of protected works was itself copyright in its new context, the aggregate recombination (e.g., the whole cento, or the particular selection and sequence of inclusions in a *Gleanings* volume, along with the collator's interstitial text) was protected.
60. Emerson, "Quotation and Originality," 427.
61. Lang, "Literary Plagiarism," 834; H. M. Paull, *Literary Ethics: A Study in the Growth of the Literary Conscience* (London: Thornton Butterworth, 1928), 103.
62. Ford, "That 'Bugbear,' Plagiarism," 36; Ellmann, *Oscar Wilde*, 376.
63. Edmund Wilson, *Axel's Castle: A Study in the Imaginative Literature of 1870–1930* (New York: Macmillan, 1991), 111.
64. See Regenia Gagnier, "On the Insatiability of Human Wants: Economic and Aesthetic Man," *Victorian Studies* 36 (1993): 126, and Heinzelman, *Economics of the Imagination*, 85–87. Gagnier's discussion is developed further in *The Insatiability of Human Wants: Economics and Aesthetics in Market Society* (Chicago: University of Chicago Press, 2000). In his *Copyrighting Culture: The Political Economy of Intellectual Property* (Boulder: Westview Press, 1996), Ronald V. Bettig writes about how neoclassical economic analysis limits our thinking about intellectual property by failing to account and provide for information's nonmarket value—e.g., its "nonproprietary value," or value beyond what the state can delimit and enforce; its "positive externalities," or value above cost ("its ability to produce wisdom, to reduce conflict, to encourage sharing relations, to promote democracy, to entertain, to promote employment and productivity"); and its intrinsic relation to human welfare (Bettig, *Copyrighting Culture*, 106–7).
65. Jevons, *Theory of Political Economy*, 27.
66. Gagnier, "On the Insatiability of Human Wants," 145. See also John Dupré and Regenia Gagnier, "The Ends of Economics" and "Reply to Amariglio and Ruccio" in Martha Woodmansee and Mark Osteen, eds., *The New Economic Criticism: Studies at the Intersection of Literature and Economics* (London: Routledge, 1999).

67. Unsigned, "Plagiarism," *Leisure Hour,* 213-14.
68. Ford, "That 'Bugbear,' Plagiarism," 35.
69. Adams, "Imitators and Plagiarists," 512. Adams's rejection of the Victorian "Great Man" theory of ideas seems to result from another characteristically late-century anxiety about the exhaustion of all new ideas. Adams writes, "Dr. Hook, one of the founders of the Royal Society, and a mathematician of credit and renown, throws out a fanciful calculation on the number of ideas of which the human mind, in the aggregate, is capable; he arrives at a total of 3,655,760,000. We should suppose that so respectable a figure is not yet exhausted; and though a time must come when nothing new will be left under the sun, we may still hope (some of us) to catch a floating idea or two, of a practical kind, for current use" (Adams, "Imitators and Plagiarists," 510).

2. Committing Copyright: The Royal Copyright Commission of 1876-78

1. Matthew Arnold, "Copyright," *Fortnightly Review* (1880); rpt. in *The Complete Prose Works of Matthew Arnold,* Vol. IX: *English Literature and Irish Politics,* ed. R. H. Super (Ann Arbor: University of Michigan Press, 1973), 117.
2. *Copyright Commission: The Royal Commissions and the Report of the Commissioners* in *Sessional Papers of the House of Commons* 1878 [C.2036] XXIV.171. Hereafter cited parenthetically in the text as *Rep.,* followed by page number.
3. [J. A. Froude], Untitled, *Edinburgh Review* 148 (1878): 311. The article was unsigned, but its authorship was apparently an open secret. Arnold connects Froude with the article in his later discussion of copyright (see Arnold, "Copyright," 122, 365 n. 122: 33-35).
4. Yet most scholars pass quickly over the Commission on the way to discussing legislative debates and reforms. To my knowledge, John Feather's *Publishing, Piracy, and Politics: An Historical Study of Copyright in Britain* (London: Mansell, 1994) contains the least cursory treatment of the 1876-78 Commission. Concluding his able summary of the hearings, Feather claims that the Commissioners fell short of a practical solution because "they failed, or were perhaps unable, to formulate a conceptual approach which might have guided their pragmatism towards the uniformity and consistency which they so genuinely desired and so painstakingly sought" (Feather, *Publishing, Piracy, and Politics,* 194). The image Feather paints of an earnest-but-misguided collaboration, however, misses the deep factionalism of the Commission and the animus it could provoke (Froude's unsigned article in *The Edinburgh Review,* for example, is nothing short of vitriolic in its indictment of the anti-copyright party of Farrer, Macfie, Trevelyan, and Mallet). The Commissioners and their witnesses frequently addressed various "conceptual approaches" but failed to adopt a common one out of fundamental differences in their views on private property, the public domain, and value. N. N. Feltes, in *Literary Capital and the Late Victorian Novel* (Madison: University of Wisconsin Press, 1993), 57-63, focuses on the Commission's treatment of international copyright and its implicit renegotiations of the book trade's temporal and spatial parameters. And in his *Authorship and Copyright* (London: Routledge, 1992), David Saunders touches briefly on the Commission and the proposed royalty system in a chapter on British copyright in the nineteenth century.
5. J. M. Lely, *Copyright Law Reform: An Exposition of Lord Monkswell's Copyright Bill Now before Parliament* (London: Eyre and Spottiswoode, 1891), 20; Augustine Birrell, *Seven Lectures on The Law and History of Copyright in Books* (London: Cassell, 1899), 207.
6. Brad Sherman and Lionel Bently, *The Making of Modern Intellectual Property Law: The British Experience, 1760-1911* (Cambridge: Cambridge University Press, 1999), 6, 134.
7. Adam Smith, *Lectures on Jurisprudence,* ed. R. L. Meek, D. D. Raphael, and P. G. Stein (Oxford: Oxford University Press, 1978), 472.
8. Chris R. Vanden Bossche, "The Value of Literature: Representations of Print Culture in the Copyright Debate of 1837-1842," *Victorian Studies* 38 (1994): 42, 47-48.
9. Cf. Macaulay's statement during the Talfourd debates that a copyright extension was a "tax on readers for the purpose of giving a bounty to writers." Thomas Babington Macaulay, *Prose and Poetry,* ed. G. Young (London: Rupert Hart-Davis, 1952), 731.
10. Richard Cobden, letter to John Bright, 22 November 1853, British Library Add. Mss.

Notes to Pages 57–61

43650; quoted in Wendy Hine, *Richard Cobden: A Victorian Outsider* (New Haven: Yale University Press, 1987), 239–40.

11. 3 *Hansard*, CXXII.838; quoted in W. Cunningham, *The Rise and Decline of the Free Trade Movement* (Cambridge: Cambridge University Press, 1905), 101.

12. R. A. Macfie, "Notes of Speech of Mr. Macfie, M.P.," William Armstrong et al., *Recent Discussions on the Abolition of Patents for Inventions in the United Kingdom, France, Germany, and the Netherlands* (London: Longmans, Green, Reader, and Dyer, 1869), 63. The collection seems to have been compiled by Macfie, who also penned the bulk of its contents. The volume bears the legend, "No rights are reserved. Mr. Macfie will be glad to be favoured . . . with a copy of any transcripts made or any printed matter illustrating the question of Patents."

13. Fritz Machlup and Edith Penrose, "The Patent Controversy in the Nineteenth Century," *Journal of Economic History* 10 (1950): 1, 4–5. See also Victor M. Batzel, "Legal Monopoly in Liberal England: The Patent Controversy in the Mid-Nineteenth Century," *Business History* 22 (1980): 189–202; and Moureen Coulter, *Property in Ideas: The Patent Question in Mid-Victorian Britain* (Kirksville: Thomas Jefferson University Press, 1991).

14. John Stuart Mill, *Principles of Political Economy* (London: Longmans, Green, 1909), 933.

15. See Macfie, "Notes," 69–73.

16. Untitled articles from the *Economist*, 5 June 1869, and the *Times* [London] 29 May 1869; quoted in Armstrong et al., *Recent Discussions*, 255, 251.

17. Machlup and Penrose, "Patent Controversy," 4, 6.

18. See Cunningham, *Rise and Decline*, 85–99.

19. See Coulter, *Property in Ideas*, 2.

20. Macfie, "Notes," 10.

21. *Minutes of the Evidence Taken Before the Royal Commission on Copyright*, in *Sessional Papers of the House of Commons* 1878 [C.2036.-I] XXIV.395. Hereafter cited parenthetically in the text as *Min.*, followed by page number.

22. Thomas Watts, untitled article in *Mechanics Magazine* 27 & 29 (1837), excerpted in Armstrong et al., *Recent Discussions*, 297–300. Macfie mentioned the article and identified Watts in his Commission testimony (*Min.* 141).

23. "If the system of patents were abandoned for that of rewards by the state, the best shape which these could assume would be that of a small temporary tax, imposed for the inventor's benefit, on all persons making use of the invention. To this, however, or to any other system which would vest in the state the power of deciding whether an inventor should derive any pecuniary advantage from the public benefit which he confers, the objections are evidently stronger and more fundamental than the strongest which can possibly be urged against patents." Mill, *Principles*, 933. The first sentence is from the original 1848 edition; the remainder was added in 1862.

24. R. A. Macfie, "International Copyright," in Armstrong et al., *Recent Discussions*, 294.

25. Macfie makes specific mention of the Irish colonial situation: "Before the Union the publishers of Dublin used to drive a useful business in reprinting British works which they have, under the present system, been deprived of, to their own loss and the incalculable disadvantage of their countrymen." Macfie, "International Copyright," in Armstrong et al., *Recent Discussions*, 294–95.

26. See George Moore, *Literature at Nurse or Circulating Morals* (London: Vizetelly, 1885; rpt., New York: Garland, 1978).

27. In 1872, the *Spectator* estimated that only 60,000 of Britain's 4,600,000 families—about 1.3 percent—could afford Mudie's yearly rate of one guinea. The number that could afford to purchase triple-deckers at 31*s. 6d.*, then, would have been dramatically smaller. "The Numbers of the Comfortable," *Spectator* 45 (30 November 1872): 1518; quoted in Guinevere L. Griest, *Mudie's Circulating Library and the Victorian Novel* (Bloomington: Indiana University Press, 1970), 79.

28. Macfie, "International Copyright," in Armstrong et al., *Recent Discussions*, 294, 295.

29. 38 Victoria c. 88, modified by ratifying imperial act in 38 & 39 Victoria c. 53; see also Feather, *Publishing, Piracy, and Politics*, 185; [Froude], Untitled, 308–9.

30. For Charles Reade's plagiarisms, see Thomas Mallon, *Stolen Words: Forays into the Origins and Ravages of Plagiarism* (New York: Ticknor & Fields, 1989).

31. "The Copyright Laws," *Times* [London], 11 May 1875: 10. See also Feather, *Publishing, Piracy, and Politics*, 183–85.

32. Farrer: "Nothing . . . can be more intolerable than a system of copyright law under which the inhabitants of the mother country, in which the books are produced, would be the only persons in the world who are prevented from obtaining cheap editions of them." *Min.*, Appendix XI. H.

33. [Froude], Untitled, 295.

34. On Trevelyan's Treasury career, see Jennifer Hart, "Sir Charles Trevelyan at the Treasury," *English Historical Review* 75 (1960). As head of British relief operations for the Irish and Scottish Famines, Trevelyan let his laissez-faire economics endorse a criminal parsimony on the part of the Treasury. Paraphrasing his letters, Hart writes, "Trevelyan believed the Irish famine was the judgment of God on an indolent and unselfreliant people, and as God had sent the calamity to teach the Irish a lesson, that calamity must not be too much mitigated . . . . He regarded deaths by starvation as 'a discipline,' a painful one, admittedly, but nevertheless a discipline, and he considered that they were a smaller evil than bankruptcy, for through them a greater good was to be obtained for Ireland and the whole British nation" (Hart, "Sir Charles Trevelyan," 99). See also Terry Eagleton, *Heathcliff and the Great Hunger: Studies in Irish Culture* (London: Verso, 1995), 16. For his "services" during the Famines, Trevelyan was knighted and awarded an extra year's salary (*DNB*).

35. See Trevelyan's "On the Education of the People of India" (1838), which extended the cultural imperialist project of T. B. Macaulay's 1835 "Minute on Indian Education." (Trevelyan was close friends with Macaulay; he married Macaulay's sister Hannah Moore in 1834, and their son George Otto Trevelyan published *The Life and Letters of Lord Macaulay* in 1876.) According to the *DNB*, it was "largely owing to his eagerness and persistence [that the] government was led to decide in favour of the promulgation of European literature and science among the natives of India." Trevelyan's educational drive continued during his Treasury years: officials on sick leave were prescribed a regimen of Adam Smith, and the Dublin office was asked to bone up on *Wealth of Nations* and Burke's *Thoughts on Scarcity* (Hart, "Sir Charles Trevelyan," 96).

36. [Archibald Alison], "The Copyright Question," *Blackwood's* 51 (1842): 108, 116–17.

37. Trevelyan refers here to Macaulay's "Minute on Indian Education" of February 1835, in which Macaulay recommended that colonial tax revenues be withdrawn from Indian-language education and used to fund only English-language colleges. Macaulay wrote, "I am quite ready to take the Oriental learning at the valuation of the Orientalists themselves. I have never found one among them who could deny that a single shelf of a good European library was worth the whole native literature of India and Arabia. The intrinsic superiority of the Western literature is, indeed, fully admitted by those members of the Committee who support the Oriental plan of education." Given what he regarded as the superiority of Western languages, literature, thought, and belief, Macaulay argued that giving Indians a Western education in English would improve them intellectually and morally. It would also assist in the administration and ideological penetration of empire by creating "a class who may be interpreters between us and the millions whom we govern; a class of persons, Indian in blood and colour, but English in taste, in opinions, in morals, and in intellect." Thomas Babington Macaulay, "Minute of 2 February 1835 on Indian Education," *Macaulay, Prose and Poetry*, ed. G. M. Young (Cambridge: Harvard University Press, 1967), 721, 729.

38. Mill, *Principles*, 200.

39. On several points, Trevelyan's critique of absolute property rights was drawn from a contemporary statement on the copyright debate from another quarter: journalism. On the eve of the Commission's first meeting, Edward James Stephen Dicey, who edited the *Observer*, had published an article on "The Copyright Question" in *The Fortnightly Review*. Written as a kind of primer on the subject for the Commissioners, the essay attacked the "divine right of authordom"—the notion "that property has some inherent indefeasible title of existence derived from some higher than human authority"—upheld by Reade and other members of the Association

for the Protection of the Rights of Authors. Presaging Trevelyan, Dicey argued that all property was the creation of law, both tenable and modifiable for the good of the community. He also gestured toward the "bundle" theory of property rights, pointing out that even landowners could be dispossessed of their holdings if they failed to rent or cultivate, or if the land were required for public purposes. In an extreme moment, Dicey opined that "there is no abstract reason why copyright should exist at all," though he conceded that it could be an expedient compromise between private incentive and public good. Most heretically, from the "divine right" point of view, he claimed that limited copyright terms were safeguards, rather than impediments, to literary immortality: "Fancy what would be the fate of Gibbon, if the 'Decline and Fall' was the property of Archbishop Manning . . . !" Happily for the Gibbons of the world, "after a certain brief interval, the perpetual publication of their writings is provided for by the ordinary laws of supply and demand." In the Talfourd Bill debates, Wordsworth and other authors had lobbied for extended or perpetual copyright terms in order to protect their works from the ravages of a literary market driven by "supply and demand." Now, under the *doxa* of free trade, those dread forces could be invoked as the arbiters of taste and fair distribution. The *Fortnightly* article resulted in Dicey's appearing as a witness before the Commission. There, he spoke on the strategic advantages of a royalty system of international copyright but skirted the more philosophical critique of monopoly copyright mounted by his essay. Edward Dicey, "The Copyright Question," *Fortnightly Review* 19 (1876): 126–27, 128, 131. Dicey was related to Commissioner James Fitzjames Stephen; he should not be confused with the liberal lawyer, E. V. Dicey, who celebrated the "manifest destiny" of British imperial rule in "Mr. Gladstone and Our Empire," *Nineteenth Century* 11 (1877): 292–308.

40. [Froude], Untitled, 315.

41. Ibid., 295.

42. Spencer may also have adopted his argument from Commissioner William Smith, who used it while questioning T. H. Farrer a few days before Spencer's second appearance: "But is not an author exposed to unrestricted competition? Directly he publishes a work on a particular subject, may not another author immediately publish another book on the same subject? Is it not the fact that directly one publisher brings out a book which proves successful, another publisher endeavours to bring out another and better book on the same subject and at a lower price? Do not therefore both author and publisher work under the stimulus of open and free competition? Would it not therefore, be more correct to say that there is free trade in the production and sale of books rather than monopoly?" (*Min.* 532).

43. Herbert Spencer, letter to J. A. Froude, date unknown; quoted in [Froude], Untitled, 329–30. Spencer's letter reprises and dilates on his testimony to the Commission, where he denounced the terms "free trade" and "monopoly," in the sense intended by the royalty proponents, as "question-begging terms" (*Min.* 540).

44. Interpolating several sources, Griest puts prose fiction at about one-third of Mudie's total stock between the 1860s and the 1880s (Griest, *Mudie's*, 38).

45. Though see *Min.* 527, where Farrer confusingly argues that Spencer's testimony (about the perils of self-financing with a commission to the publisher) "is an illustration of the way in which a royalty would work, *viz.*, that it would not interfere with an author at all, unless he has miscalculated the demand, or had failed to supply it; and then the royalty would compensate him."

46. "The Copyright Commission," *Times* [London], 13 July 1877: 11.

47. "The Copyright Commission," *Times* [London], 26 April 1878: 12, and 24 May 1878: 9.

48. Asked by Commissioner Wolff what changes in copyright law would significantly lower book prices, Bosworth replied, "I should allow after a very short period, at the most 12 months, any publisher to reprint any book upon paying a royalty to the author" (*Min.* 570).

49. Lely, *Copyright Law Reform*, 79; original emphasis.

50. See Feather, *Publishing, Piracy, and Politics*, 196–203.

51. Mallet's dissent on the topics of domestic and colonial copyright is discussed above. He objected to the Commission's suggestions for international copyright on the grounds that they

would merely extend the territory of the British monopoly form without any proportional reduction in term or price to benefit the consumer. Instead, he favored the royalty system for international copyright, along with the abolition of import duties and restrictions (see *Rep.* 218–19).

52. "Copyright Commission," *Times* [London], 24 May 1878: 9.

53. The conviction of a widespread error in value theory was central to Mallet's economics. He spent much of his retirement developing this notion in an unfinished treatise called "The Law of Value and the Theory of the Unearned Increment." The *DNB* says of him, "As an economist he had always been, like Jevons, in sympathy with the French school and in disagreement with Mill, and these chapters are an attempt to trace the common economic errors on the land question to their true source—a mistaken theory of value—and to place on a scientific basis the opposition to schemes of ill-considered reform." The entry was penned by Mallet's son, Bernard Mallet.

54. [Froude], Untitled, 339, 329.

55. The Council of Trent, which met between 1545 and 1563, consolidated papal authority and Catholic doctrine and attempted to reform abuses within the Church. It was the last such council to meet until the Vatican Council of 1870, where the doctrine of papal infallibility was established. Conspicuously, the Council of Trent made no accommodations to Protestants, especially Calvinists. Carlyle had been raised Calvinist before his apostasy; Froude had written against the Anglo-Catholic Oxford Movement.

56. [Froude], Untitled, 299.

57. Ibid., 342, 312, 343.

58. T. H. Farrer, "The Principle of Copyright," *Fortnightly Review* 30 (1878): 837, 848, 842. In the last instance, Farrer quotes Louis Blanc, *Organisation du travail* (Brussels, 1839), 233; my translation.

59. Arnold, "Copyright," 115, 125, 127, 125.

60. Ibid., 132–33.

61. Ibid., 120, 118.

62. In T. N. Talfourd, *Three Speeches Delivered in the House of Commons in Favour of a Measure for an Extension of Copyright* (London: Edward Moxon, 1840), 126–27.

63. See Ronald V. Bettig, *Copyrighting Culture: The Political Economy of Intellectual Property* (Boulder: Westview Press, 1996), 127–29.

64. Arnold Plant, "The Economic Aspects of Copyright in Books," *Economica* 1 (1934): 193–95, 189. See also Plant's 1953 Stamp Memorial Lecture, published as *The New Commerce in Ideas and Intellectual Property* (London: Athlone Press, 1953).

65. Denis Thomas, *Copyright and the Creative Artist* (London: Institute of Economic Affairs, 1967), 21.

66. Stephen Breyer, "The Uneasy Case for Copyright: A Study of Copyright in Books, Photocopies, and Computer Programs," *Harvard Law Review* 84 (1970), 281 n. 4; 283 n. 8; 300 n. 77; 311 n. 119; 313 n. 125; 314 n. 130. Breyer's essay provoked a less equivocally pro-copyright response from Barry Tyerman, "The Economic Rationale for Copyright Protection: A Reply to Professor Breyer," *UCLA Law Review* 18 (1971), which in turn elicited a response from Breyer in his "Copyright: A Rejoinder," *UCLA Law Review* 20 (1972). For a more extended discussion of Breyer's piece and the controversy it provoked, see Paul Goldstein, *Copyright's Highway: The Law and Lore of Copyright from Gutenberg to the Celestial Jukebox* (New York: Hill and Wang, 1994), 22–26.

67. Breyer, "Uneasy Case," 288–89, 322, 286, 322. The last instance quotes Shakespeare's *Hamlet,* III.i.79–82. Breyer's article did come down against term extension and in favor of broader fair use provisions. It also recommended that "Computer programs should not receive copyright protection at the present time" (Breyer, "Uneasy Case," 350–51).

68. See Feather, *Publishing, Piracy, and Politics,* 174–76.

69. Farrer, "Principle of Copyright," 851.

70. James D. A. Boyle, *Shamans, Software, and Spleens: Law and the Construction of the Information Society* (Cambridge: Harvard University Press, 1996), 49.

Notes to Pages 85–91

71. This paragraph attempts to summarize two chapters in Boyle, *Shamans, Software, and Spleens:* "Intellectual Property and the Liberal State" (47–50) and "Copyright and the Invention of Authorship" (51–60).

72. Fred Pearce, "Science and Technology: Bargaining for the Life of the Forest—Poor Nations Want Drug and Food Companies to Pay for the Plants They Plunder," *Independent* 37 (17 March 1991); quoted in Boyle, *Shamans, Software, and Spleens,* 128. Peter Jaszi and Martha Woodmansee also discuss the rosy periwinkle case in "The Ethical Reaches of Authorship," *South Atlantic Quarterly* 95 (1996): 965–66.

73. Boyle, *Shamans, Software, and Spleens,* 128–29; original emphasis.

74. Jaszi and Woodmansee, "Ethical Reaches of Authorship," 960–64.

75. See Vandana Shiva, *Biopiracy: The Plunder of Nature and Knowledge* (Boston: South End Press, 1997); Rosemary J. Coombe, *The Cultural Life of Intellectual Properties: Authorship, Appropriation, and the Law* (Durham: Duke University Press, 1998) and "The Properties of Culture and the Possession of Identity: Postcolonial Struggle and the Legal Imagination," in B. Ziff and P. V. Rao, eds., *Borrowed Power: Essays on Cultural Appropriation* (New Brunswick: Rutgers University Press, 1997), 74–93.

76. Two years after Boyle's book was published, the U.S. copyright term was extended 20 years, bringing it into harmony with U.K. and European Union copyright terms. I discuss the 1998 Sonny Bono Copyright Term Extension Act in chapter 4 and in the conclusion.

77. Predictably, bills proposing to plough intellectual property revenues back into noncorporate creative sources have fared badly in the U.S. In 1994 Senator Christopher J. Dodd submitted the "Arts Endowing the Arts Act," which proposed to use revenues from a 20-year copyright term extension to fund new art and scholarship (e.g., through the National Endowment for the Arts and the National Endowment for the Humanities). The 1998 Act that finally extended the copyright term did not use the revenues from the extension to underwrite new creation.

78. Boyle, *Shamans, Software, and Spleens,* 172. Lawrence Lessig has recently proposed a rather different series of copyright and patent reforms, including the reinstatement of mandatory copyright registration and the abandonment of the 70-year postmortem term in favor of a maximum of 16 renewable 5-year terms, for a total protection of 80 years from publication. See Lawrence Lessig, *The Future of Ideas: The Fate of the Commons in a Connected World* (New York: Random House, 2001), 240–61.

79. *Graham v. John Deere Co.,* 383 U.S. 1 (1966); quoted in Thomas M. S. Hemnes, "Three Common Fallacies in the User Interface Copyright Debate," *Computer Lawyer* 7 (1990).

80. Boyle, *Shamans, Software, and Spleens,* 44–45, 177.

81. Arnold, "Copyright," 120.

3. Oscar Wilde: Literary Property, Orality, and Crimes of Writing

1. The publisher was William Blackwood, the tale "The Portrait of Mr. W. H.," which appeared in *Blackwood's Edinburgh Magazine* in July, 1889. See Oscar Wilde, *The Letters of Oscar Wilde,* ed. Rupert Hart-Davis (London: Rupert Hart-Davis Ltd., 1962), 244.

2. In the landmark case *Burrow-Giles Lithographic Co. v. Sarony,* 111 U.S. 53 (1884), the U.S. Supreme Court established that photographers were the legal authors of their photographs, which the Court affirmed as "original works of art." The particular photos in question were Napoleon Sarony's lavish portraits of Wilde, taken during the latter's American tour. For discussions of the Sarony case, see Mark Rose, *Authors and Owners: The Invention of Copyright* (Cambridge: Harvard University Press, 1993), 135–36; and Jane M. Gaines, *Contested Culture: The Image, the Voice, and the Law* (Chapel Hill: University of North Carolina Press, 1991).

3. Oscar Wilde, *Reviews by Oscar Wilde,* Vol. 13 in *The First Collected Editions of the Works of Oscar Wilde,* ed. Robert Ross (London: Dawsons of Pall Mall, 1969), 90–91.

4. Wilde, *Letters,* 507.

5. See Wilde, *Letters,* 835–44, and H. Montgomery Hyde's Introduction to Frank Harris, *Mr. and Mrs. Daventry* (London: Richards Press, 1956).

6. Max Beerbohm, *Letters to Reggie Turner*, ed. Rupert Hart-Davis (Philadelphia: Lippincott, 1965), 36.

7. Merlin Holland, "Plagiarist, or Pioneer?" in C. George Sandulescu, ed., *Rediscovering Oscar Wilde* (Gerrards Cross: Colin Smythe, 1994), 208.

8. Oscar Wilde, *The Artist as Critic: Critical Writings of Oscar Wilde*, ed. Richard Ellmann (Chicago: University of Chicago Press), 257.

9. Deirdre Toomey, "The Storyteller at Fault," in Sandulescu, ed., *Rediscovering Oscar Wilde*, 406. See also Davis Coakley, *Oscar Wilde: The Importance of Being Irish* (Dublin: Town House, 1994); and contributions by Declan Kiberd ("Oscar Wilde: The Artist as Irishman") and Owen Dudley Edwards ("Impressions of an Irish Sphinx") in Jerusha McCormack, ed., *Wilde the Irishman* (New Haven: Yale University Press, 1998).

10. W. R. Wilde, *Irish Popular Superstitions* (Totowa: Rowman and Littlefield, 1973), vi. After William's death, Speranza edited and published two additional volumes of lore her husband had collected in *Ancient Legends, Mystic Charms, and Superstitions of Ireland* (1887) and *Ancient Cures, Charms, and Usages of Ireland* (1890).

11. W. R. Wilde, *Irish Popular Superstitions*, 10.

12. Charles Gavan Duffy, *Young Ireland: A Fragment of Irish History, 1840–1850* (London: Cassell, Petter, Galpin & Co., 1880), 89.

13. Wilde, *The Artist as Critic*, 351.

14. Wilde, *Letters*, 862.

15. W. B. Yeats, *The Autobiography of William Butler Yeats* (Garden City: Doubleday, 1958), 90, 93. Elsewhere in the *Autobiography*, Yeats mentions hearing Wilde tell a tale later published as "The Doer of Good." Yeats complains that in writing out the tale Wilde had "spoiled it with the verbal decoration of his epoch, and I have to repeat it to myself as I first heard it, before I can see its terrible beauty" (190).

16. W. W. Ward, "Oscar Wilde: an Oxford Reminiscence," in E. H. Mikhail, ed., *Oscar Wilde: Interviews and Recollections* (London: Macmillan, 1979), 1: 12–13.

17. Wilde, *Letters*, 427, 429.

18. Yeats, *Autobiography*, 90.

19. Toomey, "The Storyteller at Fault," 411.

20. Hesketh Pearson, *Oscar Wilde: His Life and Wit* (New York: Harper and Brothers, 1946), 87. Wilde often professed his aversion to writing, thus perpetuating his reputation for literary wastrelsy. After captivating listeners with an impromptu story, he fended off Bernard Partridge's suggestion that he publish it by saying, "I don't think so, my dear fellow: it's such a bore writing these things out." To demonstrate this boredom, he spoke of writing only in rote mechanical terms, as "putting black upon white." Even his jokes about his facility as a playwright couched his dislike of writing in avowals of laziness. Asked by director George Alexander to cut a scene from *The Importance of Being Earnest*, he complained, "This scene that you feel is superfluous cost me terrible exhausting labour and heart-rending nerve-racking strain. You may not believe me, but I assure you on my honour that it must have taken fully five minutes to write" (Pearson, *Oscar Wilde,* 120, 147, 225). Still, as much as the supposed meagerness of Wilde's literary production may have stemmed from his resistance to writing, his preference for talk over text comports with the little philosophy he did write down. In the 1889 essay "Pen, Pencil, and Poison," Wilde implicitly defends himself alongside the poet/forger/poisoner Wainewright: "it is only the Philistine who seeks to estimate a personality by the vulgar test of production. This young dandy sought to be somebody, rather than to do something." See "Pen, Pencil, and Poison: A Study," *Fortnightly Review* 51 (1889): 43; Wilde published a revised version of this essay in *Intentions*.

21. Toomey, "The Storyteller at Fault," 407.

22. Wilde, quoted in W. B. Maxwell, *Time Gathered: Autobiography* (New York: D. Appleton-Century, 1938), 97.

23. "The Sphinx without a Secret: An Etching" was published in *Lord Savile's Crime and Other Stories* (1891) but first appeared as "Lady Alroy" in *The World: A Journal for Men and Women* in May 1887. *The Picture of Dorian Gray* first appeared in the July number of *Lippincott's Monthly Magazine* in 1890 and was published in book form the following year.

24. I undertake such an argument advisedly. Josephine Guy has warned against what she sees as a critical tendency to read Wilde's plagiarism and self-plagiarism as consistent, deliberate, political practices, suggesting that they may equally have resulted from the time and money pressures under which Wilde frequently wrote. Discerning a political gesture behind every writerly move, Guy admonishes, risks letting Wilde-the-genius back in through the kitchen door: who besides an infallible master-orchestrator could plan every appropriation? The virtuoso must at least be counterbalanced by the journeyman, the political Wilde by the writerly Wilde. Though such an argument begs the question of whether acts born of carelessness might not, after all, produce subversive ends, I take Guy's cautionary gesture seriously. Without suggesting that Wilde's lifelong attitudes toward literary crime and property were consistent and consistently politicized, however, I persist in seeing the Chatterton manuscript as one of several important contributions on Wilde's part toward a deeply rooted critique of private literary property and its ideological mascot, the figure of the individual genius. (I differ from Guy in finding no ironclad correspondence between intentionality and consecration; a writer may mean without winning worship.) See Josephine M. Guy, "Self-Plagiarism, Creativity and Craftsmanship in Oscar Wilde," *English Literature in Transition, 1880–1920* 41 (1998): 10. Guy's essay deals strictly with Wilde's self-plagiarism; her warning against the easy politicization of Wilde's plagiarism occurs in an unpublished early version of this essay given at the International Oscar Wilde Conference at the University of Birmingham in 1997.

25. William Wordsworth, "Resolution and Independence," in *"Poem in Two Volumes," and Other Poems, 1800–1807*, ed. Jared Curtis (Ithaca: Cornell University Press, 1983), 125 lines 43–44. Keats also dedicated his *Endymion* (1817–18) to Chatterton, and Shelley lists him among "The inheritors of unfulfilled renown" who rise from their thrones to welcome the soul of Keats in *Adonais,* his 1821 elegy for the poet; see *Adonais,* in *Shelley's Poetry and Prose,* ed. Donald H. Reiman and Sharon B. Powers (New York: W. W. Norton, 1977), 403 line 397. In "Keats' Grave," a sonnet included in a June 1877 letter to Lord Houghton, Wilde unites Keats (whom he glosses as "a Priest of Beauty slain before his time") with Guido Reni's St. Sebastian under the Chattertonian icon of the martyred ephebe, "killed by the arrows of a lying and unjust tongue" (Wilde, *Letters,* 41).

26. Quoted in T. Hall Caine, *Recollections of Dante Gabriel Rossetti* (London: Elliot Stock, 1882), 185; original emphasis. The Wildean theme and practice of misattribution have proven contagious in the limited reception of his Chatterton notes: in his Wilde biography, Richard Ellmann misattributes to Wilde the Dante Gabriel Rossetti sonnet on Chatterton which concludes the lecture manuscript. See Richard Ellmann, *Oscar Wilde* (New York: Alfred A. Knopf, 1988), 285; and Roger Lewis, "A Misattribution: Oscar Wilde's 'Unpublished Poem on Chatterton,'" *Victorian Poetry* 28 (1990): 164–69. Another Rossetti sonnet, "Tiber, Nile, and Thames" (1881), mourns for Chatterton, along with Keats and Coleridge, as a poet whose "sweet speech" London scorned.

27. [Robert Browning], unsigned review of *Conjectures and Researches concerning the Love Madness and Imprisonment of Torquato Tasso* by Richard Henry Wilde, *Foreign Quarterly Review* 29 (1842): 471.

28. For a more extended discussion of Wilde's debt to Browning's Chatterton essay, see Rodney Shewan, *Oscar Wilde: Art and Egotism* (New York: Harper & Row, 1977), 70–73.

29. Susan Stewart, *Crimes of Writing: Problems in the Containment of Representation* (New York: Oxford University Press, 1991), 149. Stewart is writing here of Chatterton, arguing that the textual apparatus he forged to authenticate his Rowley poems is "designed to serve as a genealogy for Chatterton's own situation," which she partly describes as being "caught between two models of authorship: the medieval and Renaissance model of the patron, and the newly emerging contemporary schema of commercial publishing centered in London"—hence Chatterton's simultaneous reverence for and willingness to make free with the past (Stewart, *Crimes of Writing,* 149–50).

30. The audience count is Wilde's, from a 7 December 1886 letter to Horne; see Wilde, *Letters,* 192. Wilde evidently gave the lecture a second time, on 7 April 1888, under the title "Thomas Chatterton: The Boy-Poet of the Eighteenth Century," in Shaftesbury Hall, Bournemouth. He agreed to do it ("If I must, I must!") in a letter to the lecture's hostess, postmarked

19 March 1888; see Oscar Wilde, *More Letters of Oscar Wilde,* ed. Rupert Hart-Davis (London: John Murray, 1985), 73. Ellmann places it in March in his *Oscar Wilde,* 284.

31. It is not known exactly what relation the Chatterton manuscript bears either to the lectures Wilde gave or to the article slated for the *Century Guild Hobby Horse.* I find persuasive Lawrence Danson's reasons for thinking the manuscript a probable lecture transcript: "It would be nice to think that this was merely a source-book, but Wilde's finicky alterations of a word here or a phrase there suggest that it is the text of the lecture pretty much as he delivered it, with notes to himself about subjects to elaborate either extempore during delivery or later in revision." See Lawrence Danson, *Wilde's Intentions: The Artist in His Criticism* (Oxford: Clarendon Press, 1997), 90. If Wilde did in fact appropriate most of an *orally* delivered speech from written sources, we are left with the still-thorny ethical question of whether such a plagiarism is a violation of the same order as a *published* appropriation from written sources.

32. Ellmann, *Oscar Wilde,* 284–85; Shewan, *Oscar Wilde: Art and Egotism,* 70.

33. Holland, "Plagiarist, or Pioneer?" 203.

34. Oscar Wilde, [*Essay on Chatterton*], unpublished manuscript at William Andrews Clark Memorial Library, University of California, Los Angeles, Wilde W6721M3. E78 [1886?]; Finzi 2440; [3–7]. Most of the text is written in pencil on recto pages, and the manuscript is not paginated; subsequent citations will be given in square brackets in the text. The Wilde excerpts from the Chatterton manuscript are © 2003 held by the Estate of Oscar Wilde. I wish to thank the Estate of Oscar Wilde and the William Andrews Clark Memorial Library for their kind permission to quote from the Chatterton notebook.

35. Chatterton was hoping for a lucrative reward. Burgum, however, paid his "genealogist" one lone crown, for which tight-fistedness Chatterton later took him to task: "Gods! What would Burgum give to get a name, / And snatch his blundering dialect from shame! / What would he give to hand his memory down / To time's remotest boundary? A crown!"

36. Daniel Wilson, quoted in Wilde, [*Essay on Chatterton*]. The Chatterton lecture notes challenge our usual practices of scholarly citation; since one might more properly be keyed directly to Daniel Wilson, *Chatterton: A Biographical Study* (London: Macmillan, 1869).

37. Wilde subtly alleges homosexuality in Chatterton by eroticizing the bosom friendship between Thomas Rowley and his historical contemporary William Canynge[s] (1399?–1474), mayor of Bristol. At the end of one Rowley manuscript, Chatterton describes how the two friends had lived together in their dotage. Wilde writes, "So ended this marvellous romance which Chatterton not only wrote but lived—it is his own story—but he had not yet *found* his Canynge" [81–83]. When Walpole later rejects the Rowley manuscripts as inauthentic, Wilde frames Chatterton's tragic fate as romantic defeat: "Walpole accordingly returned the MSS. Chatterton's dream of a real Canynge was over." In "Mr. W. H." Wilde takes up and intensifies the theme of male friendships that are interdependently intertextual and homosexual.

38. On the verso [150] Wilde writes in ink: "there was something in him of 'the yearning of great Vishnu to create a world.'"

39. Wilde emphasizes the connection between genius and affectation by repeating his phrase in the manuscript, underscoring "affect": "Importantly—'a great genius can *affect* anything'" [155].

40. Wilde's own voice was among those he appropriated: in one of his innumerable self-plagiarisms, he lifted the Chatterton lecture's opening lines on "the conditions that precede artistic production" for a review of Joseph Skipsey's *"Carols from the Coal Fields" and Other Songs and Ballads;* see *Pall Mall Gazette* [London], 1 February 1887: 5.

41. The Chatterton lecture's exclusively oral delivery also determined its copyright status: though the manuscript was Wilde's property, neither the content of the lecture nor its particular expressions were copyright under Victorian laws. In 1899, Augustine Birrell wrote that "in the present states of the law (see 5 and 6 William IV., c. 65) (1835) no lecture is protected unless notice in writing of its delivery shall have been given to two justices living within five miles of the place where such lecture shall be delivered two days at least before delivering the same. As this statutory notice is rarely if ever given, the vast majority of lectures are unprotected, at all events from verbatim reports in the newspapers, and if lecturers ever grumble it is rather with the scantiness than with the profusion of the space allotted to them in the Press." Augus-

tine Birrell, *Seven Lectures on The Law and History of Copyright in Books* (London: Cassell, 1899), 191–92.

42. Wilde, "The Portrait of Mr. W. H.," *Blackwood's Edinburgh Magazine* 146 (1889): 1. Henceforth cited parenthetically in the text. Wilde's references to Macpherson, Ireland, and Chatterton in the passage not only constitute a short history of British literary forgery but also illustrate forgery's relation to history. The Scot James Macpherson (1736–96) published a cycle of poems about Finn MacCool, the ancient Celtic hero who crossed from Scotland to Ireland to fight the invading Danes; claiming only to have discovered and translated the poems, Macpherson attributed them to Finn's son, the poet Ossian. In the 1790s, William Henry Ireland (1777–1835) forged a small archive of "recovered" Shakespeare works, including the plays *Vortigern and Rowena* and *Henry II,* to impress his bookseller father. Both Macpherson and Ireland were exposed during their lifetimes, though neither committed Chattertonian suicide. Like Chatterton, though, they lent legitimacy to their own works by borrowing the aura of historical figures—Finn MacCool and Shakespeare—central to national literatures. For all three of the forgers whom Wilde names, history was at once a legitimizing authority and a narrative that could be rewritten to suit their own aims. Such literary forgeries erode the very authority by which they seek to establish their authenticity. In addition, a contemporary authority was also being undermined through forgery while Wilde was writing "Mr. W. H." In 1887 Charles Stewart Parnell, the Irish statesman who was spearheading the Home Rule initiatives in Parliament, was connected through a letter to an infamous political murder in Dublin's Phoenix Park. As supporters of Parnell, Wilde and his brother followed the ensuing investigations, attending meetings of the Parnell Commission (see Ellmann, 289–90). In February 1889, five months before "Mr. W. H." was published, Parnell was exonerated from the charges when the Dublin publisher Richard Pigott confessed to having forged the incriminating letter. Like Chatterton, Pigott killed himself soon after his exposure. I am indebted for aspects of my reading of "Mr. W. H." to Simon Stern.

43. "Oscar Wilde and Mr. W. H.," *Tablet* 42 (1889): 89, 88; Cecil W. Franklyn, "William Shakespeare, Gentleman," *Westminster Review* 132 (1889): 361.

44. [Oscar Wilde,] "A Few Maxims for the Instruction of the Over-Educated," *Saturday Review* 78 (1894): 533.

45. At the time "Mr. W. H." was published, British copyright law allowed the copyright in paintings, drawings, and photographs to circulate separately from the physical artifact (this is still the case today in British and U.S. copyright law). The painter Augustus Egg, for example, purchased Henry Wallis's *The Death of Chatterton* for £200 and subsequently sold the copyright for £150 to a publisher in Newcastle while retaining the actual painting. The law also possessed a bizarre loophole by which the copyright could be lost—again, as if it were a physical object—to all parties. J. M. Lely wrote in 1891, "if the artist sells [paintings, drawings, or photographs] without having the copyright reserved to him by written agreement he loses it, but it does not vest in the purchaser unless there is an agreement signed in his favor. If therefore there is no agreement in writing—a very frequent occurrence—the copyright is altogether lost on a sale, though if the work be executed on commission, instead of being sold after being executed, the copyright in the absence of agreement vests in the person for whom it was executed"; see J. M. Lely, *Copyright Law Reform: An Exposition of Lord Monkswell's Copyright Bill Now Before Parliament* (London: Eyre and Spottiswoode, 1891), 7–8. The notion of a copyright not only dissociable from the artifact it protects but capable of being lost provides an extreme case of the commodification of information. The copyright no longer simply protects a property; it behaves fully *as* property.

46. It is unclear whether or not Cyril loses his faith in the theory before his death. His suicide letter to Erskine claims that "he believed absolutely in Willie Hughes . . . and that in order to show [Erskine] how firm and flawless his faith in the whole thing was, he was going to offer his life as a sacrifice to the secret of the Sonnets" (10). But Erskine accuses Cyril of losing faith: "You never even believed in it yourself. If you had, you would not have committed forgery to prove it." He also warns the narrator, "You forget that a thing is not necessarily true because a man dies for it" (9–10). That Erskine's own "suicide" note appears to counterfeit his belief in the theory suggests the same of Cyril.

[252]

47. William A. Cohen makes a similar point, though without dilating on the connection between credence and property: "To put the theory into a letter is not simply to transcribe it: more than its literal epistolary location, the Willie Hughes theory has the material qualities of a letter, in that only one person at a time can possess (that is, believe) it. It can be passed from one person to another, but it cannot be shared or divided." See William A. Cohen, "Willie and Wilde: Reading *The Portrait of Mr. W. H.*," *South Atlantic Quarterly* 88 (1989): 228–29.

48. Charles Coquelin, *Dictionnaire de l'économie politique* (Paris, 1873), 217; quoted in Fritz Machlup and Edith Penrose, "The Patent Controversy in the Nineteenth Century," *Journal of Economic History* 10 (1950): 12 n. 39.

49. Wilde, quoted in H. M. Swanwick [Helena Sickert], *I Have Been Young* (London: V. Gollancz, 1935), 66; quoted in Ellmann, *Oscar Wilde*, 297.

50. Oscar Wilde, *The Picture of Dorian Gray: Authoritative Texts, Backgrounds, Reviews and Reactions, Criticism*, ed. Donald L. Lawler (New York: W. W. Norton, 1988), 30.

51. Oscar Wilde, "Phrases and Philosophies for the Use of the Young," *Chameleon* 1 (1894): 2.

52. Lord Alfred Douglas, *The True History of Shakespeare's Sonnets* (London: Martin Secker, 1933), 34.

53. See Cohen, "Willie and Wilde," 241.

54. Karl Beckson, ed., *Oscar Wilde: The Critical Heritage* (New York: Barnes & Noble, 1970), 245–47, 251, 243–44.

55. Wilde, *The Artist as Critic*, 286, 288.

56. Wilde, *Letters*, 473, 509, 498, 501, 491. The prelapsarian Wilde had made general sport of his outstanding debts through his quips and characters. In *A Woman of No Importance*, a fictional Lord Alfred says of his gold-tipped cigarettes, "They are awfully expensive. I can only afford them when I'm in debt. . . . One must have some occupation nowadays. If I hadn't my debts I shouldn't have anything to think about. All the chaps I know are in debt." Wilde had also poked fun at debt-collectors, such as *The Importance of Being Earnest*'s kid-gloved solicitor, Mr. Gribsby, who appears (in a scene cut from the performance script) with a writ of attachment against Ernest Worthing for £762 14s. 2d. worth of Savoy suppers. Algernon replies with the Wildean debtor's panache: "Pay it? How on earth am I going to do that? You don't suppose I have got any money? How perfectly silly you are. No gentleman ever has any money." Wilde, *Complete Works*, 439, 350.

57. See Reginia Gagnier, *Idylls of the Marketplace: Oscar Wilde and the Victorian Public* (Stanford: Stanford University Press, 1986), 179–95.

58. Wilde, *Letters*, 451, 428, 444, 507.

59. In a phrase that invokes *The Picture of Dorian Gray*, Wilde calls Bosie's habit of getting his emotions on credit "the secret of eternal youth" (Wilde, *Letters*, 501). Wilde's novel might well be read as a morality tale about the abuses of credit: by transferring his own aging process onto the portrait, Dorian lives on "borrowed time" which he eventually repays—and with interest.

60. Wilde, *Letters*, 422, 452, 421, 470, 462, 447, 470.

61. Wilde, *The Artist as Critic*, 258, 288.

62. Wilde, *Letters*, 479, 467.

63. Ibid., 506–7, 480, 460.

64. Ibid., 502–3, 511, 501, 479.

65. Walter Pater, *Selected Writings of Walter Pater*, ed. Harold Bloom (New York: Columbia University Press, 1974), 108–10.

66. George Meredith, *The Ordeal of Richard Feverel* (New York: Modern Library, 1927), 266.

67. Wilde, *Letters*, 512.

68. H. Montgomery Hyde, "The Riddle of *De Profundis*: Who Owns the Manuscript?" *Antigonish Review* 54 (1983): 112.

69. Quoted in Philip Hoare, *Oscar Wilde's Last Stand: Decadence, Conspiracy, and the Most Outrageous Trial of the Century* (New York: Arcade Publishing, 1997), 137. See also Michael Kettle, *Salome's Last Veil: The Libel Case of the Century* (London: Hart-Davis/Granada, 1977).

70. Walter Kirn, "Wilde About Oscar," *Time,* 4 May 1998.
71. See George Sylvester Viereck, "Oskar Wilde Redivivus," *Berliner Tageblatt* [Berlin], 15 May 1905, trans. as "Is Oscar Wilde Living or Dead?" *Critic* 47 (1905): 86–88.

4. The Reign of the Dead: Hauntologies of Postmortem Copyright

1. The European Union copyright term of author's life plus 70 years resulted from the Union's commitment not to rescind rights already granted its citizens by extant national laws. Thus, the longest copyright term of all the E.U. nations prevailed: the 70-year postmortem term shared by Germany and Austria. That term evidently originated in a 1960s provision to compensate literary estates for the untimely deaths of numerous writers during the two world wars. As Patrick Parrinder writes, "Thus a decision in its nature local and temporary, taken without any reference to the present and future 'development of creativity' . . . became the direct cause of European legislation intended to be universal and permanent." Patrick Parrinder, "Introduction: Literary Copyright and the Public Domain," in Patrick Parrinder and Warren Chernaik, eds., *Textual Monopolies: Literary Copyright and the Public Domain* (London: Office for Humanities Communication, 1997), 6–7. One might add that the E.U. adoption of the German and Austrian term has permanently enlisted the copyright world in the griefwork of two traumatized wartime generations: special provisions made to compensate survivors and thereby, presumably, to assist the work of mourning, have become part of the permanent architecture of a nearly globalized copyright regime.

France and Belgium also added the "*années de guerre*" to their normal copyright terms. These extensions held World War I to have lasted from August 2, 1914, to December 31, 1919, and World War II from September 3, 1939, to January 1, 1948, for a total extension of 14 years 272 days. Though the Belgian *années de guerre* provision was explicitly dropped under the E.U. directive, the French ratification did not address that country's *années de guerre* extension, with the result that several authors' estates have since sued—and so far successfully—to have that extension upheld *in addition to* the 70-year postmortem copyright term, for a total postmortem term of just under 85 years. The French ratification also failed to evacuate a special 30-year copyright bonus granted to writers killed in action, to compensate their heirs for the loss of works and revenues that would have been generated had the author's life not been foreshortened. The estates of French writers killed in the world wars, then, might enjoy a postmortem copyright term of 70 + 30 + nearly 15 years, or a total of just under 115 years after the author's death. By surviving subsequent term extensions, these site-specific *années de guerre* compensations in France have effectively been superadded to the universalized German and Austrian *années de guerre* provisions, doubly and even trebly compensating estates for their testator's death in war.

2. In October 1998, the *Chicago Tribune* reported of Disney's lobbying efforts: "In addition to its face-to-face lobbying campaign, Disney made campaign contributions. Of the 13 initial sponsors of the House bill, 10 received contributions from Disney's political action committee. The largest donations, $5,000 each, went to [House Judiciary Committee Intellectual Property Subcommittee Chairman Howard] Coble and Rep. Howard Berman (D-Calif.), a senior member of the Judiciary Committee. On the Senate side, 8 of the 12 sponsors received Disney contributions. Judiciary Committee Chairman Orrin Hatch (R-Utah), the bill's chief sponsor, received $6,000, second only to Democratic Sen. Barbara Boxer, who represents Disney's home state of California and who is up for re-election this fall. Disney gave $1,000 to [Senate Majority Leader Trent] Lott on June 16, the day he signed up as a bill co-sponsor and a week after Lott met with [Disney Chairman Michael] Eisner." "Disney Lobbying for Copyright Extension No Mickey Mouse Effort: Congress OKs Bill Granting Creators 20 More Years," *Chicago Tribune,* 17 October 1998.

3. *Congressional Record* (105th Congress, 2d Session) 144 (7 October 1998) H9946, 9951–52.

4. U.S. Constitution, Article I, § 8, cl. 8; emphasis added.

5. United States Senate Committee on the Judiciary, Report 104-817. Hearing on S. 483 (20 September 1995), 123. Testimony of Songwriter Patrick Alger. Quoted in Timothy R. Phil-

lips, "The Unconstitutionality of the Copyright Term Extension Act of 1998," Draft Brief in Support of the Constitutional Challenge to the CTEA. See http://www.law.asu.edu/HomePages/Karjala/OpposingCopyrightExtension/constitutionality/phillips02.html.

6. United States Senate Committee on the Judiciary, Report 104-817, Hearing on S. 483 (20 September 20 1995), 68; passage from Arnold Schoenberg's *Style and Idea* submitted as part of the testimony of E. R. Schoenberg; quoted in Phillips, "Unconstitutionality."

7. Quoted in Robert Kolker, "Theaters on Alert as Congress Looks at Copyright Law," *Back Stage* 36 (1995): 3.

8. Thomas Jefferson, Letter to James Madison (6 September 1789), in *The Portable Thomas Jefferson*, ed. Merrill D. Peterson (Harmondsworth: Penguin Books, 1977), 447.

9. Daren Fonda, "Copyright Crusader," *Boston Globe Magazine*, 29 August 1999. *Eldred v. Reno* argued that the CTEA's extension of subsisting copyrights exceeded Congress's power under the Copyright Clause of the Constitution as well as violating the First Amendment and the public-trust doctrine, and that its prospective extension of the copyright term violated the First Amendment. See *Eldred v. Reno*, 239 F. 3d 372 (D.C. Cir., 2001). Having been rejected twice by lower federal courts, the case—now *Eldred v. Ashcroft*, No. 01-618—was granted certiori in February 2002 by the U.S. Supreme Court, which heard oral arguments on 9 October 2002 and upheld the CTEA's constitutionality on 15 January 2003 in a 7-2 ruling. A brief account of the early stages of the case can be found in Lawrence Lessig, *The Future of Ideas: The Fate of the Commons in a Connected World* (New York: Random House, 2001), 196–99. Lessig is also one of several plaintiffs' lawyers in *Golan v. Ashcroft*, a case that assails both the CTEA and § 514 of the Uruguay Round Agreements Act on constitutional grounds. The complaint argues that the CTEA neither "promote[s] the progress of science and useful arts" nor creates a "limited" copyright term; that § 514's restoration of lapsed copyrights violates the Copyright Clause's requirement that the public be allowed to use freely all work in the public domain; that both acts violate the originality requirement for copyright protection by extending the protection in existing works; that they violate the First Amendment by producing speech restrictions; and that they violate the Due Process Clause's requirement that retroactive legislation not so disrupt settled expectations as to be fundamentally unfair. See *Golan v. Ashcroft*, No. 01-B-1854 (D. Colo. filed 19 Sept. 2001).

10. Susan Eilenberg, "Mortal Pages: Wordsworth and the Reform of Copyright," *English Literary History* 56 (1989): 354.

11. Thomas Noon Talfourd, *Three Speeches Delivered in the House of Commons in Favour of a Measure for an Extension of Copyright* (London: Edward Moxon, 1840), 143; quoted in Eilenberg, "Mortal Pages," 365.

12. Talfourd, *Three Speeches*, 112; quoted in Eilenberg, "Mortal Pages," 354.

13. *The Letters of William and Dorothy Wordsworth: The Middle Years*, ed. Ernest De Selincourt (Oxford: Oxford University Press, 1937), 2:845.

14. See Eilenberg, "Mortal Pages," 365–66.

15. Warren Montag, "Spirits Armed and Unarmed: Derrida's *Specters of Marx*," in Michael Sprinker, ed., *Ghostly Demarcations: A Symposium on Jacques Derrida's* Specters of Marx (London: Verso, 1999), 71.

16. Jacques Derrida, *Specters of Marx: The State of the Debt, the Work of Mourning, and the New International*, trans. Peggy Kamuf (London: Routledge, 1995), 160.

17. Jacques Derrida, "Marx & Sons," in *Ghostly Demarcations*, 248–49.

18. Nina Auerbach, *Our Vampires, Ourselves* (Chicago: University of Chicago Press, 1995), 109. Auerbach's reading takes up the homoerotics of the text, observing that the young Wildean ephebes Ernest and Jack read poetry to one another while "twitching with a strange ascetic passion" (Auerbach, *Our Vampires*, 103). She also notes a foreshadowing of Reginald Clarke's explicitly Wildean—and thus implicitly homosexual—fall from grace: "Many years later, when the vultures of misfortune had swooped down upon him, and his name was no longer mentioned without a sneer, he was still remembered in New York drawing rooms as the man who had brought to perfection the art of talking." See George Sylvester Viereck, *The House of the Vampire* (New York: Moffat, Yard, 1907), 4. Hereafter, page references to this work are given parenthetically in the text.

19. See Niel M. Johnson, *George Sylvester Viereck: German-American Propagandist* (Urbana: University of Illinois Press, 1972) and Phyllis Keller, "George Sylvester Viereck: The Psychology of a German-American Militant," *Journal of Interdisciplinary History* 2 (1971): 59–108.

20. Oscar Wilde, "*Olivia* at the Lyceum," *Dramatic Review* 30 May 1885; reprinted in *The First Collected Edition of the Works of Oscar Wilde,* ed. Robert Ross (London: Dawsons of Pall Mall, 1969) 13: 29.

21. Alternately, one might view the *Vampire* as a parable about the near-absence of international copyright protection in the U.S. in which it is set. Just as Ernest possesses no legal defense against Clarke's psychic plagiarisms, European authors had no legal means by which to protect their work published in the States or to collect royalties from its sale—a situation decried by Dickens, James, Trollope, Joyce, and many other professional writers on both sides of the Atlantic.

22. T. Everett Harry, "Souls of the Dead Alive in This Poet: Grandson of Wilhelm I, Spiritual Grandson of Edgar Allan Poe Is George Sylvester Viereck, Socialist," *North American* [Philadelphia], 11 August 1907. Harry responds sarcastically, "Ah, I thought, remembering Mr. Viereck's claim of inspiration from Poe, Wilde, Swinburne, I have guessed it. Mr. Viereck, like a sun glass, is gathering the rays of lesser lights, of the living and dead to focus into great works of his own, which he will give to the world clothed in purer poetry and possessing greater power than the less endowed mortals whom he will vampire."

23. "The Absorptive Nature of Genius," *Current Literature* [New York], 4 January 1908.

24. "'Vampire' Stolen, Stringer Declares," *New York Times,* 20 January 1909.

25. In some cases, storylines and other structural elements of novels that would seem to qualify as ideas rather than expression have found a degree of protection under copyright. Judge Learned Hand made clear in *Nichols v. Universal Pictures Corp.*, 45 F.2d 119, 121 (2d Cir. 1930) that characters, situations, and plots can be protected under copyright if they are sufficiently delineated, and that those same elements can be infringed by substantial copying (see my discussion of *The Wind Done Gone* in the conclusion). See also *Stewart v. Abend,* 495 U.S. 207, 238 (1990), which recognized that motion pictures may infringe a book's copyright by using its "unique setting, characters, plot, and sequence of events."

26. William Bullock wrote for the *New York Press:* "It happens that Wilde as an artist is a trifle too tall and imposing for imitators to approach; his shadow enfolds them completely. The world is fast coming to know Wilde, not for one of the biggest men of his generation, but of his century, and if Viereck continues to ape him, as he has been doing in his drama and prose, he will end by stringing his artistic self up by the toes.") But even Bullock's criticism ratified Viereck's theory of history by attacking him in absorptive, monumentalist—that is, Viereckian—language: the titanic Wilde towers over, engulfs, and finally executes his puny imitators. Others accepted the book's Great Man thesis only to deny Viereck membership in the pantheon. But while Viereck's absorptive theories lived on in the mouths of his detractors, his self-appointed "great American novel" was slowly killed in its westward trek through the U.S. by damning reviews. Under the heading "How Not to Write English," a *New York Times* reviewer called Viereck "a besotted phrase-monger. Here and there he strikes off a neat epigram. Occasionally he hits on a happy conceit. But for weary pages he labors among words with axes and hammers and implements of torture with most melancholy result." The *Tribune News* of Duluth, Minn., belittled the *Vampire* as "a verbose efflorescence that conceals a remarkable paucity of thought." Most critics found the book well-enough conceived but weak in style, execution, and technique. The San Francisco *Argonaut* hammered home the last nail: "It is a pity that some such vampire did not steal Mr. Viereck's idea before he spoiled it. . . . It must, however, be said in fairness that the book has only 190 pages and that the type is large." See William Bullock, untitled review in *New York Press,* 9 July 1909; untitled review in *New York Times,* 5 October 1907; "*The House of the Vampire,*" *Tribune News* [Duluth], 6 October 1907; untitled review in *Argonaut* [San Francisco], 12 October 1907. Reviews collected in George Sylvester Viereck, ed., unpaginated *Scrapbook* 14 in Miscellaneous Papers of George Sylvester Viereck, Hoover Institution Archives, Stanford University.

27. Decades later, Woolf would be one of the screenwriters of MGM's *The Wizard of Oz* (1939). In his revisions, Woolf let love triumph over vampirism, making the heroine rescue the

endangered young poet in the final scene, but he also foregrounded the vampire's vitalist setpieces and soliloquies. And he gave the main characters more glamorous names: Reginald Clarke was upgraded to Paul Hartleigh, Ernest to Caryl, Ethel to Allene.

28. Woolf altered the relationship between vampire and heroine in his reworking of the novel: where Ethel had been a rejected lover of Clarke's, Allene is the daughter of an old lover of Hartleigh's and now his ward, addressing him as "father." He vamps her, but then sends her away out of respect for her mother. At the dénouement of the play, Allene rescues Caryl from the vampire by throwing herself between them, and the lovers escape unharmed. (I have gleaned the plot changes from newspaper summaries of the play; the script was never published, and no performance copy seems to have survived.)

29. Allan Dale, untitled review in *Evening Post* [New York], 22 January 1909, in Viereck, ed., *Scrapbook 15*.

30. Undated reviews in *New York Commercial* and the *Morning Telegraph* [New York], in Viereck, ed., *Scrapbook 15*.

31. Jefferson wrote: "If nature has made any one thing less susceptible than all others of exclusive property, it is the action of the thinking power called an idea, which an individual may exclusively possess as long as he keeps it to himself; but the moment it is divulged, it forces itself into the possession of everyone, and the receiver cannot dispossess himself of it. Its peculiar character, too, is that no one possesses the less, because every other possesses the whole of it. . . . Inventions then cannot, in nature, be subject of property." Thomas Jefferson, Letter to Isaac McPherson, 13 August 1813, in *Thomas Jefferson: Writings,* ed. Merrill D. Peterson (New York: Literary Classics of the U.S., 1984), 1291.

32. "'Vampire' Stolen, Stringer Declares."

33. "'Vampire' Authors Will Sue Stringer," *New York Times,* 31 January 1909.

34. See *Journal* [Atlanta], 3 February 1909, in Viereck, ed., *Scrapbook 15*.

35. Untitled article in *New York American,* 18 January 1909, in Viereck, ed., *Scrapbook 15*.

36. Untitled article in *Telegraph* [New York], 29 November 1909, in Viereck, ed., *Scrapbook 15*.

37. Brad Sherman and Lionel Bently, *The Making of Modern Intellectual Property Law: The British Experience, 1760–1911* (Cambridge: Cambridge University Press, 2000), 20.

38. Untitled article in *New York Press,* 29 January 1909, in Viereck, ed., *Scrapbook 15*. The article reports that slips bearing the question "Do you believe in the Vampire?" were distributed to the hundred-plus poets, and ninety-seven out of the hundred returned answered "yes." "One facetious poet wrote that he suspected Milton, Kipling, and Tennyson of robbing him of his brainchildren."

39. Untitled review in *Register* [New Haven], 27 December 1909, in Viereck, ed., *Scrapbook 15*. Several newspaper advertisements for the play featured the testimony of another mind expert, George Trumbull Ladd, Professor of Psychology at Yale University: "The meaning is that disinterested love alone can guard against the hideous effects of overbearing ambition, and that the baleful effects of the robberies of humanity by the 'Overman' are averted by the ties of love which bind together the rank and file of humanity, while this rank and file, after all, reaps the fruits of the conquests of his genius" (Viereck, ed., *Scrapbook 15*). Ladd's redemptive humanist interpretation of the play weirdly upends Viereck's overman, whose illuminating powers justify his expropriations from the "rank and file."

40. Augustine Birrell, *Seven Lectures on the Law and History of Copyright in Books* (London: Cassell, 1899), 195–98.

41. See Ronald V. Bettig, *Copyrighting Culture: The Political Economy of Intellectual Property* (Boulder: Westview Press, 1996), 103–10.

42. Stanley M. Besen, *New Technologies and Intellectual Property: An Economic Analysis* (Santa Monica: Rand, 1987), 45; quoted in Bettig, *Copyrighting Culture,* 104.

43. Robert E. Babe and Conrad Winn, *Broadcasting Policy and Copyright Law* (Ottawa: Department of Communications, Government of Canada, 1981), 28; quoted in Bettig, *Copyrighting Culture,* 106–7.

44. See Bettig, *Copyrighting Culture,* 106–8.

45. For exceptions to this convention, see above, note 25.

Notes to Pages 148–156

46. Fiona Macmillan Patfield, "Legal Policy and the Limits of Literary Copyright," in Parrinder and Chernaik, eds., *Textual Monopolies,* 122.

47. Patfield quotes a 1985 U.S. Supreme Court brief that makes explicit what has long been an implicit function of the idea/expression dichotomy: it strikes "a definitional balance between the First Amendment and the Copyright Act by permitting free communication of facts while still protecting an author's expression." *Harper and Row Publishers, Inc. v. Nation Enterprises* 471 US 539, 556 (1985), quoting 723 F.2d 195, 203 (2d Cir. 1983); quoted in Patfield, "Legal Policy," 121.

48. Jefferson, *Thomas Jefferson: Writings,* 1291.

49. Boyle articulates this duality in the following compact formulation: "Perfect information is a defining conceptual element of the analytical structure used to analyze markets driven by the absence of information in which the imperfect information itself is a commodity." James D. A. Boyle, *Shamans, Software, and Spleens: Law and the Construction of the Information Society* (Cambridge: Harvard University Press, 1996), 35.

50. Rosemary J. Coombe, *The Cultural Life of Intellectual Properties: Authorship, Appropriation, and the Law* (Durham: Duke University Press, 1998), 266.

51. Thomas Edward Scrutton, *The Laws of Copyright: An Examination into the Principles Which Should Regulate Literary and Artistic Property in England and Other Countries* (London: John Murray, 1883), 290–92.

52. Birrell, *Seven Lectures,* 206.

53. In his 1917 essay, "Mourning and Melancholia" (trans. Joan Riviere), Freud describes the work of mourning as follows: "The testing of reality, having shown that the loved object no longer exists, requires forthwith that all the libido shall be withdrawn from its attachments to this object.... The normal outcome is that deference for reality gains the day. Nevertheless its behest cannot be at once obeyed. The task is now carried through bit by bit, under great expense of time and cathectic energy, while all the time the existence of the lost object continues in the mind. Each single one of the memories and hopes which bound the libido to the object is brought up and hyper-cathected, and the detachment of the libido from it accomplished.... when the work of mourning is completed the ego becomes free and uninhibited again." In Sigmund Freud, *General Psychological Theory: Papers on Metapsychology,* ed. Philip Rieff (New York: Macmillan, 1963), 165–66.

54. Title V of the 1994 Uruguay Round Agreements Act restored the U.S. copyright in foreign works whose protection had lapsed due to "noncompliance with formalities imposed at any time by United States copyright law." See Robert Spoo, "Copyright and the Ends of Ownership: The Case for a Public-domain *Ulysses* in America," in Thomas F. Staley, ed., *Joyce Studies Annual* 1999 (Austin: University of Texas Press, 1999) 36 n. 144.

55. The European Community Directive on harmonization was adopted on 29 October 1993 and put in effect in 1995. Britain complied with the term extension in 1996, and the U.S. in 1998.

56. By Spoo's reckoning, the first arguably copyrightable *Ulysses* in the U.S. was the 1961 Random House edition. The 1934 Random House *Ulysses* was set from Samuel Roth's pirated 1927 edition, which was a type-facsimile of the second impression of the second (1926) Paris edition; as *this* edition was essentially uncopyrightable because obscene (see chapter 5), its facsimiles were also ineligible for copyright. According to the Bono Act, the 1961 *Ulysses* would enter the public domain at the end of 2056 (the Bono Act extends the copyright on works published before 1978 to a flat term of 95 years; 1961 + 95 = 2056). See Spoo, "Copyright and the Ends of Ownership," 61. Unless the copyright term is again extended, *Finnegans Wake* will enter the public domain in the U.S. at the end of 2034 (1939 + 95 = 2034).

57. In 1999 the Joyce Estate refused permission for a special children's reading at the Dublin Writers' Museum of "The Cat and the Devil," a story Joyce had dedicated to his grandson. The Estate did initially grant permission for a staged reading from *Ulysses* by Nobel Laureate Seamus Heaney on Bloomsday 2000 but eventually demanded a prohibitively high royalty of £27,000 sterling. The Opera Theatre Company was prevented by the Estate from commissioning an opera by Irish composer Seoirse Bodley, to be based on Joyce's play *Exiles.* The Swedish/Finnish James Joyce Society had to abandon plans to translate the same play into Swedish for

internal use, discouraged by the Estate's fee of £2,000 sterling. In the fall of 2000, the Joyce Estate obtained an interim injunction preventing Cork University Press from printing excerpts from *Ulysses* when the press refused to pay the £7,500 copyright fee requested by the Estate. See Medb Ruane, "The war of words over Joyce's literary legacy," *Irish Times* [Dublin], 10 June 2000; "Hearing on Joyce excerpts resumes," *Irish Times*, 3 October 2000; and "Court urges talks in dispute over *Ulysses*," *Irish Times*, 4 October 2000. In November 2001, the Joyce Estate won an injunction in the English High Court against editor Danis Rose's 1997 Picador/ Macmillan imprint of *Ulysses: The Reader's Edition*. The court found that while the majority of the 250,000 words in Rose's *Ulysses* did not violate copyright owing to the "reliance party" provisions for revived copyrights, some 250 words taken from manuscripts reproduced in the *James Joyce Archive*, published during the 1970s, did infringe the Estate's copyright sufficiently to enjoin the edition.

58. Peter Carty, "Never on a Bloomsday," *Independent* [Dublin], 12 January 2000.

59. Catherine Bédarida, interview with Stephen Joyce, *Le Monde* [Paris], 22 March 1995: 26; trans. and quoted in Patrick Parrinder, "Licensing Scholarship: Some Encounters with the Wells Estate," in Parrinder and Chernaik, eds., *Textual Monopolies*, 57.

60. Vanessa Thorpe, "Joyce bans Molly's musical climax," *Observer* [London], 30 July 2000. Newspaper reports varied as to whether these comments were made by Stephen Joyce or by the Joyce Estate's trustee, Sean Sweeney.

61. Ruane, "War of words."

62. Bédarida, [interview with Stephen Joyce], 26.

5. *James Joyce, Copywright: Modernist Literary Property Metadiscourse*

1. James Joyce, *Finnegans Wake* (London: Faber and Faber, 1939), 185, lines 30–31. Henceforth cited parenthetically in the text as *FW*, followed by page and line number(s).

2. James Joyce, *Ulysses: The Corrected Text*, ed. Hans Walter Gabler et al. (New York: Vintage Books, 1984), chapter 9, line 309. Henceforth cited parenthetically in the text as *U*, followed by chapter number and line number(s).

3. Mark Osteen has persuasively traced the "twosome twiminds" of Joyce's economic and artistic attitudes in the service of an ultimately biographical observation: that Joyce never reached a compromise between "his desire to be a solvent member of the European bourgeoisie and his contrary desire to remain separate from the middle class, to defy bourgeois values, to spend his money and remain on the fringes of this community." Mark Osteen, *The Economy of Ulysses: Making Both Ends Meet* (Syracuse: Syracuse University Press, 1995), 2.

4. Sherman and Bently describe the period 1860–1911 as one of "consolidation and retrenchment" in British copyright law, "a time in which gradually, haphazardly and following no particular logic, the categories of modern intellectual property came to take on an institutional reality." Brad Sherman and Lionel Bently, *The Making of Modern Intellectual Property Law: The British Experience, 1760–1911* (Cambridge: Cambridge University Press, 1999), 129.

5. U.S. Constitution, article I, § 8, cl. 8.

6. Under the current U.S. law, registration remains a prerequisite to infringement suits for works of U.S. origin; it is also a precondition to obtaining statutory damages and attorney's fees. See Robert Spoo, "Copyright and the Ends of Ownership: The Case for a Public-domain *Ulysses* in America," in Thomas F. Staley, ed., *Joyce Studies Annual* 1999 (Austin: University of Texas Press, 1999): 12 nn. 32–34.

7. According to the "manufacturing clause" of the 1909 Copyright Act, English-language works of foreign origin had to be deposited at the Copyright Office in Washington, D.C., within 60 days of their first foreign publication and had to be accompanied by a request for reservation of copyright. Compliance with this procedure gained the work a four-month "*ad interim*" copyright, during which time the U.S. imprint of the work was expected to appear. Books that met these stringent requirements obtained the copyright protection of 28 years from date of first foreign publication, plus the option of an additional 28-year renewal. However, if the *ad interim* protection were not properly requested, or if U.S. publishers refused to print the work

once it had entered the *ad interim* period, the chance of obtaining a U.S. copyright was forfeited. See Spoo, "Copyright and the Ends of Ownership," 18–21, and Bruce Arnold, *The Scandal of Ulysses* (London: Sinclair-Stevenson, 1991), 81.

8. See, for example, Arnold, *The Scandal of Ulysses;* Paul Vanderham, *James Joyce and Censorship* (New York: New York University Press, 1998); Lawrence Rainey, *Institutions of Modernism: Literary Elites and Public Culture* (New Haven: Yale University Press, 1998); Jay A. Gertzman, *Bookleggers and Smuthounds: The Trade in Erotica, 1920–1940* (Philadelphia: University of Pennsylvania Press, 1999). In her essay "Joyce's Will," in *Novel* 21 (1995): 114–27, Carol Shloss discusses the distinction between copyright and *droit moral* in French civil code and the bearing of that distinction on Joyce's will and the disposal of his literary estate. See also Carol Shloss, "Privacy and Piracy in the Joyce Trade: James Joyce and *Le Droit Moral*"; David Weir, "What Did He Know, and When Did He Know It: *The Little Review,* Joyce, and *Ulysses*"; and Paul K. Saint-Amour, "Soliloquy of Samuel Roth: A Paranormal Defense," all in *James Joyce Quarterly* 37 (2000).

9. Robert Spoo, "Copyright Protectionism and Its Discontents: The Case of James Joyce's *Ulysses* in America," *Yale Law Journal* 108 (1998): 633–67. The essay in *Joyce Studies Annual* 1999 is a revised and expanded version of this article.

10. Somewhat similarly, Paul Vanderham has suggested that the 1921 U.S. obscenity verdict influenced the subsequent composition and revision of *Ulysses:* that Joyce compiled and circulated his schemata to the novel in order to nudge public focus away from the book's purported obscenity and toward its deliberate, elaborate formal devices and symbolic correspondences. Vanderham goes on to speculate that Joyce subsequently revised *Ulysses* in accordance with the schemata so as to foreground the book's "literary" attributes further over its supposed obscenity; see Vanderham, *James Joyce and Censorship,* 74–82. My contention about the legibility of an intellectual property regime in the body of *Ulysses* is at once more structural and less directly causal. Although I do not speculate as to whether Joyce deliberately composed or modified the text to engage contemporary copyright law, I do suggest that as a structuring force in the literary marketplace, copyright law inscribed its categories, metaphysics, and master narratives in varying degrees on Joyce's novel as well as on a host of contemporary texts.

11. T. S. Eliot, "*Ulysses,* Order, and Myth," *Dial* 75 (1923): 480.

12. See, for example, Rainey, *Institutions of Modernism;* Michael North, *1922: A Return to the Scene of the Modern* (Oxford: Oxford University Press, 1999); Douglas Mao, *Solid Objects: Modernism and the Test of Production* (Princeton: Princeton University Press, 1998); Michael Tratner, *Modernism and Mass Politics: Joyce, Woolf, Eliot, Yeats* (Stanford: Stanford University Press, 1995) and *Deficits and Desires: Economics and Sexuality in Twentieth-Century Literature* (Stanford: Stanford University Press, 2001); Pericles Lewis, *Modernism, Nationalism, and the Novel* (Cambridge: Cambridge University Press, 2000); Derek Attridge and Marjorie Howes, eds., *Semicolonial Joyce* (Cambridge: Cambridge University Press, 2000).

13. A letter from Joyce to Harriet Shaw Weaver puts the completion of "Oxen" in May 1920. James Joyce, *Letters of James Joyce, Vol. II,* ed. Richard Ellmann (New York: Viking Press, 1966), 464.

14. On the Continental *droit d'auteur* or *droit moral* doctrine, see my introduction, notes 1 and 2.

15. Early versions of several *Dubliners* stories appeared in 1904 in the *Irish Homestead,* and in 1915 H. L. Mencken's magazine the *Smart Set* printed three stories. The full collection had been published the year before by Grant Richards in England and appeared two years later in the U.S. under the imprint of B. W. Huebsch, who also brought out the first edition of *A Portrait of the Artist as a Young Man* in volume form. That novel had already appeared serially in a British review called the *Egoist,* which later printed episodes II, III, VI, and X of *Ulysses*—the only episodes the printer deemed "decent" enough to set. And of course it was in the Chicago-based *Little Review* that *Ulysses* appeared in serial form—at least, up through "Oxen of the Sun," the last episode published before the obscenity injunction. See Richard Ellmann, *James Joyce: New and Revised Edition* (Oxford: Oxford University Press, 1982), 443.

16. See Spoo, "Copyright and the Ends of Ownership," 9–10. Anderson held the copyright in the *Ulysses* serializations not because Joyce had produced them as "work-for-hire" on behalf

of the journal as corporate author, but because under the 1909 Copyright Act, when an author sold or gave a manuscript to the publisher of a periodical, the publisher typically acquired the copyright in the individual work unless special arrangements were made to reserve or return the copyright to the author. In the absence of such special arrangements, the publisher would hold the copyrights in both the collective work (i.e., the full issue of the periodical) and its individual component works. The 1976 Copyright Act, however, reversed this presumption, with the result that authors retain copyrights in individual works published in periodicals unless express agreements are made to the contrary. Absent such agreements, the publisher holds copyrights only in the collective work and any individual works made for hire.

17. Published internationally on 2 February 1927, the protest began with an invocation "in the name of that security of works of the intellect and the imagination without which art cannot live," going on to allege that Roth had taken advantage of *Ulysses'* uncopyrighted status "to deprive [Joyce] of his property and to mutilate the creation of his art." James Joyce, *Letters of James Joyce Vol. III*, ed. Richard Ellmann (New York: Viking Press, 1966), 151–52.

18. Ironically, all overt references in this passage to the outhouse and Bloom's defecation were expurgated by Ezra Pound for its serialization in the *Little Review*. See Vanderham, *James Joyce and Censorship*, 19–25, 170.

19. See, for example, *Moore v. The Regents of the University of California*, 793 P.2d 479 (Cal. 1990), *cert. denied*, 111 S. Ct. 1388 (1991). The plaintiff sued for—and was denied—ownership in the intellectual property legacy of his spleen, which was removed for medical reasons, and from whose T-lymphocytes researchers had extracted a profitable, patented cell line. James D. A. Boyle argues in *Shamans, Software, and Spleens: Law and the Construction of the Information Society* (Cambridge: Harvard University Press, 1996) that the court's verdict illustrates the persistence of a problematic Romantic concept of authorship in intellectual property law—a concept that sees scientists as authors of a cell line, but does not regard a patient as author of his spleen.

20. James Joyce, *Letters of James Joyce, Vol. I*, ed. Stuart Gilbert (New York: Viking Press, 1957), 130. Joyce was fond of exaggerating the intellectual property status of his formal innovations, confiding in a letter to Harriet Shaw Weaver that the nascent *Finnegans Wake* "really has no beginning or end (Trade secret, registered at Stationers Hall). It ends in the middle of a sentence and begins in the middle of the same sentence" (Joyce, *Letters, Vol. I*, 246).

21. John Gordon, "The Multiple Journeys of 'Oxen of the Sun,'" *English Literary History* 46 (1979): 159.

22. Osteen, *Economy of Ulysses*, 232, 228.

23. A. M. Klein, "Oxen of the Sun," 1949, reprinted in *Literary Essays and Reviews*, ed. Usher Caplan and M. W. Steinberg (Toronto: University of Toronto Press, 1987), 315. Intriguingly, the right of paternity is rooted not in the Anglo-American common-law regime, but in the French moral right tradition, whose principle of the rights of personality includes the right to paternity (i.e., the right to be identified as a work's originator). Celia Lury writes that "within this tradition, the work of art could be legally defined as property because it was regarded as the creative expression of what the artist already owned: his self or personality. Thus, it was in relation to the rights of personality that the rights of reproduction were contained in France"; see Celia Lury, *Cultural Rights: Technology, Legality, and Personality* (London: Routledge, 1993), 24. See also Bernard Edelman, *Ownership of the Image: Elements of a Marxist Theory of Law*, trans. E. Kingdom (London: Routledge & Kegan Paul, 1979).

24. This is the Gorman-Gilbert schema; the earlier Linati schema lists the episode's organ as "matrix/uterus," its technic as "prose (embryo-foetus-birth)," and its symbol as "fecundation, frauds, parthenogenesis." Both schemata are reproduced in the appendix of Richard Ellmann, *Ulysses on the Liffey* (Oxford: Oxford University Press, 1972).

25. *Ulysses* was published without episode titles, but Joyce took care to publicize those titles in the schemata he circulated and in the subsequent critical studies he endorsed.

26. James Joyce, *Selected Joyce Letters*, ed. Richard Ellmann (New York: Viking Press, 1975), 251.

27. See, for example, Karen Lawrence, *The Odyssey of Style in Ulysses* (Princeton: Princeton University Press, 1981), 145; and Osteen, *Economy of Ulysses*, 228–29.

Notes to Pages 176–182

28. Robert Janusko, "Another Anthology for 'Oxen': Barnett and Dale," *James Joyce Quarterly* 27 (1990): 261.

29. Janusko, *Sources*, 61–62.

30. James Joyce, *Joyce's Ulysses Notesheets in the British Museum*, ed. Phillip F. Herring (Charlottesville: University Press of Virginia, 1972), 83.

31. Quoted in Mark Rose, *Authors and Owners: The Invention of Copyright* (Cambridge: Harvard University Press, 1993), 124–25.

32. Rose, *Authors and Owners*, 125, 128.

33. The 1710 Statute of Anne bore the full title *An Act for the Encouragement of Learning, by Vesting the Copies of Printed Books in the Authors or Purchasers of such Copies, during the Times therein mentioned*. The first draft of the legislation was entitled *A Bill for the Encouragement of Learning and for Securing the Properties of Copies of Books to the Rightful Owners thereof*. One can read, in the title of this first draft, a conceptual tension between indwelling authorial property rights on the one hand and state-created rights for the fructification of the public domain on the other.

34. J. S. Atherton, "The Oxen of the Sun," in Clive Hart and David Hayman, eds., *James Joyce's Ulysses: Critical Essays* (Berkeley: University of California Press, 1974), 330, 332.

35. See aforementioned studies by Klein, Atherton, and Janusko. In addition, see J. S. Atherton, "The Peacock in the Oxen," *A Wake Newslitter* 7 (1970): 77–78 and "Still More Peacock in the Oxen," *A Wake Newslitter* 8 (1971): 53; Phillip F. Herring, "More Peacock in the Oxen," *A Wake Newslitter* 8 (1971): 51–53; Robert Janusko, "Another Anthology for 'Oxen'" and "Yet Another Anthology for the 'Oxen': Murison's *Selections*," in Thomas F. Staley, ed., *Joyce Studies Annual* 1990 (Austin: University of Texas Press, 1990): 117–31. Although it addresses a different register of the episode, my own argument here is partly homologous with Robert Spoo's contention that "Oxen" parodies the authorizing narratives of its source anthologies; see Robert Spoo, *James Joyce and the Language of History: Dedalus's Nightmare* (Oxford: Oxford University Press, 1994), 137–50.

36. W. Peacock, *English Prose from Mandeville to Ruskin* (London: Oxford University Press, 1903), v.

37. In 1911, after the publication of the Peacock and Murison volumes but before the appearance of Barnett and Dale's *Anthology of English Prose*, the copyright term in Britain and its colonies was extended to the length of the author's life plus 50 years. As a result, works by authors who died after 1861 (e.g., Landor, Dickens, Carlyle, Newman, Pater, Huxley, Ruskin) were once again copyright. This is likely the reason Barnett and Dale's 1912 collection stopped at 1740 rather than continuing up to its own moment; the term extension had made the inclusion of a large number of nineteenth-century stylists prohibitively expensive.

38. Osteen, *Economy of Ulysses*, 232.

39. See Rose, *Authors and Owners*, 12; and J. Litman, "The Public Domain," *Emory Law Journal* 39 (1990): 965.

40. See Janusko, *Sources*, 154–55.

41. See Janusko, "Yet Another Anthology for the 'Oxen,'" 126–28.

42. Catherine Seville, *Literary Copyright Reform in Early Victorian England: The Framing of the 1842 Copyright Act* (Cambridge: Cambridge University Press, 1999), 240.

43. 17 U.S.C. § 107 (1990).

44. Paul Edward Geller, "Must Copyright Be For Ever Caught between Marketplace and Authorship Norms?" in Brad Sherman and Alain Strowell, eds., *Of Authors and Origins: Essays on Copyright Law* (Oxford: Clarendon Press, 1994), 195. The House Report that accompanied the 1976 U.S. Copyright Act did, however, note that the Register of Copyright's 1961 Report gave as one example of fair use "use in a parody of some of the content of the work parodied"; see H.R. Rep. No. 1476, 94th Cong., 2d Sess. 65 (1976). Canadian fair dealing provisions are both narrower and more exclusively interpreted than U.S. fair use provisions; they do not permit parody, which would likely be held to violate the artist's "moral right of integrity," a category Canada inherits from the French legal tradition that consecrates the *droit d'auteur*. See Wendy Gordon, "Touring the Certainties of Property and Restitution: A Journey to Copyright and Parody," *Oxford Intellectual Property Research Centre Electronic Journal of Intellectual*

Notes to Pages 182–191

Property Rights (November 1999): 8–9; see *http://www.oiprc.ox.ac.uk/EJINDEX.html*. German "free utilization" laws afford copyright protection to parodies, but exempt "recognizably borrowed" melodies from protection, while British and Japanese copyright laws make no specific fair dealing provisions for parody. Spanish moral rights permit the author to restrain "any distortion, modification, or alteration . . . that is likely to prejudice his legitimate interests or threaten his reputation"; many parodies would be seen to violate this right. See David Goldberg and Denise L. Bricker, "That's Not Funny: The Limitations on Parody as a Defense to Copyright Infringement in International Forums," *New Matter* (Fall 1996), n.p.

45. *Benny v. Loew's Inc.*, 239 F.2d 532 (9th Cir. 1956), aff'd by an equally divided court, without opinion, sub nom. *Columbia Broadcasting System, Inc. v. Loew's Inc.*, 356 U.S. 43 (1958); cited in Benjamin Kaplan, *An Unhurried View of Copyright* (New York: Columbia University Press, 1967), 69.

46. See *Campbell v. Acuff-Rose Music, Inc.*, 510 U.S. 569 (1994).

47. Joyce, *Letters, Vol. III*, 15–16; *Letters, Vol. I*, 140.

48. Atherton, "The Oxen of the Sun," 334.

49. Kenner, *Ulysses* (Baltimore: Johns Hopkins University Press, 1987), 110. See also Stuart Gilbert, *James Joyce's Ulysses: A Study* (New York: Vintage Books, 1955), 312; Anthony Burgess, *Re:Joyce* (New York: W. W. Norton, 1965), 156; and Osteen, *Economy of Ulysses*, 228.

50. Richard Ellmann, *The Consciousness of Joyce* (London: Faber & Faber, 1977), 136. See also Klein, "Oxen of the Sun," 293; and Janusko, *Sources*, 52–53.

51. For important early modern studies scholarship on this subject, see Janet Adelman, *Suffocating Mothers: Fantasies of Maternal Origin in Shakespeare's Plays, Hamlet to The Tempest* (London: Routledge, Chapman & Hall, 1992); Avi Erlich, *Hamlet's Absent Father* (Princeton, N.J.: Princeton University Press, 1977); and Patricia Parker, "Othello and Hamlet: Dilation, Spying, and the 'Secret Place' of Woman," *Representations* 44 (1993).

52. William Shakespeare, *The Tragedy of Cymbeline*, ed. Samuel B. Hemingway (New Haven: Yale University Press, 1924).

53. The theme of male parthenogenesis is developed in "Scylla and Charybdis," where Stephen notes that Christianity is founded on the "mystical estate" of fatherhood rather than on maternity, and reads this "apostolic succession" into the life and works of Shakespeare, who "was and felt himself the father of all his race, the father of his own grandfather, the father of his unborn grandson" (*U* 9.838; 9.868–69). Mulligan parodies Stephen's parthenogenetic fantasy: "Wait. I am big with child. I have an unborn child in my brain. Pallas Athena! A play! The play's the thing! Let me parturiate!" (*U* 9.875–77). The play to which he gives birth further mocks at the notion of all-male reproduction in its titles: "*Everyman His Own Wife or A Honeymoon in the Hand*" (*U* 9.1171–73).

54. Ellmann, *Ulysses on the Liffey*, 135.

55. The case that established the merger doctrine was the 1879 Supreme Court case *Baker v. Selden*, a case that pivoted, suggestively, around the copyright status of blank accounting matrices. The court decided that the plaintiff did not possess copyright in blank accounting matrices he had published in a work describing a bookkeeping system he had developed, primarily because the ideas (i.e., public property) embodied in the matrices could not be separated from their expressive fixation: "The very object of publishing a book on science or the useful arts is to communicate to the world the useful knowledge which it contains. But this object would be frustrated if the knowledge could not be used without incurring the guilt of piracy of the book. And where the art it teaches cannot be used without employing the methods and diagrams used to illustrate the book, or such as are similar to them, such methods and diagrams are to be considered as necessary incidents to the art, and given therewith to the public; not given for the purpose of publication in other works explanatory of the art, but for the purpose of practical application." *Baker v. Selden*, 101 U.S. 103; quoted in Litman, "Public Domain," 981. On the merger doctrine, see Scott Abrahamson, "Comment: Seen One, Seen Them All? Making Sense of the Copyright Merger Doctrine," *UCLA Law Review* 45 (1998): 1125–66.

56. Fredric Jameson, "Postmodernism and Consumer Society," in *The Cultural Turn: Selected Writings on the Postmodern, 1983–98* (London: Verso, 1998), 18.

57. Linda Hutcheon, *A Theory of Parody: The Teachings of Twentieth-Century Art Forms* (Urbana: University of Illinois Press, 2000), 38, 6, 33, 38.

58. Jameson, "Postmodernism," 19.

59. Rosemary Coombe, *The Cultural Life of Intellectual Properties: Authorship, Appropriation, and the Law* (Durham: Duke University Press, 1998), 54.

60. See Hutcheon, *Theory of Parody*, xiv.

61. Pamela Samuelson, "Copyright, Commodification, and Censorship: Past as Prologue—But to What Future?" revised version of a paper presented at the Commodification of Information Conference at Haifa University, Israel, May 20–21, 1999; online version at http://www.sims.berkeley.edu/~pam/papers/haifa_priv_cens.pdf.

62. James Joyce, *Ulysses* (Paris: Shakespeare and Company, 1922). In English: "All rights of reproduction, translation, and adaptation reserved for all countries including Russia" (my translation).

63. These notices are a cento of actual warnings found in recently published books.

64. The assignees listed herein are fictitious. Names used either are the product of the author's imagination or are used fictitiously, and any resemblance to actual persons, living or dead, is entirely coincidental and not intended by the author.

65. Goldberg and Bricker, "That's Not Funny."

Conclusion: Copyright, Trauma, and the Work of Mourning

1. For an excellent example of this argument, see Owen Fiss, *Liberalism Divided: Freedom of Speech and the Many Uses of State Power* (Boulder: Westview Press, 1996). A supplemental, and in some degree alternate, argument recognizes the existence and necessity of multiple subaltern counterpublics that host oppositional counterdiscourses to which a single, generalized public sphere is often inhospitable. See Steven Gregory, "Race, Identity, and Political Activism: The Shifting Contours of the African American Public Sphere," *Public Culture* 7 (1994): 147–64. One notes that these counterpublics, no matter how numerous and oppositional, will nonetheless be subject to the same intellectual property laws, and thus mutually threatened by the possibility of private censorship those laws raise.

2. Rosemary Coombe, *The Cultural Life of Intellectual Properties: Authorship, Appropriation, and the Law* (Durham: Duke University Press, 1998), 170.

3. Michael Warner, "The Mass Public and the Mass Subject," in Bruce Robbins, ed., *The Phantom Public Sphere* (Minneapolis: University of Minnesota Press, 1993), 234; Coombe, *Cultural Life of Intellectual Properties*, 170.

4. Quoted in Coombe, *Cultural Life of Intellectual Properties*, 252 n. 28.

5. *San Francisco Arts & Athletics, Inc., et al. v. United States Olympic Committee*, 483 U.S. 522, 532–33; quoted in James D. A. Boyle, *Shamans, Software, and Spleens: Law and the Construction of the Information Society* (Cambridge: Harvard University Press, 1996), 145–46.

6. Boyle, *Shamans, Software, and Spleens*, 146.

7. Coombe, *Cultural Life of Intellectual Properties*, 137. See also R. N. Kravitz, "Trademarks, Speech, and the Gay Olympics Case," *Boston University Law Review* 69 (1989): 131.

8. On Southey and perpetual copyright, see Mark Rose, *Authors and Owners: The Invention of Copyright* (Cambridge: Harvard University Press, 1993), 110–12. On Wordsworth's advocacy, see chapters 1 and 4, and on the Bonos', chapter 4. Siva Vaidhyanathan discusses Mark Twain's support of perpetual copyright in *Copyrights and Copywrongs: The Rise of Intellectual Property and How It Threatens Creativity* (New York: New York University Press, 2001), 62, 78–80.

9. Spider Robinson, "Melancholy Elephants" (1982); reprinted in *Melancholy Elephants* (New York: Tor Books, 1985), 6, 7–8.

10. Ibid., 16–17, 18–19.

11. The scarce-resource critique of copyright is, one should note, significantly more persuasive with respect to music, the central example in Robinson's story, than to literature. Popular music, in particular, possesses a fairly circumscribed vocabulary of basic song structures, chord

progressions, bass lines, hooks, and riffs. Because greater profits tend to be at stake in popular music than in classical, the large financial rewards for prosecuting infringements make popular music's more limited formal lexicon a more vigilantly policed one as well.

12. In the story, Martin tells the Senator, "Now go back to the 1970s again. Remember the *Roots* plagiarism case? And the dozens like it that followed? Around the same time a writer named van Vogt sued the makers of a successful film called *Alien,* for plagiarism of a story forty years later. Two other writers named Bova and Ellison sued a television studio for stealing a series idea. All three collected. That ended the legal principle that one does not copyright *ideas,* but *arrangements of words.* The number of word-arrangements is finite, but the number of *ideas* is *much* smaller" (Robinson, "Melancholy Elephants," 14, original emphasis). Robinson's protagonist overstates the case that these suits and rulings totally collapsed the idea/expression dichotomy, though they may well testify to the colonizing of ideas, which are public goods, by expression, which is copyrightable. Nonetheless, the wholesale privatization of ideas has had its advocates. In 1982, the same year Robinson's story was published, David B. Hopkins lamented the fact that copyright law offers no protection for "a game concept, the system that goes into legal papers, or the ideas comprising the methodology or processes adopted within a computer program," adding that "the very fact that ideas are free creates a disincentive to the development of ideas. It is only when people can fully exploit the benefits of their ideas and receive protection in these endeavours that they will donate the product of their work process to the public domain." See David B. Hopkins, "Ideas, Their Time Has Come: An Argument and a Proposal for Copyrighting Ideas," *Albany Law Review* 46 (1982): 453.

13. Andrea Sachs, "Galley Girl: 'Gone With the Wind' Revisited," *Time,* 26 April 2001.

14. Randall took the name of her narrator, Cynara, from the same Ernest Dowson poem, "Non Sum Qualis Eram Bonae Sub Regno Cynarae" (1896), from which Mitchell took the title of *Gone With the Wind.* Luckily for Mitchell, U.S. copyright law has never protected the titles of works (though titles *can* acquire trademark protection).

15. Sachs, "Galley Girl"; Bill Rankin and Jill Vejnoska, "Fiddle-de-dee! What would Scarlett think of 'TWDG'?" *Atlanta Journal-Constitution,* 28 March 2001.

16. David D. Kirkpatrick, "Court Halts Book Based on 'Gone With the Wind,'" *New York Times,* 21 April 2001.

17. "Morrison weighs in on 'Wind'y tiff," *MSNBC,* 18 April 2001.

18. Rankin and Vejnoska, "Fiddle-de-dee!"; press release by Walter Vatter, Senior Publicist, Houghton Mifflin, 4 April 2001.

19. *Suntrust Bank v. Houghton Mifflin, Co.,* 136 F.Supp.2d 1357, 1369 (N.D. Ga. 2001).

20. See *Suntrust Bank v. Houghton Mifflin, Co.,* 136 F.Supp.2d (N.D. Ga. 2001); also, "Federal judge sides with 'Gone With the Wind,'" *MSNBC,* 23 April 2001, and Houghton Mifflin press release, 5 April 2001.

21. Kirkpatrick, "Court Halts Book."

22. "'Gone With the Wind' wins copyright battle," *MSNBC,* 20 April 2001.

23. See 17 U.S.C. § 101 (1990).

24. See 17 U.S.C. § 106 (1990).

25. Kirkpatrick, "Court Halts Book."

26. *The New York Herald Tribune,* July 1936.

27. Barnini Chakraborty/Associated Press, "They've Inherited the 'Wind,'" *MSNBC,* 25 May 2001.

28. Margaret Mitchell, *Gone With the Wind* (New York: Charles Scribner's Sons, 1996), 639.

29. Rankin and Vejnoska, "Fiddle-de-dee!"

30. *Suntrust Bank v. Houghton Mifflin, Co.,* 252 F.3d 1165 (11th Cir. 2001). Although the Eleventh Circuit's reversal of the initial decision referred to the latter's violation of the First Amendment, the reversal was technically based in the Court's finding that the plaintiff had not met the stringent prerequisites for a preliminary injunction.

31. See *Suntrust Bank v. Houghton Mifflin Co.,* No. 01-12200, 2001 WL 1193890 (11th Cir. 10 Oct. 2001).

32. David D. Kirkpatrick, "'Wind' Book Wins Ruling in U.S. Court," *New York Times,* 26 May 2001; "Media Joins in Support of Novel," *MSNBC,* 16 May 2001.

Notes to Pages 214–224

33. Kirkpatrick, "'Wind' Book Wins Ruling."
34. "Appeals Court OKs 'Gone With the Wind' Parody," *MSNBC,* 25 May 2001.
35. James Berger, *After the End: Representations of Post-Apocalypse* (Minneapolis: University of Minnesota Press, 1999), 80.
36. See Ray Sawhill, "Sneak Preview of New Books for the Year 2001," *Newsweek,* 1 January 2001.
37. Martin Garbus, "*Lolita* and the Lawyers," *New York Times,* 26 September 1999. Pia Pera's *Lo's Diary,* an appropriative rejoinder to Nabokov's *Lolita,* was written in Italian and published in Italy in 1995; the Nabokov estate sued only when an English translation of the book was set to appear. The English translation's would-be publishers, Farrar, Straus and Giroux, dropped the book as a result of the suit, but after Garbus's negotiations, the Nabokov estate permitted Foxrock, Inc., to publish the novel on the condition that it contain a preface by Dmitri Nabokov and that half of Pera's royalties be donated to PEN.
38. One also notes that Garbus, who represented the Mitchell trusts in their suit against *The Wind Done Gone,* took a rather different view of literary borrowing in that case, pronouncing Pannell's decision "wonderful . . . it protects authors and publishers" (Associated Press, "'Gone With the Wind' Wins Copyright Battle").
39. Testimony of Professor Peter Jaszi, "The Copyright Term Extension Act of 1995: Hearings on S.483 Before the Senate Judiciary Committee," 104th Cong. (1995), available at 1995 WL 10524355, at *6.

Appendix. A Collection of Nineteenth-Century Centos

1. Address: Spoken to the Literary Friends assembled at Westfelton, on Shakspeare's Birth-Day, 1814

This early-nineteenth-century cento seems typical enough of the Bardolatry that had been building during the previous century. However, like any single-author cento, its form is necessarily ambivalent: however worshipful the overall tone, consecutive lines or blocks of text have been lifted from such comically incompatible contexts, and so baldly altered to suit the occasion, as to make the poem seem an act of equal parts adulation and desecration. The last eight lines of the fourth stanza—where Shakespeare's sentences are cut out in little stars to rain down, blessing "both him that gives, and him that takes"—seems obliquely to celebrate the cento form itself, however loosely it has been practiced here.

The poem expands on and partly replicates an earlier cento, "On the Birthday of Shakespeare: A Cento taken from his Works," in Robert Dodsley, ed., *Collection of Poems by Several Hands* (London: Robert Dodsley, 1748). According to Dodsley, the older poem was composed by a member of a Shakespeare Society that met annually to commemorate Shakespeare's birth. William T. Dobson reprints the earlier cento in his *Literary Frivolities, Fancies, Follies, and Frolics* (London: Chatto and Windus, 1880), 178–79, adding that it "appears to be the earliest English Cento."

2. Ode to the Human Heart

The next four inclusions are from Laman Blanchard, ed., *George Cruikshank's Omnibus* (London: Tilt and Bogue, 1842), appearing in a chapter entitled "Original Poetry," also "edited" by Blanchard and attributed to "The Late Sir Fretful Plagiary, Knight, Member of the Dramatic Authors' Association, Fellow of the Parnassian Society, &c." All four centos are embedded in a running commentary by the editor, who writes of his "considerable pleasure in discharging the duty imposed upon us, of transcribing the MSS. which one of Sir Fretful Plagiary's numerous living descendants has placed in our hands, and of submitting to the public the following specimens of 'something new.'"

Sir Fretful Plagiary is a character in Sheridan's *The Critic,* one who boasts that "authors serve your best thoughts as gipsies do stolen children, they disfigure them to make them pass as their own." The name flags the chapter as a joke at the expense of original genius, and the editor's

Notes to Pages 226–227

tongue-in-cheek protestations of Sir Fretful Plagiary's "striking originality" and "connectedness" point up the poems' appropriations without ever using the terms "cento" or "mosaic poetry": "a distinguished living critic, to whom [a cento stanza] was shown, remarked that it did remind him a little of something in some other author—and he rather thought it was Goldsmith; a second critic, equally eminent, was forcibly reminded by it of something which he was convinced had been written by Rogers. *So much for criticism!* To such treatment is original genius ever subjected. Its traducers cannot even agree as to the derivation of the stolen property; they cannot name the author robbed. One cries, Spenser; another, Butler; a third, Collins. We repeat, it is the fate of Originality."

Blanchard lampoons the notion that even celebrated writers leave idiosyncratic stylistic thumbprints on their language—a notion central to nineteenth-century pro-copyright discourse. Suggestively, Sir Fretful Plagiary's centos first appeared in 1842, the year the Talfourd Bill finally passed, considerably extending the British copyright term (see chapter 1). "Original Poetry" may be Blanchard's riposte to the Talfourd Bill. Sir Fretful Plagiary's more substantial centos, along with excerpts of the editorial commentary, are reprinted in Dobson, *Literary Frivolities*, 185–88.

The note following the asterisk is in the original.

6. *"'Tis distance lends enchantment to the view"*

This couplet and the four-line cento that follows appear in Uncle George [George Frederick Pardon], ed., *Parlour Pastime for the Young: Consisting of Pantomime and Dialogue Charades, Fire-Side Games, Riddles, Enigmas, Charades, Conundrums, Arithmetical and Mechanical Puzzles, Parlour Magic, Etc. Etc.* (London: James Blackwood, 1857). Uncle George writes of the cento form: "Great and celebrated persons have thought this game worthy of occupying their time and attention; and although it is scarcely ever used now, except as a pastime for young people, yet is there much in it that is commendable as an agreeable and instructive mental recreation. It is pleasant in this way to collect and string together lines of poetry which have grown into proverbs and 'household words' amongst us, and much ingenuity may often be exhibited in placing these so that one line shall illustrate, or enforce the sentiment expressed in the foregoing line; or, perhaps, in some ludicrous way travestie, or flatly contradict it; giving, thus, occasion for merriment: and even where this is not attempted, the jumble of familiar lines and phrases cannot fail to excite a laugh in the circle of hearers."

8. *"The curfew tolls the knell of parting day"*

This untitled cento appeared in Frederick Saunders's popular "consarcination of many good things for the literary palate," *Salad for the Solitary: By an Epicure* (New York: Lamport, Blakeman & Law, 1853). In later editions of the miscellany, which he expanded to *Salad for the Solitary and the Social* (New York: De Witt C. Lent and Company, 1872; New York: Thomas Whittaker, 1886), Saunders referred to the poem's "mongrel stanzas." The cento also appears in Dobson, *Literary Frivolities*, 191, and in James Appleton Morgan, *Macaronic Poetry Collected* (Cambridge: Riverside Press, 1872), 90–91. Morgan's version is reprinted here.

9. *[Mosaic Poetry]*

In C. C. Bombaugh, *Gleanings from the Harvest-Fields of Literature, Science, and Art; A Melange of Excerpta, Curious, Humorous, and Instructive* (Baltimore: T. Newton Kurtz, 1860), 48–49. Also reprinted in Morgan, *Macaronic Poetry*, 88–90. Tony Augarde calls this "one of the best-known centos" in *The Oxford Guide to Word Games* (Oxford: Oxford University Press, 1984), 139. The title "Mosaic Poetry" is given only by Bombaugh and is likely a generic. Fittingly enough, Bombaugh's description and history of the cento form is plagiarized almost verbatim from the "Literary Follies" entry in Isaac D'Israeli's *Curiosities of Literature* (rpt., London: Frederick Warne and Co., 1881), I: 299–300.

Notes to Pages 228–233

10. Cento from Pope

In Bombaugh, *Gleanings,* 49.

11. "When first I met thee, warm and young,"

In Morgan, *Macaronic Poetry,* 90.

12. Life

"Life" appeared in *Notes and Queries,* 4th Series IX (1972): 451, beneath the following note: "Mrs. H. A. Deming, of San Francisco, is said to have occupied a year in searching for and fitting together the following thirty-eight lines from thirty-eight English and American poets." Dobson, who reprints "Life" in his *Literary Frivolities,* 180–81, adds that the cento first appeared in the *San Francisco Times.* Bombaugh also reprints "Life," with spaces between each couplet, in the 1890 edition of *Gleanings,* 75–76.

13. The Poets' "Essay on Man"

"The Poets' 'Essay on Man,'" "Marriage," and "The Fate of the Glorious Devil" are taken from Dobson, who reports that the first of the three centos was published in *Notes and Queries* "in a communication signed James Monk" (Dobson, *Literary Frivolities,* 181). William Walsh gives the title as "What Is Life?" See William Shepard Walsh, *Handy-Book of Literary Curiosities* (Philadelphia: J. B. Lippincott Co., 1893), 747.

14. Marriage

According to Dobson (*Literary Frivolities,* 184), "Marriage" appeared in "a very scarce work called *The Lonsdale Magazine.*"

15. [The Fate of the Glorious Devil]

Dobson (*Literary Frivolities,* 188–89) remarks that "this laborious trifling appeared in the *People's Friend* of May 1871, evincing great patience and research." The title appears only in Walsh's reprinting of the poem (Walsh, *Handy-Book,* 748).

16. "Breathes there a man with soul so dead"

This cento is taken from Bombaugh, *Gleanings* (1890), 74–75. A shorter version, omitting the final two stanzas, appears in Blanchard, ed., *George Cruikshank's Omnibus,* 37; in Dobson, *Literary Frivolities,* 187–88; and in Walsh, *Handy-Book,* 749.

Index

Adams, W. H. Davenport, 37, 42, 241n37, 243n69; "Imitators and Plagiarists," 40, 50–51
Aeschylus, as borrower, 217, 218
Agreement on Trade-Related Aspects of Intellectual Property Rights (TRIPS), 194
Alexander, George, 249n20
Alger, Patrick, 123, 124
Alison, Archibald, 64
Allan, Maud, 119
Anderson, Margaret, 165, 260–61n16
Anderson, Paul, 211–12
appropriation: Anglo-American writers with bent for, 47, 51; appropriative artists, modern, listing of, 13. See also appropriative rejoinder genre; genius, appropriative; "Great Man" theory of history
appropriative rejoinder genre: critics of, 216–17; as engaged with copyright issues, 216; prominent examples, 215; use of works in public domain, 217; works of, 214–16
Arnold, Matthew, 53, 61; "Copyright," 79, 80–81; doctrine of cultivation, tied to copyright, 80–81, 86; and conversation, 88–89
Arnold, Thomas, 12, 32, 81
Association for the Protection of the Rights of Authors, members in, 61, 245–46n39
Atherton, J. S., 179, 184
Auerbach, Nina, 132, 255n18
Ausonius, 41, 47, 241n51
author, authorship, 237n15; Anglo-American vs. Continental law, 235n1; and concept of individual ownership, 3, 11, 81, 100; as consumptive act, 40; copyright tied to, 30, 65, 82; as miscellanist, 44; perceived as greedy, 143–44; and Renaissance system of patronage, 165–66; varied views of, 43–44; and works of visual art, 235n2; writerly profession, studies of, 11. See also genius, individual creative; Romanticism

Bailey, Samuel, 34
Baker v. Selden, 263n55
Barnett, Annie, and Lucie Dale, Anthology of English Prose, 179; and effect of copyright term extension, 262n37
Bate, Walter Jackson, 239n21
BBC v. Time Out, 148
Beach, Sylvia, 194
Beerbohm, Max, 112
Benjamin, Walter, 84
Benny, Jack, 182
Benson, E. F., 37, 241n37; "Plagiarism," 26, 38
Bently, Lionel. See Sherman, Brad, and Lionel Bently
Berger, James, 214
Berne Convention, 14, 72, 194
Besen, Stanley, 145–46
Bettig, Ronald V., 145, 146, 242n64
Bible, Exodus 34, and Ulysses, 187
Billing, Noel Pemberton, 119
Bingham, G. Clifton, "Love's Old Sweet Song," 196
Birrell, Augustine, 54, 143–44; on no copyright protection for lectures, 251–52n41
Bismarck, Otto von, chancellor, 57
Blackwood, John, 53
Blackwood, William, 248n1
Blanc, Louis, 78–79, 80, 83

[269]

Index

Blanchard, Laman, 266–67 note to #2
Board of Trade, 74, 79; role in Royal Commission, 62, 71, 76, 77
Bodley, Seoirse, 258n57
Bombaugh, Charles, *Gleanings*, 40–43; expanded edition, 44–45
Bono, Mary, 123, 124, 145, 155, 202, 205, 212
Bono, Sonny, 122, 123, 126, 202
Bono Act. *See* Sonny Bono Copyright Term Extension Act
Boosey, John, 53
Borciani, Mario, *Molly Bloom: A Musical Dream*, 157
Bosworth, Thomas, 72, 73, 246n48
Boyle, James, 11, 19, 150, 258n49, 261n19; *Shamans, Software, and Spleens*, copyright reforms, xi, 84–87
Brennan, William J., justice, 201
Breyer, Stephen, justice, "The Uneasy Case for Copyright," 20, 82–83, 240n31, 240n67; response to, 247n66
Bright, John, 56
Brontë, Charlotte, 215, 217
Browning, Robert, 32; essay on Chatterton's forgeries, 98, 101
Bullock, William, 256n26
Burgum, Mr., and Chatterton's forgery for, 101, 102, 251n35
Burnet v. Tonson, 29–30
Burns, Robert, 127
Burrow-Giles Lithographic Co. v. Sarony, 248n2
Butler, Samuel, 111

Campbell v. Acuff-Rose Music, Inc., 182, 193, 194, 197, 204, 220, 236n5; cited in Mitchell trust case, 209
Canada, copyright in: Copyright Act of 1875, and Royal Commission, 61, 62; Copyright Act of 1889, 72; strict fair use provision for parody, 197, 262n44
Cantillon, Richard, 28, 29
Carey, Peter, *Jack Maggs*, 215, 217
Carlyle, Thomas, 12, 32, 76, 78; copyright status, 180, 181, 197, 198; Joyce's parody of, 180, 181, 183
Caygill, Howard, 15–16, 27
censorship, private: examples of, 18, 210–11, 219; increasing role of, 200–201; and intellectual property, 204–5, 210–11
censorship, state, and Joyce, 161, 162, 194
"cento": and copyright, 46, 242n59; creating of, 45, 241n51, 268 notes to #12, #15; defined and described, 26, 40–43, 266 note to #1, 267 note to #6; and idea of literary property, 12–13, 46; as justification for textual appropriation and plagiarism, 47, 219; modern legacy, 242n58; and other miscellanea, 44–45; provenance explained and justified, 45; use by Chatterton, 98; as varied and popular, 40, 43, 44, 241n52
centos, examples of, 224–27, 229–33; from English and American poets, 41–42, 228–29; lines from Pope, 228; lines from Shakespeare, 221–24, 266 note to #1; mosaic poetry, 41–42, 227–28
Century Guild Hobby Horse, and Wilde's Chatterton lecture, 98–99, 105, 251n31
Chatterton, Thomas, 103; forgeries of, 98, 100, 106, and role of environment in, 101, 250n29; Romantic tradition of, 97–98, 250n25; Wilde's lecture on, 98–99, repeated, 250–51n30; will as libelous and satirical, 102–3; works on, plagiarized by Wilde, 99. *See also* Wilde, Oscar, Chatterton lecture notes
Chatterton, Thomas, Sr., 101
circulating libraries, 60; criticism of, 74, 79; founded on monopoly copyright, 63
Clarke, Hal, 211, 212
Cobden, Richard, 56, 57, 74, 77
Coetzee, J. M., *Foe*, 215, 217, 218
Cohen, William A., 111, 253n47
Coleridge, Samuel Taylor, 98, 250n26; plagiarisms by, 103
communism: and literary property, 152–53; in Royal Commission debates, 67, 69
Conroy, Pat, 210
Coombe, Rosemary, 5–6, 11, 86, 151, 152; on trademarks, 200; *The Cultural Life of Intellectual Properties*, 19, 192–93
copyright law
  basic general issues: and concept of creativity, 6, 240n31; and concept of originality, 7; evaluation, 3–4; legal and extralegal functions, x–xi; and reproducibility, 240n33; technological changes to effect, 21–22; topics for discussion concerning, 154. *See also* idea/expression dichotomy; intellectual property law; public domain
  criticism of: case against and move to abolish, 20, 58–61, 68, 69, 82–83; modern proposals for reform, x–xi, 86–89, 248n78; parables about, and literary expression concerning, 16–17

[270]

copyright law (continued)
  cultural role, 10–12, 214–15; and collaborative invention, 11; and ethical issues, 21, 22; and historical trauma, 18, 214; legacy for the dead, 124, 128; within literary texts, 12, 97; as potentially negative, 199–200; studies of, 12, 14, 19–21
  definitions, and thoughts about: as changing concept, 144–45; as dominant discourse, 15; extended meditation on, by Mallet, 76; as having clear, straightforward bases, 130; historical significance and consequences of, 3; and idea of civilized society, 80–81, 82; and issue of tangible vs. intangible property, 3, 128–29, 132; meaning of, 90; notion of standoff between authors and public, 3, 81, 145; vs. patent, 1–2, 58–59; as posthumous commemoration and legacy, 127, 128, 129; private property/free speech mediation, 201; varying views over the years, 81–82; warnings about collectivist bases, 152–53
  hauntology: examples, 149; meaning of, 129–30, 141; perpetual copyright as specter, 153; reinstatement of copyrights, 156; and Viereck's novel/play, 151
  history: development and influence, 28, 215; as increasingly regulated, 14; in 19th century, as dominant discourse, 15. See also under copyright law, by jurisdiction
  maximalism: benefits and losses, 199; and dominant economic and political influence and control, 218–19; as leading to annihilation of public domain, 156; potential dangers of, 215, 217, 219, 220; supporters of, 212; way to unchallenged consecration of texts, 217, 218. See also term extensions, infra; public domain
  perpetual: advocates of, 29, 123, 124, 126, 153, 202; as dead issue in Britain, 81, 153; fictional futuristic view of, 202, 205–6; potential for, 236n4. See also mourning
  postmortem: abuse of, 156–58; and appeal of maximalist idea, 155; assessment, 120, 201; and authors as eternal, 128, 201–2; first laws, in Britain, 55, 125, 127; first laws in U.S., 125; and idea of mourning, 154–55, 157–58; limited vs. overextended, 17; longstanding tradition of, 122, 127
  protection: in computer programs, 247n67; in databases, 236n4, 236n8;

for film and recorded music, 140; lack of, in cases of appropriation and for lectures, 85–86, 251–52n41; for musical compositions, 82; for TV transmission rebroadcasts, 82; for visual art, 73, 235n2, 252n45
  reform: arguments for, 84–85; modern proposals for, 86–89, 248n78
  term: as lengthening, 125, 131; proposals to shorten, 86; today, in U.S., U.K., and EU, 125. See also copyright law, perpetual, and copyright law, postmortem, supra
  term extensions: in Britain, and colonies, 32, 258n55, 262n37; in EU, 254n1; opposition to, and support for, 122–24; proposed legislation for use of revenues from, 248n77; results of, 4, 6; retroactive, in Britain and EU, 156; in U.S., 20, 82, 121, 131, 235–36n3, 248n76, in agreement with EU, 122, 258n54, and cases concerning, 255n9. See also Sonny Bono Copyright Term Extension Act
  theories, in Royal Commission: "bundle" theory, 65, 68, 69, 81, of property rights, 85, 86, 246n39; issue of value, novel vs. improving literature, 70–71; issues of monopoly, 68–69, 81
  today, general issues: expansion of legal protection, 192–93; need for permissions, 196–97; shift of emphasis from tangible to intangible property, 192; weakening of fair use provisions, 194
copyright law, by jurisdiction
  Anglo-American, 235n1; copyright behaving like property, 252n45; early legislation, and history, 125; as failing in its ideals, 150; original laws, valorization of ideas over expression, 190; in transition, 144–45
  British: earliest form, 180–81; 18th-century cases, 29–30; as established, 55; history of, 28–29, 32, 81-82, 125, 160, 161, 180, 259n4; for paintings, drawings, photographs, 252n45; studies of, 14, 51, 238n21; tied to imperial governance, 63–65, 73; today, 197. See also term extensions under copyright law; copyright legislation, British
  Continental tradition, 235n1; extension for war years, 254n1; fair use protection for parody, 263n44
  French: concept of natural rights, 163, 195, 235n1, 260n8; legal tradition, 264n44; and parody, 182, 197; term

Index

copyright law, by jurisdiction (*continued*)
extensions for war years, 254n1. *See also droit d'auteur; droit moral*
international, 236n4; agreement weakening fair use, 194; as increasingly standardized, 14; late-19th-century developments, 72
U.S.: concerning "derivative works," 209–10; major overhaul, 1905–1909, 140; maximalist tendency in, 4–5, 10, 21, 125, 236nn7, 8; 237n13; merger doctrine today, 190; no legal protection for European authors, 256n21; protective and disciplinary role, 161, 220; requirement of registration, 259n6; and titles of works, 265n14; for works published in periodicals, 260–61n16. *See also* term extensions *under* copyright law; copyright legislation, U.S.

copyright legislation, British
Statute of Anne (1710): limited copyright term of, overridden, 153; profound significance of, 180, 215; provisions, 239n15; title of, 28, 236n6, 262n33
Copyright Bill (1837): introduction, 32; fair use clause, 182
Copyright Act of 1842 (Talfourd Act), 46, 267 note to #2; authors' support of, 12, 32, 81; debates over, 32–33, 246n39; durability of, 56; and the empire, 64; and free trade issues, 56; opponents, 49–50, 56; passage, 32, 51; post-mortem copyright, 55–56, 127
Copyright Act of 1911: fair use clause adopted, 182; passage and provisions, 72–73; royalty system part of, 82; term extended, and consequences, 131, 262n37

copyright legislation, U.S.
Copyright Act (1790), term lengths, 125
Chace Act of 1891, 72
Copyright Act (1909): deposit and registration of work, 160; and power of censorship, 161; royalty system in, 82; term extended, 131; works published abroad, 160–61, 259–60n7; works published in periodicals, 260–61n16
Copyright Act (1976), 121; and fair use, 182, 262n44; term extension, 212; and works published in periodicals, 260–61n16

copyrights, reinstatement of: for anthology authors, 262n37; in Britain and EU, 156, 197; of Joyce estate, 156, 157–58; in U.S., 236n4, 258n54

copywrights, meanings and uses of term, ix–x
Coquelin, Charles, 109
Corn Laws: agitation against, and free trade, 56; assault on, 87; repeal of, 56
Cornell, Drucilla, 21, 22
Council of Trent, 77, 247n55
CTEA. *See* Sonny Bono Copyright Term Extension Act
Cunningham, Michael, *The Hours,* 217
cyberlaw organizations, xi

Daldy, F. R., 73
Danson, Lawrence, 251n31
Darwinism, 67, 68, 78, 87
De Quincey, Thomas, 197
Defoe, Daniel, 215, 217
Dekker, George, 241n52
Derrida, Jacques, *Specters of Marx,* 129
Dicey, Edward James Stephen, 81, 245–46n39
Dickens, Charles, 12, 32, 215, 217; Joyce's parody of, 169, 177, 181; as public domain author and Joyce's use of, 181, 197, 198
Disney, Walt. *See* Walt Disney Company
Disraeli, Benjamin, 57, 61–62; plagiarism of, 39
Dobson, William T., *Literary Frivolities,* 45
Dr. Seuss Enterprises, 236n5
"Doctrinaire party," 56
Dodd, Christopher J., U.S. senator, 248n77
Donald v. Becket, 177
Douglas, Lord Alfred, 95; belief in Wilde's fictional Shakespeare theory, 111; *De Profundis* used in lawsuit of, 119; Wilde and, 95, 111, 113–15
Dowson, Ernest, "Non Sum Qualis Eram Bonae Sub Regno Cynarae," 265n14
droit d'auteur, 163, 236n1
droit moral, 260n8; and paternity, 261n23; regulations today, 197, 198
Duffy, Charles Gavan, 93

Eldred v. Ashcroft (formerly *Eldred v. Reno*), 125, 255n9
Edgeworth, Francis, 26, 238–39n7
Egg, Augustus, 252n45
Eilenberg, Susan, 126, 127
Eliot, T. S., 47, 51, 162
Ellmann, Richard, 99, 184, 186–87, 250n26
Ely Lilly, 85
Emerson, Ralph Waldo, 39, 47
Enfield, William, 29
expression. *See* idea/expression dichotomy

[272]

Index

fair dealing. *See* fair use
fair use: adopted in copyright law, 182; broadening of, 236n5; centos as anticipation of, 46; for parody, 182, 193, 194, 197, 209, 213, 217, 235n5, 262–63n44; for parody, denied, 5, 148, 236n5; as part of copyright reform, 86, 207; provisions, described, 2, 46; and public domain, 130, 207; testing of, in *Ulysses,* 170; weakened, 194, 204
fanzine art, 242n58
Farrer, T. H., 76; and issue of royalties, 57, 62, 245n32; questioning of, 70, 246n42; testimony, 69–70, 72, 73, 246n45; "The Principle of Copyright," 78–79, 84
Feather, John, 243n4
Feist Publications, Inc. v. Rural Telephone Service Co., Inc., 204, 236n8
Feltes, N. N., 19
Fennessy, David, 157
First Amendment, 200, 213, 255n9, 265n30
Fiss, Owen, 151, 152
Ford, Fred, 38, 47, 50, 241n37
forgery: British literary, history of, 252n42; by Chatterton, 98, 100, 106; by Ireland, 241n43; vs. plagiarism, 100, 103
Foucault, Michel, 46; "Qu'est-ce qu'un auteur?" 11, 21
Fournier d'Albe, Edward, 141
Foxrock, Inc., 216, 266n37
Franklyn, Cecil W., 106–7
free speech: vs. copyright, debates about, 213; as imperiled, 148, 200; vs. intellectual property law, 5; interpretations of, 151; stronger opportunities for, 200
free trade: acceptance of, 57; diverse views of, 67–68, 69, 87; issues concerning, 56, 57; meaning today, 87; principles, for Royal Commission, 58; as providing affordable mass literature, 63; and royalty system, 58–61, 62; supporters of, 67–68, 74
Freud, Sigmund, on mourning, 258n53
Froude, J. A., 62; assessment of Royal Commission's debates and decisions, 54, 66, 76–78, 243n3; as Report signatory, 54, 76; views on copyright, 54, 70
Fuji-ko, Madame, 140

Gagnier, Regenia, 48, 114
Garbus, Martin, 213–14, 216–17, 266nn37, 38
Gardner, John, *Grendel,* 215
Gaslight, 182

GATT (General Agreement on Tariffs and Trade), 14; and U.S. copyright code, 156
genius, appropriative, 104; as vampire taking ideas, property of others, 137–38, 139–40; vampire-geniuses, listing of, 136, 142. *See also* appropriation
genius, individual creative: authorship as divine right, 245–46n39; authorship as unique, 7, 8, 267 note to #2; and copyright law, 6; vs. imitation, 31, 44; vs. public, 6; rejection of political economy, 31; and theory of value, 30–31, 239–40n22. *See also* original genius/author, Romantic model
Gilliam v. American Broadcasting Cos., Inc., 235n1
Goethe, Johann Wolfgang von, 31, 32
Gogarty, Oliver St. John, 197; "Medical Dick and Medical Davy," 197, 198; "Song of the Cheerful (but Slightly Sarcastic) Jesus, 196, 197, 198
Golan v. Ashcroft, 255n9
Gordon, John, 169
Gossen, Hermann Heinrich, 36, 37
Grazia, Margareta de, 19
"Great Man" theory of history, 120, 131–32, 138, 256n26; appropriation as a right, 130, 138, 139–40; rejection of, 243n69; and stealing of ideas, 138–39
Guillory, John, 15–16, 27, 28
Guy, Josephine, 250n24
Gyles v. Wilcox, 30

Hand, Learned, judge, 7–8, 256n25
Hargrave, Francis, 177–78
Harris, Frank, 96; *Mr. and Mrs. Daventry,* 91
Harrison, George, "My Sweet Lord," 236n10
Harry, T. E., 256n22
Heaney, Seamus, 258n57
Heilbroner, Robert, 24
Heinzelman, Kurt, *The Economics of the Imagination,* 25
Homer: borrowings from, 216, 217; intertext(s) in *Ulysses,* 172; Wilde and, 94
Holland, Merlin, 92, 99
Hood, Thomas, 126
Hopkins, David B., 265n12
Horne, Herbert, 98
Houghton Mifflin Co., 208, 212, 213; and case against, 265n30
Hudleston, F. J., 37, 241n37
Hume, David, 27
Hutcheon, Linda, 192

[273]

Index

Hutchinson, Alan, 151
Huxley, Aldous, 180, 181, 197
Huxley, T. H., 53, 65, 68, 71, 81; *Man's Place in Nature,* 68
Hyde, Douglas, 165, 167; *The Love Songs of Connacht,* 165, 196
Hyde, Lewis, 27

idea/expression dichotomy: and copyright protection, 188; copyright's legal function concerning, 147, 256n25, 258n47; extant expressions copied into new work, 188; "Oxen" episode as critique, 188–90; problematic cases for, 147–48; theme of its breakdown, 205, 265n12
India: and copyright accords, 80; education in, policies, 64, 245n37
infringement of copyright, 7, 214; boundary with fair use, and *Ulysses,* 170; charge of, by Mitchell estate, 208–9, 214; examples of, 236n10, 256n25; vs. plagiarism, 19, 49, 173
intellectual property: changes in, between 1878 and today, 83; as communal, 153, 246n39; consequences of maximalism for, 218; meaning and role of, 2; private, oral discourse becoming, 93, 164; studies of, 14
intellectual property law: areas needing reform, 85–86; assaults on, 51–52; author as owner of text, 100; authorship as unique, 7, 8; changes in, and Viereck's novel/play, 140–41, 142, 144–45; development of, 28; and economic issues, 20–21, 145–46; vs. free speech, 5; reform of, arguments and suggestions for, 84–89, 151; roles of, 150–51, 258n49; stipulations, 109–10; strict regulations concerning, 19–20; suits concerning, 242n58. *See also* copyright law
intellectual property regimes, less-extensive: advantages, 206–7; reconception of public sphere, 200, 206
Internet, role in copyright, 21–22
Ireland, William Henry, 106, 241n43, 252n42
Ireland: and being Irish, 241n43; and book trade, 244n25; folklore collections, 92–93; Home Rule initiatives, 252n42; oral tradition, 92–93

James, Henry, "An Animated Conversation," 237n20
James Joyce Estate: court injunction by, 259n57; permissions denied by, 156–57, 258–59n57; use deterred by high royalty fees, 258–59n57
Jameson, Fredric, 191–92
Janusko, Robert, 174, 176
Jaszi, Peter, 11, 86, 220
Jefferson, Thomas: on copyright term, 125, 127; on ideas, 139, 149, 257n31
Jenkins, Edward, 61–62, 72
Jevons, William Stanley, marginalism of, 24, 26, 36, 142; concept of utility, 34–35, 38; and ethical issues, 48; Mallet as follower of, 74; *The Theory of Political Economy,* 36
Joyce, James: as benefiting from and parodying copyright, 183, 189, 220; character, 259n3; tension between individual and collective models of authorship, 159–60. *See also* James Joyce Estate
—works
Dubliners, 176, 260n15
Finnegans Wake, 157, 159, 261n20; and copyright, 258n56; discourse about literary property, 166–67
Portrait of the Artist as a Young Man, A, 260n15
See also Ulysses (James Joyce)
Joyce, Stephen, 156, 157–58

Kant, Immanuel, *Critique of Judgment,* 31–32
Kaplan, Benjamin, *An Unhurried View of Copyright,* 10–11, 21–22, 237n13
Keats, John, 103, 250nn25, 26
Kenner, Hugh, 184
Kirn, Walter, 119
Klein, A. M., 169–70

Ladd, George Trumbull, 257n39
Lamb, Charles, 197
Landor, Walter Savage, 197
Lang, Andrew, 37, 39–40, 47, 241n37
Lely, J. M., 252n45
Lessig, Lawrence, 125–26, 127, 255n9; *The Future of Ideas,* proposed copyright reforms, xi
Lévy, Michel, 79
literary estates: case of Charles Dickens, 198; case of Margaret Mitchell, 211–12; case of Vladimir Nabokov, 266n37; general nature of, 211; and prolonging life after death, 128, 201–2. *See also* James Joyce Estate
literary property: as belonging to author, 178; common-fund model, 50–51; as debatable, 18; debates over, 12; described, 141; idea of antiproperty, 51; individual

literary property (*continued*)
vs. communal, 50–51; texts that disrupt protection codes, 97; ties to modernism, 13; works aware of their status as, 13; works that question private literary property, 16–17. *See also* copyright law

literary works: affordable, for the public, 63, 73, 74, 75, 77, 79–80; and concept of innovation, 178, 240–41n33; literature vs. "useful" works, 190–91; tied to the right to rule, 64–65; value as including individual genius and collective sources, 16; vs. visual arts, 240n33; writing as borrowing, 178–79

Little Review, serialization of *Ulysses* in, 161, 162, 260n15; copyright for, 165, editing by Pound, 261n18

Locke, John, 28; *Two Treatises of Government,* 29, 239n15

Longman, William, 53

Lucas, E. V., 111–12

Lury, Celia, 261n23

Lyons, Maurice, 140

Macaulay, Thomas Babington, 33, 56, 64, 69, 180, 197, 198, 243n9, 245n35; education policies in India, 64, 245n37

Macclesfield, Lord Chancellor, 29

McCulloch, J. R., 34

Macfie, Robert Andrew: case against copyright and for royalties, 58–61, 73, 75, 79, 83; as Cobdenite radical, 57, 77, 244n12; and free trade, 67–68, 76; opposition to patent law, 57–58; role in Royal Commission debates, 66, 69, 72, 73; testimony, assessment of, 66

Machlup, Fritz, and Edith Penrose, 57

Mack, Ronald, "He's So Fine," 236n10

Macmillan, Alexander, 53

Macpherson, James, *Ossian*: defense of, 39, 50; forgeries of, 104, 105, 252n42

Mallet, Sir Louis, 81, 87; critique of copyright law, 20, 54, 86, 246–47n51; economics of, 74–75, 76, 247n53; and movement to abolish copyright, 56, 57, 153; role in Royal Commission, 70, 73, 74–76; Separate Report, afterlife of, 82–83

Malory, Sir Thomas, *Le Morte d'Arthur,* Joyce's parody of, 173–76

Mansfield, Lord, 30

marginalists. *See* neoclassical economics

Markham, Edwin, 141

Masson, David, *Chatterton,* 99, 101, 102

Melville, Herman, 215, 217

Menger, Carl, 24, 26, 34

Meredith, George, *The Ordeal of Richard Feverel,* 117; used in *Ulysses,* 169, 188, 196

"merger doctrine," 190, 263n55

metafiction, defined, and *Ulysses* as key work of, 17

Mickey Mouse, copyright extension for, 5

Mill, John Stuart, 48; *Principles of Political Economy,* 57–58, 59, 65

Millar v. Taylor, 29, 153

Milton, John, 64, 98

Mitchell, A., 37, 38, 241n37

Mitchell, Margaret, efforts to memorialize, 210, 211–12; *Gone With the Wind*: attempts to protect and sanctify, 217; authorized sequels, rights and restrictions, 209–11; copyright extended, 212; Randall's treatment of, 207–8; success and legendary status of, 211, 212–14; title, 265n14. *See also* Mitchell estate

Mitchell estate, suit against *The Wind Done Gone,* 148, 208, 215; as example of private censorship and copyright dominance, 210–11, 219; and parody/fair use defense, 209; lawyers for, 211, 213; national debate about, 213; slavery and racism issue, 209, 210, 213–14; upheld, 209, 266n37, and injunction later overturned, 213–14

modernism: Anglo-American writers with appropriative bent, 47, 51; characterized, 162; ties to intellectual property law, 13

monopoly copyright. *See* copyright

Montag, Warren, 129

Monty Python, 235n1

Moore, George, 47, 60, 96

Morley, John, 74

Morris, William, 48, 103

mourning: Freud on, 258n53; role of postmortem copyright in, 154–56, 205–6, 214

Mudie, Charles Edward, 60

Mudie's Circulating Library: as dominant and a consumer monopoly, 60; as expensive, 74, 244n27; novels as largest single genre at, 70; objections to, 73

Murison, A. F., *Selections from the Best English Authors,* 179, 181

Murray, John, 53

musical compositions, copyright protection for, 82; and question of scarce resources, 204, 264–65nn11, 12; as more strictly policed, 265n11

[275]

Index

Nabokov, Dmitri, 216, 266n37
Nabokov, Vladimir, *Lolita,* 216
Nabokov estate, 266n37
Napoleon, 138, 142
Naslund, Sena Jeter, *Ahab's Wife,* 215, 217
National Socialism, Viereck as defender of, 132
neoclassical (marginalist) economics, 24–25, 26; assessments of, 47–49, 242n64; and copyright law, 145–46; critique of private literary property, 35–36; and plagiarism, 35–36, 48–49; rise of, 34; shift to individual consumption and utility, 34–35, 74, 76
neoclassicism, literary: apology for novelty, plagiarism, pleasure, consumption, 36, 37–40, 41–42, 47, 142; centos and miscellanea, 40, 44–45; and ethical issues, 48, 242n64; influence and legacy of, 47, 51; originality as a commodity, 37; popular forms, 40–41, 43, 44
neoclassicisms, two kinds, 16, 26–27; and Viereck's novel/play, 142–43, 149. *See also* neoclassical (marginalist) economics; neoclassicism, literary
Newman, John Henry, 180, 181, 197
Nietzsche, Friedrich, 138

O'Connor, Sandra Day, justice, 240n31
"Oh Pretty Woman," 182
oral discourse, as not protected by copyright, 93, 164, 184–85; and lectures, 251–52n41
original expression and originality: accounting for, 9–10; as basis for copyright law, 6, 7, 177; as commodity, 37; innovation, protection of, 1; potential overevaluation of, 8; vs. social nature of creation, 3
original genius/author, Romantic model, 6–7, 31, 32, 142, 143, 261n19; and copyright, 7–8, 14, 32, 85, 216; overhauling of, 37–38, 40
Ossian. See Macpherson, James
Osteen, Mark, 169, 180, 259n3
"Oxen of the Sun" episode, in *Ulysses*
basic general issues: discussion of, 17–18; events and discourses of, 170–71, 183; major attributes and content, 169
binary structure: central incongruity between form and content, 188–89; and idea of public domain, 189–90; male appropriation of female creation, 187–88; as trope of patriarchal ideal, paternity, 185–86

borrowings and imitations: anthology sources for, 179–80, 181, and parodizing of, 262n35; authors in public domain, 180–81, 217; Bible, 187; as parody, 18, 171, 172, 173, 181–83; primary texts, including "Malory" paragraph, 171, 172–77
and copyright: and fair use doctrine, 173; metadiscourses of, 192, 193; and subject of literary property, 169–70
oral tailpiece: as free from copyright, 184–85; as portrait of public domain and orality, 18, 181, 183–84; as present-day talk and chaotic jumble, 184; quotations from written texts, 185
as postmodernist text: and growth of intellectual property law regime, 192–93; pastiche vs. parody, 191–92
style: appropriation of, and charges of plagiarism discussed, 173, 174, 175–79; as commentary on individual styles vs. public domain, 185, 189–90; episode as pastiche, 173; running chronology of English prose parodies, 171, 172–76, 219

Pannell, Charles, judge, 209–10, 213, 217, 266n38
Parnell, Charles Stewart, 252n42
parody: connected to public domain, 181–82, 183; established as potential form of criticism or comment, 182–83; fair use exemptions for, 5, 182, 193, 194, 197, 209, 213, 217, 236n5, 262n44; fair use provisions, as deteriorating, ignored, 5, 148, 193; "Oxen" episode as, 18, 171, 172, 173, 182–83, 191–92; vs. pastiche, 191, 192; vs. satire, 236n5; and U.S. copyright law, 182
Parrinder, Patrick, 254n1
patent law: and copyrights, 58–59; criticisms of, opposition to, 57–58; movement to abolish, losing strength, 58; suggested reform, 86
patents: vs. copyrights, 1–2, 58–59; as enabling biopiracy, 218–19; Mill on, 244n23; proposed part of public domain, 86; reform proposals, 248n78
parthenogenesis, male, theme in *Ulysses,* 186, 263n53
pastiche, 191–92
Pater, Walter, 48; parody of, in Joyce, 180, 181, 197, 198; "Style," 117
Patfield, Fiona Macmillan, 148

[276]

Peacock, William, *English Prose,* and use of works in public domain, 179–80; as source for Joyce, 179, 181; under today's restrictions, 197
Pearson, Hesketh, 96
PEN International, 266n37; Paris club, lecture by Joyce, 159, 197
Penrose, Edith. *See* Machlup, Fritz, and Edith Penrose
Pera, Pia, *Lo's Diary,* 216, 266n37
Petty, William, 28
photographs: copyright as circulating separately, 252n45; copyright protection for, 91, 248n2
Pigott, Richard, 252n42
plagiarism: apologists, listing, of, 241n37; characterized, 19, 95–96, 177, 178; charges of, discussed in *Ulysses,* 173, 174, 175–79; consumerist apologies, 26, 37–40; essays defending, 16; vs. infringement, 19, 29, 173; presented as virtue, 104–5; promotion of, 47, and ethical and economic considerations, 48–49, 51; reevaluation of, 219; Voltaire on, 237n13. *See also* Wilde, Oscar
Plant, Arnold, 20, 82
Pope, Alexander, cento based on, 228
postmodernism: appropriationist artists, 13; dominance of intellectual property law as condition of, 163; and "Oxen" episode, 191–93; and works of appropriation, 214–16. *See also* modernism
Pound, Ezra, 47, 51, 261n18
public: affordable literature for, 63, 73, 74, 75, 77, 79–80; discourse of, mourning as part of, 206; forums of, conception of broader, 200; as greedy consumer, 143–44
public domain: as area of true commemoration, 157; and copyright law, 2, 5, 124; defined, 1, 180–81; efforts to protect, 84; fair use and, 130, 207; as frozen, 121–22; impoverishing, restriction of, 5, 88, 127, 156, 193, 199, 220, 255n9; portraits of, in Joyce, 18, 185, 189–90; proposal to make patents part of, 86; as rich and dynamic source, 217; seen as troublesome, as piracy, 123–24; theme in Joyce, 167–68, 181
public goods: appropriations of bioknowledge and cultural lore, examples, 85–86; defined, 88; and protection of, 85–86, 88–89
public property: published material as, 90, 96; unpublished oral tales as, 96

public sphere: as being marginalized, 206; issue of private censorship, 201; need for more broadly conceived, 206–7
publishing industry in 19th century, British: and circulating library, 60; and copyright debates, 60–61; literature as affordable, 73, 74, 75, 77, 79, 80, 246n48
Putnam, G. H., 53

Queensberry, Marquess of, 111; Wilde's suit against, 114, 115

Randall, Alice, *The Wind Done Gone:* in appropriative rejoinder genre, 215–16, 217; attempted censorship of, 18; as counternovel to *Gone With the Wind,* 207–8, 210, 212–13; infringement charge, 208–9; injunction against, overturned, 213–14; well-known defenders of, 209, 213. *See also* Mitchell estate
Ransome, Arthur, *Oscar Wilde,* libel suit against, 119
Reade, Charles, 61, 62, 245–46n39
recordings: music, copyright protection, 140; in royalty system and later regulation, 82
Reni, Guido, *St. Sebastian,* 250n25
Report of Royal Commission on Copyright, 53–54
  appendixes, and postmortem analyses: articles of criticism, 76–78; essay by Arnold, 79–82; Separate Reports of dissent, 73–76
  completion and recommendations, 71–72
  dissenting statements, 54
  later use and afterlives, 54–55; extension of, 83; intellectual property, changes in, 83–84; intellectual property law, arguments and suggestions for reform, 84–89; legislation based on, 72–73, 82; suggestions for reform, 86–89
  signatories, 54
Rhys, Jean, *Wide Sargasso Sea,* 215, 217, 218
Ricardo, David, 33–34, 239n14; shift away from, 34–35
Richardson, Samuel, 239n21
Ripley, Alexandra, *Scarlett,* 210
Robinson, Spider, "Melancholy Elephants," 18; assessment of copyright issues, 204–5; copyright, and role of mourning, 205–7, 212; futuristic vies of copyright law, 202; plot, 202–4
Rockefeller, John, 137, 138, 142
Rodgers, Mary, 124

[277]

Index

Romanticism: Chatterton as key figure of, 98; in Germany, 31; as legacy of debts to other authors, 103; rejection of political economy, 31; value of literary labor, 240n31. *See also* original genius/author, Romantic model
Rorty, Richard, 9
Rose, John, 73
Rose, Mark, *Authors and Owners,* 11, 12, 19, 177–78, 239n15
Ross, Robert, 94, 111, 112, 116; as Wilde's executor, 118, 119
Rossetti, Dante Gabriel, 98, 250n26
rosy periwinkle case, 85
Roth, Samuel, pirated serialization of *Ulysses,* 161, 194; Joyce's protest and injunctions against, 166, 197, 261n17
Routledge, R. W., 53
Royal Commission on Copyright: background factors, 20, 55–62; convening of, and proceedings, 62, 71; issues discussed, 54, 61; major disagreements and contention, 54, 243n4; major witnesses, 53, 88; pro-copyright witnesses and arguments, 68–69, 70, 73; pro-royalty arguments, 63–68, 69–71; results, significance of, 20, 54–55, 82; studies of, 243n4. *See also* copyright theories, in Royal Commission; Report of Royal Commission on Copyright
royalty system, and the Royal Commission: in Canadian Copyright Act, 61, 62; as doomed, 71, 72; and the empire, 59, 63–65, 69; proposals for, 58–59, 65, 66–67; supporters of, 63, 66, 70, 72, 75; testimony for, 69–71, 72; versions of, as law, 82; views of, 67–68, 75–76
Ruskin, John, 48, 240n32; parodied in *Ulysses,* 180, 181

Samuelson, Pamela, 193
Sand, George, 79
Sarony, Napoleon, photographs of Wilde, 248n2
Sarraute, Raymond, 235n1
Saunders, Frederick: *Mosaics,* 43–44; *Salad for the Solitary,* 43, 267 note to #8
Sayre v. Moore, 30
Schoenberg, Arnold, 122; opinion on public domain, 123–24
Schoenberg, E. R., 122, 123
Scott, Sir Walter, 60, 103
Senior, Nassau William, 34
Shakespeare, William, 31, 64, 98, 144; centos from, 221–24, 266 note to #1; forgeries of, 241n43, 252n42; and patronage system, 165–66; as plunderer of sources, 138, 142, 147; role in *Ulysses,* 165–66, 186, 263n53; Wilde's fictional theory about, 108, 109, 110–11
Shaw, George Bernard, 112, 216, 217
Shelley, Percy Bysshe, 98, 250n25
Sheridan, Richard, *The Critic,* 266–67 note to #2
Sherman, Brad, and Lionel Bently, 54–55, 141, 235n1, 238n21, 259n4
Shewan, Rodney, 99
Shiva, Vandana, 86, 87
Shloss, Carol, 260n8
Simpson, O. J., 236n5
Smith, Adam, 34, 48, 69
—works
  Lectures on Jurisprudence, on copyright, 28–29, 56
  Theory of Moral Sentiments, 27, 28, 30, 31
  Wealth of Nations, 23–24, 28, 239n14
Smith, William, 70, 246n42
socialism: and literary property, 152–53; for Oscar Wilde, 92, 96; in Royal Commission debates, 78–80
Society for the Diffusion of Useful Knowledge, 33
Sonny Bono Copyright Term Extension Act (CTEA), 4; arguments for and against, 122–24, 154, 156; consequences of, 5, 122, 124, 125, 212; debates over, and rhetoric surrounding, 145, 202; lawsuits concerning, 125–26, 255n9; provisions, 121–22. *See also* mourning
Southey, Robert, 12, 32, 202
Spencer, Herbert, 53, 54, 81, 87; letter to Froud, 246n43; testimony of, 67–69, 153, 246nn42, 45, and its significance, 69, 71, 77
Speranza. *See* Wilde, Jane Francesca
Spoo, Robert, 161, 258n56, 262n35
Stationers' Company, 261n20; licensing monopoly, 180, 181
Stephen, James Fitzjames, 54, 70–71, 246n39; objections to Royal Commission Report, 73; questioning of Farrer, 70
Stewart, Susan, 98
Strauss, Richard, *Salome,* 119
Stringer, Arthur, *The Silver Poppy (The Yellow Vampire),* 139; suit against, 140
Strothman, Wendy, 212
style: as determinant of textual ownership, 178; 18th-century arguments of, 177–78; original, vs. copy, 178. *See also*

style (*continued*)
  idea/expression dichotomy; *and under*
    "Oxen of the Sun" episode, in *Ulysses*
Sullivan, Arthur, 53
Suntrust Bank v. Houghton Mifflin Co., 213, 265n30
Symons, Arthur, 96

Talfourd, Thomas Noon, 12, 32, 56, 182
Talfourd Bill. *See* Copyright Act of 1842 *under* legislation, British
"Taxes on Knowledge," 56, 74, 87; abolition of, 56–57, 60
Tennyson, Alfred, Lord, 103
Terdiman, Richard, 15
Thiers, Louis Adolphe, 39
Thomas, Denis, 82
Tonson v. Collins, 29
Toomey, Deirdre, 92, 95
trademarks, and copyrighted characters: appropriation of, 85–86; corporate control of, 200–201; as immune to parody, 5; role in public sphere, 200
Trevelyan, Charles, 77–78, 81; character, career, family, 62, 254nn34, 35; and free trade, 67–68, 69; and laissez-faire economics, 76–77, 245n34; testimony of, 62–66, 72, 73, 77–78, 86–87
Trollope, Anthony, 54, 62, 73
Twain, Mark, 12, 202
2 Live Crew, 182
Tyndall, John, 53, 68

Ulysses (James Joyce)
  "Aeolus," "Calypso," "Circe," and "Lestrygonians" episodes, 167
  basic general issues: as inspirational, living work, 157; as radically intertextual, 47; schemata for, 171, 261nn24, 25; singularity of, 162; structure, and episode titles, 261n25
  complex publishing history, 17: first imprint in France, 163; obsenity ban in U.S., and consequences, 161, 162, 194, 260n10; in public domain and unprotected, 168; serialized versions, 165, 260n15, 261n17, and ensuing protest and injunction, 161, 162, 166, 194, 197; studies on, 161, 194; and today's regulations, hypothetical publication under, 193–98
  and copyright: Bono Act extension, and return to copyright, 156, 258n56; first copyrightable edition in U.S., 258n56; for serialized version, 165; two cultures of copyright, 195
  copyright law, Anglo-American, reflected in, 163, 195, 260n10: appropriation, plagiarism, 47; complaints about uncopyrightability, 167; critique of, 14, 15, 195; and digestion/gestation theme, 167–68, 181; as governing anthologies used, 180; ideas vs. expression, 189–91; and literary property awareness, 13, 162; metadiscourses in "Oxen" episode, 192, 193; and oral expression, 164; as parody, 183; recompense for writing, 164, 165
  "Nausicaa" episode, 168
  "Scylla and Charybdis" episode, 165–66; Shakespeare's *Cymbeline* as key text, 186; theme of male parthenogenesis in, 263n53; and Wilde's Shakespeare story, 111
  "Telemakhos" episode, 164.
  See also "Oxen of the Sun" episode, in *Ulysses*
United States Olympic Committee (USOC), trademark control, 200–201
Uruguay Round Agreements Act, 255n9; restoration of copyright, 236n4, 258n54

value, aesthetic, 25–26: art tied to labor, 28, 30, 32, 34, 239n14; celebration of originality and genius, 30–31; in consumer utility, 33, 34, 35; as function of scarcity, 35; of private literary property, 29; production and plagiarism promoted as consumer pleasure, 26, 37–40, 47, 143, consequences, 48–49
value, theories of, 23–25; art vs. market, 27; exchange value, 27, 74–75, vs. use value, 28, 129; idea of public sovereignty, 87; labor theory of, 24, 26, 28, 33–34, 240n31; model tied to public interest, 85; shift from production to consumption, 33, 34, 40; subjectivist, 24
vampire, theme of, 135–38; vampire-geniuses, listing of, 142
Vanden Bossche, Chris, 19, 32, 56
Vanderham, Paul, 260n10
Viereck, George Sylvester: comment on, 256n22; political views and acts, 132; rumor about Wilde, 120
—works
  House of the Vampire, The: as celebration of plagiarism and appropriation, 131, 138; central issues of, 131, 155–56,

Index

Viereck, George Sylvester: works: (*continued*) 257n39; copyright themes in, 142, 149, 219, 256n21; and critique of copyright, 13, 14, 17, 120, 146; links to Wilde, 133–34, 138, 255n18; main character, considerations about, 141–42, 145; plot, 133–36; reception and reviews, 138, 256n26; and state of copyright law, 140, 142, 144–45; theme of authors vs. readers, 145–46; theme of consumption, 142–45; theme of Great Man, master-spirit, 135, 136, 137; ties to literary property law, 131
Nineveh and Other Poems, 133
Viereck, George Sylvester, and Edgar Allan Woolf, *The Vampire,* 131; accusations of plagiarism and infringement suits, 139–40; critical responses, 138–39, 141, 149; idea/expression dichotomy, theme of, 148–49; reworking of novel, 131, 256–57n27, 257n28; questions raised by, 141, 257n38
Villiers, C. P., 56
Virgil, appropriation of, 41, 47, 241n51
visual art, works of, copyright protection for, 235n2, 252n45; objection to, 73. *See also* photographs
Voltaire, 237n13

Wallis, Henry, *The Death of Chatterton,* 98; and copyright, 252n45
Walpole, Horace, 101, 251n37
Walras, Léon, 34
Walsh, William S., *Handy-Book of Literary Curiosities,* 39; defense of plagiarism, 38–39, 241nn37, 43
Walt Disney Company, support of Bono Act, 5, 122, 254n2
Ward, William, 94–95
Warner, Michael, 200, 212
Watts, Thomas, 59
Waugh, Evelyn, 96
Wilde, Oscar: bankruptcy, 114–15, 118; celebration and commission of plagiarism, 16, 47, 50, 91–92, 96, 99, 117, 241n43, 250n24, 251n31; as Chatterton's heir, 98, 103; and collectivism in language and ideas, 92, 110, 111; and copyright, 13, 14, 91, 97, 118; heritage, life, career, 91, 92; importance of orality for, 92–95, 96–97; and intellectual property, 91, 94, 110; as Irish, 92, 95, 241n43; lectures on Chatterton, 98–99, 250–51n30; legacy, and reemergence of, 118–20, 256n26; self-plagiarism,
251n40; themes of debt, credit, 110, 113, 115, 253n56; work of appropriation and recombinations, 27, 51; writing for, 96, 249n20
—works
Chatterton lecture notes, 16–17; content, 99; as critique of private literary property and individual genius, 103–6, 250n24, 251n39; description of, 105, 251nn31, 34, 36; as discourse on plagiarism and intellectual property issues, 99–101, 103–4; interpolations in own style, 102; plagiarized material in, 92, 99, 101; reception and assessment of, 105–6, 250n26; as self-justification, 104; suggestion of homosexuality, 251n37; as unpublished, 105
"Critic as Artist, The," 93–94
De Profundis (Epistola: In Carcere et Vinculis), 17, 97, 219; as change in thinking, 112; as discourse on property, 115–18; intertexuality of, 117; posthumous publication, and afterlife, 111, 118–19; reviews of, 111–12; theme of debts and losses, 91, 112–15; and value of public domain, 97, 113–14
"Doer of Good, The," 249n15
"Few Maxims for the Instruction of the Over-Educated, A," 107
Importance of Being Earnest, The, 249n20, 253n56
Intentions, 112, 249n20
"Keats' Grave," 250n25
"Pen, Pencil, and Poison," 99, 103–4, 249n20
Picture of Dorian Gray, The, 96–97, 110, 138, 249n23, 253n59, 256n26
"Portrait of Mr. W. H., The," 16–17, 97, 134, 137, 248n1; assessment and reception, 106; basic ideas, from Chatterton notes, 105–6; fictional Shakespeare theory, 108, 109–11; and intellectual property law, 109–10, 219; links to Chatterton, 106, 107, 108; parable about forgery/property, 107–8; significance of "belief," 109, 110, 111, 137; theme of homosexuality, 251n37
Ravenna, and prize for, 90–91
Salomé, 119, 134
scenario to *Mr. and Mrs. Daventry,* 91, 96
"Soul of Man under Socialism, The," 92, 112, 115–16
"Sphinx without a Secret, The," 96, 249n23
Woman of No Importance, A, 253n56

[280]

Wilde, Jane Francesca (pseud. Speranza), 92, 249n10
Wilde, William, 92–93
Wilson, Daniel, *Chatterton*, 99, 101, 102
Wilson, Edmund, *Axel's Castle*, 47
Wolff, H. D., 61, 63, 246n48; arguments against copyright, 73–74, 75
Woodmansee, Martha, 7, 86; "The Genius and the Copyright," 11, 12, 19
Woolf, Edgar Allan, 131, 138, 256–57n27. *See also* Viereck, George Sylvester, and Edgar Allan Woolf, *The Vampire*
Wordsworth, William: on Chatterton, 98; and copyright protection, 12, 30, 32, 246n39; definition of poet, 8; and original genius, 7, 31–32, 142; for postmortem copyright, 126–28, 202; *Prelude*, as published posthumously, 127

World Intellectual Property Organization (WIPO), 14, 236n4
Wright, Edward, 241n37; "The Art of Plagiarism," 40

Yeats, William Butler, 94; "The Doer of Good," 249n15; "Sonnet to Chatterton," 98; "Who Goes with Fergus Now?" 196
Young, Charles, 73
Young, Edward, 44; *Conjectures on Original Composition*, 239n21; author as genius, 6–7, 30–31, 40, 44, 239–40n22; and German Romanticism, 31; production as creation, 32, 142; and theories denied, 37, 38

www.ingramcontent.com/pod-product-compliance
Lightning Source LLC
Chambersburg PA
CBHW030131240426
43672CB00005B/96